Today's Civil Rights and Liberties Issues

Today's Civil Rights and Liberties Issues

Democrats and Republicans

KARA E. STOOKSBURY

Across the Aisle

BLOOMSBURY ACADEMIC
NEW YORK • LONDON • OXFORD • NEW DELHI • SYDNEY

BLOOMSBURY ACADEMIC
Bloomsbury Publishing Inc
1385 Broadway, New York, NY 10018, USA
50 Bedford Square, London, WC1B 3DP, UK
29 Earlsfort Terrace, Dublin 2, Ireland

BLOOMSBURY, BLOOMSBURY ACADEMIC and the Diana logo are trademarks of
Bloomsbury Publishing Plc

First published in the United States of America 2023

Copyright © Bloomsbury Publishing Inc, 2023

Cover image © Daniel Templeton/Alamy Stock Photo

Library of Congress Cataloging-in-Publication Data

Names: Stooksbury, Kara Elizabeth, 1969- author.
Title: Today's civil rights and liberties issues : Democrats and
Republicans / Kara E. Stooksbury.
Description: New York : Bloomsbury Academic, [2023] | Series: Across the
aisle | Includes bibliographical references and index.
Identifiers: LCCN 2022051564 | ISBN 9781440868344 (hardcover) | ISBN
9798216172413 (ebook) | ISBN 9781440868351 (ePDF)
Subjects: LCSH: Civil rights—Political aspects—United States. | United
States—Politics and government—21st century. | BISAC: LAW / Civil
Rights | POLITICAL SCIENCE / Political Freedom
Classification: LCC KF4750 .S766 2023 | DDC 342.7308/5—dc23/eng/20230403
LC record available at https://lccn.loc.gov/2022051564

ISBN: HB: 978-1-4408-6834-4
       ePDF: 978-1-4408-6835-1
       eBook: 979-8-216-17241-3

Series: Across the Aisle

Typeset by Amnet ContentSource

To find out more about our authors and books visit www.bloomsbury.com and sign up
for our newsletters.

To Joe Bill, with gratitude

Contents

Acknowledgments

I am indebted to many people who have helped me in the process of writing this book. First, and most importantly, I would like to thank my family for their love, encouragement, and support.

Thanks also to Kevin Hillstrom at Bloomsbury for his excellent feedback and patience while I completed this project.

I am very grateful to have the support of the administration of Carson-Newman University and my department colleagues Beth Vanlandingham, Amanda Ford, and Stephen Joiner, who encouraged me as I attempted to juggle too much.

Several Carson-Newman University students have been extremely helpful in providing research assistance for this project. Thanks to Krista Adams, Hunter Carr, Joey Clemmer, Thomas Fodor, Trent Lovelace, Skye McCarter, Savannah McMillan, Derick Marlow, Conner Miller, Angelica Montes, Gracie Keel, Kelsey Smith, and Haley Swecker. Amanda Ford went above and beyond with her helpful comments on early drafts and by providing much needed moral support. Mike Sobiech's professional writing class provided very useful feedback on portions of the manuscript. Thanks also to my administrative assistant, Baylie Lawhon, who helped me when I needed it most.

Finally, I would like to thank Joe Bill Sloan, not only for encouraging my interest in the study of politics when I was his student but also for being a valued mentor and friend and for providing constructive feedback on this manuscript.

While I'm grateful for the support of so many individuals who have helped make this project better, any errors contained herein are my own.

Introduction

The two-party system has been a key feature of American politics since the early days of the republic. The framers of the U.S. Constitution did not make any mention of political parties in the founding document, but America's two-party political system originated in the administration of the very first U.S. president, George Washington. This division of the young nation's political thinkers and lawmakers into opposite factions evolved from disputes concerning the role of government between two of Washington's cabinet members: Secretary of Treasury Alexander Hamilton and Secretary of State Thomas Jefferson.

Even as these political divisions were widening and hardening, though, the Founding Fathers recognized the perils of partisanship. Upon his retirement from political life, Washington offered a farewell address in which he warned "in the most solemn manner against the baneful effect of the spirit of party." Hamilton and Jefferson expressed similar views. Hamilton stated that "[n]othing could be more ill-judged than that intolerant spirit which has at all times characterized political parties." Jefferson quipped, "If I could not go to heaven but with a party, I would not go there at all."

Nonetheless, political parties quickly became integral to American campaigns and elections, and they remain central to American government and politics in the twenty-first century.

The goal of a political party is to establish and maintain the laws and policies of government—and the way to do that is by winning elections. To achieve that goal, parties articulate positions on a range of issues important to voters. This volume of Bloomsbury's *Across the Aisle* series provides authoritative summaries of Democratic and Republican parties' positions—and actual voting records—on important civil rights and civil liberties issues confronting the United States today. It provides an overview of each issue and explains how the parties' positions have evolved over time. The volume canvases party platforms, legislation, statements and speeches by presidents, presidential candidates, and key party leaders, along with views of those who identify with each party as indicated in public opinion polls.

The Infrastructure of Party Politics

Political parties are complex entities. Political scientist V. O. Key suggested that there are three distinct aspects to American political parties: the party in the electorate, the party in government, and the party as an organization. The party in the electorate consists of individuals who identify with a political party. In the United Kingdom, individuals wishing to join a party must apply and pay annual dues, while in the United States, there are no formal requirements to be a member of a political party.

Party affiliation is a psychological attachment to a political party. A 2022 Gallup poll found that 43 percent of the electorate identifies as Independent, while 24 percent consider themselves Democrats and 30 percent are Republicans. There are differences in party support among demographic groups. Women, minorities (including Black, Hispanic, and Asian American voters), individuals with a four-year college degree or postgraduate degree, and younger voters tend to affiliate with the Democratic Party. The Republican Party receives its strongest support from white, male, and noncollege-educated voters.

The party in government is comprised of elected officials who attempt to enact policies to advance the party's agenda. The U.S. Congress is organized along party lines. The Speaker of the House is the leader of the political party that holds the majority of seats in the House of Representatives, and the senate majority leader is a member of the majority party in the Senate. This organizational structure allows for the majority party to have the upper hand in implementing its agenda. It can also result in partisan gridlock when different parties hold the chambers. Elected officials are also influenced by interest groups and their constituents.

Party organizations are formal bodies that administer the day-to-day activities of each party. The national committees perform several important functions, including writing the party platform and planning the party's national convention held during the summer of a presidential election year, where the party's presidential nominee is formally announced. Each party has a platform committee that is tasked with drafting the platform, a document setting forth the party's positions on current political issues. The delegates attending the national convention must then approve the platform. Each issue is referred to as a plank (i.e., the abortion plank), and occasionally there is disagreement among the delegates as to the wording of planks.

For example, in 2016, some Republicans wanted the platform to include language more inclusive of the LGBTQ community. While their efforts garnered media attention, they ultimately failed, and the platform committee produced what some critics suggest is the most anti-LGBTQ plank in Republican history.

Critics have suggested that party platforms are irrelevant since they are nonbinding, meaning that candidates, whether for the presidency or for Congress, can take positions that differ from those expressed in the platform. Others have suggested that the length of the documents, sometimes reaching forty thousand words, deters even party members from reading the platforms. Indeed, at the 2012 Republican National Convention, Speaker of the House John Boehner said, "Have you ever met anybody who read the party platform?"

Scholars have countered that platforms matter because they emphasize differences between the parties. Scholars have also found that goals outlined in platforms are important indicators of the party's policy agenda. For example, the 1976 Republican platform supported the Equal Rights Amendment (ERA) and recognized that there was disagreement within the party over abortion rights for women; the 1980 platform neither supported the ERA nor abortion rights for women, which was consistent with a conservative shift within the party. The platforms also allow the party to provide a detailed explanation of their positions on issues that may not receive much attention during the campaign.

Evolving Party Positions on Civil Rights and Liberties

Civil rights involve claims to political, legal, and social equality. They are protected by several constitutional provisions as well as federal and state laws. The Fourteenth Amendment's Equal Protection Clause prohibits states from discriminating against a particular class of individuals (i.e., racial discrimination). Voting is also a civil right.

Civil liberties involve the extent to which individual freedoms can be limited by the government. This includes the guarantees in the Bill of Rights, such as freedom of speech. As Justice Oliver Wendell Holmes Jr. famously stated, "The most stringent protection of free speech would not protect a man in falsely shouting fire in a theatre and causing a panic." The First Amendment protects free speech, but this protection is limited as the government may in some instances have an interest in limiting that freedom.

Slavery was the first civil rights issue addressed by political parties. In its first-ever platform in 1844, the Democratic Party stated that any attempt to encourage Congress to "interfere" with slavery would "lead to the most alarming and dangerous consequences." Civil liberties issues were not consistently addressed by the parties until the twentieth century. Both parties referenced various guarantees of the Bill of Rights in their early platforms as those provisions related to the debate over slavery. In the first Republican platform in 1856, the party cited numerous provisions of the Bill of Rights and claimed that the citizens of Kansas had been denied these liberties because they were at the center of the fight over the expansion of slavery. The 1868 Democratic Party platform, meanwhile, accused Republicans of violating the civil liberties of individuals in the states that seceded, including their rights to freedom of speech, freedom of the press, and freedom from unreasonable searches and seizures.

Civil liberties issues rose to national prominence and became campaign issues due to the nationalization of the Bill of Rights. The framers of the Constitution added the Bill of Rights in 1791 to address fears of the Anti-Federalists during the debate over the ratification of the Constitution. The Anti-Federalists at the Virginia ratifying convention were concerned that without a Bill of Rights, the newly formed federal government posed too great a threat of becoming tyrannical—just as they felt the British Crown had become. James Madison agreed to add a Bill of Rights to the federal constitution if the Virginia ratifying convention would ratify. Thus, the Bill of Rights was intended to serve as a limit on the federal government.

After the ratification of the Fourteenth Amendment in 1868, the U.S. Supreme Court gradually expanded the protections of the Bill of Rights to the states in a series of rulings over many decades. The Due Process Clause of the Fourteenth Amendment provides, "[N]or shall any State deprive any person of life, liberty, or property, without due process of law." The Court has engaged in a process called selective incorporation, or the incorporation doctrine, in which it has applied most of the provisions of the Bill of Rights to the states through the Due Process Clause. This process has nationalized the Bill of Rights so that it prevents state governments from unduly restricting civil liberties. Thus, a state school board policy promoting prayer in public school was no longer a local issue but a national issue because (1) the Supreme Court could determine whether the policy violated the First Amendment's Establishment Clause, and (2) other states were obligated to abide by the Court's ruling. The Court applied the incorporation doctrine in 1897 in *Chicago, Burlington, and Quincy Railroad v. City of Chicago*, which dealt with Just Compensation under the Fifth Amendment. The Court continued this process with *Gitlow v. New York* in 1925 when it held that the First Amendment's free speech guarantee applied to the states. Currently, only the Third Amendment's ban on quartering of troops, the Fifth Amendment's grand jury requirement, and the Seventh Amendment's right to a jury trial in civil cases have not been incorporated. Those concerns along with civil rights issues also gained attention due to the increasing politicization of judicial appointments.

Civil rights issues became politically prominent in the 1950s due to the emergence of the African American Civil Rights Movement after decades of oppression and segregation, especially in the Jim Crow South. As the movement continued in the 1960s, civil rights leaders staged marches and peaceful protests that were often met with violence and hostility by Southern whites, including many members of law enforcement. When the relatively new medium of television broadcast footage of these ugly attacks all across the country, public support for the movement's goals rose.

When Lyndon B. Johnson became president after the assassination of John F. Kennedy in 1963, he pushed a landmark law, the Civil Rights Act of 1964, through Congress to honor Kennedy's commitment to civil rights. The next year, Johnson worked with Congress to enact the Voting Rights Act of 1965. These laws were part of an overall expansion in the power of the national government during the 1960s into areas that states had traditionally regulated. The significance of these laws is underscored by the fact that extending the Civil Rights Act to include protection for LGBTQ individuals and the renewal of the Voting Rights Act were issues during the 2020 presidential campaign.

Political Battles over the Supreme Court

The U.S. Supreme Court's role in defining civil rights and civil liberties during the 1960s and 1970s has led to greater public scrutiny of a president's judicial nominations. During the 1960s, under the leadership of Chief Justice Earl Warren, the Court expanded constitutional protections for criminal defendants. In *Mapp v. Ohio* (1961), for example, the Court applied the exclusionary rule to the states. The exclusionary rule prevents the state from using evidence illegally obtained by law enforcement to prosecute a defendant. In *Miranda v. Arizona* (1966), the Court held that law enforcement must apprise suspects who have been placed under arrest of their constitutional rights to remain silent and to legal representation. These rulings along with others led Republican presidential nominee Richard Nixon to run a campaign based on "law and order," arguing that the Court's rulings were counter to that principle.

After the Supreme Court legalized abortion in *Roe v. Wade* in 1973, political parties have been forced to take a position on abortion rights. Since the 1980 Republican platform pledged to appoint federal judges who promote the sanctity of human life, presidential candidates have often been asked whether abortion is a "litmus test" for their judicial nominees. While states impose most abortion restrictions, the president's role in appointing justices who determine the constitutionality of those restrictions has become a campaign issue. The president's ability to effect policy through the appointment of Supreme Court justices has made civil rights and civil liberties issues important in many presidential campaigns since the 1960s.

America's politics continue to orbit around the Republican and Democratic parties today. This volume analyzes the stated positions and actual voting records of both Democrats and Republicans on the most important civil rights and civil liberties issues in contemporary American politics.

Each chapter is devoted to a specific topic related to civil rights and civil liberties, such as gun policy, information privacy, freedom of speech, and LGBTQ rights. Each contains a section entitled "At a Glance" that provides the reader with a brief overview of the topic and the parties' prevailing position on that issue. An "Overview" section follows, highlighting important historical developments, including key legislation, court rulings, and shifts in party positions. The last two sections of each chapter provide a factual, objective summary of the record of each party on the issue in question. Each entry concludes with a "Further Reading" section pointing readers to other worthwhile informational resources.

Chronology

1791: The Bill of Rights is ratified.

1848: The Declaration of Sentiments and Resolutions asserts that women should have the right to vote.

1865: The Thirteenth Amendment is ratified, abolishing slavery.

1868: The Fourteenth Amendment is ratified. Its Equal Protection Clause has been an important cornerstone of civil rights lawsuits alleging discrimination on the basis of race, sex, and sexual orientation.

1870: The Fifteenth Amendment is ratified, extending voting rights to Black men.

1914: Congress passes the Harrison Narcotic Tax Act, the first federal drug law, which regulates opium and cocaine.

1920: The Nineteenth Amendment is ratified, extending voting rights to women.

1923: An Equal Rights Amendment guaranteeing equal rights for women is introduced for first time in the House of Representatives.

1934: The National Firearms Act is signed by President Franklin Roosevelt. The first federal law regulating guns, it was amended by Congress in 1968 and 1986.

1954: The U.S. Supreme Court unanimously rules in *Brown v. Board of Education* that segregated public schools violate the Equal Protection Clause of the Fourteenth Amendment.

1955: The Civil Rights Movement begins when Rosa Parks refuses to give up her seat on a Montgomery, Alabama, bus.

1964: Congress enacts the Civil Rights Act of 1964. This landmark law prohibits discrimination on the basis of race, color, religion, or national origin in places of public accommodation and employment. It also prohibits sex discrimination in employment and was interpreted by the U.S. Supreme Court in *Bostock v. Clayton, County, Georgia* (2020) to prohibit employment discrimination against LGBT individuals.

1965: Congress enacts the Voting Rights Act (VRA) of 1965. This law is based on the power of Congress to enforce the Fifteenth Amendment and prohibit states or state officials from enacting policies that prevent Blacks from voting. The reach of the VRA was dramatically limited by the U.S. Supreme Court's 5-4 ruling in *Shelby County v. Holder* (2013) that the law's coverage formula was unconstitutional.

1965: The Elementary and Secondary Education Act becomes law, providing new federal funding for K–12 public education.

1969: The Stonewall Riots erupt in Greenwich Village in New York City. The demonstrations, a response to a police crackdown on a gay bar called the Stonewall Inn, was a galvanizing event in the early Gay Rights Movement.

1971: President Richard Nixon announces a "war on drugs" declaring that drug abuse was "public enemy number one." He creates the Special Action Office of Drug Abuse Prevention to coordinate drug policy.

1972: The Equal Rights Amendment is approved by the U.S. Senate by a vote of 84-8. The House of Representatives had previously approved it by a vote of 354-24. Ultimately, thirty-five states ratify the amendment, three short of federal ratification.

1973: The U.S. Supreme Court decided *Roe v. Wade* by a 7-2 vote. This ruling held the women had a constitutional right to terminate their pregnancy.

1976: Democrat Jimmy Carter was elected president by defeating Gerald Ford.

1980: Republican Ronald Reagan defeated Jimmy Carter.

1984: Ronald Reagan was reelected president by a landslide over Democratic challenger and former vice president Walter Mondale. Mondale's running mate was Geraldine Ferraro, the first female vice-presidential candidate.

1988: Republican George H. W. Bush was elected president over Democratic nominee Massachusetts governor Michael Dukakis.

1990: The Americans with Disabilities Act is passed. This landmark civil rights law protects individuals with physical or mental disabilities from discrimination. It also requires employers to make reasonable accommodations for disabled employees.

1992: The Supreme Court upholds *Roe v. Wade* in *Planned Parenthood v. Casey* (1992), which held that states can implement abortion restrictions only if those regulations do not create an "undue burden" for a woman seeking an abortion.

1992: Democrat Bill Clinton defeats incumbent President George H. W. Bush.

1993: Congress passes the Religious Freedom Restoration Act, which attempts to overturn the U.S. Supreme Court's ruling in *Employment Division v. Smith* (1990).

1993: Congress enacts the Brady Handgun Violence Prevention Act of 1993, which requires background checks on gun purchasers.

1994: A U.S. military policy toward LGBTQ soldiers commonly known as "Don't Ask, Don't Tell (DADT)" is implemented. President Bill Clinton campaigned on a promise to end a ban supported by most Republicans on openly gay soldiers serving in the military. DADT was a compromise allowing gay soldiers to serve if they kept their sexual orientation a secret.

1994: Violent Crime Control and Law Enforcement Act was passed by Congress. The largest crime bill in American history accomplished several objectives. It also contained the Violence Against Women Act (VAWA) which provided legal and social resources to combat the issues surrounding gender-motivated violence.

1994: Public Safety and Recreational Firearms Use Protection Act, better known as the Assault Weapons Ban, was passed by Congress. The law prohibited the manufacture, sale, and possession of certain semiautomatic weapons. It expired after ten years and efforts to reenact it have been unsuccessful.

1996: Congress passes the Anti-Terrorism and Effective Death Penalty Act. This law expands the types of crimes for which the federal death penalty can be imposed.

2000: Republican George W. Bush is elected president in a closely contested race over Democratic vice president Al Gore.

2004: George W. Bush is reelected president defeating Democratic senator John Kerry.

2008: Democratic senator Barack Obama is elected president by defeating Republican senator John McCain.

2008: In *District of Columbia v. Heller*, the U.S. Supreme Court ruled by a 5-4 margin that the Second Amendment protects an individual's right to keep and bear arms.

2010: The U.S. Supreme Court ruled by a 5-4 vote in *Citizens United v. FEC* that for purposes of campaign contributions, corporations are people and have First Amendment protections.

2011: President Barack Obama repeals the U.S. military's DADT (Don't Ask, Don't Tell) policy toward LGBTQ military personnel in 2011.

2012: Barack Obama is reelected president, defeating Republican Mitt Romney.

2012: President Obama announces an immigration policy, Deferred Action for Childhood Arrivals (DACA), that allows undocumented immigrants who arrived in the United States as children a path to citizenship.

2015: In *Obergefell v. Hodges*, the U.S. Supreme Court legalizes same-sex marriage in a 5-4 ruling.

2016: Republican Donald Trump wins the presidency, defeating Democratic nominee and former secretary of state Hillary Rodham Clinton.

2020: Democrat Joe Biden is elected president, defeating incumbent Donald Trump.

2021: On January 6, a violent mob attempted to prevent Congress from counting valid electoral votes submitted by the states. The group was urged to take such action at a rally by outgoing President Trump, who falsely claimed there was widespread voter fraud and that he was the winner of the 2020 election. No evidence of voter fraud in the 2020 election has ever been found.

2022: The U.S. Supreme Court overturns *Roe v. Wade* in a 6-3 decision in *Dobbs v. Jackson Women's Health Organization*. The decision leaves abortion regulations to the states, approximately half of which ban or criminalize abortion.

2022: The U.S. Supreme Court expands Second Amendment rights in *New York State Rifle & Pistol Association, Inc. v. Bruen* by invalidating restrictions on concealed carry laws in six states.

2022: President Joe Biden signs a bipartisan gun control bill, the Bipartisan Safer Communities Act, into law after nineteen children and two teachers were murdered at a school in Uvalde, Texas. This is the first federal gun control legislation to be enacted since 1994.

Abortion

At a Glance

Abortion regulations were first implemented in the United States in the late nineteenth century. During the 1960s, many states began to reform their abortion statutes. By the early 1970s, political parties began to address the issue, but it was not until after the U.S. Supreme Court issued a ruling in *Roe v. Wade* (1973) that legalized abortion across the country that the nation's two major political parties formally articulated their positions. The moral complexity and differing perspectives regarding debates over abortion rights initially roiled both parties as they struggled to reach internal consensus on the issue. The role of the Supreme Court in defining abortion rights also politicized judicial appointments to a greater extent than had historically been the case.

Since the 1970s, the parties have defined their stance on abortion more clearly. Today, few Democrats identify as pro-life, while Republicans with pro-choice views are similarly rare. The Republican Party is thus strongly unified in opposing abortion rights and vowing to protect unborn children. The Democratic Party is similarly united but on the other side of the issue. Democratic lawmakers and officials overwhelmingly support a woman's right to abortion, characterizing it as a fundamental right of bodily autonomy.

According to many Republicans . . .

- An unborn child has a fundamental right to life protected by the U.S. Constitution.
- A human life amendment is necessary to protect the rights of the unborn.
- Public funding should not be used to facilitate abortions.

According to many Democrats . . .

- Women have a constitutionally protected right to make medical decisions about their own bodies, including the decision to terminate a pregnancy.

- Abortion should be available to all women regardless of their ability to pay.
- A ban on abortion will cause women to terminate unwanted pregnancies under dangerous circumstances.

––––––––––

Overview

Till the nineteenth century, abortion was legal in the United States until "quickening," the point at which a pregnant woman could detect fetal movement. If a woman had an abortion after quickening, it was only a misdemeanor offense. By 1880, however, every state outlawed abortion unless it was deemed necessary to save the mother's life. Restrictions were enacted for many reasons. The American Medical Association (AMA) was concerned that individuals other than physicians were performing abortions and lobbied for the restrictions to preserve physicians' professional status. Facilities in which abortions were performed were often dangerous. Finally, nativist and racist attitudes emerged as a growing factor; concerns were raised that if white women had abortions, the number of immigrants as a proportion of the overall population would grow, and whites could lose their higher status in American society.

During the 1960s, attitudes toward abortion restrictions began to change. The highly publicized 1962 case of Sherri Chessen, an Arizona children's television host, who had taken a tranquilizer containing thalidomide to quell the morning sickness associated with her pregnancy, helped change public attitudes about abortion. After reading about the severe deformities in children born to mothers who had taken the drug, Chessen sought an abortion. The procedure was canceled, however, after the hospital in which it was scheduled became concerned about getting into legal trouble. Chessen ultimately had the abortion in Sweden, where she was informed that the baby was so severely deformed it would not have survived. In a Gallup poll conducted at the time, 55 percent of Americans agreed with her decision.

An outbreak of German measles from 1962 to 1965, which caused the birth of severely deformed children and a significant number of stillbirths, also contributed to changing attitudes. The women's rights movement led by the National Organization for Women (NOW) supported abortion rights and campaigned against restrictive abortion laws. States began reforming their abortion laws during the late 1960s. In 1970, the AMA's position changed to allow doctors and patients to make decisions regarding terminating pregnancies. From 1965 to 1972, thirteen states liberalized their laws, while others retained their bans on the procedure. An active pro-life movement was instrumental in defeating abortion reform legislation in twenty-five states in 1971. It was against this broader period of social and legal debate and change that the U.S. Supreme Court became involved in defining abortion rights.

In *Roe v. Wade*, the U.S. Supreme Court, by a 7-2 margin, invalidated an 1854 Texas law that prohibited abortion except in cases where the woman's life was in danger. Justice Harry Blackmun, writing for the majority, stated that the constitutional right to privacy was broad enough to include a woman's decision to terminate her pregnancy. This right, however, was not unlimited. The Court's ruling was based on a trimester framework. During the first trimester, the decision was left to the discretion of a woman and her doctor. During the second trimester, the state could regulate abortion as long as the regulations put in place were reasonably related to maternal health. For example, the state could specify the types of facilities where abortions could be performed. During the third trimester, once the fetus was viable (able to live outside the womb), the state had a compelling interest in protecting potential life and could prohibit abortion entirely unless the woman's life was endangered.

To limit *Roe* and prevent abortions, Congressman Henry Hyde (R-IL) introduced an amendment to the Department of Health, Education, and Welfare's budget in 1976 prohibiting Medicaid funds from being used to pay for abortions. Medicaid is a program jointly funded by the federal government and the states for indigent health care. The so-called Hyde Amendment took effect in 1980. The only exceptions that allowed for a federally funded abortion procedure under the law were cases in which the mother's life would be endangered if the fetus was carried to term. Since 1994, Medicaid funds can only be used for abortions when the pregnancy is a result of rape or incest or when it endangers the mother's life. This amendment must be approved by Congress every year as part of the budget process.

After *Roe*, many states enacted restrictions on abortion that were challenged in court. Almost twenty years after the *Roe* ruling, the Court fundamentally altered its approach to abortion cases in *Planned Parenthood v. Casey* (1992). A plurality of three justices, all Republican appointees, reaffirmed the central holding of *Roe*, which had three aspects: (1) a woman had the right to a pre-viability abortion without undue interference from the state, (2) the state could restrict abortions after viability if the mother's life was not in danger, and (3) the state's interest in the life of both the woman and the fetus started at pregnancy, not viability. The *Casey* ruling replaced the trimester framework, which the Court argued was not part of *Roe*'s central holding, with the "undue burden" test. This approach allows states to restrict abortions before viability unless the regulation imposes a "substantial obstacle" in the path of the woman seeking an abortion.

The Court applied the undue burden test when it evaluated the Partial-Birth Abortion Ban Act of 2003 in *Gonzales v. Carhart* (2007). This law prohibited a specific type of abortion known as dilation and extraction, which is performed during the second and third trimesters of pregnancy. "Partial-birth abortion" is not a medical term but rather a political term often used by pro-life supporters. Abortion rights supporters use the term "late-term abortion" instead. By a 5-4 vote, the

Court upheld the law stating that it did not create an undue burden because the procedure was not used to save the mother's life, nor was it a commonly used one.

In *Whole Woman's Health v. Hellerstedt* (2016), however, the Court applied the undue burden standard to invalidate a controversial Texas law that required physicians who performed abortions to have admitting privileges at a hospital within thirty miles of where the abortion was performed. The law also required abortion clinics to meet the same standards as ambulatory surgical centers. The Court held that the admitting privileges requirement did not advance women's health but caused half of the state's abortion clinics to close. Similarly, requiring abortion clinics to meet ambulatory surgical center requirements made it more difficult for them to remain open.

Although the Court had generally held that state restrictions on abortion were constitutional, it had upheld *Roe v. Wade*. In 2022, however, the Court overturned *Roe* in *Dobbs v. Jackson Women's Health Organization* holding that abortion was not a protected constitutional right. It upheld Mississippi's law that banned abortion after fifteen weeks of pregnancy. Justice Samuel Alito wrote the majority opinion in which he stated that there was no constitutional basis for the right to privacy on which abortion decisions had been legally protected. He stated that abortion is an issue that should be left to the states and that women who wanted abortion to be legal could lobby their state legislatures. Chief Justice John Roberts wrote a concurring opinion because he would have also upheld the Mississippi law but would not have overturned *Roe*. The three dissenting justices, all Democratic appointees, argued that many other rights, including same-sex marriage, were also based on the right to privacy and were now under threat. The dissenters also stated that the ruling "would allow States to ban abortion from conception onward because it does not think forced childbirth at all implicates a woman's rights to equality and freedom. Today's court, that is, does not think there is anything of constitutional significance attached to a woman's control of her body and the path of her life. A State can force her to bring a pregnancy to term, even at the steepest personal and familial costs." Before the Court's decision was announced in June, a draft of Justice Alito's opinion was leaked to the public—a very unusual occurrence.

Abortion and Political Partisanship

The abortion issue has played a significant role in presidential politics over the past half century. For example, according to Gallup, abortion was a threshold issue for one in six voters in the 2012 election. Both parties have emphasized the role of presidential appointments to the Supreme Court in their presidential campaigns and their platforms. Interest groups on both sides have attempted to influence the parties' positions on abortion and other reproductive rights issues. Catholics and evangelical Christians are the most supportive of overturning *Roe* and outlawing abortion, while women's rights groups have been vocal in their support of *Roe* and "personal choice."

Public opinion polls have consistently indicated that a majority of Americans favor abortion rights, with some limitations. While these views have remained relatively stable overall, the partisan gap in attitudes about abortion has widened since the mid-1990s. According to one Pew Research Center poll, in 1995, Republicans were evenly divided in terms of whether abortion should be illegal in all or most cases (with 49 percent supporting legalization and 48 percent calling to make it illegal). A 2018 Pew poll found that those percentages had changed to 59 percent of self-identified Republicans who believed it should be illegal and 36 percent who thought it should be legal. Pew found similar shifts for Democrats. According to its 2018 poll, 76 percent of Democrats believed abortion should be legal in most cases, up from 64 percent in 1995. Overall, Pew found that attitudes about abortion had not changed much in the United States. In 1995, 60 percent of Americans believed that abortion should be legal in all/most cases; the percentage was virtually the same—58 percent—in 2018 (Pew Research Center 2018). After the *Dobbs* ruling, which overturned *Roe*, a Pew survey found that 62 percent of Americans believed abortion should be legal in all or most circumstances (Pew Research Center 2022). The poll also indicated that 57 percent of Americans disagreed with the *Dobbs* decision. There were stark differences between Republicans and Democrats with 29 percent of Republicans and those who lean Republican disapproving of the ruling and 82 percent of Democrats and those who lean Democratic disapproving of the ruling.

Both parties were initially reluctant to take a definitive stand on the abortion issue; however, since the 1980s, the Republican Party has taken an increasingly pro-life stance while the Democratic Party has consistently supported abortion rights. Not all Republicans are pro-life, nor are all Democrats pro-choice. In 1988, Republican Majority for Choice was formed to support pro-choice Republicans, and in 1999, Democrats for Life was formed to support pro-life Democrats. Given the significance of abortion as a political issue, however, these groups have been marginalized within each party.

Republicans on Abortion

The Republican Party has officially taken the position of opposing abortion rights in favor of the rights of the unborn since the 1976 presidential election. It has become more strongly pro-life since 1980 and has advocated for a human life amendment to be added to the Constitution. Since 1980, Republican presidential nominees have opposed *Roe v. Wade*, even if they had supported it earlier in their careers. Religious organizations, particularly Catholics and Evangelical Protestants, along with pro-life interest groups have played a significant role in shaping the party's abortion policies. While the party's platforms have consistently supported banning abortion, public opinion polls indicate that a majority of Republican voters favor abortion rights in certain circumstances.

Prior to *Roe v. Wade*, while campaigning for reelection in 1972, Republican president Richard Nixon stated that he could not support abortion because it conflicted with his belief in the sanctity of human life. He was concerned that if he supported abortion reform, he would lose Catholic votes. After *Roe*, the party was divided on the issue. The 1976 platform stated that abortion was "one of the most difficult and controversial issues of our time" and that some Republicans support *Roe*, others oppose *Roe*, and yet others are undecided or take a moderate approach.

The next statement, however, strongly condemned *Roe*: "We protest the Supreme Court's intrusion in to the family structure through its denial of the parents' obligation and right to guide their minor children. The Republican Party favors a continuance of the public dialogue on abortion and supports efforts of those who seek enactment of a constitutional amendment to restore protection of the right to life for unborn children."

In 1976, President Gerald Ford was challenged for the Republican nomination by California governor Ronald Reagan, whose delegates had significant influence in shaping that year's official party platform. One of the positions taken in the party platform was a clear "pro-life" plank or statement. Many Republican women were opposed to the pro-life plank and attempted to have it removed from the platform but were unsuccessful. They feared spending too much effort fighting to remove it would jeopardize the inclusion of a pro–Equal Rights Amendment plank, which Republicans supported at the time. Ford's views were different from those articulated in the platform. While he was opposed to "abortion on demand," he supported it in cases of rape or when the woman's health was in jeopardy. He opposed a constitutional amendment banning abortion and believed that the issue should be left to the states.

In 1980, the party's statement on abortion still contained conciliatory language acknowledging that Americans in general and Republicans in particular held various views on abortion. The platform continued to support a constitutional amendment to protect the right to life for unborn children, though, and to restrict the use of taxpayer money to fund abortions. The 1984 platform added a provision commending religious entities and private organizations for providing alternatives to abortion.

The 1988 Republican presidential nominee, Vice President George H. W. Bush, articulated a pro-life stance as Reagan's vice president; however, in his earlier years as a congressman, he had supported abortion rights. In 1988, his views differed from those of Reagan because Bush supported an abortion exception for rape, incest, and life of the mother. As the 1988 election drew closer, Bush stated that his views on the subject were evolving. The 1988 platform applauded Reagan's appointment of federal judges who "respect traditional family values and the sanctity of human life." The human life amendment, support of the Hyde Amendment, and appointment of pro-life judges are the most consistent aspects of the

Republican stance on the issue and appear in every platform from 1988 through 2020. The 1992 abortion plank did not differ significantly from the views stated in 1988.

In 1996, there was a contentious debate within the party over the abortion plank. Republican presidential nominee Bob Dole asserted that he thought the platform should recognize exceptions for rape and the health of the mother. Dole also wanted to include a "Declaration of Tolerance," which contained language similar to the 1976 and 1980 platforms, both of which recognized that Republicans held a wide variety of views on the legality of abortion. After an intense debate among party leaders, Dole's proposed language was not included with the abortion plank. For the first time the platform emphasized Republican policies such as congressional support for adoption and compassion toward "women with problem pregnancies." The party also criticized President Clinton for vetoing a ban on partial-birth abortions.

Four years later, pro-life activists threatened to drop their support for nominee George W. Bush if he chose a pro-choice running mate. This was also a concern for Republicans in the electorate. A Gallup poll conducted in July 2000 indicated that 39 percent of Bush's supporters would be disturbed if he chose a pro-choice running mate. The platform, as in previous years, supported a human life amendment, the appointment of pro-life judges, and the prohibition of federal funds for abortion. It based the right to life in the Declaration of Independence and stated the pro-life agenda did not include punishment for women who had abortions. Finally, it emphasized Republican support for adoption, including tax credits for adoptive parents. The 2004 platform praised President Bush for supporting crisis pregnancy programs, parental notification laws, extending health care to unborn children, and signing the Born-Alive Infants Protection Act, which considers every child born alive as a person under federal law. The law was intended to provide infants who had survived abortion procedures with legal protection after hospital employees testified before Congress that infant abortion survivors had been allowed to die (Pear 2005). Critics, however, noted that this was a political ploy as it was extremely rare for an infant to survive an abortion and that state law already criminalized murder making the law unnecessary. The platform praised Congressional Republicans for the Partial-Birth Abortion Ban Act, which had been enacted with bipartisan support but had been particularly popular with Republicans.

The 2008 platform cited many of the same policies detailed in 2004. However, a statement was added that "Women deserve better than abortion" and that "Every effort should be made to work with women considering abortion to enable and empower them to choose life." However, no specific policies that would help achieve the stated goal were enumerated in the platform. The Republican presidential nominee, Senator John McCain, had supported *Roe* due to the danger its repeal would pose to women who would seek illegal abortions. However, while running for president, he changed his stance and stated that *Roe* should be overturned.

McCain's running mate, Alaska governor Sarah Palin, had consistently stated that she was opposed to abortion with no exceptions. While Palin helped appease concerns of pro-life voters, abortion received little attention in this election. According to a 2008 Gallup poll, only 15 percent of pro-life voters indicated that a candidate must share their views on abortion for them to vote for the candidate—down from 28 percent in a 2004 Gallup survey (Saad 2008a).

Abortion was a more significant issue in the 2012 presidential campaign, when reproductive health issues became entangled in the controversial Affordable Care Act, a sweeping health-care law strongly opposed by the GOP that President Barack Obama and his fellow Democrats had narrowly passed into law in 2010. This law, called Obamacare by critics, required businesses to provide health-care coverage for various types of contraceptives. The 2012 GOP platform asked for an expansion of the Born-Alive Infants Protection Act by enacting civil and criminal penalties for health-care providers who did not provide care for an infant who survived an abortion. There were several new pro-life policies addressed in the platform, including legislation banning sex-selective abortions, protections for unborn children who are capable of feeling pain, and a ban on the use of body parts from aborted fetuses for research.

The 2012 Republican nominee, Mitt Romney, had a complicated record on abortion. As Massachusetts governor, he had supported abortion rights. When running for president, he changed his position to restricting abortion except in cases of rape or incest or to save the life of the mother. However, in a 2007 debate, he had stated that he would be "delighted" to sign legislation banning all abortions but believed the country was not ready for such an action. Romney was one of only three Republican candidates who did not sign a "Pro-Life Presidential Leadership Pledge" authored by Susan B. Anthony List (SBA List), a prominent pro-life group. While the group was formed in 1997, the 2012 election marked the first time it asked candidates to sign the pledge, which was characterized by historian Christine Stansell (2011) as "a radical escalation in the war against abortion." The pledge's provisions were similar to the views outlined in the platform: it called on signees to appoint pro-life judges and bureaucrats, eliminate federal funding for hospitals or clinics that performed abortions, and advance a Pain-Capable Unborn Child Protection Act. The Pain-Capable Unborn Child Protection Act proposed the banning of abortions after twenty weeks of pregnancy. The bill assumed that a fetus could feel pain at twenty weeks. Many states enacted similar laws, but these ideas were criticized by physicians in the *Journal of the American Medical Association* as being misleading. In a review of research on the topic, they stated that it is unlikely a fetus can feel pain until the third trimester of pregnancy—not at twenty weeks as this type of legislation suggests.

The 2016 abortion plank in the Republican Party's platform was the party's most comprehensive statement at that point on abortion. In 2020, the Republican Party passed a resolution to retain its 2016 platform rather than create a new one. This

The GOP Describes Abortion Stance as a Constitutional "Right to Life" Issue

In this excerpt from the Republican Party's 2016 platform (which it also used as its 2020 platform), the GOP frames abortion as a moral issue and criticizes the Democratic Party's stance as being "extreme."

The Constitution's guarantee that no one can "be deprived of life, liberty or property" deliberately echoes the Declaration of Independence's proclamation that "all" are "endowed by their Creator" with the inalienable right to life. Accordingly, we assert the sanctity of human life and affirm that the unborn child has a fundamental right to life, which cannot be infringed. We support a human life amendment to the Constitution and legislation to make clear that the Fourteenth Amendment's protections apply to children before birth.

We affirm our moral obligation to assist, rather than penalize, women who face an unplanned pregnancy. In order to encourage women who face an unplanned pregnancy to choose life, we support legislation that requires financial responsibility for the child be equally borne by both the mother and father upon conception until the child reaches adulthood.

The Democratic Party is extreme on abortion. Democrats' almost limitless support for abortion, and their strident opposition to even the most basic restrictions on abortion, put them dramatically out of step with the American people. Because of their opposition to simple abortion clinic safety procedures, support for taxpayer-funded abortion, and rejection of pregnancy resource centers that provide abortion alternatives, the old Clinton mantra of "safe, legal, and rare" has been reduced to just "legal." We are proud to be the party that protects human life and offers real solutions for women.

Source

Republican Party Platforms. 1976–2020. American Presidency Project. Accessed November 21, 2022. https://www.presidency.ucsb.edu/people/other/republican-party-platforms.

was the first time since 1856 that the party had not issued a new platform. Prior to the 2020 Republican National Convention, the resolution stated that "[t]he Republican Party has and will continue to enthusiastically support the president's America-first agenda" (Epstein 2020). The party continued to support a human life amendment to the Constitution to protect the unborn. It modified its stance on the Hyde Amendment to make it permanent. As in 2008 and 2012, the platform expressed a "moral obligation" to help women with unwanted pregnancies find alternatives to abortion. It also indicated Republican support for legislation requiring financial support for a child, from conception to adulthood, to be shared equally by both parents. There was also a strong statement opposing the sale of fetal body parts from elective abortion for research.

In 2015, a secretly recorded video released by an antiabortion group purported to show Planned Parenthood discussing the sale of fetal tissue for profit. Later, it was found that the recording was edited to make it look like the officials were discussing making a profit from the sale when they were actually discussing how to cover the costs of providing the tissue to medical researchers. The use of fetal tissue for medical research is legal. The video led to investigations of Planned Parenthood organizations in several red states in early 2016; however, no evidence of Planned Parenthood selling fetal tissue for profit was discovered.

The platform, unlike in previous years, praised states for implementing various restrictions on abortion, including parental consent laws for minors and Pain-Capable Unborn Child Protection laws.

Pro-life groups did not support Donald Trump before he became the party's 2016 nominee to run against Democratic nominee Hillary Clinton. Trump was dubbed a "Manhattan pro-choice liberal" by some pro-life conservatives. During the campaign for the Republican nomination, he had difficulty stating a consistent opinion on abortion. Trump was able to shore up pro-life support after the second presidential debate, however, when he stated that he was pro-life. He insisted that *Roe* would automatically be overturned by the justices he appointed to the Supreme Court. He also stated his opposition to partial-birth abortion, saying that the practice allowed babies to be "ripped out of the womb" in the ninth month of pregnancy.

With the growing influence of SBA, the decline in the number of pro-choice Republican voters, and the hostility of party members to pro-choice views, pro-choice Republicans have become relative rarities. Leaders of the Republican Majority for Choice dissolved the organization in 2018, claiming in an op-ed in the *New York Times* that the party's pro-life stance was "anti-woman and anti-common sense" (Bevan and Cullman 2018). They stated that true conservatives should support family planning because it reduces poverty and increases educational opportunities, which in turn can lead to better economic conditions. They also asserted that family planning services save the taxpayers billions of dollars that would otherwise be spent on the welfare state and that the "far right was more interested in conflating abortion and birth control for political purposes. It is fiscally disingenuous to deny birth control coverage and then bemoan unintended pregnancies and abortion" (Bevan and Cullman 2018).

Congressional Republicans applauded the *Dobbs* ruling in 2022. The Republican House leadership issued a statement that provided that "[e]very unborn child is precious, extraordinary, and worthy of protection" and the Court was right to return the power to protect the unborn to Congress and state legislatures. The statement claimed that this would allow them to prevent "extreme" policies such as late-term abortions that were funded by taxpayers even though those procedures are very rare and seldom funded by taxpayers (Scalise 2022). Republican Senator Lindsay Graham proposed a federal ban on abortions after fifteen weeks of pregnancy that would include an exception for rape, incest, and to save the mother's life. This proposal divided Republicans as many argued that the issue should be handled by the states, not the federal government. Graham defended the proposal, which had no chance of passing a Democratically controlled House and an evenly divided Senate, as a response to the "extreme" Women's Health Protection Act passed by House Democrats. That bill would have codified *Roe* and limited the states' ability to restrict abortion. Graham suggested that his proposed bill was consistent with how other countries treat abortion (Breuninger 2022).

Public opinion polls indicate that most Republicans (67 percent) believe that abortion should be legal only under certain conditions, while only 22 percent support an outright ban on abortion. Only 10 percent of Republicans believe that abortion should be legal under any circumstances (Gallup 2022).

Democrats on Abortion

Since the Democrats first addressed the abortion issue, the party's support for a woman's "right to choose" whether to end or continue a pregnancy has strengthened over time. Democrats have consistently supported abortion rights, including abortions for indigent women unable to pay for the procedure. In the 1990s, Democratic candidates touted legislative success in protecting abortion rights and supported holistic policies for family planning and adoption. Most recently, the party has addressed abortion in the context of women's health care.

Prior to *Roe*, the Democratic Party struggled with the abortion issue. A rule change regarding delegate selection at the 1968 Democratic National Convention resulted in more diverse delegates attending the 1972 Convention. At this meeting, an unprecedented number of women delegates proposed an abortion rights plank, which was the subject of a contentious debate on the convention floor. The proposed plank read, "In matters relating to human reproduction each person's right to privacy, freedom of choice and individual conscience should be fully respected, consistent with relevant Supreme Court decisions." This was ultimately voted down due to concerns at the time (*Roe v. Wade* had not yet become the law of the land) that the party's presidential nominee, Senator George McGovern, would be perceived as an extremist.

In 1976, Democratic candidates were forced to address abortion due to *Roe* and the candidacy of Ellen McCormack, a pro-life Democrat who ran for the party's presidential nomination solely on the abortion issue. The eventual Democratic nominee, Jimmy Carter, a born-again Christian, was personally opposed to abortion. He ultimately supported abortion rights, but not to the extent some had hoped. The party platform acknowledged the religious and moral concerns Americans held regarding abortion but did not directly endorse abortion rights. It merely stated that it was "undesirable" to attempt to overturn *Roe* through a constitutional amendment.

During the 1980s, Democratic platforms devoted limited attention to abortion rights but took a pro-choice stance. In 1980, Jimmy Carter was challenged for the Democratic presidential nomination by Senator Edward "Ted" Kennedy. Kennedy was unsuccessful in securing the nomination, but he was able to get concessions in the platform, including stronger pro-choice language in the abortion plank. The NOW lobbied for the language. The platform, like the 1976 statement, acknowledged religious and ethical concerns about abortion but opposed a constitutional amendment overturning *Roe*, which it characterized as the "law of the land." The Democrats' 1984 platform did not specifically mention abortion but emphasized that reproductive freedom could disappear if President Reagan were reelected because he would appoint judges opposed to abortion rights. In 1988, the platform stated that the fundamental right of reproductive choice should be guaranteed, regardless of the woman's ability to pay for the procedure.

The 1992 platform contained a more elaborate abortion plank than in prior years. The position outlined in this platform formed the core of the Democratic Party's abortion stance for the next twenty years; namely, that women have a right to choose an abortion regardless of their ability to pay and that this choice belongs to the woman and not the government. Democratic nominee Bill Clinton had been criticized for his lack of strong support for abortion rights as governor of Arkansas. During the 1992 presidential campaign, however, he vowed to support abortion rights and promised to appoint Supreme Court justices who would uphold *Roe*.

The party's 1996 platform highlighted President Clinton's role in protecting abortion rights. He vetoed legislation banning partial-birth abortions because the measure did not include an exception to save the life of the mother, signed the Freedom of Access to Clinic Entrances Act to protect abortion clinics and women seeking abortions from harassment and violence at those facilities, and rescinded the "gag rule" that prohibited health professionals at family planning clinics receiving government funds from providing information about, or referrals for, abortion. The platform echoed the 1976 platform, however, by describing the Democratic Party as a party of inclusion that respected those with differing opinions on this "difficult" issue. Finally, the platform noted that the abortion rate was dropping and offered support for family planning and other efforts to further prevent unwanted pregnancies and encourage personal responsibility. Clinton coined the phrase "safe, legal, and rare" to describe the party's views on abortion.

In 2000, the party continued to articulate its support for *Roe* and for women who could not afford to pay for the procedure. The platform emphasized the importance of the Supreme Court and stated that "eliminating the right to choose is only one justice away." The most notable change in the platform was that an entire section of the abortion plank adopted the language that Republican presidential nominee Bob Dole wanted to include in the Republican's 1996 platform—a Declaration of Tolerance. The platform again characterized the Democratic Party as a "party of inclusion" and stated, we are very proud to put into our platform the very words which Republicans refused to let Bob Dole put into their 1996 platform and which they refused to even consider putting in their platform in 2000: "While the party remains steadfast in its commitment to advancing its historic principles and ideals, we also recognize that members of our party have deeply held and sometimes differing views on issues of personal conscience like abortion and capital punishment. We view this diversity of views as a source of strength, not as a sign of weakness, and we welcome into our ranks all Americans who may hold differing positions on these and other issues. Recognizing that tolerance is a virtue, we are committed to resolving our differences in a spirit of civility, hope and mutual respect."

The abortion planks in the Democratic platforms of 2004, 2008, and 2012 were much less detailed than in 2000. They all supported *Roe* and abortion rights for indigent women, however, and emphasized strategies to reduce abortion, such as family planning and adoption. In 2004, John Kerry became the first Catholic to be the party's presidential nominee since John F. Kennedy. Like many other Catholic Democrats, Kerry was personally opposed to abortion but supported *Roe*. The 2008 platform characterized the party's support for *Roe* as unequivocal. The abortion plank was brief and couched within comprehensive family planning policies such as sex education, health care, and education to help reduce the need for abortions. For the first time in a platform, the Democrats also promoted policies, including prenatal care, income support, and programs to help build parenting skills to support women who chose to have a child.

The 2012 abortion plank was very similar to the stance articulated in 2008. In addition to its support for *Roe*, the Democratic platform that year stressed "strong and unequivocal support" for a woman's decision to have a baby by providing affordable health care and access to health services throughout pregnancy. Democrats also pledged to fight Republican efforts to defund Planned Parenthood, an organization that provides a wide variety of health-care services to women, including abortion.

The 2016 platform contained the most comprehensive statement on abortion and reproductive rights the party has offered to date. With regard to abortion, the platform provided that "[w]e believe unequivocally, like the majority of Americans, that every woman should have access to quality reproductive health services, including safe and legal abortion." The party pledged to oppose and overturn both federal and state laws that limit abortion rights, including an outright repeal of the Hyde Amendment. It advocated programs to reduce unwanted pregnancies, including sex education and family planning, and "strongly and unequivocally" supported a woman's decision to have a child by providing social support services throughout pregnancy and after the birth of the child. For the first time, the platform urged repeal of the Helms Amendment, a law first passed in 1973 that prohibited U.S. foreign aid from being used for abortion services overseas.

The 2016 Democratic nominee, former first lady and secretary of state Hillary Clinton, was a longtime supporter of *Roe*. As a presidential candidate in the 2008 campaign, Clinton reiterated her husband's statement that abortion should be "safe, legal, and rare," with emphasis on the latter. During the second presidential debate against Republican nominee Donald Trump in 2016, she stated that the abortion decision "is one of the worst possible choices that any woman and her family has to make. And I do not believe the government should be making it."

These stances fit with the generally pro-choice perspective of most Democratic voters. Some pro-life Democrats, however, characterized the pro-choice views of Clinton and other Democrats as "an outright betrayal of millions of Democrats" (Day and Camosy 2016). That accusation was made in a *Los Angeles Times* guest editorial by Kristen Day, president of Democrats for Life, an organization founded in 1999 to help pro-life Democrats get elected; and Professor Charles Camosy of Fordham University. They asserted that repealing the Helms Amendment would force them and other Democrats to contribute to government-sponsored killing. They also argued that Democrats were losing supporters over the abortion issue and that the 2016 platform language on the issue would jeopardize the party's ability to win in swing states.

In 2020, Democrats for Life sent a letter to the Democratic National Committee's Platform Committee urging the party to change its 2016 stance on abortion. In its place, the letter urged the committee to adopt the party's 2000 platform plank language, which described internal party differences on the issue as a "source of strength." The 2020 abortion plank that was ultimately approved, however, was very similar to the 2016 platform. It linked abortion to wider health-care issues, indicated support for repealing the Hyde Amendment, and called for new legislation protecting abortion rights.

The 2020 Democratic nominee, Joe Biden, supported the platform's views on abortion. Additionally, during the Democratic debate in New Hampshire, Biden promised that any potential Supreme Court justices he nominated would have a strong record of support for the belief that the Constitution protects unenumerated rights, including the right to an abortion. He also claimed that he played a key role in protecting abortion rights years in the 1980s by leading the fight against President Ronald Reagan's failed Supreme Court nominee Robert Bork, who did not support the idea that the Constitution contained unenumerated rights. Biden was criticized for changing his views on the Hyde Amendment. Prior to the 2020 presidential campaign, he had supported the amendment limiting taxpayer funding for abortions. He was criticized for caving in to the more progressive wing of the Democratic Party by supporting the repeal of the amendment.

In 2022, Democrats decried the Supreme Court's ruling overturning *Roe v. Wade*. President Biden accused the Court of taking away a constitutional right and stated that the ruling endangered the lives of women who needed medically necessary

Democrats Oppose Supreme Court Ruling
Overturning *Roe v. Wade*

After the U.S. Supreme Court's ruling in Dobbs v. Jackson Women's Health Organiza-tion *overturning* Roe v. Wade, *Democratic President Joe Biden delivered remarks at the White House criticizing the decision. This is an excerpt from those remarks.*

Make no mistake: This decision is the culmination of a deliberate effort over decades to upset the balance of our law. It's a realization of an extreme ideology and a tragic error by the Supreme Court, in my view . . .

The court's decision to do so will have real and immediate consequences. State laws banning abortion are automatically taking effect today, jeopardizing the health of mil-lions of women, some without exceptions.

So extreme that women could be punished for protecting their health.

So extreme that women and girls who are forced to bear their rapist's child—of the child of consequence.

It's a—it just—it just stuns me.

So extreme that doctors will be criminalized for fulfilling their duty to care . . .

This a sad day for the country, in my view, but it doesn't mean the fight is over.

Let me be very clear and unambiguous: The only way we can secure a woman's right to choose and the balance that existed is for Congress to restore the protections of *Roe v. Wade* as federal law.

No executive action from the President can do that. And if Congress, as it appears, lacks the vote—votes to do that now, voters need to make their voices heard.

This fall, we must elect more senators and representatives who will codify a woman's right to choose into federal law once again, elect more state leaders to protect this right at the local level.

Source
Biden, Joe. 2022. "Remarks by President Biden on the Supreme Court Decision to Overturn *Roe v. Wade*." Accessed November 21, 2022. https://www.whitehouse.gov/briefing-room/speeches -remarks/2022/06/24/remarks-by-president-biden-on-the-supreme-court-decision-to -overturn-roe-v-wade/.

abortions. Democratic Speaker of the House, Nancy Pelosi, crafted a multifaceted response to the ruling. In a letter she penned to fellow House Democrats, Pelosi outlined a legislative agenda, including passage of the Women's Health Protec-tion Act in 2022, that would protect abortion rights. This passed the House in a party line vote with all Republicans and one Democrat voting against it. Repub-licans argued that the federal government did not have the power to supersede state abortion regulations. Pelosi also proposed legislation to guarantee the right to travel so that pregnant women could leave a state where abortion was criminal-ized to go to another where it was not, and legislation to protect the personal data stored in reproductive health apps to prevent law enforcement from using that information "against women by a sinister prosecutor in a state that criminalizes abortion" (Pelosi 2022).

According to Gallup polls from 1975 to 2019, Democrats who think abortion should be illegal in all circumstances fluctuated from a high of 25 percent in 1975 to a low of 8 percent in 2017 and 14 percent in 2019. However, the majority of Democrats favor abortion rights, including almost 40 percent in 2019 who agreed that abortion should be allowed under any circumstances (Gallup 2022). After a draft of the *Dobbs* ruling was leaked prior to its official release, the percentage of Democrats who agreed that abortion should be allowed under any circumstances increased to 57 percent with 38 percent who agreed that abortion should be allowed with some limitations. Only 4 percent think abortion should be made illegal (Gallup 2022).

Further Reading

Bacon, Perry. 2018. "The Abortion Debate Isn't as Partisan as Politicians Make It Seem." FiveThirtyEight, July 10. Accessed July 23, 2019. https://fivethirtyeight.com/features/the-abortion-debate-isnt-as-partisan-as-politicians-make-it-seem/.

Bevan, Susan, and Susan Cullman. 2018. "Why We Are Leaving the GOP." *New York Times*, June 24. Accessed July 12, 2019. https://www.nytimes.com/2018/06/24/opinion/abortion-rights-republican-party-women.html.

Birenbaum, Gabby. 2020. "Democrats for Life Urge DNC to Change Party Platform on Abortion." *The Hill*, August 14. Accessed December 1, 2020. https://thehill.com/policy/healthcare/abortion/511967-democrats-for-life-dnc-change-party-platform-abortion.

Breuninger, Kevin. 2022. "Lindsey Graham's Abortion Ban Bill Baffles Some Republicans as Democrats Sharpen Attacks in Key Midterm Races." *CNBC*, September 16. Accessed September 20, 2022. https://www.cnbc.com/2022/09/16/lindsey-graham-abortion-ban-bill-splits-gop-on-midterm-message.html.

Bump, Phillip. 2016. "Trump's Ever Shifting Positions on Abortion." *Washington Post*, April 3. Accessed July 20, 2019. https://www.washingtonpost.com/news/the-fix/wp/2016/04/03/donald-trumps-ever-shifting-positions-on-abortion/.

Day, Kristen, and Charles Camosy. 2016. "Op-Ed: How the Democratic Platform Betrays Millions of the Party Faithful." *LA Times*, July 25. Accessed July 21, 2019. https://www.latimes.com/opinion/op-ed/la-oe-day-and-camosy-democratic-platform-abortion-20160725-snap-story.html.

Democratic Party Platforms. 1976–2020. American Presidency Project. Accessed November 21, 2022. https://www.presidency.ucsb.edu/people/other/democratic-party-platforms.

Epstein, Reid J. 2020. "The G.O.P. Delivers Its 2020 Platform: It's from 2016." *New York Times*, August 25. Accessed September 1, 2022. https://www.nytimes.com/2020/08/25/us/politics/republicans-platform.html.

Gallup. 2022. "Abortion: Trends by Party Identification." Accessed September 20, 2022. https://news.gallup.com/poll/246278/abortion-trends-party.aspx.

Hoffman, Jan. 1992. "'Romper Room' Host on Her Abortion Case." *New York Times*, June 16. Accessed July 19, 2019. https://www.nytimes.com/1992/06/16/movies/romper-room-host-on-her-abortion-case.html.

Jones, Jeffrey. 2000. "Abortion a Major Issue, but Not Critical to Presidential Vote of Most Americans." Gallup, May 1. Accessed July 19, 2019. https://news.gallup.com /poll/2953/abortion-major-issue-critical-presidential-vote-most-americans.aspx.

Kurtzleben, Danielle. 2016. "Planned Parenthood Investigations Find No Fetal Tissue Sales." National Public Radio, January 28. Accessed September 1, 2022. https://www .npr.org/2016/01/28/464594826/in-wake-of-videos-planned-parenthood-investigations -find-no-fetal-tissue-sales.

Lee, Susan, Henry J. Peter Raulston, Elizabeth Drey, et al. 2005. "Fetal Pain: A Systematic Multidisciplinary Review of the Evidence." *Journal of the American Medical Association*, August 24/31. Accessed July 20, 2019. https://jamanetwork.com/journals/jama /fullarticle/201429.

Lett, Phoebe. 2015. "The Endangered Pro-Choice Republican." *New York Times*, December 24. Accessed July 23, 2019. https://takingnote.blogs.nytimes.com/2015/12/24 /the-endangered-pro-choice-republican/.

"New Hampshire Democratic Debate Transcript." 2020. February 7. Accessed December 1, 2020. https://www.rev.com/blog/transcripts/new-hampshire-democratic-debate-transcript.

Pear, Robert. 2005. "New Attention for 2002 Law on Survivors of Abortions." *New York Times*, April 23. Accessed September 1, 2022. https://www.nytimes.com/2005/04/23 /politics/new-attention-for-2002-law-on-survivors-of-abortions.html.

Pelosi, Nancy. 2022. "Dear Colleague on Legislative Response to Supreme Court Overturning Roe." Speaker Nancy Pelosi, June 27. Accessed September 20, 2022. https://www .speaker.gov/newsroom/62722-0.

Pew Research Center. 2018. "Nearly Six-in-Ten Americans Say Abortion Should Be Legal in All or Most Cases." Pew Research Center, October 17. Accessed June 27, 2019. https://www.pewresearch.org/fact-tank/2018/10/17/nearly-six-in-ten-americans-say -abortion-should-be-legal/.

Pew Research Center. 2022. "Majority of Public Disapproves of Supreme Court's Decision to Overturn *Roe v. Wade*." Pew Research Center, July 5. Accessed September 1, 2022. https://www.pewresearch.org/politics/2022/07/06/majority-of-public-disapproves-of -supreme-courts-decision-to-overturn-roe-v-wade/.

Republican Party Platforms. 1976–2020. American Presidency Project. Accessed November 21, 2022. https://www.presidency.ucsb.edu/people/other/republican-party-platforms.

Riffkin, Rebecca. 2015. "Abortion Edges Up as Important Voting Issue for Americans." Gallup, May 29. Accessed July 19, 2019. https://news.gallup.com/poll/183449/abortion -edges-important-voting-issue-americans.aspx.

Robertson, Nan. 1972. "Democrats Feel Impact of Women's New Power." *New York Times*, July 15. Accessed July 20, 2019. https://www.nytimes.com/1972/07/15/archives /democrats-feel-impact-of-womens-new-power-womens-power-has-an.html.

Ross, Janell. 2015. "How Planned Parenthood Actually Uses Its Federal Funding." *Washington Post*, August 4. Accessed July 19, 2019. https://www.washingtonpost.com/news /the-fix/wp/2015/08/04/how-planned-parenthood-actually-uses-its-federal-funding.

Saad, Lydia. 2000. "Pro-Choice VP Selection Carries Risk for Bush." Gallup, July 21. Accessed July 19, 2019. https://news.gallup.com/poll/2713/prochoice-selection-carries -risks-bush.aspx.

Saad, Lydia. 2004. "Abortion Issue Guides One in Five Voters." Gallup, October 26. Accessed July 19, 2019. https://news.gallup.com/poll/13786/abortion-issue-guides -one-five-voters.aspx.

Saad, Lydia. 2008a. "Abortion Issue Laying Low in 2008 Campaign." Gallup, May 22. Accessed July 19, 2019. https://news.gallup.com/poll/107458/abortion-issue-laying -low-2008-campaign.aspx.

Saad, Lydia. 2008b. "Will the Abortion Issue Help or Hurt McCain?" Gallup, September 3. Accessed July 19, 2019. https://news.gallup.com/poll/110002/will-abortion-issue-help -hurt-mccain.aspx.

Saad, Lydia. 2012. "Abortion Is Threshold Issue for One in Six U.S. Voters." Gallup, October 4. Accessed July 19, 2019. https://news.gallup.com/poll/157886/abortion-threshold-issue -one-six-voters.aspx.

Saad, Lydia. 2016. "Most 'Pro-Life' Americans Unsure About Trump's Abortion Views." Gallup, May 17. Accessed July 19, 2019. https://news.gallup.com/poll/191573/pro -life-americans-unsure-trump-abortion-views.aspx.

Scalise, Steve. 2022. "House Republican Leadership's Statement on Dobbs Decision." Republican Whip. Accessed September 1, 2022. https://www.republicanwhip.gov /news/house-republican-leaderships-statement-on-dobbs-decision/.

Seelye, Katharine. 1995. "Dole's Switch on Abortion Leads Quickly to Furor on G.O.P. Right." *New York Times*, December 19. Accessed June 27, 2019. https://www.nytimes .com/1995/12/19/us/dole-s-switch-on-abortion-leads-quickly-to-furor-on-gop-right .html.

Stansell, Christine. 2011. "Meet the Anti-Abortion Group Pushing Presidential Politics to the Extreme Right." *The New Republic*, July 11. Accessed June 20, 2019. https://new republic.com/article/91669/abortion-pledge-susan-b-anthony-republicans-romney.

Taranto, Stacie. 2018. "How Abortion Became the Single Most Important Litmus Test in American Politics." *Washington Post*, January 22. Accessed July 19, 2019. https:// www.washingtonpost.com/news/made-by-history-wp/2018/01/22/how-abortion -became-the-single-most-important-litmus-test-in-american-politics/.

Capital Punishment

At a Glance

Capital punishment has been a method of punishment in the United States since the colonial era. The issue gained national prominence in the 1970s but has only been consistently addressed by both parties since the 2008 election. The Republican Party has unfailingly supported the death penalty, while the Democratic Party has come full circle in its stance over the past fifty years. Democrats initially advocated abolishing the death penalty in 1972, shifted to supporting it under various circumstances throughout the 1990s and 2000s, then once again argued for its abolition in its 2016 and 2020 platforms.

According to many Democrats . . .

- The death penalty should be abolished because it is "cruel and unusual" and violates the Eighth Amendment's guarantee preventing such punishment.
- The death penalty is an ineffective policy because it costs more to implement than life sentences without the possibility of parole.
- The number of exonerations of death row inmates shows that capital punishment takes the lives of people who have been unjustly convicted for crimes they did not commit.
- Capital punishment is not an effective deterrent in preventing future murders or other serious crimes.

According to many Republicans . . .

- The death penalty is the only appropriate punishment for murder.
- The death penalty is an effective deterrent.
- The death penalty should be extended to individuals who commit heinous crimes other than murder.
- The death penalty is part of a broader goal to ensure just punishments for criminals.

Overview

The death penalty has been a significant aspect of the American criminal justice system at both the federal and the state levels since the founding of the country. Commonly used as a method of punishment throughout Great Britain, British settlers brought the practice with them to the American colonies. When the Constitutional Convention drafted the U.S. Constitution in 1787, all thirteen colonies provided for the death penalty. In 1790, the first Congress enacted the federal death penalty for crimes committed against the United States, including treason, piracy, murder, and forgery. The use of the death penalty at the state level steadily increased throughout the eighteenth and nineteenth centuries, primarily because most crimes are violations of state law. In the twentieth century, over seven thousand individuals were executed before the U.S. Supreme Court issued its landmark ruling in *Furman v. Georgia* (1972).

In *Furman v. Georgia*, the Court held that the way the death penalty was being implemented violated the Cruel and Unusual Punishment Clause of the Eighth Amendment. The Court's complex ruling was decided by a 5-4 margin with each member of the majority writing a separate opinion. While two justices argued that the death penalty itself was cruel and unusual punishment, three justices argued instead that the *process* by which the death sentence was imposed was constitutionally problematic. The laws at issue in this case did not specify the crimes for which a defendant could receive a death sentence. As a result, said the Court, juries had "unfettered discretion" in deciding when to impose capital punishment. This situation led specifically to racially discriminatory sentencing and more generally to death sentences being "wantonly and freakishly imposed."

The immediate effect of this ruling was the invalidation of death sentences at both the state and the federal levels because none of the capital punishment statutes would have survived review by the Court. After *Furman*, thirty-five states revised their capital punishment statutes. Georgia's revised statutory scheme was challenged in *Gregg v. Georgia* (1976), which also reached the U.S. Supreme Court. The revised law specified six categories of crime for which the death penalty could be imposed. The law also provided for a bifurcated, or two-stage, trial. In the first phase, the guilt of the defendant was determined. In the second phase, the jury imposed the sentence. During the sentencing phase, the jury was required to determine that at least one statutory aggravating factor existed before it could impose the death penalty. The Supreme Court rejected the argument that the death penalty in and of itself was cruel and unusual and upheld the law because it created the type of clear guidelines lacking in *Furman*. This ruling led to the reinstatement of capital punishment across the country.

In defining "cruel and unusual" punishment, the Court has held that "the Amendment must draw its meaning from the evolving standards of decency that mark the progress of a maturing society." Using this standard in *Coker v. Georgia*

(1977), the Court held that executing someone who has committed rape is unusual, and thus unconstitutional, because the number of states executing defendants for rape declined from eighteen in 1925 to only one (Georgia) in 1976. Employing the same rationale, the Court has held that mentally incapacitated defendants, juveniles, and child rapists are not eligible for the death penalty. Indeed, the Court's jurisprudence indicates that capital punishment can be imposed only for crimes in which the victim was murdered.

Congress reinstated the federal death penalty in 1988 with the Anti-Drug Abuse Act. In addition to enacting policies related to the Reagan administration's War on Drugs, this law provided for the death penalty when a defendant was convicted in federal court of a murder committed while engaging in a continuing criminal enterprise, such as killing or ordering killings while committing drug-related felonies. The federal death penalty was expanded in the Violent Crime Control and Law Enforcement Act of 1994, the largest crime bill in U.S. history. Among its many provisions was a significant expansion of the federal death penalty to include sixty crimes related to terrorism, murder of a federal law enforcement officer, civil rights–related murders, fatal drive-by shootings, and fatal carjackings. After the bombing of the Alfred P. Murrah Federal Building in Oklahoma City in 1995, Congress enacted the Anti-Terrorism and Effective Death Penalty Act of 1996, which limited federal habeas corpus relief for death penalty appeals. This legislation placed stringent limits on state cases in which defendants sentenced to death could have their appeals heard in federal court.

Since most crimes, including first-degree murder, are violations of state law, presidents have limited influence on death penalty policies. Even at the federal level, Congress must act to modify federal death penalty statutes. The president can influence both state and federal capital punishment laws, however, through the appointment of federal judges, especially Supreme Court Justices. Consequently, the death penalty has played an important role in presidential politics.

The Democratic and Republican parties began to incorporate their views on this issue into their platforms in the 1970s. In 1972, the Democratic Party became the first of the parties to take a stand on the death penalty when it stated in its official party platform that it should be abolished. The issue was not specifically addressed in a Democratic platform again until 1996. In the intervening years, Democratic presidential candidates took varying positions on the issue. When he ran for president in 1976, Jimmy Carter supported it in limited instances, while Walter Mondale, the party's 1984 nominee, was opposed to it. In 1988, Democratic contender Michael Dukakis's dispassionate answer to a question about his opposition to capital punishment during a presidential debate was seized on by Republicans to paint him as "soft on crime." Since that campaign, every Democratic nominee has supported the death penalty, albeit to varying degrees until 2020. The 2020 Democratic nominee, former senator and vice president Joe Biden, supported the death penalty throughout his time as a senator; however, during the 2020 presidential campaign, he changed his stance on the issue.

The Republican Party has consistently supported the death penalty since the Court's ruling in *Furman*. The party first addressed the issue in its 1976 platform with the assertion that states have the power to institute capital punishment laws within their borders. In subsequent platforms, the party reiterated its support for the death penalty and advocated expanding it to include drug traffickers throughout the 1980s, 1990s, and early 2000s. Beginning in the late 1990s the death penalty plank of the GOP platform criticized Supreme Court rulings limiting capital punishment, even though the Court also consistently upheld its constitutionality. More recent Republican platforms have continued to advocate for the death penalty as one aspect of a broader criminal justice strategy. While a majority of Republicans support the death penalty for defendants who commit first-degree murder, surveys indicate that a growing number are concerned that its cost and its ineffectiveness in reducing murder rates violate basic conservative principles against big government programs.

Democrats and Capital Punishment

The Democratic Party's view on the death penalty has shifted dramatically since 1972, when its platform explicitly advocated for its abolition. In the 1990s, however, the party supported capital punishment and even supported its expansion, at least partly to insulate itself from Republican criticisms that Democrats were "soft" on crime. During the 2000s, the Democratic platform supported the death penalty but also emphasized procedural safeguards, including DNA testing, effective counsel, and post-conviction review to make sure innocent people were not put to death. In 2016, the platform unequivocally supported abolishing the death penalty despite the views of Democratic presidential nominee Hillary Clinton, who argued that it was appropriate for certain crimes. The 2020 Democratic presidential nominee, Joe Biden, reversed his earlier support for capital punishment. The 2020 platform stated simply that "Democrats continue to support abolishing the death penalty."

The first mention of the death penalty in the Democratic Party platform was in 1972. Capital punishment was a pressing issue of public concern after the U.S. Supreme Court's ruling in *Furman v. Georgia*. The Democratic platform stated that justice "expresses the moral character of a nation and its commitment to the rule of law, to equality of all people before the law." The platform characterized the death penalty as being incompatible with justice and stated that it was "an ineffective deterrent to crime, unequally applied and cruel and excessive punishment."

After this bold statement, the Democratic platform did not address the issue again until 1996. The Democratic presidential nominees from 1976 to 1992 did not have a consistent stance on the death penalty. In 1976 and 1980, Jimmy Carter,

Statement from Joe Biden's 2020 Presidential Campaign Website on Capital Punishment

The following statement from 2020 Democratic nominee Joe Biden's website summarizes the key reasons that Democrats have come to oppose the death penalty.

Over 160 individuals who've been sentenced to death in this country since 1973 have later been exonerated. Because we cannot ensure we get death penalty cases right every time, Biden will work to pass legislation to eliminate the death penalty at the federal level, and incentivize states to follow the federal government's example. These individuals should instead serve life sentences without probation or parole.

Source

Biden, Joe. n.d. "Joe Biden's Criminal Justice Policy." Joe Biden for President: Official Campaign Website. Accessed December 17, 2022. http://joebiden.com/justice.

who as governor of Georgia signed the revised death penalty legislation upheld by the Court in *Gregg v. Georgia*, favored the death penalty for a few specific crimes. In 1984, the party's nominee, former vice president Walter Mondale, opposed it.

So did the 1988 nominee, Massachusetts governor Michael Dukakis. In fact, many observers believe that Dukakis paid a political price for his stance that alarmed Democratic Party lawmakers and strategists. During the 1988 campaign, presidential debate moderator Bernard Shaw of CNN asked Dukakis if he would support the death penalty for an individual who raped and murdered his wife. Dukakis answered, "No, I don't, Bernard, and I think you know that I've opposed the death penalty during all of my life. I don't see any evidence that it's a deterrent and I think there are better and more effective ways to deal with violent crime" (Simon 2007). Dukakis's unemotional response to this horrific scenario involving his wife proved costly to his campaign. The Republicans used his stance on the death penalty to portray him as being soft on crime.

Subsequent Democratic candidates sought to avoid that label—often by declaring their support for capital punishment. The 1992 Democratic platform did not specifically address the death penalty. However, three of the five leading contenders for the Democratic nomination supported it. The eventual nominee, Arkansas governor Bill Clinton, even interrupted his campaign just before the New Hampshire primary to return to Arkansas for the execution of an Arkansas inmate, Ricky Ray Rector, despite serious concerns that had been raised about Rector's mental condition. Clinton ran his campaign as a "new Democrat," meaning that he was a more moderate, centrist Democrat who would take more conservative stances on some social issues than other members of his party.

In 1996, a Gallup poll indicated that 78 percent of Americans believed that the death penalty was an appropriate punishment for convicted murderers. That same year, the Democratic platform expressed the party's strongest support yet for the death penalty. "We believe that people who break the law should be punished, and people who commit violent crimes should be punished severely." The platform also touted the passage (with Clinton's signature) of the Violent Crime Control and Law Enforcement Act of 1994 that expanded the death penalty by making it an option for sixty additional federal crimes. Although the law had bipartisan support, Democrats controlled both Houses of Congress and the presidency.

In 2000, the Democratic platform recounted the Clinton administration's efforts to expand the death penalty to include "cop killers and terrorists" and stated that the party's 2000 presidential nominee, Vice President Al Gore, would continue to "move America forward." Gore had supported capital punishment since he was a Tennessee congressman in 1976. But in recognition of the advent of DNA testing, which had exonerated a number of death row inmates in the United States, the Democrats' 2000 platform also advocated new procedural safeguards when individuals were charged with murder to make sure no innocent people were executed. These safeguards included DNA testing, effective assistance of counsel, and post-conviction review, which helps to ensure the fairness of the sentencing process.

The 2004 Democratic platform marked a significant change in the party's approach to the death penalty. For the first time since 1992, it did not address the issue. The Democratic presidential nominee, Senator John Kerry, had opposed the death penalty throughout his political career. Kerry cited his military service in Vietnam, during which he had witnessed the deaths of many people, as the basis for his views. After the September 11 attacks, however, Kerry altered his position by supporting capital punishment in terrorism cases. As a senator, Kerry cosponsored the National Death Penalty Moratorium Act of 2001 and the National Death Penalty Moratorium Act of 2003. This proposed legislation would have suspended the federal death penalty until a commission could study whether its implementation comported with principles of due process.

The death penalty plank returned in the 2008 platform. Democratic nominee Senator Barack Obama was a longtime supporter of the death penalty. He argued that there were some crimes so heinous that death was the only appropriate punishment, but he also argued that procedural safeguards should be implemented to prevent innocent people from being executed. While campaigning for president, Obama expressed disagreement with the Supreme Court's ruling in *Kennedy v. Louisiana* (2008), which invalidated laws allowing child rapists to be sentenced to death. He believed that death was the appropriate punishment for this crime.

The death penalty was not a significant issue in the 2012 campaign. As in the 2000 and 2008 platforms, the 2012 Democratic platform supported the death penalty with safeguards. By 2016, however, public support for the death penalty was at an historic low, particularly among Democratic and Independent voters, according to a Gallup poll. From 1996 to 2016, support for the death penalty dropped from 71 percent to 34 percent among Democrats and from 79 percent to 44 percent for Independents (Jones 2020). The Democratic Party returned to its 1972 view of the death penalty as a cruel and unusual form of punishment in its 2016 platform. The platform cited its lack of a deterrent effect, its cost, its arbitrary and unjust use, and the fact that exonerations of innocent defendants made it an unreliable form of punishment.

Although the Democratic platform called for abolishing capital punishment, 2016 Democratic nominee Hillary Clinton took a different approach. She stated that there were problems with the death penalty because it had been "too frequently applied and too often in a discriminatory way." She also stated that she would welcome a Supreme Court ruling or efforts by the states to eliminate the death penalty; however, she argued that the federal death penalty should still be available for crimes such as terrorism.

The 2020 Democratic platform only stated that the party favored abolishing capital punishment. The party's nominee that year, former senator and vice president Joe Biden, had supported the death penalty in the past. Biden was even an architect of the 1994 Violent Crime Control and Law Enforcement Act, which expanded the number of crimes subject to a federal death penalty. In a 2000 Senate Judiciary Committee hearing, Biden stated that "I don't oppose the death penalty on moral grounds, but I have been fastidious . . . that if you are going to have a death penalty, you had better go out of your way to make sure you don't execute an innocent person." On his 2020 campaign website, Biden pledged to eliminate the federal death penalty and incentivize the states to do the same. He suggested replacing the death penalty with life imprisonment without the possibility of parole.

After he was elected, Biden came under fire from death penalty opponents for not eliminating the federal death penalty during the first one hundred days of his presidency. Critics contended that he could commute the sentences of death row inmates. While Biden remained silent on the issue, Congressional Democrats introduced legislation to abolish the federal death penalty and to commute the sentences of current federal death row inmates to life imprisonment without the possibility of parole.

Republicans and Capital Punishment

The Republican Party has consistently favored the death penalty since it became a salient national political issue in the 1970s. Republican platforms and presidential nominees have long focused on the alleged deterrent effect of the death penalty and protecting the rights of crime victims. Since the early 2010s, however, public opinion polls and actions by Republican public officials in several states indicate a potential shift in the party's stance on the death penalty.

Immediately after the Supreme Court's ruling in *Furman v. Georgia*, Republican president Richard Nixon stated that he hoped the decision did not foreclose capital punishment for kidnapping and hijacking. Later, when it became clear that it did, Nixon stated in a Special Message to Congress that "the death penalty is not a sanction to be employed loosely or considered lightly, but neither is it to be ignored as a fitting penalty, in exceptional circumstances, for the purpose of preventing or deterring crime." Nixon also believed that Congress should reinstate the federal death penalty for treason, assassination, acts of sabotage and espionage, and instances in which violations of federal law resulted in death. Leading anti–death penalty scholar Hugo Adam Bedau criticized the Nixon administration's argument that the death penalty was an effective deterrent. Bedau noted that the study cited by the administration was based more on anecdotal evidence than actual statistical evidence (Bedau 1973).

The Republican Party Platform addressed capital punishment for the first time in 1976. The platform emphasized that law enforcement was primarily a local responsibility and that the states have the power to decide whether they want to impose capital punishment. The party took a similar stance in 1980 but added that the death penalty was "an effective deterrent to capital crime" that both the states and the federal government should permit.

The party's 1984 platform promised to restore a constitutionally valid federal death penalty. The GOP platform framed the party's stance on capital punishment within the broader context of public opinion supporting it. President Ronald Reagan employed this approach in his 1985 State of the Union Address when he called for reinstating the federal death penalty, despite its limited applicability, because Americans overwhelmingly supported it. During the mid-1980s, public opinion polls showed that approximately 70 percent of Americans supported the death penalty.

In 1988, the Republican Party platform not only pledged to reestablish the federal death penalty but also stated that major drug traffickers and individuals who kill federal agents should be eligible for that punishment. Republican nominee and vice president George H. W. Bush drew a distinction between his views and those of his Democratic opponent, Michael Dukakis, in his acceptance speech at the Republican National Convention. Bush asked, "Should society be allowed to impose the death penalty on those who commit crimes of extraordinary cruelty and violence? My opponent says no, but I say yes." Further, Bush stated, "And I'm the one who says a drug dealer who is responsible for the death of a policeman should be subject to capital punishment." The death penalty, along with the parties' respective approaches to dealing with crime, became a key topic in the presidential election—particularly after the final presidential debate. After Dukakis failed to show any emotion when asked whether he would favor the death penalty if an individual raped and murdered his wife, Bush extended his lead in the polls by seven points.

In 1992, both parties' presidential candidates favored capital punishment, so the Republican platform attacked Congressional Democrats for refusing "to enact effective procedures for reinstating the death penalty for the most heinous crimes." As in 1988, the 1992 GOP platform advocated capital punishment for major drug traffickers.

In 1994, the Republicans regained control of the House and Senate for the first time in forty years. Thus, the 1996 platform touted the legislative accomplishments of the party in the area of criminal justice. The death penalty plank was much stronger than in previous years. The platform stated that it was time to revisit the Supreme Court's "arbitrary" ruling in *Coker v. Georgia*, which prevented convicted rapists from being executed, and boasted of "our strong support of capital punishment for those who commit heinous federal crimes—including drug kingpins." The platform directly attacked President Clinton, accusing him of "hypocrisy" in supporting the 1994 Violent Crime Control and Law Enforcement Act and then appointing federal judges who opposed capital punishment. The platform pledged that 1996 Republican presidential nominee Bob Dole would "end that nonsense and make our courts once again an instrument of justice."

The 2000 GOP platform claimed that the federal death penalty was an effective deterrent against crime. It also renewed the support it had expressed in previous platforms for capital punishment for drug traffickers who "take innocent life." The Republican presidential nominee, Texas governor George W. Bush, had presided over more executions than any other governor since the death penalty was reinstated, including the highly publicized execution of Karla Faye Tucker in 1998. Convicted of brutally murdering two people, Tucker became a Christian in prison and many evangelical Christians considered her a role model for rehabilitation; however, Bush denied her pleas for forgiveness and clemency, even though religious leaders such as Pat Robertson and Pope John Paul II supported her.

During the 2000 election campaign, Bush issued a rare stay of execution for a defendant when questions were raised about the DNA evidence introduced during the sentencing phase of his trial. Bush's critics argued that he was attempting to insulate himself against any political backlash for the number of executions over which he presided. Although a majority of Americans (66 percent) supported the death penalty in 2000, the number was down fourteen points from just six years prior (Pew Research Center 2018).

In 2004, the Republican platform limited its support for the death penalty to instances of capital murder for the first time ever. It made no mention of supporting the death penalty for drug traffickers and less of the platform was devoted to the issue than in previous years. In 2008, both Republican nominee John McCain and Democratic nominee Barack Obama supported the death penalty. The GOP platform in 2008 criticized the U.S. Supreme Court's rulings limiting capital punishment and emphasized the party's belief that the death penalty must be an option for capital murder cases and other heinous crimes. The platform advocated streamlined federal review of deaths sentences to only focus on claims of innocence. In 1994, McCain voted against a Senate bill that would have prohibited African

Americans sentenced to death from introducing evidence of racial discrimination in capital punishment. In *McKleskey v. Kemp* (1987), the Supreme Court had barred the use of aggregate statistics to show that Black defendants were significantly more likely to be sentenced to death than white defendants. Republicans in Congress feared that if this type of data were introduced at trial, it would make it impossible for prosecutors to secure a capital conviction. McCain also favored banning the death penalty for minors.

When the 2012 Republican nominee, Mitt Romney, was governor of Massachusetts he had appointed a commission to revisit the death penalty, which the state had abolished in 1984. The goal was to create a "virtually foolproof" system so that only those individuals who were guilty were sentenced to death. The bill crafted from the commission's findings included several unique provisions. For example, it would require conclusive scientific evidence such as DNA linking a defendant to a crime; that a jury found the defendant guilty with "no doubt," a higher standard than "beyond a reasonable doubt"; and that a defendant have at least two attorneys to represent them. Romney's critics asserted that since there was little chance of the bill passing in a state legislature controlled by Democrats, his motive had little to do with reinstating capital punishment in Massachusetts and more to do with demonstrating to conservatives across the country that he supported the death penalty. During the campaign, Romney did not devote much time to discussing his proposal choosing instead to focus on the economy.

In 2013, conservatives who were critical of the Republican Party's support for the death penalty formed Conservatives Concerned About the Death Penalty. This organization cites its high cost, the possibility of executing an innocent person, and the questionable deterrent effect as key reasons for opposing capital punishment. The high costs of the death penalty stem from the intensive trial and appellate process for capital cases. States that have the death penalty spend millions more in prosecuting these cases than noncapital cases resulting in a sentence of life without the possibility of parole.

There is also growing concern over executions of innocent people. In a 2016 Pew poll, 84 percent of those who opposed the death penalty and 63 percent of those who supported it believed there was a risk of executing someone who was innocent of the crime. Many Republicans have come to express uneasiness with how support for capital punishment can be reconciled with the overall pro-life views of the party. Thus, some conservatives are critical of the death penalty as an inefficient, costly government program.

According to polling by the Pew Research Center and Gallup, by 2016, public support for capital punishment had fallen to a near historic low with 56 percent supporting it (Jones 2020); however, 77 percent of Republicans were in favor of it (Pew Research Center 2018). In 2020, support for the death penalty had fallen to 55 percent with 79 percent of Republicans supporting it (Jones 2020).

The 2016 and 2020 platforms (which are identical) stated that the death penalty's constitutionality was firmly settled by its explicit mention in the Fifth Amendment.

The Republican Party Position on the Death Penalty

The following statement from the 2016 Republican Party Platform outlines the primary GOP arguments in favor of the death penalty.

> The constitutionality of the death penalty is firmly settled by its explicit mention in the Fifth Amendment. With the murder rate soaring in our great cities, we condemn the Supreme Court's erosion of the right of the people to enact capital punishment in their states.

Source

Republican Party Platform. 2016. American Presidency Project. Accessed November 22, 2022. https://www.gop.com/the-2016-republican-party-platform/.

The platforms condemned the Supreme Court's limitations on the right of the people to enact capital punishment laws in their states. Republican Donald Trump, who had not held public office prior to winning the presidency in 2016, did not have an official record on the death penalty prior to his first presidential campaign. However, as a high-profile real estate developer in New York City, he called for the death penalty for several Black and Latino youths known as the Central Park Five in 1989 after they had been accused of the brutal rape of a jogger in Central Park. Trump spent $85,000 on a full-page ad published in New York City newspapers titled "BRING BACK THE DEATH PENALTY. BRING BACK THE POLICE!" The ad argued that the Black teenagers (aged fourteen to sixteen) should be executed. Although they were convicted, they were exonerated in 2002.

In February 2020, Trump praised Chinese president Xi Jingpeng's use of the death penalty for drug dealers. The Trump administration ended a seventeen-year hiatus on federal executions in 2020 and executed more federal death row inmates than had been executed in the previous fifty years (Editorial Board 2020). Ten executions were carried out from July 2020 to December 2020, and three in January 2021 during the waning days of the Trump administration. This action was unprecedented not only in terms of numbers but also because outgoing presidents have historically deferred those types of decisions to their successors. The last time a lame-duck president presided over an execution was in 1889. Critics noted that the number of federal executions ran counter to public opinion and to the trend of state executions, which had been postponed due to the COVID-19 pandemic.

Further Reading

Abramson, Paul R., John H. Aldrich, and David W. Rohde. 2007. *Change and Continuity in the 2004 and 2008 Elections.* Washington, DC: CQ Press.

Arango, Tim. 2019. "Democrats Rethink the Death Penalty, and Its Politics." *New York Times*, April 7. Accessed June 17, 2019. https://www.nytimes.com/2019/04/07/us/politics/death-penalty-democrats.html?searchResultPosition=1.

Baker, Peter. 2018. "Bush Made Willie Horton an Issue in 1988, and the Racial Scars Are Still Fresh." *New York Times*, December 13. Accessed June 11, 2019. https://www.nytimes .com/2018/12/03/us/politics/bush-willie-horton.html?searchResultPosition=1.

Bedau, Hugo Adam. 1973. "The Nixon Administration and the Deterrent Effect of the Death Penalty." *University of Pittsburgh Law Review* 34, no. 4: 557–566. Accessed December 17, 2022. https://heinonline.org/HOL/Page?handle=hein.journals/upitt34 &page=557&collection=journals.

Caldiego, Christopher. 2019. "Biden Appears to Be Softening His Stance on the Death Penalty." *Politico*, June 20. Accessed December 13, 2020. https://www.politico.com /story/2019/06/20/joe-biden-death-penalty-1371932.

Carrega, Christina. 2021. "Biden Vowed to End the Death Penalty: Activists Are Demanding Action as He Nears the 100-Day Mark." *CNN*, April 25. Accessed September 1, 2022. https://www.cnn.com/2021/04/25/politics/death-penalty-biden-100-days/index.html.

Democratic Party Platforms. 1972–2020. American Presidency Project. Accessed November 22, 2022. https://www.presidency.ucsb.edu/people/other/democratic-party-platforms.

Editorial Board of the *Washington Post*. 2020. "Trump Pushes an Unprecedented and Unjust Wave of Executions." *Washington Post*, November 29. Accessed December 13, 2020. https://www.washingtonpost.com/opinions/trump-pushes-an-unprecedented-and -unjust-wave-of-executions/2020/11/26/e8d06606-2f59-11eb-bae0-50bb17126614 _story.html.

Ford, Matt. 2018. "The Trump Administration's Death Penalty Daydream." *New Republic*, March 21. Accessed July 16, 2019. https://newrepublic.com/article/147608 /trump-administrations-death-penalty-daydream.

Fournier, Ron. 2015. "The Time Bill Clinton and I Killed a Man." *National Journal*, May 28. Accessed June 20, 2019. https://www.nationaljournal.com/s/26479/time-bill-clinton -i-killed-man.

Honderich, Holly. 2021. "In Trump's Final Days, a Rush of Federal Executions." *BBC*, January 16. Accessed September 2, 2022. https://www.bbc.com/news/world-us-canada -55236260.

Jones, Jeffrey M. 2020. "U.S. Support for Death Penalty Holds Above Majority Level." *Gallup*, November 19. Accessed December 13, 2020. https://news.gallup.com/poll/325568 /support-death-penalty-holds-above-majority-level.aspx.

Montgomery, David. 2019. "Death Penalty Opponents Gain Unlikely Allies: Republicans." *Stateline*, March 20. Accessed June 11, 2019. https://www.pewtrusts.org/en/research -and-analysis/blogs/stateline/2019/03/20/death-penalty-opponents-gain-unlikely -allies-republicans.

Moore, Solomon. 2008. "Records of Obama and McCain as Lawmakers Reflect Differences on Crime." *New York Times*, October 31. Accessed June 20, 2019. https:// www.nytimes.com/2008/10/31/world/americas/31iht-31crime.17405569.html? searchResultPosition=1.

Pew Research Center. 2018. "U.S. Support for Death Penalty Ticks Up in 2018." June 11. Accessed June 20, 2019. https://www.pewresearch.org/fact-tank/2018/06/11/us -support-for-death-penalty-ticks-up-2018/.

Republican Party Platforms. 1972–2020. American Presidency Project. Accessed November 22, 2022. https://www.presidency.ucsb.edu/people/other/republican-party-platforms.

Simon, Roger. 2007. "Questions That Kill Candidates' Careers." *Politico*, April 20. Accessed June 27, 2019. https://www.politico.com/story/2007/04/questions-that-kill -candidates-careers-003617.

Slisco, Alia. 2020. "Trump Praises China's 'Powerful Death Penalty' for Drug Dealers, Says He's Unsure If America's 'Ready for That.'" *Newsweek*, February 2. Accessed December 13, 2020. https://www.newsweek.com/trump-praises-chinas-powerful-death-penalty -drug-dealers-says-hes-unsure-if-americas-ready-1486604.

Yardley, Jim. 2000. "ON THE RECORD/Bush and the Death Penalty; Texas' Busy Death Chamber Helps Define Bush's Tenure." *New York Times*, January 7. Accessed June 27, 2019. https://www.nytimes.com/2000/01/07/us/record-bush-death-penalty-texas -busy-death-chamber-helps-define-bush-s-tenure.html?searchResultPosition=1.

Disability Rights

At a Glance

Disabled Americans have endured discrimination since the earliest days of the nation, but legal protections and rights for people with disabilities became a growing social cause in the mid-twentieth century. The federal government responded to this public pressure by enacting several laws to protect the rights of disabled Americans in the 1970s; in 1990, the landmark Americans with Disabilities Act (ADA) was passed with strong bipartisan support in Congress.

While disability rights legislation has traditionally enjoyed bipartisan support, more recently the parties have differed in their approaches to protecting those rights. Republicans have supported placing new limits on the ADA's authority and reach, while Democrats argue that the ADA should be *more* vigorously enforced. The parties have focused on differing aspects of health care for disabled Americans, with Republicans concentrating on issues such as opposing euthanasia and Democrats emphasizing access to health care through the Affordable Care Act (ACA; 2010).

Republicans and Democrats also disagree on formal U.S. ratification of the UN Convention on the Rights of Persons with Disabilities (CRPD). This treaty, modeled after the ADA, would provide more protection for disabled individuals around the world, including Americans working and traveling abroad. Democrats support the treaty because it would extend ADA protections across the globe, but Republicans oppose it, claiming it would infringe on U.S. sovereignty.

According to many Republicans . . .

- The ADA's regulatory power should be limited to protect businesses.
- Disabled Americans should be protected from attempts to legalize euthanasia.
- The United States should reject the UN CRPD because it jeopardizes the sovereignty of U.S. law.

According to many Democrats . . .

- The ADA should be more vigorously enforced.
- The ADA should continue to protect access to health care for disabled Americans.
- The United States should ratify the UN CRPD to ensure protections of disabled Americans abroad.

Overview

Living in a World without Rights or Legal Protection

For centuries, individuals with physical and mental disabilities have been stigmatized and denied rights available to nondisabled Americans. The care of disabled individuals was largely left to their families until the nineteenth century when social reformers established schools and institutions for their benefit and care. In 1854, due largely to Dorothea Dix, an advocate for the indigent mentally ill, Congress passed the Land-Grant Bill for Indigent Insane Persons. This bill dedicated federal land for mental hospitals and directed that the proceeds from the sale of additional federal land be awarded to the states for the construction of asylums. President Franklin Pierce vetoed the bill, arguing that assistance for disabled individuals was not a federal issue. Pierce's veto appeased Southern congressmen who were concerned that any expansion of federal power into areas traditionally governed by the states could establish a precedent that would limit slavery.

The federal government began providing services to physically disabled individuals after soldiers returned from World War I with debilitating injuries. Congress enacted the Smith-Sears Veterans Rehabilitation Act of 1918 (also known as the Soldiers Rehabilitation Act), which provided federal funds for vocational rehabilitation of disabled veterans. Two years later, in 1920, Congress passed the Smith-Fess Act, also known as the Civilian Vocational Rehabilitation Act. This important legislation provided federal matching funds to states to support vocational rehabilitation programs for Americans with physical disabilities.

Among the many provisions of the Social Security Act of 1935 were those that expanded vocational rehabilitation programs and provided income support for blind Americans. Congress extended income support to disabled Americans in the Social Security Disability Insurance program as part of the 1956 amendments to the act.

While federal programs addressing physical disabilities steadily expanded during the twentieth century, individuals with mental disabilities received no legal protection or federal assistance due to entrenched social stigma associated with those illnesses. Indeed, in *Buck v. Bell* (1927), the U.S. Supreme Court upheld the constitutionality of a Virginia law authorizing the forced sterilization of women deemed to be "feeble minded" in order to prevent them from passing the condition on to their offspring. In the ruling, Justice Oliver Wendell Holmes stated that "[i]t is better for all the world, if instead of waiting to execute degenerate offspring for crime, or to let them starve for their imbecility, society can prevent those who are manifestly unfit from continuing their kind. . . . Three generations of imbeciles are enough."

Now widely denounced, Holmes's opinion was a product of the eugenics movement, which was prevalent in the United States and Europe during the late nineteenth and early twentieth centuries. Eugenics proponents distorted Charles Darwin's theory of evolution and the concept of "survival of the fittest" to justify policies such as forced sterilization to prevent "unfit" or "defective" individuals from reproducing and passing on defective traits to their children. These individuals included epileptics, women of questionable moral character, alcoholics, immigrants, and criminals. Over thirty states enacted forced sterilization laws in the early twentieth century. Historians say these laws provided a model for Adolph Hitler's extermination of six million Jews and millions of physically and mentally disabled and LGBT individuals, political opposition groups, and other "undesirables" in Nazi Germany.

In 1963, President John F. Kennedy signed the first federal legislation aiding the intellectually disabled and mentally ill. Shortly after he became president, Kennedy established a twenty-seven-member commission to study issues affecting those Americans and to provide policy recommendations to solve those issues. His commitment was inspired by one of his sisters who was intellectually disabled. The Maternal and Child Health and Mental Retardation Planning Amendment to the Social Security Act provided grants to states to update their programs for the intellectually disabled and increased funding for programs geared toward preventing intellectual disabilities.

Disability Policies at the Federal Level

Federal legislation addressing disabilities significantly increased in the 1960s and 1970s. In 1966, Congress amended the Elementary and Secondary Education Act of 1965 to provide funding for states to start, expand, and improve educational opportunities for mentally and physically disabled children. The Architectural Barriers Act of 1968 required buildings owned or leased by the federal government to be handicapped accessible. In 1972, Congress created Supplemental Security Income, which authorized benefits, subject to a needs test, for the indigent, blind, aged, and disabled.

The Rehabilitation Act of 1973 was another significant milestone in federal lawmaking pertaining to disability rights. Republican president Richard Nixon vetoed two previous versions of the bill because of their cost, but he signed the law after demonstrations by disabled Americans, including activists who parked their wheelchairs in the middle of Madison Avenue in New York City during rush-hour traffic, brought increased public attention to the legislation. The law prohibited disability discrimination in federal programs and programs that received federal funds. It also prohibited disability discrimination in federal employment and in employment practices by federal contractors.

In the late 1970s, lackluster enforcement of the Rehabilitation Act spurred further protests by disabled Americans. In 1975, Congress enacted the Education for All Handicapped Children Act, which was later renamed the Individuals with Disabilities Education Act. The original law forbade discrimination against disabled students and required their inclusion in mainstream public-school classrooms. The updated law required the development of an individual education plan with parental involvement for students with disabilities.

Until the 1980s, disability rights legislation was enacted through a piecemeal approach. At that time, activists sought the enactment of comprehensive disability rights legislation. The National Council on Disability, then known as the National Council on the Handicapped, an independent federal agency that provides advice to the president and Congress on disability issues, released a report in 1986 recommending comprehensive disability civil rights legislation. During the 1988 presidential campaign, Vice President George H. W. Bush pledged to sign a disability rights law.

Help for People with Disabilities with the ADA and the ACA

The Americans with Disabilities Act passed the House of Representatives by a vote of 377-28 and the Senate by a vote of 91-6. It was signed into law by Republican president George H. W. Bush in July 1990. This landmark law bans discrimination on the basis of disability in four broad areas: employment, state and local government, public accommodations, and telecommunications. Due to the breadth of the law, federal courts, including the U.S. Supreme Court, limited its scope by using a narrow definition of "disability." In response to these decisions, the Americans with Disabilities Amendments Act was passed with bipartisan support and signed into law by Republican president George W. Bush in 2008. The law overturned Supreme Court rulings using a narrow definition of disability and gave courts greater guidance on evaluating disability discrimination claims under the ADA.

The ADA did not, however, address a very significant aspect of disability rights: health care. The Patient Protection and Affordable Care Act, or Affordable Care Act of 2010, sought to provide greater access to health care for Americans, including those with disabilities. Prior to the enactment of this legislation, many disabled individuals had great difficulty securing health-care benefits. ACA benefited disabled individuals in many ways. The law prevented insurance companies from denying care based on preexisting conditions and from denying coverage to individuals who became disabled. The law also prohibited insurance companies from raising rates on health-care coverage to disabled persons, and it expanded Medicaid programs providing in-home care. It required insurance companies to cover "essential services," which included mental health care and substance abuse treatment. The ACA was enacted without any Republican support in either chamber of Congress. Republicans argued that the law gave the federal government too much authority over health-care regulations, while Democrats argued that the law would increase access and decrease costs of health care.

The parties also disagreed over a treaty modeled after the ADA. In 2006, the Bush administration negotiated the UN Convention on the Rights of Disabled Persons. It was signed by Democratic president Barack Obama in 2009. When the treaty was submitted to the Senate for ratification in 2012, it was defeated by a vote of 61-38 with the split occurring along party lines; the U.S. Constitution requires 66 votes for treaty ratification. Democratic senators supported the treaty arguing that ratification demonstrated the United States' leadership on this issue. Despite strong lobbying efforts by former president George H. W. Bush and former Republican senate majority leader Bob Dole, who lost the use of an arm in World War II, only eight Republican senators supported the treaty. Republican opposition stemmed from a concern that the UN could interfere with U.S. law. In 2014, Democratic senator Tom Harkin attempted to bring the treaty back to the Senate floor for a vote, but that effort was blocked by conservative Republicans.

Disability rights garnered unprecedented attention during the 2016 presidential campaign. While campaigning in South Carolina in November 2015, Republican nominee Donald Trump mocked a *New York Times* reporter, Serge Kovaleski, with a congenital joint condition limiting the range of motion in his arms. Trump also drew the ire of disability rights activists for titling his campaign book "Crippled America." Of the other candidates for the Republican nomination, only Jeb Bush, whose father and brother supported the ADA, devoted any attention to disability rights on their campaign websites.

While Trump touted advances for disability rights during his administration, critics argued that his support for repealing ACA would harm millions of disabled Americans. During the 2020 campaign, Democratic candidates emphasized their support for ACA and the expansion of Medicare to ensure health-care access for all Americans. Since defeating Trump in the 2020 election and moving into the White House in January 2021, President Joe Biden and his administration have vowed to continue defending the ACA and other laws and programs benefitting people with disabilities.

Republicans

ADA Liability

Following the passage of the ADA, some Republicans raised concerns regarding the liability businesses faced under the law. Under Title III of the ADA, places of public accommodation can be required to make repairs or modifications necessary for their premises to become compliant with the law. Those who violate Title III can be liable for the attorneys' fees of those who file a suit against them. Some

Republicans feared that trial lawyers were using Title III lawsuits as an opportunity to charge high fees.

In 2000, Republican representatives Mark Foley and Clay Shaw proposed the ADA Notification Act. The law was designed to provide noncompliant businesses a ninety-day period in which to rectify ADA violations prior to a lawsuit being filed. Republicans argued that the amendment would inhibit some lawyers from suing businesses for ADA infractions and collecting expensive attorneys' fees that could exceed the cost of repairing the infraction (Mezey 2005, 113). During hearings on the bill, actor Clint Eastwood testified that he was sued $25,000 for Title III violations and $577,000 in legal fees for a hotel he owned (113–114). While a companion bill was introduced in the Senate by Republican Tim Hutchinson, Congress did not approve either bill.

Republican president George W. Bush opposed the ADA Notification Act on the grounds that changes to the ADA could ultimately result in reduced protections for those with disabilities (National Council on Disability 2001). Despite President Bush's opposition, similar ADA Notification Acts were unsuccessfully proposed by House Republicans in each of the 106th-114th Congresses.

In 2015, Representative Ted Poe introduced a revised version of the bill styled as the ADA Education and Reform Act of 2015. While this bill did not pass the House, it became the basis for the ADA Education and Reform Act of 2017. According to this GOP -crafted bill, the owner/operator of a place of public accommodation must be given notice prior to a lawsuit that includes when an individual was denied access to public accommodation and what barriers were present. Upon receipt of this notification, the owner/operator of the public accommodation has sixty days to respond detailing how they will fix the accommodation and an additional sixty days to make the modifications (U.S. Congress 2017).

The bill passed the House with broad Republican support, but Democratic opposition prevented its consideration in the Senate. Disability rights organizations also opposed the bill. The Consortium for Citizens with Disabilities, the largest coalition of national disability rights organizations, wrote a letter to the House Judiciary Committee in which it charged the bill would make it much harder for persons with disabilities to "engage in daily activities and participate in the mainstream of society" (ACLU 2017). The group argued that the bill shifted the burden to the person with the disability to ensure access to public accommodations when it should be with the business owner.

Euthanasia

In 1992, the GOP platform pledged opposition to euthanasia and assisted suicide as a reflection of Republican support for the ADA and the party's opposition to involuntarily refusing medical care to individuals because of disability and other conditions. Republicans and other pro-life advocates were concerned that if disabled individuals were allowed to end their own lives or if medical care could be withdrawn, society would devalue their lives, eventually leading us down a path to involuntary euthanasia. The George W. Bush administration opposed efforts to legalize euthanasia and assisted suicide throughout his two terms in office.

In 2005, in a particularly high-profile case, the Bush administration fought attempts by Michael Schiavo to have the feed tube of his wife, Terri Schiavo, removed after she suffered severe brain damage. Schiavo requested the removal of his wife's feeding tube, asserting she would not have wanted to continue living in her condition. The case gained national attention when Terri Schiavo's parents disagreed. After a Florida court permitted the removal of the feeding tube, Congress enacted legislation allowing the case to be heard in a federal court. Federal courts do not normally have jurisdiction in these matters; however, Congress determines which types of cases federal courts can decide. Congressional Republicans, including Republican senate majority leader and physician Bill Frist, argued that this unusual intervention was necessary to protect "the sanctity of life." Republicans drafted what became known as Terri's Law, a one-page bill giving jurisdiction to the federal courts to decide whether a feeding tube could be removed. The vote took place during the Easter holiday, so most members of Congress had to fly back to Washington, DC, to vote on the law, which passed 203-58 in the House. It was approved by a voice vote in the Senate. President Bush flew from his home in Texas back to Washington, DC, to sign the bill. At the signing of the law, Bush framed the legislation as committed to protecting the lives of disabled individuals: "I will continue to stand on the side of those defending life for all Americans, including those with disabilities" (Bush 2007, 500). The federal courts upheld the ruling of the Florida courts and when the U.S. Supreme Court declined to hear the case, Schiavo's feeding tube was removed.

The 2008–2020 GOP platforms pledged support for those living with disabilities. In 2016, for example, the GOP included the following statement in its official platform:

Under the last two Republican presidents, landmark civil rights legislation affirmed the inherent rights of persons with disabilities. Republicans want to support those rights by guaranteeing access to education and the tools necessary to compete in the mainstream of society. This is not just a moral obligation to our fellow Americans with disabilities. It is our duty to our country's future to tap this vast pool of talented individuals who want to work and contribute to the common good. . . . The Individuals with Disabilities Education Act (IDEA) has opened up unprecedented opportunities for many students. Congressional Republicans will lead in its reauthorization, as well as renewal of the Higher Education Act, which can offer students with disabilities increased access to the general curriculum. Our TIME Act (Transition to Integrated and Meaningful Employment) will modernize the Fair Labor Standards Act to encourage competitive employment for persons with disabilities. We affirm our support for its goal of minimizing the separation of children with disabilities from their peers. We endorse efforts like Employment First that replace dependency with jobs in the mainstream of the American workforce. (Republican Party Platform 2016)

In addition, the platform included language affirming the party's continued staunch opposition to assisted suicide and euthanasia. "We oppose the non-consensual withholding of care or treatment from people with disabilities, including newborns, the elderly, and infirm, just as we oppose euthanasia and assisted suicide, which endanger especially those on the margins of society. We urge the Drug Enforcement Administration to restore its ban on the use of controlled substances for physician-assisted suicide" (Republican Party Platform 2016).

GOP opposition to euthanasia and assisted suicide was further reflected in President Donald Trump's appointment of Neil Gorsuch to the U.S. Supreme Court in 2017. Euthanasia was a topic familiar to Justice Gorsuch, who extensively researched the legal and ethical ramifications of euthanasia and assisted suicide. As part of his study, Gorsuch noted the impact of euthanasia and assisted suicide upon individuals living with disabilities. He asserted that euthanasia legalization could encourage disabled individuals to end life out of peer pressure, when they might otherwise continue leading productive lives (Gorsuch 2006, 125–128).

In addition to judicial appointments, Republican opposition to euthanasia and assisted suicide has also been reflected by GOP efforts to prevent the District of Columbia from legalizing assisted suicide. Following the passage of DC's Death with Dignity Act in 2016, Republicans sought to prevent the law from taking effect. Republican floor speeches opined that legalization of assisted suicide in the nation's capital could contribute to an environment in which assisted suicide became the only affordable option for many individuals. Republicans expressed concerns that those living with disabilities could be targeted (Congress.gov 2017). Ultimately, however, this effort to thwart implementation of the law failed to garner enough congressional support, and the measure took effect on February 18, 2017.

However, public opinion polls have consistently shown that GOP lawmakers are out of step with Republican voters on this issue. Poll after poll shows that a majority of Republican voters favor allowing a terminally ill person to end his or her life with the aid of a doctor. A 2018 Gallup poll, for example, found that 62 percent of Republicans were in favor of such a policy. The only demographic group opposed to the policy was weekly church attenders, 60 percent of whom opposed the policy (Brenan 2018).

While disability rights activists are concerned about euthanasia, the Republican opposition to ACA has resulted in a new wave of activism. Republican proposals for repealing ACA included cuts to Medicaid, which is the primary insurer of disabled Americans. This has led to an increase in membership and donations to disability rights groups and a wave of protests such as "die-ins" at the offices of Congressional Republican leaders (Abrams 2018).

Republicans Oppose Assisted-Suicide

In a 2017 Congressional debate over a proposed assisted-suicide policy in the District of Columbia, Republican Representative Keith Rothfus argued that the policy could hurt disabled Americans.

. . . D.C.'s assisted suicide law, Mr. Speaker, threatens the inalienable rights of vulnerable citizens. Not only does the new D.C. statute tear at the tapestry of our Nation's founding, it directly contradicts the Hippocratic oath every physician takes, to do no harm. I shudder to think of the lives that will be lost because our society tells the weak, the despairing, the suffering, or the hopeless that suicide is the best option for them. Laws similar to the D.C. Death with Dignity Act in the U.S. and Europe have resulted in individuals being pressured to end their lives, and insurance companies covering the reimbursements for suicide treatment but not for other care.

If patients find themselves unable to pay for expensive treatments out-of-pocket, they may find their options severely limited when facing a new diagnosis, facing a disability, or struggling with mental illness. In some cases, death may become the only affordable option. Proponents of physician-assisted suicide point to real and tragic stories of suffering individuals at the end of their lives. However, according to a report by the National Institutes of Health, pain is not the primary factor motivating patients to seek a lethal dose of medication. More commonly cited motivations include depression, hopelessness, and the loss of control or autonomy. Allowing physicians to prescribe lethal medications to these patients would mean we are abandoning our Nation's most vulnerable citizens and, instead, succumbing to a culture that is worse than the disease.

Source

Congress.gov. 2017. "Expressing Strong Opposition to D.C.'s Assisted Suicide Program." Congressional Record. February 16. Accessed December 21, 2022. https://www.congress.gov/congressional-record/volume-163/issue-20/house-section/article/H998-1.

United Nations CRPD

In 2003, international negotiations began for the UN CRPD. Many Republicans opposed ratification of the treaty, claiming that it threatened to undermine American sovereignty, nullify parental rights, and loosen abortion restrictions overseas. During the treaty's development, the George W. Bush administration played a limited role, while offering advice based on U.S. disability rights law. This position reflected the Bush State Department's view that "it would be more productive for nations to strengthen their domestic legal frameworks related to non-discrimination and equality than to negotiate a new UN Convention" (U.S. Department of State 2008, 79). When the treaty was adopted in 2006 at the UN General Assembly, the Bush administration voted to adopt the treaty even as it voiced objections to the CRPD Preamble's reference to "reproductive health," which the administration feared could be construed to support abortion (79–80).

In 2009, Barack Obama signed the CRPD and submitted it for Senate ratification in 2012. When the treaty was brought before the U.S. Senate, thirty-eight Republicans voted against the treaty, highlighting a variety of justifications for their positions. For example, opposition was raised regarding the CRPD's creation of an international Disabilities Committee to monitor the treaty's enforcement. Republican senator Mike Lee (2012) claimed that this oversight could threaten American sovereignty and parental rights by permitting "an international body to define our own domestic law." He argued that such a committee could be tasked with drafting and enforcing regulations and could deem parental decisions such as homeschooling children with disabilities outside the "best interests of the child" (Lee 2012). Assurances from legal experts and diplomats that the committee had no such power were ignored or discounted by critics.

Besides American sovereignty, Republicans also expressed opposition on the grounds that the treaty could result in abortion funding. The senators based their argument on the inclusion of "sexual and reproductive health" in the treaty's explanation that individuals living with disabilities should be afforded the same quality of health care as other individuals (U.S. Congress 2012, 17–18). Without being defined, the senators feared this provision could be interpreted as providing support for abortion. Regarding the potential impact of the treaty on the United States' capacity to lead other nations in the promotion of disability rights, the Republican senators argued that it was unnecessary to ratify the treaty because they believed the United States already led the world in promoting rights for the disabled. Following the CRPD's defeat in 2012, the 2016 and 2020 Republican platforms continued to express the GOP's opposition to the treaty on the grounds that it threatened the sovereignty of the United States.

Despite Republican opposition for the CRPD's ratification, some members of the party came out in support of it. President George H. W. Bush, who signed the ADA into law, expressed support for the treaty. Former senator and 1996 Republican presidential nominee Bob Dole, a disabled World War II veteran, personally came to the Senate floor to advocate for the treaty's passage in 2012. Former Republican senator John McCain echoed Dole's support for the treaty by questioning the objections of his GOP colleagues and emphasizing the treaty "would do nothing to change America's domestic laws regarding abortion" (Menendez and McCain 2013).

Democrats

ADA Liability

Congressional Democrats have opposed efforts to reduce the liability public accommodations are exposed to under Title III of the ADA. Many Democrats view the threat of lawsuits as necessary to encourage businesses to comply with the law.

Without lawsuits, they argue that places of public accommodation could simply refuse to comply with Title III until notified that they are in violation.

When House Republicans first introduced the ADA Notification Act in 2000, House Democrats were staunchly opposed to the bill's provisions limiting the liability of businesses by delaying the time a lawsuit could be filed until after a business had received ample time to make modifications. As one official for the Clinton administration said, businesses noncompliant with the ADA "should not be rewarded" or "receive an unfair competitive advantage over businesses that have already complied in good faith with the law" (U.S. Congress 2000, 140). As modifications of the ADA Notification Act were proposed by House Republicans in the 2000s and early 2010s, Democrats continued to oppose them. John Kerry's 2004 presidential campaign website expressed opposition for the ADA Notification Act as a part of Kerry's pledge to promote equality for those living with disabilities (Kerry-Edwards 2004, n.p.). Likewise, the 2012 Democratic platform promised "to oppose all efforts to weaken the landmark Americans with Disabilities Act" and to "vigorously enforce laws that prevent discrimination."

Following the proposal and eventual passage in the House of the ADA Education and Reform Act of 2017, Democrats expressed strong disapproval for changes to the public accommodation liability provisions of the ADA. For instance, Democratic congressman Jerrold Nadler argued that the bill would incentivize noncompliance with the ADA. With the notification burden placed on the victim and the waiting period for a place of public accommodation to make "substantial progress," Nadler argued the law had a chilling effect on the enforcement of the ADA. He also noted that no other civil rights law put these types of requirements on the victim of discrimination before they even file a suit (Nadler 2018).

Nadler's views were shared by his Democratic colleagues in the Senate. Senator Tammy Duckworth, a disabled veteran, expressed opposition to the reform proposal. He noted that

> Businesses have had 27 years to comply with the ADA public-access protections. Yet rather than investing time and energy to achieve this goal, they are waging a propaganda campaign to convince Congress that their own lack of accessibility isn't the problem—so-called drive-by lawsuits are. Notably, supporters of the ADA Education and Reform Act often do not dispute that they are violating the law. Rather, they simply resent being sued for what they believe are "minor" ADA infractions. (Duckworth 2017)

Duckworth's sentiments were later expressed in a letter penned by forty-three Democratic senators pledging opposition to the ADA Education and Reform Act. Since Senate rules require at least sixty votes to overcome a filibuster, the Democratic opposition to the reform prevented the Senate from acting upon the legislation. In 2020, the Democratic platform raised continued objections

---

Democrats Tout Support for Disability Rights

A 2021 Fact Sheet released by the White House on the 31st anniversary of the ADA outlined Democratic efforts to expand disability rights. This is an excerpt from that document.

The Biden-Harris Administration has taken significant steps to achieve a more inclusive, accessible, and equitable country for people with disabilities, including people with disabilities that experience multiple forms of discrimination and bias on the basis of race, gender, sexual orientation and other factors. Through quick policy action, the Administration has ensured disabled Americans are receiving resources and are included in key administrative proposals. Specifically, the Administration has:

- Centered Equity as a Priority on Day One. President Biden's Inauguration Day Executive Order 13985 on Advancing Racial Equity and Support for Underserved Communities Through the Federal Government directs the whole of federal government to pursue a comprehensive approach to advancing equity for all, including with respect to persons with disabilities. ...

- Increased Access to Democracy for Voters with Disabilities. Executive Order 14019 on Voting Access ensures people with disabilities can access key voting resources, requires an assessment of barriers to the right to vote independently and privately, and will help ensure that all Americans, including voters with disabilities, can exercise their right to vote...

- Advanced Diversity, Equity, Inclusion, and Accessibility Across the Federal Government. In June, President Biden signed Executive Order 14035 advancing diversity, equity, inclusion, and accessibility (DEIA) across the Federal government. The EO charges agencies with assessing their state of DEIA to eliminate barriers employees face. For federal workers with disabilities, the EO sets a path for the Federal government to become a model employer to improve accessibility, ensure accommodations can be requested, increase opportunities for advancement and hiring, and reducing physical accessibility barriers.

Source

"FACT SHEET: Biden-Harris Administration Marks Anniversary of Americans with Disabilities Act and Announces Resources to Support Individuals with Long COVID." 2021. The White House. July 26, 2021. https://www.whitehouse.gov/briefing-room /statements-releases/2021/07/26/fact-sheet-biden-harris-administration-marks-anniversary -of-americans-with-disabilities-act-and-announces-resources-to-support-individuals -with-long-covid/.

---

to ADA liability reforms. It vowed opposition to any efforts reducing the ADA's enforcement capabilities and pledged to defend the rights of all Americans with disabilities:

One in four American adults live with a disability. Democrats believe people with disabilities deserve to lead full, happy, and healthy lives. Democrats will fully enforce the Americans with Disabilities Act, the Individuals with Disabilities Education Act, the Fair Housing Act, the Civil Rights of Institutionalized Persons Act, Section 504 of the Rehabilitation Act, the Mental Health Parity and Addiction Equity Act, and the Help America Vote Act, among other bedrock statutes protecting the rights of people with disabilities. We will oppose any efforts to weaken enforcement of the Americans with Disabilities Act. We will ensure non-discrimination in access to health care, building on the protections for people with disabilities enshrined in the Affordable Care Act. We will ensure every federal agency aggressively enforces the integration mandate affirmed in the Olmstead decision, and repair the damage done by the Trump Administration. We will rigorously enforce non-discrimination protections for people with disabilities in health care, employment, education, and housing, and ensure equal access to the ballot box. (Democratic Party Platform 2020)

The Patient Protection and ACA

Many Democrats support the Patient Protection and ACA's provisions impacting those living with disabilities. The 2012 Democratic platform touted the ACA's capacity to extend health insurance to disabled individuals who had been denied health-care coverage because of preexisting conditions. Additionally, the platform asserted that Americans living with disabilities could benefit from the ACA's provisions for Medicaid expansion and Medicaid home and community-based services (HCBS). The 2016 platform advocated continued support for the ACA against Republican calls for the law's repeal. The platform also pledged to work to expand the ACA's Medicaid expansion program.

During the 2020 Democratic primary, several candidates presented health-care reform proposals. Vermont senator Bernard Sanders advocated a Medicare for All approach that would insure all Americans. Massachusetts senator Elizabeth Warren compiled a comprehensive disability rights proposal that included provisions for reducing the Medicare eligibility age to fifty and extending Medicare eligibility to minors under age eighteen and those making under 200 percent of the federal poverty level (Warren Democrats n.d.). During the campaign, President Joe Biden advocated for a public health-care option, instead of a single-payer system. His plan supported building upon the ACA to offer all Americans the option to buy into a public health-care system. Biden's plan also supported reduced costs and increased eligibility for Americans under the ACA (Biden Harris n.d.). The 2020 Democratic platform reflected the diverse views within the Democratic Party concerning health care: "We are proud our party welcomes advocates who want to build on and strengthen the Affordable Care Act and those who support a Medicare for All approach; all are critical to ensuring that health care is a human right."

In response to the COVID-19 pandemic, the Democratically controlled Congress passed the American Rescue Plan (ARP) without Republican support. Among its provisions, the ARP included funding for Medicaid expansion and for Medicaid HCBS, which has the potential to impact individuals living with disabilities. Medicaid provides coverage for nearly 30 percent of Americans living with disabilities

(Musumeci, Chidambaram, and Watts 2019). Medicaid expansion refers to the ACA's provision that states can extend Medicaid eligibility to adults making within 138 percent of the federal poverty level. For the thirty-eight states that have opted into the program, the federal government reimburses 90 percent of Medicaid costs. To incentivize the remaining twelve states to expand Medicaid, the ARP provides states with an additional 5 percent of funding for regular Medicaid for two years. According to the Kaiser Family Foundation, this additional funding will provide states net reimbursements of over 100 percent of the program's cost for the first two years (Rudowitz, Corallo, and Garfield 2021). Jae Kennedy and Jean Hall have noted that Medicaid expansion programs have the potential to help those living with disabilities as Medicaid eligibility requirements become less stringent. For instance, they found that those with disabilities could grow their savings more without having to keep their assets low enough to remain Medicaid-eligible (Kennedy and Hall 2019).

The ARP's provisions also provide additional funding for Medicaid HCBS. HCBS allows individuals with disabilities to live independently by providing funds for home care aids, transportation assistance, and technology upgrades that can assist those with disabilities who are working from home. During the drafting of the ARP, Senator Tammy Duckworth noted that HCBS funding was needed for Americans living with disabilities in order to prevent mass institutionalization of the disabled, which could lead to more cases of COVID-19 among that population (Duckworth 2020).

Republicans have consistently opposed the ACA. Indeed, the law was enacted without a single Republican vote in Congress. Republicans argue that the law, which requires individuals to purchase health insurance, constitutes an overreach of federal power. They have sought to repeal the law since its inception. In 2017, when Republicans controlled both chambers of Congress and the presidency, the House passed the American Health Care Act, which proposed repealing Obamacare and eliminating the Medicaid expansion. Senate Republicans introduced the Health Care Freedom Act, referred to as a "skinny" repeal of Obamacare because it eliminated a few key provisions of the law. For example, the bill eliminated the individual mandate. The skinny repeal failed by a vote of 51-49 with three Republicans, Susan Collins, John McCain, and Lisa Murkowski, voting with Senate Democrats to defeat the bill.

United Nations CRPD

The 2008 Democratic platform pledged support for passage of the 2006 UN CRPD. After his victory in the 2008 election, Democratic President Barack Obama announced that his administration would sign the CRPD on the nineteenth anniversary of the ADA in 2009. He said the date was chosen because the treaty would "guarantee rights like those afforded under the ADA" (Obama 2013, 1174). When the CRPD went to the Senate for ratification in 2012, all fifty-three Democratic senators voted in favor of the treaty. This support converged around the conviction within Democratic circles that signing the treaty would increase the United States' international influence regarding disability rights, enable American citizens with disabilities to experience greater equality abroad, and give American businesses a boost in the global marketplace.

First, Democrats argued that supporting the CRPD would increase the United States' ability to influence global disability rights discussions. Chairman of the Senate Foreign Relations Committee (SFRC) and future U.S. secretary of state John Kerry claimed that CRPD ratification "would strengthen our hand as we push for higher standards internationally" (U.S. Congress 2012, 22). This sentiment was shared by Judith Heumann, the Obama administration's special adviser for international disability rights. Heumann observed that failure to ratify the treaty could diminish the United States' ability to advocate internationally for disability rights. She pointed out that CRPD ratification had become a "prerequisite" for participation in international disability rights discussions (U.S. Congress 2012, 35). Supporters of passage emphasized that if Congress did not ratify the treaty, the United States would not even have a seat at those tables.

Next, Democratic supporters of the CRPD touted the treaty's potential to benefit American businesses. Heumann argued that American businesses could benefit from international acceptance of the treaty; American companies could export assistive technologies abroad, and U.S. industries could become more competitive globally if international competitors were forced to absorb expensive CRPD compliancy costs that U.S.-based firms had already paid for and implemented (U.S. Congress 2012, 35). Finally, Democrats argued that ratifying the treaty would make traveling abroad easier for Americans with disabilities. Democratic majority whip Richard Durbin expressed support for the CRPD on such grounds, saying that the treaty "promotes independence, dignity and inclusion while protecting the rights of Americans with disabilities when they travel abroad" (Bunis 2012).

Following the defeat of the CRPD in 2012, Democratic senate majority leader Harry Reid attempted to take up the treaty in the 113th Congress, but the treaty was not considered for a full vote in the Senate. Despite these failed attempts to ratify the treaty, the 2016 and 2020 Democratic platforms pledged continued support for the CRPD's ratification.

In 2021, President Joseph Biden's administration advocated for the execution of CRPD provisions globally by providing assistance to interested foreign countries and disability organizations through the State Department's International Disability Rights team (U.S. Department of State 2021). But while Democratic support for ratification remains high, continued unified Republican opposition has kept it from passage.

Kara E. Stooksbury and Derick Marlow

Further Reading

Abrams, Abigail. 2018. "How Donald Trump Inadvertently Sparked a New Disability Rights Movement." *Time*, February 26. Accessed May 4, 2021. https://time.com/5168472 /disability-activism-trump.

American Civil Liberties Union (ACLU). 2017. "Coalition Letter of Opposition for ADA Education and Reform Act of 2017 (H.R. 620)." Accessed May 5, 2021. https://www.aclu .org/letter/coalition-letter-opposition-ada-education-and-reform-act-2017-hr-620.

Biden Harris. n.d. "Health Care." Accessed May 3, 2021. https://joebiden.com/healthcare/.

Brenan, Megan. 2018. "Americans' Strong Support for Euthanasia Persists." Gallup, May 31. Accessed August 4, 2021. https://news.gallup.com/poll/235145/americans-strong -support-euthanasia-persists.aspx.

Bunis, Dena. 2012. "Disability Treaty Gets Bipartisan Support." *CQ Today*, May 29. Accessed November 21, 2022. https://link.gale.com/apps/doc/A291877051/ITOF?u =tel_a_rscc&sid=bookmark-ITOF&xid=3d3413f7.

Bush, George W. 2007. "Statement on Signing Legislation for the Relief of the Parents of Theresa Marie Schiavo, March 21, 2005." In *Public Papers of the Presidents of the United States: George W. Bush, 2005, Book I—January 1 to June 30, 2005*, 500. Washington, DC: Government Printing Office.

Congress.gov. 2017. "Expressing Strong Opposition to D.C.'s Assisted Suicide Program." Congressional Record. February 16. Accessed December 21, 2022. https://www .congress.gov/congressional-record/volume-163/issue-20/house-section/article/H998-1.

Democratic Party Platform. 1992–2020. American Presidency Project. Accessed November 21, 2022. https://www.presidency.ucsb.edu/documents/presidential-documents-archive -guidebook/party-platforms-and-nominating-conventions-3.

Duckworth, Tammy. 2017. "Congress Wants to Make Americans with Disabilities Second-Class Citizens Again." *Washington Post*, October 17. Accessed November 21, 2022. https:// www.washingtonpost.com/opinions/congress-is-on-the-offensive-against-americans -with-disabilities/2017/10/17/f508069c-b359-11e7-9e58-e6288544af98_story.html.

Duckworth, Tammy. 2020. "Republicans Gut Americans with Disabilities Act in Coronavirus Relief Bill." *USA Today*, August 20. Accessed November 21, 2022. https:// www.usatoday.com/story/opinion/voices/2020/08/20/ tammy-duckworth-disabilities -ada-coronavirus-republicans-column/3400566001/.

Gorsuch, Neil M. 2006. *The Future of Assisted Suicide and Euthanasia*. Princeton, NJ: Princeton University Press.

Kennedy, Jae, and Jean Hall. 2019. "For Adults with Disabilities, Medicaid Expansion Works." *The Hill*, February 1. Accessed November 21, 2022. https://thehill.com /opinion/healthcare/428137-for-adults-with-disabilities-medicaid-expansion-works.

Kerry-Edwards. 2004. "Equal Opportunity for All." Accessed April 8, 2021. https:// webarchive.loc.gov/all/20041001044110/http://www.johnkerry.com/issues/civil_rights/.

Lee, Mike. 2012. "Lame Duck Session Not the Time for New Treaty Ratifications." Mike Lee, Senator for Utah, September 24. Accessed November 21, 2022. https://www.lee.senate .gov/public/index.cfm/2012/9/lame-duck-session-not-the-time-for-new-treaty-ratifications.

Menendez, Robert, and John McCain. 2013. "Menendez and McCain: Ratify Disabilities Treaty." *USA Today*, November 3. Accessed December 21, 2021. https://www.usatoday.com /story/opinion/2013/11/03/mccain-menendez-disabilities-treaty-column/3424159/.

Mezey, Susan Gluck. 2005. *Disabling Interpretations: The Americans with Disabilities Act in Federal Court*. Pittsburgh: University of Pittsburgh Press.

Musumeci, MaryBeth, Priya Chidambaram, and Molly O'Malley Watts. 2019. "Medicaid Financial Eligibility for Seniors and People with Disabilities: Findings from a 50-State Survey." Kaiser Family Foundation, June 4. Accessed November 21, 2022. https://www .kff.org/report-section/medicaid-financial-eligibility-for-seniors-and-people-with -disabilities-findings-from-a-50-state-survey-issue-brief/.

Nadler, Jerrold. 2018. "Nadler's Statement Opposing the 'ADA Education and Reform Act of 2017.'" House Committee on the Judiciary, February 15. Accessed November 21, 2022. https://judiciary.house.gov/news/documentsingle.aspx?DocumentID=632.

National Council on Disability. 2001. *Investing in Independence: Transition Recommendations for President George W. Bush*. Washington, DC, January. Accessed November 21, 2022. https://ncd.gov/progress_reports/Jan2001.

New York Times. 2007. "The Republicans' First Presidential Candidates Debate." May 3. Accessed November 21, 2022. https://www.nytimes.com/2007/05/03/us/politics/04 transcript.html.

Obama, Barack. 2013. "Remarks on Signing a Proclamation Honoring the 19th Anniversary of the Americans with Disabilities Act, July 24, 2009." In *Public Papers of the Presidents of the United States: Barack Obama, 2009, Book II–July 1 to December 31, 2009*, 1172–1175. Washington, DC: Government Printing Office.

Peters, Jeremy W. 2014. "Dole, Slumped but Sharp, Returns to Senate to Push Disabilities Treaty." *New York Times*, July 24. Accessed November 21, 2022. https://www.nytimes .com/2014/07/24/us/politics/dole-slumped-but-sharp-returns-to-senate-to-push -disabilities-treaty.html.

Republican Party Platform. 1992–2016. American Presidency Project. Accessed November 21, 2022. https://www.presidency.ucsb.edu/documents/presidential-documents-archive -guidebook/party-platforms-and-nominating-conventions-3.

Rudowitz, Robin, Bradley Corallo, and Rachel Garfield. 2021. "New Incentive for States to Adopt the ACA Medicaid Expansion: Implications for State Spending." Kaiser Family Foundation, March 17. Accessed November 21, 2022. https://www.kff.org/coronavirus -covid-19/issue-brief/new-incentive-for-states-to-adopt-the-aca-medicaid-expansion -implications-for-state-spending/.

U.S. Congress. 2000. House. Committee on the Judiciary, *ADA Notification Act: Hearing Before the Subcommittee on the Constitution of the Committee on the Judiciary*. 106th Cong., 2d sess., May 18.

U.S. Congress. 2012. Senate. Committee on Foreign Relations, *Convention on the Rights of Persons with Disabilities: Report (to Accompany S. Treaty Doc. 112-7)*. 112th Cong., 2d sess. S. Exec. Rep. 112-6. Accessed November 21, 2022. https://www.congress .gov/112/crpt/erpt6/CRPT-112erpt6.pdf.

U.S. Congress. 2014. Senate. Committee on Foreign Relations, *Convention on the Rights of Persons with Disabilities: Report (to Accompany S. treaty Doc. 112-7)*. 113th Cong., 2d sess. Exec. Rep. 113-12. Accessed November 21, 2022. https://www.congress.gov /congressional-report/113th-congress/executive-report/12.

U.S. Congress. 2017. House. ADA Education and Reform Act of 2017. HR 620. 115th Cong., 2d sess. Accessed November 21, 2022. https://www.congress.gov/115/bills /hr620/BILLS-115hr620rds.pdf.

U.S. Department of State. 2008. *United States Participation in the United Nations, 2006*. January. Accessed November 21, 2022. https://2009-2017.state.gov/p/io/rls/rpt/c25829.htm.

U.S. Department of State. 2021. "Promoting the Rights of Persons with Disabilities." Bureau of Democracy, Human Rights, and Labor, January 20. Accessed November 21, 2022. https://www.state.gov/promoting-the-rights-of-persons-with-disabilities/#:~:text=Persons%20with%20disabilities%20have%20the,Rights%20of%20Persons%20with%20Disabilities.

U.S. Library of Congress. 2015. Congressional Research Service. *The United Nations Convention on the Rights of Persons with Disabilities: Issues in the U.S. Ratification Debate*, by Luisa Blanchfield and Cynthia Brown. R42749.

Warren Democrats. n.d. "Protecting the Rights and Equality of People with Disabilities." Accessed April 29, 2021. https://elizabethwarren.com/plans/disability-rights-and-equality.

Drug Policy

At a Glance

The federal government's increased role in drug criminalization in the 1970s has had widespread implications for civil rights and liberties. The "war on drugs" that was initiated by Republican president Richard Nixon and expanded by Republican president Ronald Reagan produced significant increases in federal spending on antidrug programs as well as law enforcement efforts that generated higher numbers of people convicted of drug-related offenses in the U.S. prison population. During the 1980s, several bipartisan laws instituting harsh punishments for drug users and drug traffickers were enacted. In the 1990s, however, several states legalized marijuana for medical purposes, starting a national debate on the extent to which the drug should be legalized for medical and recreational purposes. During the 2000s, there was considerable debate over whether mandatory minimum sentences for low-level nonviolent drug users were appropriate, given their disproportionate impact on communities of color. There was also renewed attention on civil asset forfeiture, which allows law enforcement agencies to seize the properties of individuals accused of drug crimes and liquidate those assets for their department's own financial benefit. While Democrats and Republicans disagree on the extent to which marijuana should be legalized, the parties have found some common ground on the issues of reforming mandatory minimum sentencing and civil asset forfeiture.

According to many Republicans . . .

- Marijuana use should not be legalized.
- Mandatory minimum sentencing should be modified, but not eliminated.
- Civil asset forfeiture should be reformed.

According to many Democrats . . .

- Medical marijuana should be legalized, and policies concerning recreational marijuana should be left to the states.

- Mandatory minimum sentencing for nonviolent drug offenses should be abolished.
- Civil asset forfeiture should be reformed.

Overview

The U.S. Constitution gives concurrent power over criminal justice policies to the federal and state governments. Most crimes, however, are violations of state laws. With a few notable exceptions, policies criminalizing drug use were primarily implemented by the states until the 1970s. The first federal law to regulate drugs was the Harrison Act of 1914, which regulated the production and distribution of opiates and coca products. Many other early laws targeted drugs favored by immigrants. Indeed, the first antidrug ordinance in the United States was enacted by San Francisco in 1785. The ordinance prohibited smoking opium, a common practice among Chinese immigrants. During the 1920s, several states passed laws criminalizing the use of marijuana. These measures, along with the federal Marijuana Tax Act of 1937, were aimed at stopping drug use by Mexican immigrants. Another federal measure to deter marijuana use was the 1951 Boggs Act, which established mandatory minimum sentences for marijuana possession. Those penalties were further increased in the Narcotic Control Act of 1956. These laws were based on limited knowledge about drug addiction, which was thought to be contagious and incurable, and hostility to non-white communities with different cultural practices.

During the late 1960s and 1970s, illegal drug use was rampant among college students and Vietnam War protestors. Marijuana became more popular than ever before during this period, but use of psychedelic drugs such as lysergic acid diethylamide (LSD) also became widespread. American popular culture shifted too, with an explosion of songs, art, and literature that glorified drug use as a path to greater personal freedom and awareness. In 1970, Congress enacted the Federal Comprehensive Drug Abuse Prevention and Control Act, more commonly known as the Controlled Substances Act, which categorized drugs according to their potential for abuse. Marijuana was placed in Schedule I along with other drugs, such as heroin, that have the highest potential for abuse and no accepted medical use. It was also a federal crime to possess drugs in this category. The law repealed mandatory minimum sentences for drug crimes except for large-scale drug trafficking operations because those laws failed to deter drug abuse. It also allowed federal law enforcement to engage in "asset forfeiture"—to seize drugs and the equipment used in manufacturing them to prevent dealers from continuing to operate their illegal businesses.

In 1971, Republican president Richard Nixon announced that his administration was launching a "war on drugs"; to that end, the Nixon administration established a Special Action Office of Drug Abuse to coordinate federal drug policy. In

1973, the National Institute of Drug Abuse was created to coordinate federal prevention and treatment programs. While criminal penalties were reserved for drug traffickers, prevention and treatment for drug users was a prevalent theme of drug policy in the 1970s.

When Republican Ronald Reagan was elected president in 1980, he abandoned that approach. During his presidency, Reagan declared a new "war on drugs," and Congress enacted several new federal drug laws, including the Comprehensive Crime Control Act of 1984, one of the most sweeping criminal justice reform laws in U.S. history. The law established mandatory minimum sentences for several crimes, including drug crimes. It also expanded civil asset forfeiture by allowing the federal government to confiscate property, funds, and any other assets related to criminal activity. Federal law enforcement agencies can keep all the assets they seize, and state and local law enforcement can keep 80 percent of the proceeds if they participate in a law enforcement effort leading to federal forfeiture.

In 1986, Congress passed the Anti-Drug Abuse Act, which established mandatory minimum sentences for a variety of cocaine-related offenses. The legislation was crafted in response to the highly publicized death of Len Bias, a college basketball star poised for stardom in the NBA. Bias died from cardiac arrhythmia following a cocaine overdose two days after the Boston Celtics made him the second pick in the 1986 NBA draft. Among other provisions, the Anti-Drug Abuse Act established a mandatory minimum sentence of five years without parole for possession of five grams of crack cocaine. Individuals convicted of possessing five hundred grams of powder cocaine received the same sentence. This was followed by the Anti-Drug Abuse Act of 1988, which reintroduced the federal death penalty for drug traffickers, created the Office of National Drug Control Policy headed by a Drug Czar, and made crack cocaine the only drug for which a defendant received a mandatory sentence for a first offense. It also set mandatory minimum sentences for drug offenses that involved minors.

Subsequent federal drug policy has dealt primarily with synthetic drugs. For example, the Clinton administration made methamphetamine abuse a special focus during the 1990s, when meth soared in popularity. Congress passed several laws enhancing criminal penalties for manufacturing and trafficking methamphetamine. The bipartisan 1994 Violent Crime Control and Law Enforcement Act, one of the most significant crime laws in American history, established a "three strikes" federal sentencing policy. While not specifically a drug policy, a felon convicted of a serious violent felony was eligible for life imprisonment if they committed two other crimes, one of which was a violent felony or a serious drug offense that violated either state or federal law.

Critics of the war on drugs have contended that it is rooted in racism, like early U.S. drug policy, because of the disproportionate effect it has had on minorities. For example, studies have found that prison sentences are much harsher for crimes involving crack cocaine, used primarily by Blacks, than for those involving powder cocaine, used primarily by whites. They also note that despite equal usage of marijuana, Blacks are 3.73 times more likely to be arrested than whites for possession (ACLU 2013). Black defendants have also been sentenced to longer prison terms than whites for the same crimes (Holder 2016). Recent political debate on drug policy has focused on the extent to which laws enacted during the 1980s, including marijuana legalization, mandatory minimum sentences, and civil asset forfeiture, need reform.

The starkest difference between the parties is in their respective views regarding marijuana legalization. Most Congressional Republicans are opposed to legalizing marijuana for any purpose; however, Republicans in the electorate favor it by a narrow margin. According to a 2021 Gallup poll, 50 percent of Republicans favor legalizing marijuana, while 49 percent opposes it (Gallup Poll 2021). In addition, otherwise red states such as Montana and South Dakota have passed ballot measures legalizing recreational marijuana in recent years.

Democrats have begun to support removing marijuana from the Controlled Substances Act and letting the states regulate medicinal and adult recreational marijuana use. They typically favor decriminalization, which differs from legalization. Decriminalization allows individuals to possess small amounts of marijuana without a criminal penalty, but they could be subject to a civil fine. Legalization allows marijuana to be sold, taxed, and regulated. While President Joe Biden has supported decriminalization, the party has shifted toward legalization. A 2021 Gallup Poll indicated that 83 percent of Democrats support legalization (Gallup Poll 2021). The poll also showed that support for legalization was at a record high of 68 percent of those surveyed. In October 2022, the Biden administration announced a major shift in federal marijuana policy. Biden pardoned thousands of people who had been convicted on federal charges of simple marijuana possession, urged governors across the nation to do the same with state-level simple possession convictions, and announced that his administration intended to review marijuana's classification as a Schedule I narcotic.

The marijuana legalization movement in the states has created tension between federal and state marijuana laws. In 1996, California became the first state to legalize marijuana for medical reasons. California's Compassionate Use Act allows seriously ill state residents to use marijuana and patients, doctors, and caregivers to cultivate and possess marijuana. When federal agents confiscated marijuana belonging to a California resident eligible to possess the drug under state law, the U.S. Supreme Court was asked to determine whether medical marijuana could be proscribed under federal law when it was legal under state law. In *Gonzales v. Raich* (2005), the Court held in a 6-3 ruling that Congress had the authority to regulate marijuana use—regardless of whether it was for medicinal or recreational purposes.

Congress had passed the 1970 Controlled Substances Act based on its constitutional power (detailed in Article I, Section 8, of the Constitution) to regulate interstate commerce. Raich claimed, however, that because the marijuana was cultivated and processed entirely within California, her possession and use of the product did not substantially affect interstate commerce and was beyond the regulatory power of Congress. Justice John Paul Stevens's majority opinion disagreed. He reasoned that Congress had a rational basis for believing that allowing individuals to cultivate and use their own marijuana would affect the overall price and market conditions for marijuana.

Due to *Raich* and other court rulings, the federal government retains the authority to arrest and prosecute individuals or businesses who violate federal drug laws. Both Democratic and Republican administrations have wielded this authority, albeit in different ways. The Clinton administration threatened to punish California doctors prescribing cannabis by prosecuting them for violating federal law. The George W. Bush and Barack Obama administrations took a different approach and authorized the enforcement of federal law against individuals who possessed marijuana and businesses that produced marijuana in states where it had been legalized. In 2013, however, the Obama Justice Department issued a memorandum that allowed these businesses to operate without fear of federal prosecution.

Jeff Sessions, President Donald Trump's first attorney general, rescinded that memorandum, but ultimately the administration allowed states to determine their own marijuana policies. This decision undoubtedly reflected growing support for medical and recreational marijuana use from the American public. By 2022, thirty-seven states had legalized marijuana for medical purposes and twenty-one had legalized marijuana use for recreational purposes (Avery 2022).

In 2019, a bipartisan group of representatives and senators introduced the Strengthening the Tenth Amendment Through Entrusting States (STATES) Act, which sought to amend the Controlled Substances Act to prevent federal prosecution of individuals who possess marijuana legally under state law. The bill failed to garner sufficient legislative support. However, one clear sign of changing public attitudes about marijuana came in December 2020, when House Democrats, with the crossover votes of five Republicans, passed the Marijuana Opportunity Reinvestment and Expungement (MORE) Act. The bill aimed to decriminalize marijuana by removing cannabis from the Controlled Substances Act. It also called for the elimination of low-level federal convictions for marijuana-related offenses. The Republican-controlled Senate did not consider the bill, but its passage in the House was nonetheless seen by legalization advocates as encouraging evidence of broadening public acceptance of marijuana.

The parties have also wrestled over mandatory minimum sentences for drug offenses. The bipartisan Anti-Drug Abuse Act of 1986 required the same sentence for the possession of fifty grams of crack cocaine as for five thousand grams of powder cocaine; fifty grams of crack is approximately the weight of a candy bar, while five thousand grams is enough to fill a standard briefcase (Editors, *New York Times* 2012). Several attempts were made to remedy this inconsistency during the

2000s. The Drug Sentencing Reform and Cocaine Kingpin Trafficking Act of 2007, which was introduced by Democratic senator Joe Biden, proposed eliminating the distinction between the two forms of cocaine altogether in sentencing. A different bill introduced by Republican senator Orrin Hatch and Democratic senator Ted Kennedy, also in 2007, sought to reduce the federal crack cocaine disparity from 100:1 to 20:1. A third bill introduced in 2007 by Republican senator Jeff Sessions proposed increasing the amount of crack cocaine that would subject a person to a five-year sentence from five grams to twenty grams but decreasing the amount of powder cocaine that would mandate a five-year sentence to four hundred grams. However, there was insufficient congressional support to pass any of these bills.

In 2010, President Obama signed the Fair Sentencing Act. The law, which was passed by unanimous consent in the Senate and a voice vote in the House of Representatives, changed the ratio for crack cocaine and powder cocaine in the Anti-Drug Abuse Act from a 100:1 weight ratio to 18:1. It also altered the sentences. Previously, possessing 5 grams of crack cocaine triggered a five-year minimum sentence, but the Fair Sentencing Act raised that amount to 28 grams for a five-year minimum sentence. The amount for a ten-year minimum sentence for possessing crack was also raised from 50 grams to 280 grams. The law also repealed the five-year mandatory sentence for first-time drug offenders. Another bipartisan law, the First Step Act, was signed by President Donald Trump in 2018. This law shortened mandatory minimum sentences for nonviolent drug offenses, gave judges more discretion to impose sentences that depart from mandatory minimums, and applied the provisions of the Fair Sentencing Act retroactively to individuals convicted prior to the law's implementation. The law also changed the three strikes sentencing rule so that individuals convicted of a third felony offense received a sentence of twenty-five years instead of life without parole.

Civil liberties groups from the left and the right argue that civil asset forfeiture needs reform. The 1984 Comprehensive Crime Control Act expanded the ability of federal law enforcement to seize assets related to criminal activity. However, law enforcement can also permanently seize property of individuals they merely suspect of having engaged in criminal conduct—even if the individuals are never convicted of any crime. This practice has resulted in the confiscation of property of innocent people. Once the property has been seized, the owners must demonstrate that they were not involved in criminal activity and must endure lengthy and costly legal proceedings to regain their assets. Law enforcement agencies, meanwhile, have a financial incentive to seize property because they can keep the proceeds.

Reform efforts to address this dynamic first began in 1992, when Republican representative Henry Hyde and Democratic representative John Conyers held hearings on the issue. Hyde introduced several bills to reform civil asset forfeiture regulations during the 1990s, laying the groundwork for the bipartisan Civil Asset Forfeiture Reform Act of 2000, which was signed into law by Democratic president Bill Clinton. The intent of the law was to make the civil asset forfeiture

President Trump Praises the First Step Act

In this speech, President Donald Trump highlights the bipartisan effort and cooperation involved in House passage of the First Step Act. The bill, in part, applied the Fair Sentencing Act provisions retroactively allowing individuals who had been convicted of an offense involving crack to have their sentence reduced. It also shortened or modified mandatory minimum sentences. The legislation was signed into law by Trump on December 21, 2018, a little more than a month after he delivered the remarks below.

Americans from across the political spectrum can unite around prison reform legislation that will reduce crime while giving our fellow citizens a chance at redemption. So if something happens and they make a mistake, they get a second chance at life . . .

The legislation I'm supporting today contains many significant reforms, including the following:

[R]easonable sentencing reforms while keeping dangerous and violent criminals off our streets. In many respects, we're getting very much tougher on the truly bad criminals—of which, unfortunately, there are many. But we're treating people differently for different crimes. Some people got caught up in situations that were very bad.

Today's announcement shows that true bipartisanship is possible. And maybe it'll be thriving, if we're going to get something done. When Republicans and Democrats talk, debate, and seek common ground, we can achieve breakthroughs that move our country forward and deliver for our citizens. And that's what we're doing today. And I have great respect for the people standing alongside of me.

I urge lawmakers in both the House and Senate to work hard and to act quickly and send a final bill to my desk. And I look very much forward to signing it. This is a big breakthrough for a lot of people. They've been talking about this for many, many years.

Source

Trump, Donald. 2018. "Remarks by President Trump on H.R. 5682, the FIRST STEP Act." November 14. Accessed November 21, 2022. https://www.whitehouse.gov/briefings -statements/remarks-president-trump-h-r-5682-first-step-act/.

process more efficient and equitable. Among other things, the law introduced a requirement that the government has the burden of proof to show that the property is legitimately subject to forfeiture. The law also expanded the government's forfeiture power to include additional crimes. It set forth certain requirements the government had to meet in seizing property, including establishing time limits for notification.

Ultimately, however, the 2000 legislation failed to rein in law enforcement use of civil asset forfeiture. From fiscal year 2001 to fiscal year 2014, federal law enforcement's use of forfeiture increased by over 1,000 percent, resulting in $29 billion in revenue (Institute for Justice 2020b). Obama's Justice Department took steps toward civil asset forfeiture reform, but those were reversed by President Donald Trump's attorney general Jeff Sessions in 2017. While there have been several bipartisan reform bills introduced in Congress since that time, none have been enacted. Meanwhile, groups as ideologically diverse as the conservative Heritage Foundation and the liberal American Civil Liberties Union have endorsed legislation to reform this practice. A 2020 poll conducted by YouGov for the Institute for Justice found that 56 percent of Americans oppose civil asset forfeiture and 59 percent oppose allowing law enforcement to keep the proceeds of forfeiture (Institute for Justice 2020a).

Republicans and Drug Policy

The Republican Party initiated the so-called war on drugs during the Nixon years. Ever since then, the party has opposed marijuana legalization and has generally advocated for stronger penalties for drug offenders. Republicans have supported mandatory minimum sentencing, but recently they have suggested modifications for certain types of offenders. They have also reconsidered civil asset forfeiture as a tool to combat drug crimes.

Marijuana Legalization

The 1972 Republican Party platform opposed marijuana legalization, contending that "[w]e intend to solve problems, not create bigger ones by legalizing drugs of unknown physical impact." In a 1973 speech, Nixon stated, "I oppose the legalization of the sale, possession, or use of marijuana. The line against the use of dangerous drugs is now drawn on this side of marijuana. If we move the line to the other side and accept the use of this drug, how can we draw the line against other illegal drugs?" More than three decades later, in 2016, Nixon official and Watergate coconspirator John Ehrlichman was asked about the Nixon administration's stance on drugs. He responded that the

> Nixon campaign in 1968, and the Nixon White House after that, had two enemies: the antiwar left and black people. . . . We knew we couldn't make it illegal to be either against the war or black, but by getting the public to associate the hippies with marijuana and blacks with heroin, and then criminalizing both heavily, we could disrupt those communities. We could arrest their leaders, raid their homes, break up their meetings, and vilify them night after night on the evening news. Did we know we were lying about the drugs? Of course we did. (Baum 2016)

Republicans continued to oppose marijuana legalization long after Nixon departed the White House. While campaigning for president, Ronald Reagan claimed that smoking marijuana "leads to cancer, sterility and 'irreversible effects on the mental processes'" (Dokoupil 2016). He also said that "marijuana—pot, grass, whatever you want to call it—is probably the most dangerous drug in the United States." First Lady Nancy Reagan became heavily involved with the administration's war on drugs as well. She launched a program, "Just Say No," that encouraged schoolchildren to say no to all illegal drugs, but she often focused on marijuana. She even appeared on a popular NBC television sitcom *Diff'rent Strokes* to promote that message. The Reagan administration, however, spent only 1 percent of its drug budget on prevention efforts; the rest went to interdiction and prosecution efforts.

President George H. W. Bush continued the GOP war on drugs, and both the 1988 and 1992 Republican platforms featured language that vehemently opposed legalizing or decriminalizing marijuana and other drugs. In 1996, Republican presidential nominee Bob Dole tried to make President Bill Clinton's youthful use of marijuana into a campaign issue. In 2000, Republican presidential candidate and Texas governor George W. Bush indicated that he would leave the regulation of medical marijuana to the states. During his presidency, however, federal law enforcement agencies raided marijuana dispensaries in California that were in violation of federal law.

The 2012 Republican nominee, former Massachusetts governor Mitt Romney, also opposed marijuana legalization, calling marijuana a "gateway drug." He also opposed medical marijuana but suggested it was a state issue (*Economist* 2012).

The identical 2016 and 2020 GOP platforms bemoaned that progress that had been made against drug abuse was "eroding" and the complaint specifically cited that marijuana is "virtually legalized despite its illegality under federal law." There was an intense debate over medical marijuana at the 2016 Republican Platform Committee meeting when delegate Eric Brakey, a GOP legislator from Maine, introduced a measure suggesting that the party should support the use of cannabis oil by seriously ill children as a pain management tool when no other medication was effective (Bobic 2016). The measure was voted down by his fellow Republicans due to concerns about the dangers of marijuana use. Specifically, one committee member asserted that "people who commit mass murders are 'young boys from divorced families, and they're all smoking pot,'" while another member made the false claim that researchers had found a clear link between marijuana and schizophrenia (Bobic 2016).

In January 2018, Trump administration attorney general Jeff Sessions announced that he was rescinding the Cole Memorandum. During the Obama administration in 2013, Deputy Attorney General James M. Cole issued a memorandum that the Justice Department would not sue to prevent states from legalizing marijuana but that it expected states to enforce applicable drug laws. Sessions stated that the Justice Department would be enforcing federal marijuana law even in states where the drug was legal. In response, Colorado senator Cory Gardner, a Republican, placed a hold on all Justice Department nominees until he received assurance that Colorado's marijuana laws would be respected by the federal government. He stated that he "received a commitment from the President that the Department of Justice's rescission of the Cole memo will not impact Colorado's legal marijuana industry. Furthermore, President Trump has assured me that he will support a federalism-based legislative solution to fix this states' rights issue once and for all" (Gardner 2018). John Hudak, a senior fellow in governance studies and deputy director of the Center for Effective Public Management at the Brookings Institution, was critical of Sessions's decision. He asserted that Sessions "has shown a deep ignorance of the realities of the drug war, which has been ineffective and costly and has disproportionately affected minority communities. And he has committed to numerous claims that have been dispelled by science, such as cannabis's gateway effect and the idea that marijuana is 'only slightly less awful' than heroin" (Hudak 2018).

In 2020, House Republicans condemned the MORE Act, which had been passed by the House Democratic majority with only five Republican votes, despite opposition to the legislation from the American Medical Association (Walsh 2020). Republican Greg Murphy argued that "[m]arijuana is one of the most abused substances on this planet" and that "[l]egalizing weed would create revenue from taxes, but at what cost? Do we then start legalizing cocaine? Marijuana is a gateway drug—make no mistake about that" (Parkinson 2020). Republican Matt Gaetz, one of the five Republicans who supported the bill, stated that he was the only Republican cosponsor of the bill "because the federal government has lied to the people of this country about marijuana for a generation" and that "[w]e have seen a generation, particularly of black and brown youth, locked up for offenses that should not have resulted in any incarceration whatsoever" (Brufke 2020). He also noted that House Republican arguments against marijuana legalization were "overwhelmingly losing with the American people" (Brufke 2020). Indeed, a 2020 Gallup poll indicated historically strong support overall for marijuana legalization with 68 percent of Americans favoring it, including 48 percent of Republicans (Brenan 2020).

Mandatory Minimum Sentencing

In 1976, the Republican platform advocated mandatory minimum sentencing for several crimes, including trafficking in hard drugs. Republicans also supported legislation throughout the 1980s establishing mandatory minimum sentencing for drug crimes. The 1996 Republican platform criticized President Clinton and the Democratic Party for being a "conscientious objector" in the war on drugs and indicated its strong support for mandatory minimum sentences for "drug trafficking, distribution, and drug-related crimes." In 2003, George W. Bush's attorney general, John Ashcroft, instructed prosecutors to seek mandatory minimums when possible. The 2008 GOP platform supported mandatory minimums for several crimes, such as child rape, but did not specifically mention drugs.

In 2012, the Republican platform once again expressed support for mandatory minimum sentencing for several crimes—this time including repeat drug dealers. But the party's 2016 and 2020 platforms took a decidedly different tone, applauding efforts toward "restorative justice" and criminal justice reform. Specifically, the platform urged Congress to "learn from what works" particularly for drug sentencing. Mandatory minimum sentences were still defended as a useful tool in keeping "dangerous criminals" in jail, but the Republicans endorsed changes to mandatory minimum sentences in "particular categories, especially nonviolent offenders and persons with drug, alcohol, or mental health issues." Republican support also proved crucial in passing the First Step Act in 2018. This legislation shortened federal prison sentences and allowed judges to impose sentences less than the mandatory minimum under certain conditions.

President Trump's Justice Department, however, continued to defend mandatory minimum sentences. It rescinded an Obama administration policy that minimized mandatory sentences for low-level, nonviolent drug offenses and instructed federal prosecutors to pursue the longest sentences possible except in exceptional circumstances. Nancy Gertner, a former federal judge, and Chiraag Bains, a former federal prosecutor, criticized this stance. They argued that mandatory minimums were ineffective because for drug charges, "it is the certainty of punishment—not the severity—that deters crime" (Gertner and Bains 2017). They also argued that the changes imposed by Trump's Justice Department were not cost-effective and ran counter to congressional intent for mandatory minimums—that they were for drug kingpins and middle-level dealers, not minor offenders (Gertner and Bains 2017).

Civil Asset Forfeiture

The 1988 Republican platform supported civil asset forfeiture, stating that the party would "encourage seizure and forfeiture programs by the Department of the Treasury and each State to take the profits out of illicit drug sales." By 2016, the Republican position had shifted dramatically toward one supportive of reform, noting that "civil asset forfeiture was originally intended as a way to cripple organized crime through the seizure of property used in a criminal enterprise. Regrettably, it has become a tool for unscrupulous law enforcement officials, acting without due process, to profit by destroying the livelihood of innocent individuals, many of whom never recover the lawful assets taken from them." The platform also called on "Congress and state legislatures to enact reforms to protect law-abiding citizens against abusive asset forfeiture tactics."

Despite this shift in the party's position, in 2017, Attorney General Jeff Sessions announced that he was reinstating civil asset forfeiture and eliminating reforms that had been initiated by Obama's attorney general, Eric Holder. Sessions stated that "as President Trump knows well, civil asset forfeiture is a key tool that helps law enforcement defund organized crime, take back ill-gotten gains, and prevent new crimes from being committed, and it weakens the criminals and the cartels" ("Attorney General Sessions Issues Policy and Guidelines on Federal Adoptions of Assets Seized by State or Local Law Enforcement" 2017). This decision was criticized by the editorial board of the conservative *National Review*, which characterized civil asset forfeiture as "a constitutionally questionable practice" that "produces perverse outcomes in which American citizens are punished by their government for crimes with which they have not even been charged" (Editorial Board 2017). They were particularly critical of "equitable sharing" because it allows states to bypass their own potentially restrictive state reform laws. Equitable sharing is a legal maneuver that allows state and local law enforcement authorities to transfer seized assets to the federal government. They argued that "conservatives should object to this on due-process grounds and on Tenth Amendment grounds" because it interferes with state laws (Editorial Board 2017). In 2019, Trump declared a national emergency to take control of executive branch appropriations to fund construction of a wall on the border between the United States and Mexico. He took $600 million from the Treasury Department's Forfeiture Fund as part of this scheme (Neuhauser 2019).

Despite the Trump administration's actions in support of civil asset forfeiture, Congressional Republicans have introduced legislation to limit the practice. Republican senator Rand Paul reintroduced the Fifth Amendment Integrity Restoration (FAIR) Act in 2020; he has introduced the bill in every session of Congress since 2014. This bill would eliminate the Equitable Sharing Program, raise the burden of proof so that the government would have to meet a standard of clear and convincing evidence that property was used in a crime before it could seize property, and require that funds from forfeitures be placed in the Treasury Department's general fund, which is subject to greater congressional control (Paul 2020). Paul pledged to attach the bill to other police reform bills in the wake of George Floyd's murder by police officers; however, none of the bills were enacted.

Meanwhile, Republican voters have expressed uneasiness with the practice. A 2020 poll found that 52 percent of Republicans oppose civil asset forfeiture, 50 percent oppose allowing law enforcement agencies to keep the proceeds of forfeiture, and 60 percent indicated that they were more likely to support a member of Congress who opposed civil asset forfeiture (Institute for Justice 2020a).

Democrats and Drug Policy

The Democratic Party has come full circle in its views on marijuana policy. Initially, the party advocated for decriminalization, but in the 1980s and 1990s, it supported stringent federal marijuana laws. During the Obama administration, the Justice Department initially prosecuted businesses involved in producing medicinal marijuana but later rescinded that policy. In late 2020, the Democratic-controlled House of Representatives voted to decriminalize marijuana. Meanwhile, Democrats have shifted on other drug policy issues as well. For example, the party supported strict mandatory minimum sentences for drug crimes in the 1980s and 1990s, but by 2020, it had pledged to abolish them entirely. The party has also supported reforms to civil asset forfeiture laws since 2000.

Marijuana Legalization

During the 1976 presidential campaign, Democratic nominee Jimmy Carter advocated decriminalizing marijuana possession of up to an ounce of the drug. In 1977, President Carter announced his support for a congressional bill aimed at decriminalization of marijuana by replacing the existing law, which required anyone convicted of possession of any amount of the substance to pay a $5,000 fine and face up to a year of imprisonment, with a fine for persons caught with less than an ounce. Carter emphasized that selling marijuana should still be considered a "serious federal offense" and that there needed to be greater international cooperation and investigations by the Justice Department into the link between organized crime and drug trafficking (Wooten 1977). Throughout the 1980s, Democrats supported restrictions on marijuana. In addition to supporting federal crime bills, the 1988 Democratic Party platform pledged to use all the tools necessary to fight the war on drugs and stated that "the legalization of illicit drugs would represent a tragic surrender in a war we intend to win."

In 1992, Bill Clinton became the first presidential candidate to admit to illegal drug use. Clinton claimed that he had never broken state or federal drug laws, but when asked whether he had broken the laws of another country, he admitted to marijuana use while studying at Oxford University in the United Kingdom. He claimed that he tried marijuana "a time or two" and that he neither "inhaled it" nor "enjoyed it" (Allis 1992). During his 1996 State of the Union Address, Clinton announced the appointment of four-star Army General Barry McCaffrey as his drug czar. McCaffrey fought against the legalization of medicinal marijuana in California by pledging to prosecute physicians who prescribed it, revoke their prescription licenses, and prohibit them from participating in Medicaid and Medicare. The 1996 Democratic platform outlined McCaffrey's "aggressive" four-part agenda to: (1) prevent drug use among children, (2) catch and punish drug users and dealers, (3) provide treatment to those who need it, and (4) prevent drugs from entering the United States.

During the first two decades of the twenty-first century, however, attitudes within the party about marijuana began a slow but perceptible shift toward a pro-legalization position. During the 2000 campaign, the Democratic nominee, Vice President Al Gore, voiced support for allowing doctors the flexibility to prescribe medical marijuana. Five months later stated that "[r]ight now the science does not show me, or the experts whose judgment I trust, that it is the proper medication for pain and that there are not better alternatives available in every situation" (Seelye 2000). The 2004 Democratic nominee, Senator John Kerry, pledged to end the policy of arresting patients in states with legalized medical marijuana.

While campaigning for president in 2008, Senator Barack Obama indicated that he would respect state medical marijuana laws by not following the Bush administration's policy of conducting raids on businesses that produced marijuana for seriously ill people. In March 2009, the administration stopped the raids that had been prevalent under the Bush administration, and a memo from the Justice Department stipulated that the administration would not prioritize prosecuting individuals who legally possessed medical marijuana. However, in 2011, the Justice Department reversed course and threatened to "vigorously" prosecute those individuals. The administration also made it difficult for marijuana dispensaries to operate by denying them the ability to deduct business expenses for federal income tax purposes (Kampia 2012). Obama was criticized by a marijuana advocacy group, the Marijuana Policy Project, for being "more hostile to medical marijuana patients than any president in U.S. history" (Kampia 2012). The Marijuana Policy Project's executive director Rob Kampia commented that "[t]he five presidents from Richard Nixon through George H.W. Bush allowed medical marijuana research to proceed unhindered. The three presidents from Jimmy Carter to George H.W. Bush allowed patients to apply to the federal government for waivers to use medical marijuana legally under federal law" (Kampia 2012).

The 2016 Democratic platform was critical of the war on drugs and pledged to remove marijuana from Schedule I of the Controlled Substances Act due to the conflicting federal and state laws on the legality of the drug. It also encouraged states to take the lead in being "laboratories of democracy" in creating policies for medical and recreational marijuana. These views were consistent with those of 2016 Democratic presidential nominee Hillary Clinton, who stated that she favored more research into the medicinal uses of the drug and wanted to wait and see what happened in states like Colorado that had legalized marijuana entirely (*ABC News* 2016). Clinton also noted that "significant racial disparities exist in marijuana enforcement—black men are significantly more likely to be arrested for marijuana possession than their white counterparts, despite the fact that their usage rates are similar" (Clinton 2016).

In 2020, the Democratic Party's Platform Committee rejected a proposal to include marijuana legalization in the party platform, deciding instead to leave that issue to the states. Democratic presidential nominee Joe Biden took the same stance on the issue while he was campaigning for office. The platform supported legalizing medical marijuana and decriminalizing marijuana generally. Some Democrats believed the refusal to do this signaled a retreat from the 2016 platform's "reasoned pathway to legalization." However, in December 2020, Congressional Democrats approved the MORE Act which would decriminalize marijuana at the federal level. Democrats argued that the federal government's criminalization of marijuana was out of step with most of the states who have legalized marijuana in some form. As Democratic congressman Jim Clyburn tweeted, "[P]eople of color are 4X more likely to be arrested for cannabis possession than White people despite equal usage" (Walsh 2020).

Tom Basile, who worked on the Bush-Cheney campaign, criticized the Democrats' position on marijuana as hypocritical. He asserted that "the left has willfully

Biden Announces New Approach to Marijuana Possession

In October 2022, Democratic President Joe Biden pardoned individuals convicted for simple possession of marijuana under federal law. Biden also outlined other initiatives his administration was taking to reform marijuana policy.

As I often said during my campaign for President, no one should be in jail just for using or possessing marijuana. Sending people to prison for possessing marijuana has upended too many lives and incarcerated people for conduct that many states no longer prohibit. Criminal records for marijuana possession have also imposed needless barriers to employment, housing, and educational opportunities. And while white and Black and brown people use marijuana at similar rates, Black and brown people have been arrested, prosecuted, and convicted at disproportionate rates.

Today, I am announcing three steps that I am taking to end this failed approach.

First, I am announcing a pardon of all prior Federal offenses of simple possession of marijuana. I have directed the Attorney General to develop an administrative process for the issuance of certificates of pardon to eligible individuals . . .

Second, I am urging all Governors to do the same with regard to state offenses. Just as no one should be in a Federal prison solely due to the possession of marijuana, no one should be in a local jail or state prison for that reason, either.

Third, I am asking the Secretary of Health and Human Services and the Attorney General to initiate the administrative process to review expeditiously how marijuana is scheduled under federal law. Federal law currently classifies marijuana in Schedule I of the Controlled Substances Act, the classification meant for the most dangerous substances. This is the same schedule as for heroin and LSD, and even higher than the classification of fentanyl and methamphetamine—the drugs that are driving our overdose epidemic.

Finally, even as federal and state regulation of marijuana changes, important limitations on trafficking, marketing, and under-age sales should stay in place.

Too many lives have been upended because of our failed approach to marijuana. It's time that we right these wrongs.

Source

"Statement from President Biden on Marijuana Reform." 2022. October 6. Accessed October 7, 2022. https://www.whitehouse.gov/briefing-room/statements-releases/2022/10/06/statement-from-president-biden-on-marijuana-reform/.

ignored studies like one published in 2017 in *the American Journal of Psychology* showing a strong connection between marijuana and future opioid use" (Basile 2019). Basile also cited research demonstrating that marijuana has negative physical and neurological effects such as reduced motor function and cognitive impairment. He also pointed to a study in the *New England Journal of Medicine* that found additional negative effects, including "addiction, impacts on brain development, possible mental illness and impaired driving ability" (Basile 2019). He suggested that Democrats were more interested in getting the votes of "young and minority voters" and of those involved in the marijuana industry.

In October 2022, President Joe Biden pardoned individuals who were convicted by the federal government of simple possession of marijuana. Biden argued that the action was necessary given that more people of color were convicted of possession and that this action would help right that wrong. He also encouraged governors to do the same as most marijuana crimes are violations of state laws. Biden supports decriminalization of marijuana, while other Democrats support legalization of the drug. In response to Biden's announcement, "the Republican National Committee had literally nothing to say about it. The National Republican Congressional Committee and the National Republican Senatorial Committee were silent, too" (Benen 2022).

Mandatory Minimum Sentencing

Democrats supported mandatory minimum sentences in key drug legislation passed during the 1980s and the "three strikes" policy contained in the 1994 Violent Crime Control and Law Enforcement Act. They began to support sentencing reforms, however, due to racial disparities in sentencing that became increasingly evident over time. In 2020, the party's shift on the issue became even clearer when it emphasized abolishing mandatory minimum sentences rather than merely reforming them.

In 2010 President Obama signed the Fair Sentencing Act, which attempted to reconcile the disparity in sentencing between crimes involving crack cocaine and powder cocaine. In a speech to the National Urban League, he stated that "we're taking on the structural inequalities that have held so many of our fellow citizens back, whether it's making more housing available and more affordable, making sure civil rights and antidiscrimination laws are enforced, making sure our crime policy is not only tough, but also smart. So yesterday we took an important step forward when Congress passed a fair sentencing bill that I look forward to signing into law, a bipartisan bill to help right a longstanding wrong by narrowing sentencing disparities between those convicted of crack cocaine and powder cocaine" (Obama 2010).

In 2013, Eric Holder, Obama's attorney general, announced that federal prosecutors would no longer list the quantities of drugs in indictments for low-level drug offenses, subject to certain criteria. Mandatory minimum sentences are dependent upon the amount of illegal drugs a defendant possessed at the time of arrest, so omitting the amount would avoid triggering strict mandatory sentences for those crimes. Holder stated that he and Obama were examining ways to "recalibrate" the U.S. criminal justice system. He continued that "[w]e will start by fundamentally rethinking the notion of mandatory minimum sentences for drug-related crimes. Some statutes that mandate inflexible sentences—regardless of the individual conduct at issue in a particular case—reduce the discretion available to prosecutors, judges, and juries. Because they oftentimes generate unfairly long sentences, they breed disrespect for the system. When applied indiscriminately, they do not serve public safety" (Holder 2013).

In 2016, Hillary Clinton pledged to reform mandatory minimum sentencing as part of a wider effort to end mass incarceration. Her presidential campaign website specifically linked mandatory minimum sentencing practices to racial discrimination, and she vowed to cut mandatory minimum drug sentences in half. In an op-ed for the *New York Times* that same year, Attorney General Eric Holder emphasized the racial disparities associated with mandatory minimum sentencing: "Controlling for other factors, the United States Sentencing Commission found that between December 2007 and September 2011, black male defendants received sentences 20 percent longer than their white counterparts. From 1983 to 1997, the number of African Americans sent to prison for drug offenses went up more than 26-fold, compared with a sevenfold increase for whites" (Holder 2016). Clinton also favored changing the Fair Sentencing Act by equalizing the penalties for crack and powder cocaine, rather than the 18:1 ratio in the law (Clinton 2016). The 2016 Democratic platform also stated that the party supported reforms to mandatory minimum sentences that would address racial inequities in their use.

By 2020, the Democratic Party's position on mandatory minimum sentences had shifted again, toward one of outright opposition—a position shared by the party's 2020 presidential nominee, former senator and vice president Joe Biden. The 2020 party platform pledged to "fight to repeal federal mandatory minimums, incentivize states to do the same, and make all sentencing reductions retroactive so judges can reconsider past cases where their hands were tied." According to Biden's campaign website, he "supports an end to mandatory minimums. As president, he will work for the passage of legislation to repeal mandatory minimums at the federal level. And, he will give states incentives to repeal their mandatory minimums" (Biden 2020). He also pledged to eliminate the sentencing disparity between crack and powder cocaine.

Civil Asset Forfeiture

Democrats supported the Civil Asset Reform Act of 2000. When further reform became a prominent political issue in the 2010s, the Obama administration modified the program. Attorney General Eric Holder undertook a comprehensive review of civil asset forfeiture and made significant changes to the way the Justice Department administered its Asset Forfeiture Program. In 2015, Holder modified the Equitable Sharing Program to prevent federal agencies from accepting assets seized by state and local law enforcement agencies unless the owner was actually convicted of a crime. Critics suggested that since the policy did not pertain to joint federal/state task forces, its effect might be limited (Balko 2015).

The 2016 Democratic Party platform promised to "reform the civil asset forfeiture system to protect people and remove perverse incentives for law enforcement to 'police for a profit.'" Neither the 2020 platform nor the party's nominee, Joe Biden, addressed civil asset forfeiture; however, the *National Review* noted that Biden played a central role in passing several stringent drug laws during the

1980s and 1990s: "Biden bragged about the sweeping scope of civil asset forfeiture: 'Under our forfeiture statutes, the government can take everything you own. Everything from your car, to your house, to your bank account, not merely what they confiscate in terms of the dollars of the transaction you've been caught engaging in. They can take everything!'" (Geraghty 2019). Libertarians were also critical of Biden, labeling him the "architect of the government's asset forfeiture program" for his efforts to expand the practice in 1983 (Calton 2019). Others defended Biden against these attacks, noting that many lawmakers who have had lengthy careers in public service have changed their positions on certain policy issues over time.

Further Reading

ABC News. 2016. "Good Morning America." Accessed November 21, 2022. https://abcnews .go.com/GMA/video/hillary-clinton-responds-question-legalizing-marijuana -38566835.

Allis, Sam. 1992. "Watch Yer Back." *Time*, April 13. Accessed December 12, 2020. https:// time.com/vault/issue/1992-04-13/page/22/.

American Civil Liberties Union (ACLU). 2013. "Report: The War on Marijuana in Black and White." June. Accessed December 1, 2020. https://www.aclu.org/report /report-war-marijuana-black-and-white?redirect=criminal-law-reform/war-marijuana -black-and-white.

"Attorney General Sessions Issues Policy and Guidelines on Federal Adoptions of Assets Seized by State or Local Law Enforcement." 2017. Justice.gov., July 19. Accessed December 19, 2022. https://www.justice.gov/opa/pr/attorney-general-sessions-issues -policy-and-guidelines-federal-adoptions-assets-seized-state.

Avery, Dan. 2022. "Marijuana Laws by State: Is Pot Legal in Your State?" CNET, November 9. Accessed December 19, 2022. https://www.cnet.com/google-amp/news /marijuana-laws-by-state-is-weed-legal-where-you-live/.

Balko, Radley. 2015. "More Fallout from Eric Holder's Changes to Civil Asset Forfeiture Law." *Washington Post*, January 19. Accessed December 1, 2020. https://www.washington post.com/news/the-watch/wp/2015/01/19/more-fallout-from-eric-holders-changes -to-civil-asset-forfeiture-law/.

Basile, Tom. 2019. "Marijuana Legalization Debate Prompts a New High in Democratic Hypocrisy." *Fox News*, January 6. Accessed December 21, 2022. https://www.foxnews.com /opinion/marijuana-legalization-debate-prompts-a-new-high-in-democratic-hypocrisy.

Baum, Dan. 2016. "Legalize It All: How to Win the War on Drugs." *Harpers*, April. Accessed December 3, 2020. https://harpers.org/archive/2016/04/legalize-it-all/.

Benen, Steve. 2022. "Why the GOP Response to Biden's Marijuana Pardons Was So Amazing." MSNBC, October 7. Accessed October 7, 2022. https://www.msnbc.com/rachel-maddow -show/maddowblog/gop-response-bidens-marijuana-pardons-was-amazing -rcna51178.

Biden, Joe. 2019. "The Biden Plan for Strengthening America's Commitment to Justice." Joe Biden for President. Accessed February 8, 2023. https://joebiden.com/justice/.

Bobic, Igor. 2016. "Medical Marijuana Fails to Make GOP Platform After Vigorous Debate." *HuffPost*, July 16. Accessed December 10, 2020. https://www.huffpost.com/entry /medical-cannabis-gop-convention_n_578412f1e4b07c356cfe3c55.

Brenan, Megan. 2020. "Support for Legal Marijuana Inches Up to New High of 68%." Gallup Poll, November 9. Accessed December 10, 2020. https://news.gallup.com/poll/323582/support-legal-marijuana-inches-new-high.aspx.

Brufke, Juliegrace. 2020. "Five Republicans Vote for Bill to Decriminalize Marijuana." *The Hill*, December 4. Accessed December 10, 2020. https://thehill.com/homenews/house/528806-five-republicans-vote-for-bill-to-decriminalize-marijuana.

Calton, Chris. 2019. "How a Young Joe Biden Became the Architect of the Government's Asset Forfeiture Program." Foundation for Economic Education, March 19. Accessed December 15, 2020. https://fee.org/articles/how-a-young-joe-biden-became-the-architect-of-the-governments-asset-forfeiture-program/.

Clinton, Hillary. 2016. "Criminal Justice Reform." Office of Hillary Rodham Clinton. Accessed December 10, 2020. https://www.hillaryclinton.com/issues/criminal-justice-reform/.

Democratic Party Platforms. 1976–2020. American Presidency Project. Accessed November 21, 2022. https://www.presidency.ucsb.edu/people/other/democratic-party-platforms.

Dokoupil, Tony. 2016. "Analysis: Did Nancy Reagan's War on Drugs Backfire?" *NBC News*, March 7. Accessed December 17, 2022. https://www.nbcnews.com/news/us-news/analysis-did-nancy-reagan-s-war-drugs-backfire-n533476.

Economist. 2012. "Intelligent Sentences." October 6. Accessed December 10, 2020. https://www.economist.com/united-states/2012/10/06/intelligent-sentences.

Editorial Board, *National Review*. 2017. "Jeff Sessions Should Drop His Expansion of Civil Asset Forfeiture." *National Review*, July 20. Accessed December 10, 2020. https://www.nationalreview.com/2017/07/jeff-sessions-civil-asset-forfeiture-plans-conservatives-should-oppose/.

Editors, *New York Times*. 2012. "Abiding by the Fair Sentencing Act." *New York Times*, April 17. Accessed December 3, 2020. https://www.nytimes.com/2012/04/18/opinion/abiding-by-the-fair-sentencing-act.

Gallup Poll. 2021. "Support for Legal Marijuana Holds at Record High of 68%." November 4. Accessed October 1, 2022. https://news.gallup.com/poll/356939/support-legal-marijuana-holds-record-high.aspx.

Gardner, Cory. 2018. "Gardner Protects Colorado's Legal Marijuana Industry." U.S. Senator Cory Gardner of Colorado. April 13. Accessed December 13, 2020. https://www.gardner.senate.gov/newsroom/press-releases/gardner-protects-colorados-legal-marijuana-industry.

Geraghty, Jim. 2019. "20 Things You Probably Didn't Know about Joe Biden." *National Review*, January 17. Accessed December 15, 2020. https://www.nationalreview.com/2019/01/joe-biden-twenty-things-you-probably-didnt-know/.

Gertner, Nancy, and Chiraag Bains. 2017. "Mandatory Minimum Sentences Are Cruel and Ineffective. Sessions Wants Them Back." *Washington Post*, May 15. Accessed December 17, 2022. https://www.washingtonpost.com/posteverything/wp/2017/05/15/mandatory-minimum-sentences-are-cruel-and-ineffective-sessions-wants-them-back/.

Hansen, Claire. 2019. "Bipartisan Bill Would Give States Control Over Marijuana Laws." *Newsweek*, April 4. Accessed December 10, 2020. https://www.usnews.com/news/national-news/articles/2019-04-04/bipartisan-bill-would-give-states-control-over-marjuana-legalization.

Holder, Eric H., Jr. 2013. "Remarks at the Annual Meeting of the American Bar Association's House of Delegates." U.S. Department of Justice, August 12. Accessed December 10, 2020. https://www.justice.gov/opa/speech/attorney-general-eric-holder-delivers-remarks-annual-meeting-american-bar-associations.

Holder, Eric H., Jr. 2016. "Eric Holder: We Can Have Shorter Sentences and Less Crime." *New York Times*, August 11. Accessed December 10, 2020. https://www.nytimes .com/2016/08/14/opinion/sunday/eric-h-holder-mandatory-minimum-sentences -full-of-errors.html?searchResultPosition=19.

Hsu, Spencer. 1999. "Bush: Marijuana Laws Up to States." *Washington Post*, October 22. Accessed December 1, 2020. https://www.washingtonpost.com/wp-srv/politics /campaigns/wh2000/stories/bush102299.htm.

Hudak, John. 2018. "Sessions Stands against Conservatives—Including Trump—To Fight Marijuana." *Washington Post*, January 5. Accessed December 10, 2020. https://www .washingtonpost.com/opinions/sessions-stands-against-conservatives--including -trump--to-fight-marijuana/2018/01/05/65dfc73a-f188-11e7-97bf-bba379b809ab _story.html.

Institute for Justice. 2020a. "Civil Forfeiture." n.d. Accessed December 21, 2022. https:// ij.org/wp-content/uploads/2020/11/Results-for-Institute-for-Justice-Civil-Forfeiture -245-9.30.2020-1-Civil-Forfeiture-2.pdf.

Institute for Justice. 2020b. *Policing for Profit: The Abuse of Civil Asset Forfeiture*. 2nd ed. Accessed December 15, 2020. https://ij.org/report/policing-for-profit-2/introduction/.

Kampia, Rob. 2012. "Medical Marijuana Meets Hostility from Obama Administration." *Washington Post*, May 4. Accessed December 1, 2020. https://www.washingtonpost.com /opinions/medical-marijuana-meets-hostility-from-obama-administration/2012/05/04 /gIQA80GK2T_story.html.

National Conference of State Legislatures. 2020. "State Medical Marijuana Laws." November 10. Accessed December 3, 2020. https://www.ncsl.org/research/health/state-medical -marijuana-laws.aspx.

Neuhauser, Alan. 2019. "Trump Taps Civil Asset Forfeiture to Fund Border Wall." *US News and World Report*, February 15. Accessed December 15, 2020. https://www.usnews .com/news/national-news/articles/2019-02-15/trump-taps-civil-asset-forfeiture-to -fund-border-wall.

Nixon, Richard. 1973. "Radio Address about the State of the Union Message on Law Enforcement and Drug Abuse Prevention." American Presidency Project. March 10. Accessed December 12, 2020. https://www.presidency.ucsb.edu/documents/radio -address-about-the-state-the-union-message-law-enforcement-and-drug-abuse -prevention.

Obama, Barack. 2010. "Remarks at the National Urban League Centennial Conference." July 29. Accessed December 10, 2020. https://www.govinfo.gov/content/pkg/PPP-2010 -book2/xml/PPP-2010-book2-doc-pg1104-2.xml.

Parkinson, John. 2020. "House Votes to Federally Decriminalize Marijuana." *ABC News*, December 4. Accessed November 21, 2022. https://abcnews.go.com/Politics/house -historic-vote-federally-decriminalizing-marijuana/story?id=74521976.

Paul, Rand. 2020. "Dr. Rand Paul's FAIR Act Restores Respect for 5th Amendment." U.S. Senator Rand Paul of Kentucky. Accessed December 1, 2020. https://www.paul.senate .gov/news/dr-rand-paul%E2%80%99s-fair-act-restores-respect-5th-amendment.

Republican Party Platforms. 1976–2020. American Presidency Project. Accessed November 21, 2022. https://www.presidency.ucsb.edu/people/other/republican-party-platforms.

Seelye, Katharine Q. 2000. "THE 2000 CAMPAIGN: THE EVOLUTION OF A POSITION; Gore Retreats from Earlier Signal of Support for Medical Use of Marijuana." *New York Times*, May 17. Accessed December 2, 2000. https://www.nytimes.com/2000/05/17

/us/2000-campaign-evolution-position-gore-retreats-earlier-signal-support-for.html?
searchResultPosition=1.

Southhall, Ashley, and Jack Healy. 2013. "U.S. Won't Sue to Reverse States' Legalization
of Marijuana." *New York Times*, August 29. Accessed December 2, 2020. https://www
.nytimes.com/2013/08/30/us/politics/us-says-it-wont-sue-to-undo-state-marijuana
-laws.html.

Walsh, Deirdre. 2020. "House Approves Decriminalizing Marijuana: Bill to Stall in Senate."
National Public Radio, December 4. Accessed December 10, 2020. https://www.npr
.org/2020/12/04/942949288/house-approves-decriminalizing-marijuana-bill-to
-stall-in-senate.

Wooten, James T. 1977. "Carter Seeks to End Marijuana Penalty for Small Amounts."
New York Times, August 3. Accessed December 12, 2020. https://www.nytimes
.com/1977/08/03/archives/carter-seeks-to-end-marijuana-penalty-for-small-amounts
-urges-fines.html?searchResultPosition=6.

Education Policy

At a Glance

State and local governments have historically developed and implemented education policy. The federal government became involved in public education to end segregated public schools and to enforce antidiscrimination laws. After the U.S. Supreme Court's ruling in *Brown v. Board of Education* (1954), federal judges retained authority over desegregation plans until the Court limited their role in the mid-1990s. Many scholars argue that this shift contributed to the resegregation of public schools in many parts of the country due to the overall socioeconomic disparities that persist between white and minority populations.

Democrats support federal programs to facilitate voluntary integration for public schools, while Republicans support a limited federal role. The parties have also disagreed over the implementation of Title IX of the Education Amendments Act of 1972, which prohibits sex discrimination in education programs. Democrats support a lower evidentiary standard for cases of campus sexual assault under Title IX, while Republicans support due process guarantees in those cases. The parties also differ over Title IX's definition of "sex discrimination." Democrats argue that the term includes transgender people, while Republicans argue that it does not.

According to many Democrats . . .

- The federal government should encourage voluntary socioeconomic integration in public schools.
- Title IX of the Education Amendments Act of 1972 should provide more protection for women who have been sexually assaulted on campus.
- Title IX's prohibition against sex discrimination applies to transgender persons.

According to many Republicans . . .

- The federal government should not encourage voluntary socioeconomic integration in public schools.

- Title IX of the Education Amendments Act of 1972 should provide stronger due process rights in college sexual assaults.
- Title IX's prohibition against sex discrimination does not apply to transgender persons.

Overview

Education policy has historically been implemented by state and local governments. The federal government's role in education policy increased in 1954 with the U.S. Supreme Court's ruling in *Brown v. Board of Education*. After some schools refused to comply with the ruling requiring school desegregation, Republican president Dwight Eisenhower and Democratic president John F. Kennedy used the military to enforce it. *Brown* also placed desegregation policy in the hands of federal judges who were tasked with overseeing school district desegregation plans.

The federal role further increased in the 1960s with the passage of the Civil Rights Act of 1964 and the Elementary and Secondary Schools Act (ESEA) in 1965. These laws prohibited racial discrimination in programs that received federal funds and provided federal funds to schools with low-income students, respectively. While great strides were made integrating the nation's public schools, busing policies became politically unpopular in the 1970s and 1980s because parents wanted their students to attend neighborhood schools. Although the U.S. Supreme Court had upheld busing in *Swann v. Charlotte-Mecklenburg Board of Education* (1971), politicians were concerned that they would lose votes for supporting an unpopular policy. Presidents Richard Nixon, Jimmy Carter, and Ronald Reagan voiced their opposition to busing in their presidential campaigns. In the 1990s, the U.S. Supreme Court limited federal judicial oversight of school desegregation plans, leaving much of that responsibility to the individual states. Civil rights groups and education scholars argue that this inaction in the face of continued socioeconomic disparities inevitably led to resegregation. Indeed, schools in some parts of the country are more segregated than when *Brown v. Board of Education* was decided. Democrats have advocated for a stronger federal role to promote diversity in the nation's public schools, while Republicans argue that education policies should remain under state and local control.

The parties have also disagreed about the federal role in addressing sex discrimination in education. Title IX of the Education Amendments Act of 1972 prohibits sex discrimination in education programs receiving federal assistance. Sexual harassment and sexual assault in educational settings are considered sex discrimination because those actions significantly affect a person's ability to learn. The most recent debates between the parties have focused on the guidelines colleges and universities must follow when handling sexual assault reports, and whether sex discrimination prohibits discrimination against transgender individuals.

Democrats have argued that schools should adopt a preponderance of the evidence standard of review in sexual assault cases, while Republicans argue this standard violates due process rights of students accused of those crimes. Democrats cite a 2020 U.S. Supreme Court ruling that discrimination against transgendered individuals violates federal law, while Republicans argue that the law only applies to discrimination on the basis of one's biological sex, not gender identity.

Integration Policy and Resegregation

Prior to emancipation, slaves in many parts of the United States were not only forbidden from receiving any formal education but were also prohibited from learning to read. The enactment of anti-literacy laws stemmed from the most famous slave rebellion of the pre–Civil War South, led by a literate slave named Nat Turner in 1831. Inspired by reading stories of freedom in the Bible, Turner coordinated an uprising that resulted in the deaths of at least fifty-five whites in Southampton County, Virginia. White mobs, in turn, killed or assaulted over two hundred Blacks in the region. The subsequent laws varied by state but typically involved fines for whites who taught slaves to read or write, with some states also using flogging as a punishment. Slaves who were caught learning to read or write were subject to lashings or other physical punishments.

After slavery was abolished, the Freedman's Bureau established schools, including colleges and trade schools, for former slaves. Several religious denominations, including Baptists, Episcopalians, Methodists, and Presbyterians, also created schools for that purpose. Public funding for these schools, however, was limited. The U.S. Supreme Court's interpretation of the Fourteenth Amendment's Equal Protection Clause in *Plessy v. Ferguson* (1896) allowed states to maintain a segregated society. The Court's holding that separate public facilities were constitutional if they were equal also applied to public schools.

In *Cummings v. Richmond Board of Education* (1899), the Court determined that there was no constitutional violation when the Richmond Board of Education denied Black students admission to white high schools because the county could not afford the costs associated with a separate school for Black students. The Court specifically deferred to state and local governments to establish and implement education policies.

This so-called separate but equal doctrine prevailed for decades, even though white lawmakers brazenly ignored the "equal" part. The Court did not repudiate its infamous *Plessy* decision until *Brown v. Board of Education*. The Court repudiated the separate but equal doctrine, declaring that "separate educational facilities are inherently unequal." A year later, in *Brown v. Board of Education II*, the Court held that segregated school districts must develop a plan for desegregation "with all deliberate speed." This vague language gave federal district court judges, who were charged with overseeing the plans, a great deal of discretion. During the 1970s and

1980, desegregation plans that included busing students became an increasingly controversial political issue. The Supreme Court's membership also underwent a shift during the 1980s toward more conservative justices more favorably disposed to limitations on the federal government's regulatory power. During the 1990s, the Court began to curtail the authority of federal judges to oversee school districts' integration plans. In *Freeman v. Pitts* (1992), for instance, the Court ruled that lower courts could incrementally end judicial control of desegregation, even if full compliance with *Brown* had not been achieved. This removal of federal oversight is widely recognized as a significant contributing factor in the resegregation of America's public schools.

To prevent resegregation, some school districts implemented school choice policies as a means of facilitating voluntary integration. In 2007, school choice policies in Seattle, Washington, and Louisville, Kentucky, were challenged by white students who argued that they had been denied their choice of school because of their race in violation of the Equal Protection Clause. In *Parents Involved in Community Schools v. Seattle School District No. 1* and *Meredith v. Jefferson County Board of Education*, a deeply divided Court invalidated the policies by a 5-4 vote. A plurality of four justices, including Chief Justice John Roberts, held that the school districts limited their view of diversity by only considering racial diversity and that the reliance on race as a factor in admissions violated the Equal Protection Clause of the Fourteenth Amendment. Justice Anthony Kennedy agreed that the policies here were unconstitutional, but he refused to subscribe to the plurality's view that "the Constitution mandates that state and local authorities must accept the status quo of racial isolation in school," a position he called "profoundly mistaken." The dissenting justices accused the plurality of undermining "*Brown's* promise of integrated primary and secondary education that local communities fought to make a reality."

While the judicial branch determines the constitutionality of integration policies, the executive branch determines the extent to which those policies are enforced. Despite some initial hesitation, Republican president Dwight Eisenhower and Democratic president John F. Kennedy enforced racial integration. Democratic president Lyndon B. Johnson was instrumental in securing the passage of the Civil Rights Act of 1964. This landmark law contains Title IV, which gives the Justice Department the authority to enforce the law, and Title VI, which prohibits discrimination based on race, color, or national origin to programs or activities receiving federal financial assistance. Johnson signed the ESEA in 1965, which significantly expanded the federal government's role in education policy. This law initially provided funds to local education authorities (LEAs) for several purposes, including funding programs for schools that served low-income students. For LEAs to receive ESEA funds, schools could not discriminate on the basis of race because that would violate Title VI. Connecting funding to nondiscrimination helped facilitate integration.

Republican presidents Richard Nixon and Gerald Ford were opposed to busing students to achieve integration, as was Democratic president Jimmy Carter,
but all three presidents enforced integration policies (Shah and Severns 2014).
According to a report by the Civil Rights Project at UCLA, ten years after *Brown*
was decided, 98 percent of Black students were attending segregated schools.
By the early 1970s, Southern schools were the most integrated in the country
(Frankenberg et al. 2017).

Carter replaced the Department of Health, Education, and Welfare with the
Department of Education in 1979. He argued that the change was needed so that
the federal government could supplement the states' efforts in providing education
to American students. The agency also houses an Office for Civil Rights (OCR),
which enforces civil rights statutes involving education. OCR continues to issue
policy position documents, referred to as "guidance," that represent the agency's
current position on an issue. Guidance documents lack the force of law, however,
unless specifically authorized by legislation.

During the presidency of Republican Ronald Reagan, school integration efforts
slowed. Reagan promised to eliminate the Department of Education during the
1980 presidential campaign, asserting that the agency represented an illegiti-
mate expansion of federal power into a policy area historically controlled by the
states. During this same period, Reagan and his education secretary, Terrel H. Bell,
restrained "the power of the Office for Civil Rights by cutting back its funding,
reducing investigations and reviews, and rescinding guidance" (Murphy 2017).
Bell also reduced the number of employees in the Office for Civil Rights—a trend
that has continued "across Republican and Democratic administrations: from
1981–2016, the full-time staff shrank from 1,099 to 563, even as civil-rights complaints grew from 2,887 to 16,720" (Murphy 2017). Despite the inaction of federal authorities in the Reagan administration, integration reached its zenith in the
South in 1988 with almost 44 percent of Black students attending majority white
schools (Orfield et al. 2014).

The Office of Civil Rights remained mostly forgotten under Reagan's successor,
George H. W. Bush, but it was given renewed emphasis under Democratic president Bill Clinton in the 1990s. Although OCR conducted more investigations of
alleged school discrimination during the Clinton administration, it was criticized
by civil rights groups for "failing to advance an agenda of school-desegregation and
gender equality" (Murphy 2017).

After the 2007 Supreme Court ruling imposing limits on school choice programs
that relied on the students' race, Republican president George W. Bush's Education
Department issued guidance to schools that they could only consider race-neutral
integration policies even though five members of the Court had held that race
could be considered in certain circumstances. The administration of Democratic
president Barack Obama rescinded this rule in 2011 and replaced it with guidance
to help school districts implement voluntary integration plans.

These steps failed to slide the trend toward educational resegregation. By 2011, the percentage of Black students attending majority white schools in the South had dropped to 23 percent, the same percentage as in 1968 (Orfield et al. 2014). In 2016, the Obama administration created a grant program to help schools wishing to be socioeconomically diverse. After assuming office in 2017, Republican president Donald Trump's administration rescinded the 2011 guidance and the grant program. Democratic president Joe Biden pledged to reinstate the Obama guidance during the 2020 presidential campaign.

Title IX of the Education Amendments Act

Title IX of the Education Amendments Act of 1972 was enacted to address centuries of sex discrimination in education. Congress enacted it as the Women's Rights Movement was becoming a prominent force in American politics. Title IX explicitly stipulates that "no person in the United States shall, on the basis of sex, be excluded from participation in, be denied benefits of, or be subjected to discrimination under any education program or activity receiving Federal financial assistance." The Fourteenth Amendment's Equal Protection Clause also prohibits discrimination in education; however, that provision only applies to state-funded schools, whereas Title IX applies to any school, public or private, that receives federal funds. The law prohibits discrimination in admissions, hiring and personnel practices, and student treatment. Courts have held that sexual harassment and sexual assault are considered sex discrimination under the law.

During the 1980s, public awareness grew of the sexual violence and harassment many women routinely experienced on college campuses. The 1986 on-campus rape and murder of college student Jeanne Clery highlighted this issue. After intense lobbying by a group formed by Clery's parents, Congress enacted the Jeanne Clery Disclosure of Campus Security Policy and Campus Crime Statistics Act of 1990 (Clery Act).

This law requires schools receiving federal funds to publish certain crime statistics, including the number of reported rapes. It also requires schools to provide details about campus security. In 1992, Congress enacted the Federal Campus Sexual Assault Victims' Bill of Rights, which required schools to provide information regarding procedures for reporting sexual violence, and to have a disciplinary process for handling these cases.

A 1999 U.S. Supreme Court ruling, *Davis v. Monroe County. Board of Education*, held that schools could be liable for student-on-student sexual harassment only when schools "are deliberately indifferent to sexual harassment, of which they have actual knowledge, that is so severe, pervasive, and objectively offensive that it can be said to deprive the victims of access to the educational opportunities or benefits provided by the school." This standard applies to civil suits when plaintiffs are seeking monetary damages.

In 2011, the OCR issued new guidance for schools in handling cases of sexual violence. This "Dear Colleague" letter, crafted and distributed by the Obama administration, required schools to investigate cases of sexual violence within a sixty-day time period, allow appeals for both the victim and the perpetrator, and use a preponderance of the evidence standard in determining guilt (a "preponderance" standard means that it is more likely than not that a person committed an act, as opposed to a higher "clear and convincing evidence standard"). The implementation of these new policies angered Congressional Republicans and conservative commentators who charged that they favored alleged victims at the expense of providing fair hearings for the alleged perpetrators.

President Trump's education secretary, Betsy DeVos, rescinded the Obama policies in 2017 and replaced them with new guidelines in 2020. Under the new guidelines, schools could decide whether to use the preponderance of the evidence standard or the clear and convincing evidence standard. They also allowed alleged perpetrators' advisers to cross-examine the victim, although they could be in different rooms during a hearing. The hearing could also be virtual. The new guidance further provided that colleges and universities were responsible for off-campus incidents if the school owned or was affiliated with the property. This decision was met with criticism from Democrats and women's rights groups who charged that the policies were hostile to sexual assault victims and coddled perpetrators. After Democrat Joe Biden was elected, he issued an executive order in March 2021 directing the Department of Education to review the policies concerning sex discrimination and violence in schools. During the 2020 presidential campaign, Biden pledged to reinstate the Obama-era policies, and this order was the first step in that process.

In 2022, the Biden administration proposed new guidance. The rules reinstated the clear and convincing evidence standard but only if schools used the standard in other types of discrimination cases. If it did not, it was required to use the preponderance of the evidence standard. The new rules eliminated live hearings on college campuses, and schools could investigate and punish off-campus assaults.

The parties also disagreed over another aspect of Title IX: the protection of transgender students. In May 2016, the Department of Education's Office of Civil Rights issued guidance to schools receiving federal funds that discrimination against transgender students constituted sex-based discrimination prohibited by Title IX. More specifically, the OCR's guidance provided that schools "must not treat a transgender student differently from the way it treats other students of the same gender identity." According to some legal commentators, this guidance followed rulings by the U.S. Supreme Court, lower federal courts, and federal agencies in considering transgender discrimination as sex-based discrimination. In *Price Waterhouse v. Hopkins* (1989), for example, the U.S. Supreme Court held that a company violated Title VII of the Civil Rights Act of 1964, which prohibits sex discrimination in employment, by denying a woman a promotion because she did not conform to gender norms. Other legal scholars, however, argued that sex discrimination applied only to men and women because that was the intent of the statute.

The Trump administration rescinded the Obama policies, with officials insisting that Title IX civil liberties protections did not apply to transgender individuals. Republicans were mostly unified in claiming that states and local school districts should be responsible for making and implementing policies involving transgender students, not the federal government. In 2021, however, Biden's Department of Education reverted to the Obama-era policy of requiring schools to treat transgender discrimination as sex discrimination. The administration argued that the U.S. Supreme Court's ruling in *Bostick v. Clayton County* (2020), in which the Court ruled that Title VII of the Civil Rights Act of 1964 prohibits discrimination on the basis of sexual orientation or transgender status, applies to education. The Biden policies were challenged by twenty Republican state attorneys general who argued that Title IX did not prohibit transgender discrimination. In July 2022, a federal judge temporarily blocked the policies from going into effect.

Democrats
Integration and Resegregation
Under President Obama, the Department of Education placed a renewed emphasis on civil rights. Obama's first education secretary, Arne Duncan, stated in his confirmation hearing that "[q]uality education is also the civil rights issue of our generation. It is the only path out of poverty, the only road to a more equal, just, and fair society" (Phenicie 2016).

In 2011, the Department of Education issued guidance offering its interpretation of the 2007 Supreme Court ruling, which provided practical legal strategies for school districts that wanted to pursue voluntary integration policies. The letter stated that "[t]he academic achievement of students at racially isolated schools often lags behind that of their peers at more diverse schools. Racially isolated schools often have fewer effective teachers, higher teacher turnover rates, less rigorous curricular resources (e.g., college preparatory courses), and inferior facilities and other educational resources" (U.S. Department of Education Office for Civil Rights 2011).

The letter also provided suggestions for school districts pursuing voluntary integration, including the geographical location of new schools and specialized programs to attract a diverse student body. But with Democratic policy proposals to reduce school segregation blocked by Republicans at every turn, little headway was made by the Obama White House. At the end of his tenure in late 2015, Education Secretary Duncan lamented that "I would give myself a pretty low grade on [school integration]" (Phenicie 2016).

In 2016, President Obama included a $120 million grant program, "Stronger Together," in his final budget request to Congress. This proposal would have established a competitive grant process to fund the development or implementation of local school plans to increase socioeconomic diversity. Duncan's successor, Education Secretary John King, touted the benefits of the plan: "[i]n today's economy, diversity isn't some vague ideal. It's a path to better outcomes for all of America's children. And the proposal we are announcing today will help show us the most effective ways to meet that goal" (Klein 2016). When this plan was rejected by Republicans in Congress, the Department of Education launched a smaller program to promote school integration. "Opening Doors, Expanding Opportunities" was a $12 million program modeled after the Stronger Together program. This program was ended in 2017 by Trump's education secretary, Betsy DeVos, a long-time fixture in Republican politics in her home state of Michigan.

As a candidate for the Democratic nomination in 2020, Vice President Joe Biden was criticized in a debate with fellow Democratic presidential nominees for opposing busing early in his political career. Biden responded that he opposed forced busing, not voluntary busing to increase diversity in public schools. He pledged to reinstate the Obama-era guidance on developing plans to "legally implement desegregation strategies" (Biden 2019b) and to ensure that "no child's education opportunity is determined by their zip code, parents' income, race, or disability" (Biden 2019b).

Title IX of the Education Amendments Act
The Obama administration issued new guidance on Title IX as it applied to procedures used by colleges to investigate and adjudicate sexual assault claims. In a 2011 letter, the assistant secretary of the Office of Civil Rights stated that the Department and the OCR were "deeply concerned" about sexual violence on campuses. The letter characterized education as "the great equalizer in America" and asserted that the Department and the OCR believed that "providing all students with an educational environment free from discrimination is extremely important." To that end, the OCR issued new guidance for educational institutions receiving federal funds to handle sexual violence cases. As previously noted, these policies included: lowering the evidentiary standard from that of clear and convincing evidence that a student was guilty of assaulting another student to that of a preponderance of the evidence, requiring schools to investigate assaults within sixty days, and creating an appeals process for both parties.

Vice President Joe Biden and Education Secretary Duncan introduced the new guidance at an event in 2011. Biden stated that "[t]oday we are strengthening our response to sexual assault in schools and on college campuses. Students across the country deserve the safest possible environment in which to learn. That's why we're taking new steps to help our nation's schools, universities and colleges end the cycle of sexual violence on campus" (Office of the Vice President 2011). Two years later Secretary Duncan issued additional guidance related to teen dating violence after President Obama designated February 2013 as National Teen Dating Violence

Awareness and Prevention Month. In a letter to state education chiefs, Duncan noted the serious consequences of gender-motivated violence for victims and their schools. For example, he cited research showing that "[w]itnessing violence has been associated with decreased school attendance and academic performance. Further, teenage victims of physical dating violence are more likely than their non-abused peers to smoke, use drugs, engage in unhealthy dieting (e.g., taking diet pills or laxatives, vomiting to lose weight), engage in risky sexual behaviors, and attempt or consider suicide" (United States Department of Education 2013). Duncan also cited research that female victims of dating violence suffer more severe consequences than male victims. Because research indicated that schools played an important role in preventing teen violence, he suggested that schools implement programs to prevent teen dating violence and provided information as to how they could do so.

In January 2014, President Obama directed the vice president and the White House Council on Women and Girls to lead an interagency council to "develop a coordinated Federal response to campus rape and sexual assault" ("Memorandum—Establishing a White House Task Force to Protect Students from Sexual Assault" 2014). In a statement announcing the formation of the task force, Obama noted that the Departments of Justice and Education had been working to enforce existing federal law regarding sexual violence; however, given that one in five women is a victim of sexual violence or attempted sexual violence while in college, he argued that more work was needed to address the issue and appointed the task force to facilitate that work ("Memorandum—Establishing a White House Task Force to Protect Students from Sexual Assault" 2014). By April 2014, the task force compiled a twenty-page report, and the OCR issued a question-and-answer document to provide additional clarification on the requirements of the policy. Critics of the policies charged that the Obama administration "overreached in its guidance, failed to use the proper channels to impose policies, and created kangaroo courts that shredded due process and students' rights along the way" (Camera 2020).

During the 2020 presidential campaign, Joe Biden pledged to restore the 2011 Obama guidance on Title IX, which he had played a role in developing. His campaign website stated that "any backstepping on Title IX is unacceptable" (Biden 2019a). He was hardly alone in expressing these sentiments within the Democratic Party. In fact, the 2020 Democratic platform explicitly framed the party as a desperately needed antidote to the Trump administration's misguided and uncaring education policies:

> We will enforce and provide tools and resources for schools to implement Title IX, which requires schools and institutions of higher education to properly investigate sexual misconduct, including peer-on-peer sexual harassment and violence; take appropriate action; and prevent future sexual misconduct.
> Democrats will make sure schools do not engage in, and appropriately address, discrimination, bullying and harassment related to sex, including sexual orientation

and gender identity; race; national origin; immigration or citizenship status; religion; disability; and language status. We will protect the rights of transgender students.

It is unacceptable that America's public schools are more racially segregated today than they were in the late 1960s. Schools—and classrooms and programs within schools—continue to be segregated by race and class. And, with increasing frequency, students are being unnecessarily and unlawfully segregated by disability, language status and through the use of exclusionary discipline and school-based arrests. We believe that schools must no longer engage in segregation and segregative practices. Democrats support appointing judges who will enforce the Civil Rights Act in schools. (Democratic Party Platform 2020)

The Biden administration, however, has been criticized by some women's rights organizations for not working with enough urgency to repeal the Trump-era rules. A coalition of groups had asked the administration to immediately stop enforcement of those policies. Fatima Goss Graves, president of the National Women's Law Center, stated that "students should not have to put their rights and safety on hold" (Stratford 2021).

The 2016 Education Department guidance concerning the treatment of transgender students was also criticized. President Obama stated that the guidance was issued because the Department of Education was receiving requests from states about how to accommodate transgender students in places such as bathrooms and locker rooms. He defended the policy by arguing that "I think it is part of our obligation as a society to make sure everyone is treated fairly and our kids are all loved and that they're protected and that their dignity is affirmed" (Fabian 2016b). The administration also sued North Carolina for implementing a policy requiring students to use restrooms corresponding to the sex listed on their birth certificate. Public opinion polls showed that most Americans under thirty believed that transgender individuals should be allowed to use the restroom corresponding to their gender identity, and some strategists argued that the Democrats' stance on this issue could help with younger voters (Fabian 2016a). Republicans accused Obama of executive overreach. The Republican Texas lieutenant governor Dan Patrick, when faced with the potential of losing federal funds for imposing a bathroom policy similar to North Carolina's, responded, "Well in Texas, he can keep his 30 pieces of silver. We will not yield to blackmail from the president of the United States" (Fabian 2016a).

Under President Biden, the Department of Education reversed the Trump-era policy of refusing to consider transgender discrimination actionable under Title IX in June 2021. While the administration did not specifically reinstate the Obama policy, Education Secretary Miguel Cardona stated that "[t]oday the Department makes clear that all students—including LGBTQ+ students—deserve the opportunity to learn and thrive in schools that are free from discrimination" (Associated Press 2021). The policy directed that discrimination based on sexual orientation or transgender status was sex-based discrimination prohibited by Title IX. It was

Democrats Offer Transgender Bill of Rights

In 2022, Democrats supported a Resolution outlining a Transgender Bill of Rights that included broad legal protections for transgender Americans including provisions related to Title IX.

Recognizing that it is the duty of the Federal Government to develop and implement a Transgender Bill of Rights to protect and codify the rights of transgender and nonbinary people under the law and ensure their access to medical care, shelter, safety, and economic security.

Whereas an estimated 1,400,000 transgender adults live in the United States;

Whereas Title VII of the Civil Rights Act of 1964 requires equal treatment under the law regardless of sex;

Whereas the Supreme Court affirmed in *Bostock v. Clayton County* that Federal protection against discrimination on the basis of sex includes protection from discrimination on the basis of sexual orientation and gender identity;

Whereas despite these protections, transgender people still experience discrimination in medical care, employment, housing, education, lending, and other basic necessities; . . .

Resolved, that it is the sense of the House of Representatives that—

(1) it is the duty of the Federal Government to protect the rights of transgender and nonbinary people as outlined in this Transgender Bill of Rights by—

(A) ensuring transgender and nonbinary people have equal access to services and public accommodations that align with their gender identity by— . . .

(iv) amending Federal education laws to ensure that they protect students from discrimination based on sex, including gender identity and sex characteristics, and guarantee students' right to—

(I) participate in sports on teams that best align with their gender identity; and

(II) use school facilities that best align with their gender identity; . . .

Source

Congress.gov. 2022. "Text – H.Res.1209—117th Congress (2021–2022): Recognizing That It Is the Duty of the Federal Government to Develop and Implement a Transgender Bill of Rights to Protect and Codify the Rights of Transgender and Nonbinary People under the Law and Ensure Their Access to Medical Care, Shelter, Safety, and Economic Security." November 1. Accessed January 30, 2023. https://www.congress.gov/bill/117th-congress/house-resolution/1209/text.

based on the Supreme Court's ruling equating LGBTQ discrimination with sex discrimination.

Biden was criticized for this action by Doreen Denny, a senior adviser for Concerned Women for America, a conservative women's organization. She argued that allowing transgender students to compete in sports based on their gender identity discriminated against female athletes who would be disadvantaged by competing against biological males. She stated that by pushing for inclusion, Biden and Democrats "have erased female status and ultimately rejected any meaningful difference between the sexes," which will "continue to aid and abet the erasure of women's opportunities for fair competition" (Denny 2021).

Republicans

Integration and Resegregation

One of George W. Bush's most significant achievements as president was the bipartisan No Child Left Behind Act (2001). Bush echoed President Johnson in labeling education as "the civil rights issue of our time"; however, he did not acknowledge resegregation, only "failing" and "succeeding" schools (McAndrews 2009). His administration, like previous Republican administrations, sought to limit the role of OCR in school integration (Murphy 2017). President Donald Trump's administration also devoted little attention to resegregation. Secretary of Education Betsy DeVos ended the school integration program initiated by her Democratic predecessor, John King. The same week that DeVos gave a speech in which she spoke of the benefits of racial and socioeconomic diversity in education at the Brookings Institute, an Education Department spokesperson stated that the program was discontinued because "it would not be a wise use of tax dollars, in part because the money was to be used for planning, not implementation" (Brown 2017). The decision was praised by Paul Crookston writing in the *National Review*. Crookston argued that the Opening Doors, Expanding Opportunities program was based on the "administration's flawed model: paying schools vast sums of money to implement Washington mandates" (Crookston 2017). Democratic representative and then-ranking member of the House Education and Labor committee disagreed with the decision to end the program. He reminded "President Trump and Secretary DeVos that it is the responsibility of the U.S. Department of Education to promote equity of educational opportunity in pursuit of fulfillment of the promise of *Brown v. Board*, and that despite much progress, that promise remains unfulfilled. Just last year, the Government Accountability Office found that our nation's public schools are more segregated by race and class now than they were in 1968" (Scott 2017). He also noted that there was research demonstrating that "all students are better served in diverse learning environments" and criticized the Trump administration for not affirming its commitment to civil rights by continuing the program (Scott 2017).

Title IX of the Education Amendments Act

Republican opposition to most Obama administration education policies remained strong throughout both of the Democratic president's two terms. The GOP's 2016 platform offers a fairly representative example of Republican rhetoric during this period:

> We emphatically support the original, authentic meaning of Title IX of the Education Amendments of 1972. It affirmed that "no person in the United States shall, on

the basis of sex, be excluded from participation in, be denied the benefits of, or be subjected to discrimination under any education program or activity receiving Federal financial assistance." That language opened up for girls and women a world of opportunities that had too often been denied to them. That same provision of law is now being used by bureaucrats—and by the current President of the United States—to impose a social and cultural revolution upon the American people by wrongly redefining sex discrimination to include sexual orientation or other categories. Their agenda has nothing to do with individual rights; it has everything to do with power. They are determined to reshape our schools—and our entire society—to fit the mold of an ideology alien to America's history and traditions. . . .

Sexual assault is a terrible crime. We commend the good-faith efforts by law enforcement, educational institutions, and their partners to address that crime responsibly. Whenever reported, it must be promptly investigated by civil authorities and prosecuted in a courtroom, not a faculty lounge. Questions of guilt or innocence must be decided by a judge and jury, with guilt determined beyond a reasonable doubt. Those convicted of sexual assault should be punished to the full extent of the law. The Administration's distortion of Title IX to micromanage the way colleges and universities deal with allegations of abuse contravenes our country's legal traditions and must be halted before it further muddles this complex issue and prevents the proper authorities from investigating and prosecuting sexual assault effectively with due process.

After her confirmation, Betsy DeVos, secretary of the Department of Education for the Trump administration in 2017, ordered an immediate review of the Title IX sexual violence policies because "[w]e knew the framework, as laudable as it might have been, that the Obama 'Dear Colleague' letter was simply not working" (Camera 2020).

Her plans were quickly criticized by Democrats and women's rights activists. Democratic senator Patty Murray, the ranking member of the Senate Committee on Health, Labor, Education and Pensions, sent a letter to DeVos in 2017 outlining concerns about the changes in the sexual violence policy along with broader concerns about the unwillingness of DeVos and Candice Jackson, acting assistant secretary of education, to investigate sexual violence cases. Murray reminded DeVos that "upholding civil rights, working to ensure student safety, and responding to reports of sexual violence are critical parts" of her job. Murray expressed opposition to changing the standard from preponderance of the evidence because it would make it more difficult for victims to get relief for their injuries. She criticized Jackson for not taking sexual assault claims seriously after Jackson told the *New York Times* that "the [sexual assault] accusations—90 percent of them—fall into the category of 'we were both drunk,' 'we broke up, and six months later I found myself under a Title IX investigation because she just decided that our last sleeping together was not quite right'" (Green and Stolberg 2017).

After the new regulations were released, civil rights attorneys and Democrats offered additional criticism. Four Democratic congresswomen introduced legislation to prevent the implementation of the new policies. One of the cosponsors, Democratic representative Elissa Slotkin, stated, "I cannot understand why Secretary DeVos continues to move forward with proposed changes to Title IX that make it harder for victims to come forward with a successful claim" (Gringlas 2019). According to journalist Tyler Kingkade, organizations that represented K–12 schools and colleges and universities opposed DeVos's rules "on a near universal basis" because they "were overly prescriptive, forced schools to act like courts and were 'detached from the realities' on campuses" (Kingkade 2021). Even stalwart Republican and former Liberty University president Jerry Falwell Jr. criticized the DeVos policies as being "terribly misinformed and [having a] narrow view" (Kingkade 2021).

After Biden defeated Trump in the 2020 presidential election, scholar and educator Michael Poliakoff, president of the American Council of Trustees and Alumni, urged the incoming Biden administration to provide more due process rights than the Obama administration had in Title IX investigations. He claimed that the DeVos policies provided important rights to the accused, including "the rights to present, cross-examine, and challenge evidence in campus hearings. . . . You do not have to be a constitutional scholar to recognize that Secretary DeVos was right to redress a longstanding ethical and procedural abuse. The Biden administration must not reverse her important work and bring back the guilty presuming process that the Obama administration demanded" (Poliakoff 2021).

Secretary DeVos also faced criticism for rescinding the Obama administration's Title IX rules protecting transgender students. In this case, the Trump administration did not replace the regulations but revoked them, even after a federal judge issued a stay preventing the Obama regulations from taking effect. A joint letter from the Justice Department and the Education Department stated that the policy was being rescinded because it was implemented "without due regard for the primary role of the states and local school districts in establishing educational policy" (Peters, Becker, and Davis 2017). The *New York Times* reported that there was some disagreement in the Trump White House over eliminating the protections for transgender students to use the restroom of their choice. Secretary DeVos reportedly resisted the policy change due to the potential harm to transgender students; however, after Attorney General Jeff Sessions, an opponent of LGBTQ rights, approached the president, DeVos relented. The joint letter included a statement that schools must protect transgender students from bullying. The secretary released a separate statement emphasizing that she believed every school in the United States had a "moral obligation" to protect all students from "discrimination, bullying, and harassment" (Peters, Becker, and Davis 2017).

DeVos was asked about the policy change when she testified before the House Education Committee in 2019. Democratic representative Suzanne Bonamici

---

Republicans Introduce Protection of Women and Girls in Sports Act

Republicans introduced legislation in 2021 to ensure that Title IX applied to someone's sex at birth and not their gender identity to prevent female athletes from suffering disadvantages in school sports. The text of the bill is excerpted here.

"To provide that for purposes of determining compliance with title IX of the Education Amendments of 1972 in athletics, sex shall be recognized based solely on a person's reproductive biology and genetics at birth . . ."

This Act may be cited as the "Protection of Women and Girls in Sports Act of 2021."

SEC. 2. AMENDMENT.

Section 901 of the Education Amendments of 1972 (20 U.S.C. 1681) is amended by adding at the end the following:

"(d) (1) It shall be a violation of subsection (a) for a recipient of Federal funds who operates, sponsors, or facilitates athletic programs or activities to permit a person whose sex is male to participate in an athletic program or activity that is designated for women or girls."

"(2) For purposes of this subsection, sex shall be recognized based solely on a person's reproductive biology and genetics at birth."

Source

Congress.gov. 2022. "Text – H.R.426—117th Congress (2021–2022): Protection of Women and Girls in Sports Act of 2021." April 26. Accessed January 30, 2023. https://www.congress.gov/bill/117th-congress/house-bill/426/text.

---

asked DeVos whether "she knew that harassment and discrimination can lead to poor academic performance and depression for transgender students." DeVos responded that the OCR protected the rights of all students. Bonamici then asked whether DeVos was aware of data indicating "alarming levels of attempted suicide among transgender youth." DeVos stated that she was and then repeated that "OCR is committed to ensuring all students have access to their education free from discrimination" (Anapol 2019).

While Democrats opposed the Trump policies, they were praised by many conservatives. The editorial board of the *National Review* applauded Trump's return of educational policymaking power to states and school boards, including policies related to transgender students. "Contrary to the claims of LGBT activists," wrote the board, "preserving federalism does not leave transgender students to the mercy of bullies or bigots" because the letter still said that schools were required to ensure all students "are able to learn and thrive in a safe environment" (Editorial Board 2017).

By 2020, the emphasis had shifted from bathrooms to sports. In 2020, the Trump administration's Department of Education threatened to withhold federal funding from Connecticut high schools after the state's high school athletics governing body implemented a policy allowing students to compete in sports based on their gender identity. The department argued that the policy discriminated against female students because it "denied female student-athletes athletic benefits and opportunities, including advancing to the finals in events, higher level competitions, awards, medals, recognition, and the possibility of greater visibility to colleges and other benefits" (Levenson and Vigdor 2020).

Further Reading

Anapol, Avery. 2019. "DeVos Defends Controversial Guidance on Transgender Students." *The Hill*, April 10. Accessed July 11, 2021. https://thehill.com/homenews/administration/438257-dem-asks-devos-if-she-knew-of-potential-harm-to-transgender-students.

Associated Press. 2021. "Biden Administration Extends Protections to Transgender Students." National Public Radio, June 16. Accessed April 30, 2021. https://www.npr.org/2021/06/16/1007344321/biden-admin-extends-protections-to-transgender-students.

Biden, Joe. 2019a. "The Biden Plan to End Violence against Women." Joe Biden for President. Accessed July 12, 2021. https://joebiden.com/vawa/.

Biden, Joe. 2019b. "The Biden Plan for Educators, Students, and Our Future." Joe Biden for President. Accessed July 12, 2021. https://joebiden.com/education/.

Brown, Emma. 2017. "Trump's Education Department Nixes Obama-Era Grant Program for School Diversity." *Washington Post*, March 29. Accessed July 23, 2019. https://www.washingtonpost.com/news/education/wp/2017/03/29/trumps-education-department-nixes-obama-era-grant-program-for-school-diversity/.

Camera, Lauren. 2020. "New Title IX Rules Bolster the Rights of Those Accused of Sexual Assault." *US News and World Report*, May 6. Accessed June 18, 2021. https://www.usnews.com/news/education-news/articles/2020-05-06/trump-administration-publishes-final-title-ix-campus-sexual-assault-regulations.

Cohen, Rachel. 2015. "Obama's Mixed Record on School Integration." *The American Prospect*, August 30. Accessed October 5, 2021. https://prospect.org/education/obama-s-mixed-record-school-integration/.

Crookston, Paul. 2017. "Education Department Cancels Obama-Era Diversity Grants." *National Review*, March 31. Accessed May 2, 2019. https://www.nationalreview.com/corner/betsy-devos-ends-obama-era-diversity-grants-promoting-integration/.

Democratic Party Platform. 2020. The American Presidency Project. Accessed December 16, 2022. https://www.presidency.ucsb.edu/documents/presidential-documents-archive-guidebook/party-platforms-and-nominating-conventions-3.

Denny, Doreen. 2021. "The Biden Administration Is Sending Title IX to the Ash Heap of History." *Newsweek*, December 16. Accessed January 18, 2022. https://www.newsweek.com/biden-administration-sending-title-ix-ash-heap-history-opinion-1659730.

Editorial Board of the *National Review*. 2017. "Returning Power to States and School Boards." *National Review*, February 23. Accessed April 4, 2019. https://www.nationalreview.com/2017/02/trump-administration-transgender-guidelines-title-ix-rescinds-obama-letter-federalism/.

Fabian, Jordan. 2016a. "Obama Opens New Culture War with Transgender Rights Fight." *The Hill*, May 14. Accessed July 10, 2020. https://thehill.com/homenews/administration /279882-obama-opens-new-culture-war-with-transgender-rights-fight?rl=1.

Fabian, Jordan. 2016b. "Obama Defends Actions on Transgender Policies." *The Hill*, May 16. Accessed July 13, 2020. https://thehill.com/homenews/administration /280065-obama-defends-actions-on-transgender-policies?rl=1.

Frankenberg, Erica, Genevieve Siegel Hawley, Jongyeon Ee, and Gary Orfield. 2017. "Southern Schools: More Than a Half-Century after the Civil Rights Revolution." UCLA Civil Rights Project, May 23. Accessed October 3, 2022. https://www .civilrightsproject.ucla.edu/research/k-12-education/integration-and-diversity/southern -schools-brown-83-report.

Green, Erica L., and Sherilyn Gay Stolberg. 2017. "Campus Rape Policies Get a New Look as the Accused Get DeVos's Ear." *New York Times*, July 12. Accessed September 22, 2020. https://www.nytimes.com/2017/07/12/us/politics/campus-rape-betsy-devos -title-iv-education-trump-candice-jackson.html.

Gringlas, Sam. 2019. "Democratic Bill Aims to Block Title IX Rule Changes Pushed by Trump Administration." National Public Radio, December 10. Accessed February 11, 2021. https://www.npr.org/2019/12/10/786810875/democratic-bill-aims-to-block -title-ix-rule-changes-pushed-by-trump-administration.

Kingkade, Tyler. 2021. "Activists Increase Pressure on Biden to Scrap Betsy DeVos' Title IX Rules." *NBC News*, March 15. Accessed March 5, 2021. https://www.nbcnews.com/news /us-news/activists-increase-pressure-biden-scrap-betsy-devos-title-ix-rules-n1261017.

Kingkade, Tyler. 2022. "Biden Admin Proposes Sweeping Changes to Title IX to Undo Trump-Era Rules." *NBC News*, June 23. Accessed October 4, 2022. https://www.nbcnews.com/politics /biden-admin-proposes-sweeping-changes-title-ix-undo-trump-era-rules-rcna34915.

Klein, Rebecca. 2016. "Obama Wants to Get Rich and Poor Kids in the Same Classroom." *HuffPost*, February 9. Accessed March 12, 2021. https://www.huffpost.com/entry /obama-education-budget_n_56ba0701e4b04f9b57db1fe0.

Levenson, Michael, and Neil Vigdor. 2020. "Inclusion of Transgender Student Athletes Violates Title IX, Trump Administration Says." *New York Times*, May 29. Updated June 16, 2021. Accessed July 7, 2021. https://www.nytimes.com/2020/05/29/us/connecticut -transgender-student-athletes.html.

McAndrews, Larry. 2009. "'Not the Bus, but Us': George W. Bush and School Desegregation." Educational Foundations. Accessed July 7, 2021. https://files.eric.ed.gov/fulltext /EJ869701.pdf.

"Memorandum—Establishing a White House Task Force to Protect Students from Sexual Assault." 2014. The White House, January 22. Accessed December 16, 2022. https://obamawhitehouse.archives.gov/the-press-office/2014/01/22/memorandum -establishing-white-house-task-force-protect-students-sexual-a.

Murphy, James S. 2017. "The Office for Civil Right's Volatile Power." *The Atlantic*, March 13. Accessed March 8, 2021. https://www.theatlantic.com/education/archive/2017/03 /the-office-for-civil-rights-volatile-power/519072/.

Murray, Patty. 2017. Letter to Secretary of Education Betsy DeVos. July 12. Accessed April 3, 2021. https://www.help.senate.gov/imo/media/doc/071217%20-%20DeVos%20 -%20Title%20IX.pdf.

Office of the Vice President. 2011. "Vice President Biden Announces New Administration Effort to Help Nation's Schools Address Sexual Violence." April 4. Accessed

April 5, 2021. https://obamawhitehouse.archives.gov/the-press-office/2011/04/04/vice
-president-biden-announces-new-administration-effort-help-nation-s-s.

Orfield, Gary, Erica Frankenburg, Jongyeun Le, and John Kuscera. 2014. "Brown at 60:
Great Progress, a Long Retreat, and an Uncertain Future." UCLA Civil Rights Project, May 15. Accessed December 16, 2022. https://civilrightsproject.ucla.edu
/research/k-12-education/integration-and-diversity/brown-at-60-great-progress-a
-long-retreat-and-an-uncertain-future/Brown-at-60-051814.pdf.

Peters, Jeremy W., Jo Becker, and Julie Hirschfeld Davis. 2017. "Trump Rescinds Rules on
Bathrooms for Transgender Students." *New York Times*, February 22. Accessed April 4,
2021. https://www.nytimes.com/2017/02/22/us/politics/devos-sessions-transgender
-students-rights.html.

Phenicie, Carolyn. 2016. "The 74 Interview: Arne Duncan Grades Himself—And Sees Fail-
ures on Pre-K, Safety, Desegregation." *The 74*, February 7. Accessed April 6, 2021.
https://www.the74million.org/article/the-74-interview-arne-duncan-grades-himself
-and-sees-failures-on-pre-k-safety-desegregation/.

Poliakoff, Michael. 2021. "The Biden Plan for Title IX Must Protect Due Process."
Forbes, January 25. Accessed April 6, 2021. https://www.forbes.com/sites/michael
poliakoff/2021/01/25/the-biden-plan-for-title-ix-must-protect-due-process/.

Rogers, Katie, and Erica L. Green. 2021. "Biden Will Revisit Trump Rules on Campus
Sexual Assault." *New York Times*, March 8. Updated June 16. Accessed April 7, 2021.
https://www.nytimes.com/2021/03/08/us/politics/joe-biden-title-ix.html.

Scott, Bobby. 2017. "Scott Condemns Trump Administration's Decision to Pull Funding for School Diversity." Press Release House Committee on Education and Labor,
March 30. Accessed April 7, 2021. https://edlabor.house.gov/media/press-releases
/scott-condemns-trump-administrations-decision-to-pull-funding-for-school-diversity.

Shah, Nirvi, and Maggie Severns. 2014. "60 Years On: Education, Segregation, and the
Obama White House." *Politico*, May 17. Accessed April 14, 2021. https://www
.politico.com/story/2014/05/brown-board-of-education-barack-obama-106781.

Stratford, Michael. 2021. "Biden Administration Expects to Unveil Title IX Proposals in
April." *Politico*, December. Accessed December 16, 2022. https://www.politico.com
/news/2021/12/15/title-ix-proposals-april-524871

United States Department of Education. 2013. "Key Policy Letters from the Education
Secretary and Deputy Secretary." February 28. Accessed May 17, 2021. https://www2
.ed.gov/policy/gen/guid/secletter/130228.html.

United States Department of Education Office for Civil Rights. 2011. "Dear Colleague."
April 4. Accessed May 17, 2021. https://www2.ed.gov/about/offices/list/ocr/docs
/guidance-ese-201111.pdf.

Environmental Justice

At a Glance

From the 1960s through the 1980s, researchers compiled compelling evidence that historically marginalized groups in the United States, including people of color, tribal populations, and low-income individuals, were disproportionately harmed by pollution and hazardous waste generated across the country. Civil rights and environmental activists labeled this type of discrimination "environmental racism" and urged a governmental response that would meaningfully promote what they called "environmental justice."

In the 1990s, both Republican president George H. W. Bush and Democratic president Bill Clinton took executive action to address the issue. Additional federal environmental justice legislation has been repeatedly proposed by Democrats since 1992; however, none has been enacted. This has left the executive branch and the Environmental Protection Agency (EPA) as the primary policymakers in this area.

Since the 1990s, scientists and policymakers around the world have also emphasized the need to address the growing dangers of climate change and its impact on vulnerable populations. Initially, both political parties included lawmakers and policy experts committed to reducing greenhouse gas emissions. During Democratic president Barack Obama's first term in office, the GOP became virtually unified in opposing regulatory efforts to combat climate change. The political dynamic has remained largely unchanged since then, with Democrats urging bold action to ward off a cataclysmic environmental crisis and Republicans being firmly opposed. Some Republicans even remain adamant that global warming is a myth, dismissing the overwhelming scientific evidence of anthropogenic (human-made) climate change.

According to many Democrats . . .

- The federal government should implement regulations to address environmental racism.
- The United States should enact policies to address the threat of climate change.

- Individuals should be allowed to file lawsuits even if racism is an incidental result of government action.

According to many Republicans . . .

- Federal environmental regulations often interfere with economic growth.
- Climate change is not a serious threat, and the United States should not enact regulatory policies that will harm American businesses in the process of addressing it.
- Lawsuits alleging racial discrimination should proceed only if racism is intentional and not an incidental result of government action.

Overview

Environmental justice refers to the equitable distribution of costs and benefits of environmental policy regardless of race, color, national origin, or income. The environmental justice movement is a response to policies that cause communities heavily populated by minorities and lower-income households to be disproportionately affected by air and water pollution, toxic waste disposal, and other environmental hazards. Climate change—and policy responses to its looming threat—is also part of the environmental justice debate, as the socioeconomic ripple effects of our rapidly warming world disproportionately harm vulnerable populations.

Environmental justice issues first began to gain national attention in the 1960s and 1970s, during which time air and water pollution and habitat protection emerged as increasingly prominent voting issues for many Americans. Public health concerns rose too, especially in poor and working-class neighborhoods and industries where exposure to industrial pollution was likely to be higher. In the 1960s, the United Farm Workers union drew attention to the impact of dangerous pesticides on laborers in California. In 1969, Black residents of Shaw, Mississippi, filed a lawsuit alleging that the municipal services provided to the city's white neighborhoods were superior to those provided to Black neighborhoods as the latter lacked sewage treatment facilities, street-lighting, paved roads, and drainage ditches to prevent flooding. After a U.S. district court found that the city had not violated the Black residents' constitutional rights, the U.S. Court of Appeals for the Fifth Circuit reversed that decision holding that the city's actions violated the Fourteenth Amendment.

Pursuing Environmental Justice in the Courts

The environmental justice movement gained momentum in the early 1980s primarily due to two events. In 1979, the first lawsuit alleging environmental discrimination was filed by residents of a predominantly Black community in Houston to prevent the placement of a municipal solid waste landfill in their neighborhood. In the suit, the residents cited the city's past history of locating solid waste facilities in Black communities. Although the lawsuit was unsuccessful, it drew attention to this previously commonplace practice. In 1982, protests over the placement of a hazardous landfill for polychlorinated biphenyl (PCBs) in Warren County, North Carolina, where 84 percent of the residents were Black, drew national media attention after a violent clash with police led to mass arrests of protestors. PCBs have been linked to increased cancer rates and birth defects.

These protests spurred civil rights activists and groups to document the impact of environmental policy on communities of color and low-income individuals. A 1983 Government Accounting Office report found that three of the four hazardous waste landfill sites in southern United States were in minority communities while the fourth was in a low-income community. A landmark 1987 report by the United Church of Christ Commission for Racial Justice, *Toxic Wastes and Race in the United States*, found that the race of residents was the most important factor in deciding the location of abandoned toxic waste sites across the country.

Despite this evidence of what activists called "environmental racism," the federal government was slow to respond—in part due to significant cuts to the EPA during the Reagan administration. The Reagan White House cut the EPA budget by 25 percent, and his first EPA administrator, Anne Gorsuch Burford, cut the workforce of the agency by 20 percent.

In a significant break with the policies of his predecessor, Republican president George H. W. Bush pledged to be the "environmental president." Although he clashed with environmental groups on some issues, he is credited by those same groups with signing major amendments to the Clean Air Act in 1990. After two high-profile environmental conferences in 1990 and 1991 and lobbying by environmental justice organizations, the Bush EPA established the Office of Environmental Equity in 1992. This office, now known as the Office of Environmental Justice, provides grants and technical assistance to communities working to address environmental justice issues.

In 1993, the EPA—now part of the new administration of Democratic president Bill Clinton—established the National Environmental Justice Advisory Council to advise the agency's administrator on integrating environmental justice into EPA programs. One year later, Clinton issued Executive Order 12898, *Federal Action to Address Environmental Justice in Minority Populations and Low-Income Populations*, which required federal agencies to address the effects of their policies on the environment and health of minority and low-income populations and to create strategies for implementing environmental justice. The Office of Environmental Justice is responsible for coordinating efforts to comply with the order. It defines "environmental justice" as "fair treatment and meaningful involvement of all people regardless of race, color, national origin, or income, with respect to the development, implementation, and enforcement of environmental laws, regulations, and policies" (United States Environmental Protection Agency 2021). Unlike federal legislation, executive orders apply only to administrative agencies within the executive branch, which limits their effect. Subsequent presidents can refuse to enforce or rescind prior executive orders. The absence of federal environmental justice laws, despite repeated attempts since the early 1990s to enact such legislation, has left the president and the EPA as the primary policymakers in this area.

Early in the environmental justice movement, individuals filed lawsuits alleging racial discrimination in the placement of hazardous waste sites and other environmental hazards. A 2001 U.S. Supreme Court ruling made it more difficult for individuals to file such suits. In *Alexander v. Sandoval* (2001), the Court held that plaintiffs bringing lawsuits under Title VI of the Civil Rights Act of 1964 must show that a policy intentionally discriminated on the basis of a litigant's race, color, or national origin. This ruling eliminated the use of disparate impact discrimination in which policies may appear to be neutral but when applied affect people of color in a disproportionate manner. Democrats have supported legislation to overturn this ruling arguing that disparate impact discrimination is actionable racial discrimination, while Republicans support the Court's ruling because plaintiffs should have to show that they were intentionally discriminated against.

During Republican president George W. Bush's administration, the EPA administrators shifted the focus of the Office of Environmental Justice. During the Clinton administration, the agency emphasized addressing situations in which minorities and low-income communities were disadvantaged by environmental hazards. A 2001 memorandum from Christine Todd Whitman, Bush's first EPA administrator, indicated that the agency would strive to ensure environmental justice for "all communities and persons" (United States Environmental Protection Agency 2001). Bush also withdrew the United States from the Kyoto Protocol because of its potential adverse effects on the U.S. economy.

Challenges to Reform
In his first term as president, Barack Obama held a White House Forum on Environmental Justice in 2010, bringing together community leaders and government leaders, including Cabinet heads, to discuss environmental justice issues. Ultimately, Obama devoted more attention to environmental justice during his second term. In 2016, the EPA released its 2020 Action Agenda—a four-year plan to advance environmental justice initiatives. The Obama administration also played a significant role in negotiating the Paris Climate Agreement, a treaty signed by over two hundred nations, which pledged to reduce greenhouse gas emissions.

Environmental issues were a significant part of the 2016 presidential campaign as several candidates addressed the water crisis in Flint, Michigan. Flint's population was 56 percent Black with 40 percent of the residents living below the poverty line. Due to the city's financial problems, the state assumed the management of Flint's municipal services. To save money, a state official opted to change the source of the city's drinking water from the Detroit water system to the Flint River in 2014. The water from the Flint River was contaminated with lead, and this ended up killing twelve people. When the EPA failed to investigate, Flint residents filed a series of lawsuits beginning 2016. In 2021, Flint residents settled a lawsuit with the state of Michigan for $626 million. Residents have also sued the architectural firms that designed the water pipelines and the banks that provided financing for the project. In 2021, the Michigan attorney general filed criminal charges against nine individuals who worked either for the city of Flint or for the state of Michigan for their role in the crisis, including former Michigan governor Richard Snyder (Michigan Department of Attorney General 2021). The case is pending as of 2022.

In September 2016, the construction of the Dakota Access Oil Pipeline on tribal lands drew significant media attention. Protestors opposed the pipeline due to the alleged threat it posed to drinking water and sacred Native American lands. In the last months of the Obama administration, the Army Corps of Engineers revoked the easement that had allowed construction of the pipeline on tribal lands. This action, however, was overturned along with a raft of other Obama-era environmental policies by President Donald Trump. Trump, who has claimed that global warming is a hoax, also withdrew the United States from the Paris Climate Agreement and proposed eliminating all funding for the Office of Environmental Justice (Clegg 2017).

In 2019, Democratic representative Alexandria Ocasio-Cortez and Senator Edward Markey introduced a congressional resolution known as the Green New Deal. Borrowing language from President Franklin Roosevelt's New Deal programs meant to help the economy during the Great Depression, the plan proposed significant government spending to eliminate U.S. reliance on fossil fuels, create jobs, and combat climate change. The proposal was also crafted with environmental justice concerns at the forefront: "Climate change, pollution, and environmental destruction have exacerbated systemic racial, regional, social, environmental, and economic injustices by disproportionately affecting indigenous peoples, communities of color, migrant communities, deindustrialized communities, depopulated rural communities, the poor, low-income workers, women, the elderly, the unhoused, people with disabilities, and youth" (Friedman 2019). Senate Republicans scheduled a vote on the resolution, which was voted down 57-43 along party lines. Republicans celebrated the demise of the plan, which they said was too expensive and extreme for American businesses and consumers.

During the 2020 campaign, Congressional Democrats introduced the Environmental Justice for All Act and reintroduced it in 2021. The text of the bill stated that a federal law was necessary to address environmental justice issues because federal agencies were inconsistent in complying with Executive Order 12898. The bill also provided a private right of action to bring lawsuits under Title VI against organizations that engaged in harmful environmental practices on the basis of race, color, or national origin. During his first week as president, Joe Biden rejoined the Paris Climate Agreement.

Republicans have opposed environmental regulations as an unnecessary burden on businesses, inhibiting economic growth. Democrats have been more supportive of regulations, which they say are necessary to protect public health and the environment against polluters and other threats. Republicans have also opposed treaties requiring the United States to reduce its greenhouse gas emissions, saying that they pose too great an economic burden on American businesses. Democrats argue that the United States should be a leader in reducing greenhouse gases, in part, because climate change disproportionately affects disadvantaged groups but also because investing in alternative sources of energy can create jobs. They also assert that the economic costs of effectively addressing pollution and climate change pale in comparison with the astronomical costs of adapting to a rapidly warming and resource-stretched planet.

Republicans

The Republican Party supported early landmark environmental legislation, and during the presidency of George H. W. Bush, it endorsed policies to address environmental justice and climate change. More recently, Republicans have opposed increased environmental regulations due to the costs businesses would incur in complying with them. Republicans have also reversed their stance on climate change, with many labeling it a hoax. Other Republicans argue that climate change is not man made and increasing government spending to deal with a naturally occurring phenomenon is a waste of taxpayer money.

In the 1970s, Republicans supported environmental legislation and a stronger federal role in improving environmental quality. In a February 1970 Special Message to Congress on the Environment, Republican president Richard Nixon outlined a comprehensive thirty-seven-point program detailing initiatives in five categories: air pollution, water pollution, solid waste management, parklands and public recreation, and improved government organization. This program included twenty-three legislative efforts and fourteen new administrative or executive actions. In July 1970, Nixon created the EPA through an executive order to unify environmental efforts that had been performed by numerous federal agencies. He also signed several landmark environmental laws, including the National Environmental Protection Act (1969), the Clean Air Act (1972), and the Safe Drinking Water Act (1974).

The commitment to a stronger federal role in environmental regulation, and in government regulation generally, waned during the presidency of Ronald Reagan, who believed in a limited role for the federal government. Reagan's vice president, George H. W. Bush, launched several environmental initiatives, while also arguing that federal regulation should be limited. In 1989, Bush established the U.S. Global Change Research Program (USGCRP), which was passed into law unanimously by

Congress the following year in the Global Change Research Act. The law requires the USGCRP to develop and coordinate research on global warming, including a report, the National Climate Assessment, which must be presented to the president and Congress at least once every four years. His administration was the first to formally address environmental justice through the establishment of the Office of Environmental Equity at the EPA.

During the 1992 presidential campaign, critics charged that Bush backtracked on his environmental policies by delaying the implementation of rules in the Clean Air Act and by refusing to agree to a timetable for the United States to decrease greenhouse gas emissions. His supporters, however, noted that he signed the U.N. Framework Convention on Climate Change, the outcome of the 1992 Rio Earth Summit, which was an important first step in addressing global warming. The 1992 Republican platform asserted that "[a]dverse changes in climate must be the common concern of mankind" and touted Bush's work at the Rio Conference while also insisting that a Republican Senate would not ratify any climate change treaty that "moves environmental decisions beyond our democratic process or transfers beyond our shores authority over U.S. property." Political analysts have suggested that Bush's mixed record on the environment, particularly his stance on climate change, was influenced by members of his administration. Bush's chief of staff, former New Hampshire governor John Sununu, disputed that climate change was the result of human action and prevented the administration from taking stronger action to limit greenhouse gases (Rich 2018).

During the 2000 presidential campaign, George W. Bush called for a "new era" in environmental policy, which would maintain a strong federal role but also provide regulatory authority to the states. Indeed, the 2000 Republican Party platform stated that "[s]trong leadership by governors, legislators, and local officials is the key to solving the emerging environmental issues of this new century." Bush also opposed the Kyoto Protocol because he believed it was unfair for American businesses to implement costly regulations to reduce greenhouse gases when other countries were not bound to follow the same rules. He did, however, promise during the campaign to increase regulation of carbon dioxide emissions from power plants. After he reneged on that pledge, a coalition of environmental justice groups wrote President Bush a letter in April 2001 urging him to address environmental justice issues. The letter argued that there was irrefutable evidence that global warming was occurring, despite the president's views to the contrary, and that the effects of not supporting the Kyoto Protocol would be costly, particularly to minority and low-income populations. The letter cited the United Nations Intergovernmental Panel on Climate Change's analysis that global warming would "disproportionately harm the poor" (CorpWatch 2001). Bush defended his reversal citing evidence of an energy shortage; however, critics contended that he succumbed to pressure from coal company lobbyists and from conservative Republicans who argued it would harm the economy (Jehl and Revkin 2001).

When Bush's EPA administrator, former New Jersey governor Christine Todd Whitman, issued a 2001 memorandum outlining the agency's support for environmental justice and understanding of Executive Order 12898, critics suggested that the memo instead undermined that support. During the Clinton administration, environmental justice initiatives focused on the environmental impact on people of color and lower-income households. Whitman stated that "[e]nvironmental justice is achieved when everyone, regardless of race, culture, or income, enjoys the same degree of protection from environmental and health hazards and equal access to the decision-making process to have a healthy environment in which to live, learn, and work" (United States Environmental Protection Agency 2002). A 2004 report from the EPA inspector general, an independent position within the agency, noted that the statement is identical to the EPA's overall mission. The report stated that "[w]e believe the Executive Order [12898] was specifically issued to provide environmental justice to minority and/or low-income populations due to concerns that those populations had been disproportionately impacted by environmental risk" (United States Environmental Protection Agency 2004).

The 2004 platform pledged to fight global warming but argued that the Kyoto Protocol was not an effective way to do so. It stated that "Republicans are committed to meeting the challenge of long-term global climate change by relying on markets and new technologies to improve energy efficiency. These efforts will help reduce emissions over time while allowing the economy to grow." One of the technologies of the platform involved the construction of new nuclear power plants, which would not only mitigate the effects of climate change but also reduce U.S. dependence on foreign oil. The platform also emphasized that "[o]ur President and our Party strongly oppose the Kyoto Protocol and similar mandatory carbon emissions controls that harm economic growth and destroy American jobs."

In 2008, Republican presidential nominee Senator John McCain took a distinctly different view on climate change than President Bush and many other Republicans. McCain stated that "[t]he facts of global warming demand our urgent attention. Good stewardship, prudence and simple common sense demand that we act to meet the challenge and act quickly" (Marre 2008). The 2008 platform devoted an entire section to "Addressing Climate Change Responsibly." The platform, as it had in 2004, advocated expanding nuclear energy options. It also provided that "Republicans support technology-driven, market-based solutions that will decrease emissions, reduce excess greenhouse gasses in the atmosphere, increase energy efficiency, mitigate the impact of climate change where it occurs, and maximize any ancillary benefits climate change might offer for the economy." The platform argued that since climate change is a global phenomenon, countries such as India and China should be held to the same standard as other countries.

In 2012, the tone of the platform shifted considerably. There was no section devoted to climate change. Indeed, the term was mentioned once to criticize Democrats for "elevat[ing] 'climate change' to the level of a 'severe threat' equivalent to foreign aggression. The word 'climate,' in fact, appears in the current President's strategy more often than Al Qaeda, nuclear proliferation, radical Islam, or weapons of mass destruction." The change in the party's view on climate change was also evident in the policy positions of its presidential nominees. During the 2012 Republican primaries, all of the candidates with the exception of Mitt Romney and Jon Huntsman argued that climate change was either a hoax or a naturally occurring phenomenon. The eventual Republican nominee Mitt Romney believed that climate change is a serious, man-made issue.

The Republican position shifted even further to the right in 2016 (and in 2020, when Republicans just adopted the exact platform they had used four years earlier), when it approved a platform that charged:

> The environment is too important to be left to radical environmentalists. They are using yesterday's tools to control a future they do not comprehend. The environmental establishment has become a self-serving elite, stuck in the mindset of the 1970s, subordinating the public's consensus to the goals of the Democratic Party. Their approach is based on shoddy science, scare tactics, and centralized command-and-control regulation. Over the last eight years, the Administration has triggered an avalanche of regulation that wreaks havoc across our economy and yields minimal environmental benefits . . . they routinely ignore costs, exaggerate benefits, and advocate the breaching of constitutional boundaries by federal agencies to impose environmental regulation. . . . Our agenda is high on job creation, expanding opportunity and providing a better chance at life for everyone willing to work for it. Our modern approach to environmentalism is directed to that end, and it starts with dramatic change in official Washington. We propose to shift responsibility for environmental regulation from the federal bureaucracy to the states and to transform the EPA into an independent bipartisan commission, similar to the Nuclear Regulatory Commission, with structural safeguards against politicized science. (Republican Party Platform 2016)

During the 2016 presidential campaign, Republican nominee Donald Trump denounced the science behind climate change. Beginning in 2012, Trump called global warming a hoax perpetuated by the Chinese government to hurt American businesses. After his inauguration, the climate change page was removed from the White House website (Henry 2017). Early in his presidency, Trump withdrew the United States from the Paris Climate Accord characterizing the pact as "simply the latest example of Washington entering into an agreement that disadvantages the United States to the exclusive benefit of other countries, leaving American workers—who I love—and taxpayers to absorb the cost in terms of lost jobs, lower wages, shuttered factories, and vastly diminished economic production" (Trump 2017).

While few Republicans were willing to challenge the Trump administration on climate change, Christine Todd Whitman criticized EPA administrator Scott Pruitt's increasing politicization of the agency. In an op-ed for the *New York Times*,

Trump Withdraws the U.S. from the Paris Climate Accord

In 2017, President Donald Trump withdrew the U.S. commitment to the Paris Accord. In this statement, Trump argued that the terms of the agreement hurt the United States.

. . . as of today, the United States will cease all implementation of the non-binding Paris Accord and the draconian financial and economic burdens the agreement imposes on our country. This includes ending the implementation of the nationally determined contribution and, very importantly, the Green Climate Fund which is costing the United States a vast fortune.

Compliance with the terms of the Paris Accord and the onerous energy restrictions it has placed on the United States could cost America as much as 2.7 million lost jobs by 2025 according to the National Economic Research Associates. This includes 440,000 fewer manufacturing jobs—not what we need—believe me, this is not what we need—including automobile jobs, and the further decimation of vital American industries on which countless communities rely. They rely for so much, and we would be giving them so little.

According to this same study, by 2040, compliance with the commitments put into place by the previous administration would cut production for the following sectors: paper down 12 percent; cement down 23 percent; iron and steel down 38 percent; coal—and I happen to love the coal miners—down 86 percent; natural gas down 31 percent. The cost to the economy at this time would be close to $3 trillion in lost GDP and 6.5 million industrial jobs, while households would have $7,000 less income and, in many cases, much worse than that.

Not only does this deal subject our citizens to harsh economic restrictions, it fails to live up to our environmental ideals. As someone who cares deeply about the environment, which I do, I cannot in good conscience support a deal that punishes the United States—which is what it does—the world's leader in environmental protection, while imposing no meaningful obligations on the world's leading polluters . . .

Source

"Statement by President Trump on the Paris Climate Accord—the White House." 2017. The White House, June 1. Accessed January 9, 2023. https://trumpwhitehouse.archives.gov/briefings-statements/statement-president-trump-paris-climate-accord/.

Whitman noted that while there are normally two sides to every issue, climate change is different. She argued that "[o]n one side is the overwhelming consensus of thousands of scientists at universities, research centers and the government who publish in peer-reviewed literature, are cited regularly by fellow scientists and are certain that humans are contributing to climate change" (Whitman 2017). She characterized "the other side" as "a tiny minority of contrarians who publish very little by comparison, are rarely cited in the scientific literature and are often funded by fossil fuel interests, and whose books are published, most often, by special interest groups" (Whitman 2017). Democratic cochairs of the United for

Climate and Environmental Justice Task Force criticized Trump for his inaction on climate change arguing that his administration did not "hold corporate polluters accountable" but also "actively pursued a dangerous regulatory agenda by rolling back over 100 public health and environmental safeguards" (McEachin, Barragán, and Jayapal 2021).

The 2016 and 2020 Republican platforms emphasized the protection and development of the fossil fuel industry and criticized Democrats for attempting to "smother the U.S. energy industry." They also questioned the science behind the United Nations' climate change policies and argued that market forces would mitigate the effects of global warming. The party's stance on global warming was criticized by Doug Heye, a Republican strategist, who argued that the party's unwillingness to address climate change could be problematic in the long run because it is an important issue to younger voters (Frazin 2020).

A 2019 Pew poll showed that while most Americans (67 percent) agree that the federal government is not doing enough to address climate change, the views of Republicans vary based on ideology, age, and gender. Of those who identify as moderate or liberal Republicans, 65 percent, including independents who lean Republican, say that the federal government is doing too little to reduce the effects of climate change; however, only 24 percent of conservative Republicans hold that view. Among Republicans aged 18–38, 52 percent believe the government is not doing enough to address the issue, whereas 41 percent of Generation X and 31 percent of Baby Boomers and older Americans hold that view. Female Republicans (46 percent) are more likely than male Republicans (36 percent) to say the government is not doing enough to address climate change (Funk and Hefferon 2019).

Democrats

The Democratic Party has supported policies to promote environmental justice and address climate change. President Bill Clinton's Executive Order 12898 laid the foundation for the Obama and Biden administrations to address this issue and expand federal efforts to combat environmental racism. Democrats have consistently supported policies, including international treaties, to stop climate change.

Democrats supported key environmental legislation in the 1970s. Indeed, laws such as significant updates to the Clean Air Act in 1970 were passed with near unanimous bipartisan support. The 1976 Democratic Party platform asserted that "the party's strong commitment to environmental quality is based on its conviction that environmental protection is not simply an aesthetic goal, but is necessary to achieve a more just society." Despite this statement, the party did not address environmental justice specifically until the 1990s.

Environmental issues were an important part of the 1992 presidential campaign. Democratic vice presidential nominee, Senator Albert Gore, Jr., published a book entitled *Earth in the Balance: Ecology and the Human Spirit* during the summer of 1992. The book examined the problems created by the climate crisis and offered policy recommendations to address those issues. During his presidency, Bill Clinton issued Executive Order 12898. In a memorandum accompanying the order, Clinton emphasized existing civil rights and environmental laws and stated that the "[a]pplication of these existing statutory provisions is an important part of this Administration's efforts to prevent those minority communities and low income communities from being subject to disproportionately high and adverse environmental effects." As a basis for the order, he cited Title VI of the Civil Rights Act of 1964, which requires federal agencies to ensure that programs receiving federal aid that "affect human health or the environment" do not discriminate on the basis of race, color, or national origin. He also cited the National Environmental Policy Act of 1969, which requires the federal government to consider the impact of any major federal action that significantly affects the environment.

Environmental groups applauded Clinton's actions, but the Democratic Party paid little attention to environmental justice issues and focused its attention more broadly on environmental issues such as climate change and conservation efforts. While campaigning for president in 2008, Senator Barack Obama pledged to strengthen the Office of Environmental Justice. In the Senate, he had cosponsored, with Senator Hillary Clinton, the Healthy Communities Act of 2005. This bill would have created an environmental advisory committee, supported expanded environmental health research, and provided grants for communities negatively affected by environmental hazards. In his first term, President Obama held a White House Forum on Environmental Justice in 2010 but focused more attention on the issue during his second term.

The 2012 Democratic Party platform was the first to specifically address environmental justice, although it was only briefly mentioned in its section on the environment. The platform stated, "We understand that global climate change may disproportionately affect the poor, and we are committed to environmental justice." In 2014, Obama issued a proclamation recognizing the twentieth anniversary of Executive Order 12898 in which he highlighted his administration's efforts to advance environmental justice, including working with tribal governments to reduce pollution on reservations and implementing federal limits for mercury and other pollutants from power plants. Obama also attempted to limit the emission of greenhouse gases through his Clean Power Plan, which established the nation's first-ever carbon emissions standards for power plants, and through the Paris Climate Agreement, which obligated signatory countries to gradually increase limits on greenhouse gas emissions. In 2016, the EPA issued its EJ 2020 Action Agenda. The plan focused on three goals: (1) deepening environmental justice practice within EPA programs to improve the health and environment of overburdened communities; (2) working with partners to expand the agency's positive impact within overburdened communities; and (3) demonstrating progress on national environmental justice challenges.

Despite these actions, critics countered that Democrats could have taken additional steps to guarantee environmental justice. For example, Obama could have created an Office of Environmental Justice in the White House and Congressional Democrats could have introduced environmental justice legislation when they controlled both chambers of Congress and the presidency. The latter point was noted by Republican senate majority leader Mitch McConnell in an op-ed for the *Washington Post*. McConnell (2015) suggested that while Democrats had the majority, they "used the opportunity to pass one left-wing policy after the next. But even with the left at its generational zenith, the president could not persuade his party to pass an anti-middle class energy tax that would have punished the poor and shipped more American jobs overseas." He criticized Obama for exceeding executive power with his Clean Power Plan and the Paris Climate Agreement. He also argued that the Clean Power Plan would eliminate almost 250,000 U.S. jobs and raise energy costs, which would hurt the middle class.

The 2016 Democratic platform included an entire section entitled "Securing Environmental and Climate Justice." The platform asserted the Democratic belief that "clean air and clean water are basic rights of all Americans." It noted that climate change disproportionately affected low-income and minority communities and pledged to eliminate greenhouse gases and promote clean energy alternatives for economic and public health reasons. The 2016 Democratic presidential nominee, Hillary Clinton, addressed environmental justice in the "Racial Justice" section of her campaign website. She pledged to "work to reduce air pollution, invest in the removal of toxins like lead, develop greener and more resilient infrastructure, tackle energy poverty, and boost efforts to clean up highly polluted toxic sites" (Clinton 2016). In an op-ed for MSNBC, Clinton was critical of the slow response to the Flint water crisis. She vowed to "make environmental justice a central part of my comprehensive commitment to low-income communities of color—by pursuing cleaner transportation; ambitious steps to reduce air pollution; dedicated efforts to clean up toxic sites; more resources for lead remediation; and greener more resilient infrastructure" (Clinton 2016).

Congressional Democrats introduced a wide array of environmental justice proposals after the 2016 campaign. In the House, Representatives Nanette Diaz Barragán, A. Donald McEachin, and Pramila Jayapal established the United for Climate and Environmental Justice Task Force in 2017. Composed of members of the Congressional Black Caucus, Congressional Hispanic Caucus, and the Congressional Asian Pacific American Caucus, the task force was formed after the Trump administration failed to address environmental justice issues. In the Senate, Cory Booker, Tom Carper, and Tammy Duckworth announced the formation of the Senate Environmental Justice Caucus on Earth Day in 2019 to raise awareness of those issues and to craft environmental justice legislation. After the Republican-controlled Senate voted down the Green New Deal, moderate House Democrats introduced an alternative that would impose reductions in greenhouse gases by 2050, not 2030,

Democrats Support Paris Climate Accord

In this statement released on the fifth anniversary of the Paris Climate Agreement, Democratic House Speaker Nancy Pelosi emphasized the party's support for environmental legislation to combat the climate crisis.

Five years ago, in a monumental moment in history, the nations of the world committed to working together to confront the existential threat posed by the climate crisis. Shamefully, the Trump Administration spent four years systematically undermining this historic agreement, abandoning American leadership and refusing to acknowledge the science or lift a finger to combat this growing threat.

Despite these challenges, House Democrats have stood with the American people in reaffirming our commitment to building a just, equitable and green future for all. Over the past two years, our Majority has taken decisive action by passing H.R. 9, the Climate Action Now Act, to keep America in the Paris Agreement. We passed H.R. 2, our Moving Forward infrastructure bill, and H.R. 4447, the Clean Economy Jobs and Innovation Act, strong down-payments in a clean energy future that helps solve the climate crisis. And our Select Committee on the Climate Crisis issued Solving the Climate Crisis, the most detailed, sweeping climate action plan in American history focused on immediate action, long-term results and promoting environmental justice for the most vulnerable communities.

As we mark this anniversary and look toward the future, House Democrats will work with the Biden-Harris Administration to deliver the urgently needed climate action that the American people demand. As the climate crisis continues to jeopardize our public health and our economic and national security, there is no time to waste. We will never back down from our moral responsibility to safeguard the beauty of God's creation for generations to come.

Source

"Pelosi Statement on the Fifth Anniversary of the Paris Climate Agreement." 2020. Congresswoman Nancy Pelosi, December 14. Accessed January 30, 2023. https://pelosi.house.gov/news/press-releases/pelosi-statement-on-the-fifth-anniversary-of-the-paris-climate-agreement.

as the Green New Deal had proposed. The plan, from the House Select Committee on the Climate Crisis, made several recommendations concerning environmental justice and argued that environmental justice communities should be prioritized in terms of government spending and investment (United States House Select Committee on the Climate Crisis 2020).

At a 2019 CNN climate forum, nine of the ten candidates for the Democratic presidential nomination specifically addressed or alluded to environmental justice; only former vice president Joe Biden did not. The 2020 Democratic platform contained the party's most comprehensive statement to date on environmental justice in a section entitled "Combating the Climate Crisis and Pursuing Environmental Justice."

Democrats combined environmental policies with environmental justice "because Democrats believe we must embed environmental justice, economic justice, and climate justice at the heart of our policy and governing agenda." Democratic nominee, Joe Biden, pledged on his campaign website that "[a]ny sound energy and environmental policy must advance public health and economic opportunity for all Americans, in rural, urban, and suburban communities, and recognize that communities of color and low-income communities have faced disproportionate harm from climate change and environmental contaminants for decades" ("The Biden Plan to Secure Environmental Justice and Equitable Economic Opportunity" 2019). He also noted that COVID-19 rates were higher in areas with greater amounts of air pollution. As president, Biden issued Executive Order 14008 entitled "Tackling the Climate Crisis at Home and Abroad," a wide-ranging directive on environmental issues that included provisions addressing environmental justice. It created the White House Environmental Justice Interagency Council, which was tasked with prioritizing environmental justice and "ensur[ing] a whole-of-government approach to addressing current and historical environmental injustices, including strengthening environmental justice monitoring and enforcement through new or strengthened offices" (The White House 2021). The council was also charged with finding ways to update Executive Order 12898.

According to public opinion polls, Democrats overwhelmingly believe that the federal government is not doing enough to address climate issues. A 2019 Pew poll showed that 90 percent of those identifying as Democrats or Independents who lean Democratic agree with that statement (Funk and Hefferon 2019). With virtual unanimity of opinion on the issue, the Democrats included these words in their 2020 party platform:

> Democrats are committed to curbing the effects of climate change, protecting America's natural resources, and ensuring the quality of our air, water, and land for current and future generations. From investing in clean energy to protecting our ecosystems, Democrats are working to address our biggest environmental challenges, paving the way to a more sustainable America.
>
> Under President Obama, we made great strides to combat climate change and protect our environment and public lands. . . . Democrats want to protect and build on President Obama's progress. We know that climate change is one of our nation's greatest challenges, and that addressing this urgent threat could make America the world's clean energy superpower and create millions of good-paying jobs. . . . Donald Trump, on the other hand, has called climate change "a hoax invented by the Chinese," and withdrawn from the Paris Climate Agreement. And by choosing to ignore the consensus of the scientific community on climate change, he is putting our country's health, security, and economy at risk.

Further Reading

Astor, Mary. 2019. "Environmental Justice Was a Climate Forum Theme: Here's Why." *New York Times*, September 5. Accessed May 3, 2021. https://www.nytimes.com/2019/09/05/us/politics/environmental-justice-climate-town-hall.html.

Barragán, Nanette Diaz. 2017. "Barragán, McEachin, Jayapal Announced United for Climate and Environmental Justice Congressional Task Force." Congresswoman Barragan,

May 3. Accessed May 11, 2021. https://barragan.house.gov/barragan-mceachin-jayapal
-announced-united-for-climate-and-environmental-justice-congressional-task-force/.

"The Biden Plan to Secure Environmental Justice and Equitable Economic Opportunity."
2019. Accessed December 15, 2022. Joe Biden for President: Official Campaign Website. https://joebiden.com/environmental-justice-plan/.

Bullard, Robert D. 2000. *Dumping in Dixie: Race, Class, and Environmental Quality*. 3rd ed.
New York: Routledge.

Bullard, Robert D., Paul Mohai, Robin Saha, and Beverly Wright. 2008. "Toxic Wastes and
Race at Twenty: Why Race Still Matters After All of These Years." *Environmental Law
Journal* 38: 371–412.

Clegg, Roger. 2017. "Environmental Justice and the Trump Administration." *National
Review*, March 10. Accessed February 11, 2021. https://www.nationalreview.com
/corner/epa-environmental-justice-trump-administration/.

Clinton, Hillary. 2016. "There Are Too Many Flints: Environmental Justice Can't Just Be
a Slogan." MSNBC, January 29. Accessed May 13, 2021. https://www.msnbc.com
/msnbc/there-are-too-many-flints-msna785086.

CorpWatch. 2001. "Environmental Justice Appeal to Bush on Climate Change." April 19.
Accessed May 3, 2021. https://corpwatch.org/article/environmental-justice-appeal
-bush-climate-change.

Democratic Party Platforms. 1976, 2012–2020. The American Presidency Project. Accessed
November 21, 2022. https://www.presidency.ucsb.edu/documents/presidential
-documents-archive-guidebook/party-platforms-and-nominating-conventions-3.

Fears, Darryl, and Brady Dennis. 2021. "How a Protest in a Black N.C. Farming Town Nearly
40 Years Ago Sparked a National Movement." *Washington Post*, April 21. Accessed
May 1, 2021. https://www.washingtonpost.com/climateenvironment/interactive/2021
/environmental-justice-race/.

Frazin, Rachel. 2020. "GOP Platform on Climate Risks Ceding Issue to Democrats." *The
Hill*, August 24. Accessed May 3, 2021. https://thehill.com/policy/energy-environment
/513029-gop-platform-on-climate-risks-ceding-issue-to-democrats?rl=1.

Friedman, Lisa. 2019. "What Is the Green New Deal? A Climate Proposal, Explained." *New
York Times*, February 21. Accessed May 4, 2021. https://www.nytimes.com/2019/02/21
/climate/green-new-deal-questions-answers.html.

Funk, Cary, and Meg Hefferon. 2019. "U.S. Public Views on Climate and Energy." Pew
Research Center, November 25. Accessed May 3, 2021. https://www.pewresearch.org
/science/2019/11/25/u-s-public-views-on-climate-and-energy/.

Gore, Albert, Jr. 1992. *Earth in the Balance: Ecology and the Human Spirit*. New York:
Houghton Mifflin.

Henry, Devin. 2017. "EPA Removes Climate Change Page from Website." *The Hill*, April
28. Accessed May 4, 2021. https://thehill.com/policy/energy-environment/331185-epa
-removes-climate-change-page-from-website-amid-updates.

Jehl, Douglas. 2000. "THE 2000 CAMPAIGN: THE ENVIRONMENT; On a Favorite Issue,
Gore Finds Himself on a 2-Front Defense." *New York Times*, November 3. Accessed
May 2, 2021. https://www.nytimes.com/2000/11/03/us/2000-campaign-environment
-favorite-issue-gore-finds-himself-2-front-defense.html.

Jehl, Douglas, with Andrew C. Revkin. 2001. "Bush, in Reversal, Won't Seek Cut in Emissions of Carbon Dioxide." *New York Times*, March 14. Accessed May 2, 2021. https://

www.nytimes.com/2001/03/14/us/bush-in-reversal-won-t-seek-cut-in-emissions-of
-carbon-dioxide.html.

Marre, Klaus. 2008. "McCain Wants U.S. Government to Go Green." *The Hill*, June 24.
Accessed May 3, 2021. https://thehill.com/homenews/news/15369-mccain-wants-us
-government-to-go-green.

McConnell, Mitch. 2015. "Obama Takes His Reckless Energy Plan to the United Nations."
Washington Post, November 27. Accessed May 4, 2021. https://www.washingtonpost
.com/opinions/the-president-doesnt-have-the-power-to-sign-onto-international
-environment-commitments/2015/11/27/924a45e8-92ee-11e5-a2d6-f57908580b1f
_story.html.

McEachin, A. Donald, Nanette Barragán, and Pramila Jayapal. 2021. "We Can Build the
Economy While Addressing the Climate Crisis and Environmental Injustice." *The Hill*,
February 10. Accessed May 5, 2021. https://thehill.com/blogs/congress-blog/energy
-environment/538204-we-can-build-the-economy-while-addressing-the-climate.

Meyer, Robinson. 2017. "Democrats Are Shockingly Unprepared to Fight Climate Change."
The Atlantic, November 15. Accessed May 5, 2021. https://www.theatlantic.com/science
/archive/2017/11/there-is-no-democratic-plan-to-fight-climate-change/543981/.

Michigan Department of Attorney General. 2021. "Nine Indicted on Criminal Charges
in Flint Water Crisis Investigation." January 14. Accessed September 1, 2022. https://
www.michigan.gov/ag/news/press-releases/2021/01/14/nine-indicted-on-criminal
-charges-in-flint-water-crisis-investigation.

New York Times. 1982. "55 Arrested in Protest at Toxic Dump in North Carolina." September 16. Accessed December 11, 2020. https://www.nytimes.com/1982/09/16/us/55
-arrested-in-protest-at-a-toxic-dump-in-carolina.html.

Perls, Hannah. 2020. "EPA Undermines Its Own Environmental Justice Programs." Environmental and Energy Law Program, November 12. Accessed May 4, 2021. https://eelp
.law.harvard.edu/2020/11/epa-undermines-its-own-environmental-justice-programs/.

Plautz, Jason, and *The National Journal*. 2015. "This Isn't Your Normal Bill to Gut the EPA."
The Atlantic, April 30. Accessed May 12, 2021. https://www.theatlantic.com/politics
/archive/2015/04/this-isnt-your-normal-bill-to-gut-the-epa/452514/.

Republican Party Platforms. 1992, 2000–2020. The American Presidency Project. Accessed
December 15, 2022. https://www.presidency.ucsb.edu/documents/presidential-documents
-archive-guidebook/party-platforms-and-nominating-conventions-3.

Rich, Nathaniel. 2018. "Losing Earth: The Decade We Almost Stopped Climate Change."
New York Times, August 1. Accessed May 3, 2021. https://www.nytimes.com/interactive
/2018/08/01/magazine/climate-change-losing-earth.html.

Shepherd, Marshall. 2018. "The Surprising Climate and Environmental Legacy of President George H. W. Bush." *Forbes*, December 1. Accessed May 3, 2021. https://
www.forbes.com/sites/marshallshepherd/2018/12/01/the-surprising-climate-and
-environmental-legacy-of-president-george-h-w-bush/?sh=8e9b9f0589c5.

Stracqualursi, Veronica, Adam Kelsey, and John Santucci. 2016. "On Trip to Flint, Donald
Trump Gives Stump Speech, Gets Interrupted." *ABC News*, September 14. Accessed
May 10, 2021. https://abcnews.go.com/Politics/trip-flint-donald-trump-stump
-speech-interrupted/story?id=42094796.

Suro, Robert. 1992. "The 1992 Campaign: Al Gore; Environment and Industry Can Flourish." *New York Times*, October 22. Accessed May 12, 2021. https://www.nytimes.com

/1992/10/22/us/the-1992-campaign-al-gore-environment-and-industry-can-flourish
-gore-says.html.

Trump, Donald. 2017. "Statement by President Trump on the Paris Climate Accord." The
White House, June 1. Accessed May 14, 2021. https://trumpwhitehouse.archives.gov
/briefings-statements/statement-president-trump-paris-climate-accord/.

United States Environmental Protection Agency. 2001. "Administrator Whitman Reaffirms Commitment to Environmental Justice." August. Accessed May 3, 2021. https://
archive.epa.gov/epapages/newsroom_archive/newsreleases/41a2df9798d627a185256
aaf0067e435.html.

United States Environmental Protection Agency. 2002. "Environmental Justice Collabora-
tive Model: A Framework to Ensure Local Problem Solving." Accessed May 4, 2021.
https://www.epa.gov/sites/default/files/2015-02/documents/iwg-status-02042002.pdf.

United States Environmental Protection Agency. 2004. "EPA Needs to Consistently
Implement the Intent of the Executive Order on Environmental Justice." Accessed
May 10, 2021. https://www.epa.gov/office-inspector-general/report-epa-needs-consistently
-implement-intent-executive-order.

United States Environmental Protection Agency. 2017. "Office of Environmental Justice in
Action." Accessed May 11, 2021. https://www.epa.gov/sites/production/files/2017-09
/documents/epa_office_of_environmental_justice_factsheet.pdf.

United States Environmental Protection Agency. 2021. "Environmental Justice." July 26.
Accessed May 10, 2021. https://www.epa.gov/environmentaljustice.

United States House Select Committee on the Climate Crisis. 2020. "Solving the Climate
Crisis: The Congressional Action Plan for a Clean Energy Economy and a Healthy,
Resilient, and Just America." Accessed November 21, 2022. https://climatecrisis.house
.gov/sites/climatecrisis.house.gov/files/Climate%20Crisis%20Action%20Plan.pdf.

The White House. 2021. "Fact Sheet: President Biden Takes Executive Actions to Tackle
the Climate Crisis at Home and Abroad, Create Jobs, and Restore Scientific Integrity Across Federal Government." January 27. Accessed May 3, 2021. https://www
.whitehouse.gov/briefing-room/statements-releases/2021/01/27/fact-sheet-president
-biden-takes-executive-actions-to-tackle-the-climate-crisis-at-home-and-abroad
-create-jobs-and-restore-scientific-integrity-across-federal-government/.

Whitman, Christine Todd. 2017. "Opinion: How Not to Run the EPA." New York Times,
September 8. Accessed May 3, 2021. https://www.nytimes.com/2017/09/08/opinion
/how-not-to-run-the-epa.html.

Freedom of Speech

At a Glance

Freedom of speech is an important constitutional guarantee, but apart from its relevance in arguments about campaign finance reform, it has not been consistently addressed in American presidential campaigns. The issue of campaign finance reform was framed in terms of freedom of speech in the 1970s as the U.S. Supreme Court held that campaign expenditures and donations communicated ideas or support for a candidate and were entitled to First Amendment protection. Recognizing that monetary donations to political campaigns could corrupt politicians, Congress has enacted significant campaign finance reform on several occasions, but most of it has been invalidated by the Supreme Court. The Democratic Party has supported limits on campaign donations and expenditures along with public financing of campaigns to minimize the influence of corporate donors. The Republican Party has opposed limits on campaign donations and expenditures and public funding of elections arguing that those restrictions limit freedom of speech.

The extent to which online speech is constitutionally protected became an issue in the mid-1990s with the emergence of the internet into the daily lives of Americans. The two parties agree that Section 230 of the Communications Decency Act (CDA; 1996), which protects websites from liability from third-party statements posted on their sites, needs to be reformed because of its impact on free speech; however, Republicans argue that the law allows websites to censor conservative views while Democrats argue that it allows the posting of hate speech and falsehoods.

According to many Democrats . . .

- Campaign expenditures are not protected by the Free Speech Clause of the First Amendment, and Congress should place limits on campaign donations and candidate spending.
- Section 230 of the CDA should be reformed to hold companies accountable for factually inaccurate statements and hate speech.

According to many Republicans . . .

- Campaign contributions and expenditures are protected by the Free Speech Clause of the First Amendment and should not be limited by legislation.
- Section 230 of the CDA should be reformed because it violates freedom of speech by censoring conservative views.

Overview

The First Amendment to the U.S. Constitution provides, in part, that "Congress shall make no law . . . abridging freedom of speech." As with other guarantees in the Bill of Rights, free speech is not absolute and may be limited by the government under certain conditions. As Justice Oliver Wendell Holmes famously stated in *Schenck v. United States* (1919), "[T]he most stringent protection of free speech would not protect a man in falsely shouting 'fire' in a crowded theater." The U.S. Supreme Court has afforded greater protection to political speech, speech directed at supporting or criticizing the government or public officials, than to other types of speech such as commercial advertising, obscenity, and "fighting words" (words that inflict injury or incite violence or other breach of the peace). The Court has also recognized that speech includes expressive conduct, such as burning an American flag as part of a political protest.

Free speech issues historically have not garnered much attention in presidential campaigns; however, two areas of relevance have emerged in the past few decades campaign finance reform and internet speech. Beginning with *Buckley v. Valeo* (1976), the U.S. Supreme Court has held in a series of cases that campaign contributions are the equivalent of political speech protected by the Free Speech Clause of the First Amendment.

Republicans oppose campaign finance reform because they argue that contributions and expenditures are speech. Democrats disagree that money is the equivalent of speech and argue that more regulation is needed to protect the integrity of elections.

Meanwhile, the advent of the internet in the 1990s raised concerns about freedom of speech when Congress passed a series of laws to regulate internet content. Both parties want to reform Section 230 of the CDA of 1996 but for different reasons.

Campaign Finance Reform

Concerns about the influence of money in political campaigns date back to the early days of the republic. In 1828, Andrew Jackson was the first presidential candidate to spend one million dollars on an organized campaign. Jackson instituted a "spoils system" whereby government jobs were awarded to his supporters. In the mid-1800s, Congress enacted several laws to rein in corruption. In 1867,

Congress banned contributions from naval yard workers, and in 1883, the Pendleton Act ended the spoils system by mandating that most federal employees be awarded their jobs based on merit rather than political support. Further reforms were enacted during the early twentieth century. After being criticized for accepting corporate contributions during the election of 1904, President Theodore Roosevelt supported the Tillman Act (1907), which prohibited corporate donations to political campaigns. Roosevelt, however, believed that the law did not adequately address the corrupting influence of money in elections and suggested public funding of elections and limits on campaign donations.

The Federal Corrupt Practices Act of 1910, which was amended in 1911 and 1925, was the first federal law that attempted to limit campaign spending for congressional candidates. It also required political parties and candidates to disclose information about the contributions they received. The law lacked an adequate enforcement mechanism, however, and did little to limit campaign contributions to politicians. In 1943, Congress passed the Smith-Connally Act, which prohibited unions from donating to campaigns. As a result, unions, corporations, and trade associations formed political action committees (PACs) to donate money to candidates.

Congress initiated further reform of campaign funding with the Federal Election Campaign Act (FECA) of 1971 (amended in 1974), which established limits on campaign contributions by individuals and PACs. It also placed limits on campaign expenditures and established a system of public financing for presidential elections to limit the influence of private donors. Candidates who agree to limit their total spending in the primary election and the general election are eligible for federal matching funds in each of those campaigns.

In *Buckley v. Valeo*, the U.S. Supreme Court upheld FECA's limits on campaign contributions but invalidated the law's limits on campaign expenditures. The Court reasoned that the First Amendment Freedom of Association is affected by the amount of money that an individual can donate to a candidate's campaign, but the government's interest in limiting corruption, or the appearance of corruption, resulting from large individual contributions was more significant. The provisions restricting expenditures, including limits on the overall amount of money a candidate could spend on an election and the limits an individual or a group could spend on behalf of a candidate, unconstitutionally restricted political speech. The Court invalidated the limits on a candidate using personal funds for a campaign by the same rationale. In sum, the Court found that FECA's provisions related to campaign expenditures "place substantial and direct restrictions on the ability of candidates, citizens, and associations to engage in protected political expression, restrictions that the First Amendment cannot tolerate."

FECA also unintentionally created loopholes in the federal campaign finance law. While the Court upheld FECA's limits on "hard money" (individual donations to candidates), so-called soft money limitations on donations to political parties vanished. This allows donors to give unlimited sums for party-building activities and get-out-the-vote drives. Over time, the amount of soft money has significantly increased, effectively undermining FECA. Additionally, interest groups and other organizations could air issue advertisements, which were beyond the scope of FECA regulation provided that the ads did not specifically mention a candidate. During the 1996 presidential election, both parties raised an unprecedented amount of soft money, and Republicans raised alarms about foreign contributions to Democratic president Bill Clinton's reelection campaign. Allegations were also leveled against both the Democratic National Committee (DNC) and Republican National Committee (RNC) for producing and broadcasting so-called issue ads that were thinly veiled ads in support of one candidate or another. As such, the cost of the ads should have counted as an expenditure by the campaign and not the party.

After the law was passed, candidates accepted public funding and agreed to limits on fundraising for both the primary election and the general election because it made fundraising easier. In 2000, Republican candidate, and later president, George W. Bush rejected public funding for the primaries. In 2008, Barack Obama rejected public funding for the general election. Both Bush and Obama realized that they could raise more money than the public funding would provide.

McCain-Feingold

Republican senator John McCain and Democratic Senator Russ Feingold introduced campaign finance reform legislation in 1996. In a February 1996 op-ed in the *Washington Post*, the duo argued that there was an urgent need for reform based on analyses indicating that candidates who spent the most money tended to win elections, and that incumbents raised and spent considerably more than challengers. "The people's cynicism about the way we seek office has grown into contempt for the way we retain office," they warned. "The foundations of self-government rest on the public's faith in the basic integrity of our political system. That faith is shaken today" (McCain and Feingold 1996).

Although their bill was first introduced in 1996, it was not enacted until 2002 due to repeated Republican-led filibusters in the Senate. The Bipartisan Campaign Finance Reform Act of 2002 (BCRA) sought to tighten FECA loopholes by enacting new restrictions on campaign money. The law passed the House by a 240-189 vote, with 198 Democrats and 42 Republicans voting for it and 177 Republicans and 12 Democrats voting against it. The bill passed the Senate by a 60-40 vote in which 48 of the 50 Democrats voted for it and 38 of its 49 Republicans voted against it. It was signed into law by Republican president George W. Bush. The law banned soft money, increased individual contribution limits, and restricted the ability of corporations and labor unions to air "electioneering" ads featuring the names or likenesses of candidates within thirty days of a primary election or sixty days of a general election. The law also contained a "millionaire's amendment" raising contribution limits for candidates competing against wealthy opponents who spent more than $350,000 of their own money.

The U.S. Supreme Court upheld several provisions of the law by a 5-4 margin in *McConnell v. FEC* (2003). After Justice Sandra Day O'Connor, who voted in favor of the limits, was replaced by Justice Samuel Alito in 2006, the Court invalidated most provisions of BCRA in a series of 5-4 cases, including *Citizens United v. FEC* (2010), arguably the most controversial ruling involving limits on campaign funding. In this case, the Court invalidated BCRA's limits on electioneering ads and struck down bans on corporate speech that had been in place for almost one hundred years. The Court held that corporations, like individuals, have free speech rights protected by the First Amendment. The Court also held that independent political spending that was not coordinated with a candidate's campaign did not present a "substantive threat of corruption." This has resulted in unlimited spending by groups referred to as Super PACs. These organizations can both accept and spend unlimited amounts of money if the funds are spent independently of a candidate's campaign. The ruling has also led to "dark money" because nonprofit groups that had previously not been allowed to donate to campaigns are not required by law to disclose their donors' identities.

Democrats have consistently criticized the ruling as an example of conservative judicial activism because the Court overturned one hundred years of precedent to allow an even larger influx of money threatening the integrity of the political process. Since this ruling, Democrats have introduced constitutional amendments and legislation to overturn or limit its impact. Republicans applauded the decision as a perfectly legitimate defense of constitutional free speech rights.

Most Americans voters support campaign finance reform legislation and favor overturning *Citizens United*. A 2018 Pew poll showed that 77 percent of respondents, including a majority of Democrats and Republicans, believe that there should be limits on the amount of money individuals and organizations can spend on campaigns (Jones 2018). A similar percentage, 75 percent, indicated in a University of Maryland poll that they support a constitutional amendment to overturn *Citizens United*. Again, majorities of voters from both parties agreed.

Internet Speech

The development of the internet in the mid-1990s quickly raised thorny questions about freedom of speech. Congress enacted the CDA in 1996 as part of the broader Telecommunications Act of 1996. The CDA passed with significant bipartisan support in the House (414-16) and the Senate (91-5) and was signed into law by Democratic president Bill Clinton. Section 230 of the CDA protects websites from liability for content produced by third parties and is considered the most significant law regulating the internet because it allowed websites to flourish without fear of legal action. In 2019, for example, a federal appellate court ruled that Facebook was not liable for a terrorist attack in Israel that was coordinated on the social media site. The law also allows website providers to take good faith action to limit access to materials that the provider "considers to be obscene, lewd, lascivious, filthy, excessively violent, harassing or otherwise objectionable whether or not such material is constitutionally protected." Section 230 does not protect websites that permit the posting of child pornography or that violate intellectual property or other federal laws. In 2018, the law was amended to prohibit the posting of information about sex trafficking.

Section 230 became controversial during the 2016 presidential campaign when Russian ads and posts related to the campaign appeared on Google, Facebook, and other social media sites. During the 2020 presidential campaign, both political parties criticized the law but for different reasons. Republicans argued that it allowed websites to censor conservative views. After one of his tweets was flagged for inaccurate content by Twitter, President Donald Trump issued an executive order to limit the scope of the law. Congressional Republicans also introduced legislation that would strip Section 230's liability protection for big technology companies. Democratic nominee Joe Biden also argued that Section 230 should be revoked because it provides a forum for hate speech and the spreading of false information. Congressional Democrats, however, suggested that the law should be reformed, not repealed.

Public opinion polls show that Americans are divided about whether social media platforms should be sued. In a 2021 Pew survey, 56 percent of respondents agreed that they should not. Democrats were more evenly divided in their opinion on this issue, while 60 percent of Republicans believed that the companies should not be sued (McClain 2021).

Democrats

Campaign Finance Reform

In the post-Watergate era, the Democratic Party has supported public financing for elections to limit the impact of moneyed interests in campaigns. The party favors limiting campaign contributions and expenditures, asserting that that neither qualifies as protected speech under the First Amendment and that limits would preserve the integrity of elections. Many Democrats also support reform of Section 230 of the CDA, charging that it provides cover for the posting of damaging falsehoods and the proliferation of hate speech online.

The 1976 Democratic Party platform stated that the party has "led the fight to take the presidency off the auction block by championing the public financing of presidential elections" and argued that congressional elections should also be publicly financed. It also supported "the exploration of further reforms to insure the integrity of the electoral process." The 1980 and 1984 platforms reiterated the party's support for public funding of federal election campaigns and advocated for more contribution limits for PACs. The 1988 platform contained only a brief statement that the party sought to revitalize the Democratic process in part "by minimizing the domination and distortion of our elections by moneyed interests." In 1992, the platform suggested that "[i]t's time to reform the campaign finance system, to get big money out of our politics and let the people back in. We must limit overall campaign spending and limit the disproportionate and excessive role of PACs." The 1996 platform endorsed the McCain-Feingold campaign finance reform bill and criticized Republicans for preventing a vote on it.

The 2000 platform also supported McCain-Feingold and asserted that its nominee, Vice President Al Gore, would fight for the legislation and that it would be the first bill he submitted to Congress. The platform also criticized Republicans, not only for their opposition to the bill but also for wanting to raise contribution limits when their nominee, Governor George W. Bush, was the first candidate since FECA was amended in 1974 to forgo federal funds and not abide by spending limits for the primary election. Gore made campaign finance reform a priority in his campaign and was heavily criticized by the Bush camp given the investigation into Gore's role in 1996 campaign funding abuses. The U.S. Justice Department and Congress investigated whether illegal Chinese donations to the Democratic National Committee benefited the campaign. In 2002, after years of investigations, the Federal Election Commission fined the Democratic National Committee, the Clinton/Gore campaign, and several companies for setting up or participating in meetings between candidates and Chinese nationals in return for campaign contributions. Gore acknowledged in a March 2000 speech at Marquette University that he was an "imperfect messenger" but then proposed a ban on soft money and electioneering ads calling the influx of special interest money a "cancer on our democracy" (Gore 2000).

The 2004 Democratic platform did not specifically address campaign finance reform and most of the emphasis of that campaign dealt with national security in the aftermath of the 9/11 attacks. During the 2008 campaign, Barack Obama became the first candidate to reject public financing for his general election campaign since it was instituted in 1974. As noted in the 2008 Democratic Party platform, Obama and other Democratic candidates rejected PAC money in favor of small donations from many people. The platform also "supported campaign finance reform to reduce the influence of moneyed special interests, including public financing of campaigns combined with free television and radio time."

In his 2010 State of the Union Address, held a week after the Court's ruling in *Citizens United*, President Obama stated that "[w]ith all due deference to separation of powers, last week, the Supreme Court reversed a century of law that I believe will open the floodgates for special interests, including foreign corporations, to spend without limit in our elections. I don't think American elections should be bankrolled by America's most powerful interests, or worse, by foreign entities. They should be decided by the American people. And I'd urge Democrats and Republicans to pass a bill that helps correct some of these problems" (Obama

2010). Democrats introduced the DISCLOSE (Democracy Is Strengthened by Casting Light on Spending in Elections) Act in 2010 and have introduced a version of it in every Congress since then. The bill proposed to restrict campaign spending by foreign corporations and to require certain tax-exempt organizations to disclose their list of donors who contribute $10,000 or more. Democrats argued this would promote transparency in elections.

President Obama decried *Citizens United* and the lack of disclosure requirements throughout his presidency. In his 2015 State of the Union Address, which fell on the fifth anniversary of the *Citizens United* ruling, he condemned the use of dark money to fund campaign ads. Obama was criticized by groups on the left and the right for not moving from rhetoric to action. Lisa Gilbert from Public Citizen, a nonprofit organization dedicated to promoting the public interest by limiting corporate influence, suggested that the president issue an executive order requiring government contractors to disclose their political donations. She stated that Obama's rhetoric on campaign finance reform was "clear and unwavering. But when we turn to ponder the question of legacy, what can we point to that the administration has done to curb money in politics? The answer is: nothing yet. The 'yet' is the pivotal part of that sentence, as the president has within his grasp the ability to do something meaningful on this issue" (Gilbert 2015). After Obama's presidency, Luke Wachob (2017), a policy analyst from the Center for Competitive Politics, which opposes campaign finance reform on free speech grounds, also noted Obama's inaction and stated that "[n]either conservatives nor liberals found a hero in President Obama on free speech or 'money in politics.' When the ball was in his court, Obama did little to nothing to advance the 'reform' agenda, nor did he try to roll it back."

The 2016 Democratic platform framed the party's support for campaign finance reform as a "fight to preserve the essence of the longest standing democracy in the world: a government that represents the American people, not just a handful of powerful and wealthy special interests." The platform suggested several policies "to fight back and safeguard our electoral and political integrity." These included a constitutional amendment to overturn *Citizens United* and *Buckley v. Valeo*, increased disclosure requirements through either executive order or legislation, a public financing system, strengthening the Federal Election Commission to enforce existing campaign finance laws, and eliminating Super PACs. Democratic nominee Hillary Clinton's 2016 campaign website stated that she supported "aggressive campaign finance reform," including overturning *Citizens United*. She pledged to appoint Supreme Court justices who would protect the "right to vote over the right of billionaires to buy elections" and to propose a constitutional amendment within her first thirty days in office to overturn *Citizens United*.

Congressional Democrats unveiled the Better for Democracy Agenda in 2018, a broad electoral agenda that included proposals to modify the campaign financing system. The agenda criticized *Citizens United* because it "made a bad system worse, fueling the rise of unaccountable, undisclosed secret money in our politics" ("Pelosi Remarks at Press Event to Unveil a Better Deal for Our Democracy" 2018). Nancy Pelosi (2018), the Speaker of the House, stated that Congress "must improve enforcement of campaign finance law, end the scourge of dark money and establish its authority to regulate the raising and spending of political money, by passing a constitutional amendment to overturn *Citizens United*."

In 2020, the Democratic platform stated that "[m]oney is not speech, and corporations are not people." On his 2020 campaign website, Democratic nominee Joe Biden highlighted his work in Congress to limit the influence of money in campaigns, including supporting public funding for congressional campaigns and cosponsoring a constitutional amendment to limit contributions and corporate and private spending in elections. He offered various proposals for reforming funding of campaigns. These included eliminating private dollars and foreign money from federal elections, providing federal matching funds for federal candidates receiving small-dollar donations, keeping Super PACs independent of candidates, increasing the transparency of spending on political advertising, and requiring real-time disclosure of campaign donations.

Despite these pledges, at least half of the money raised by the party and the Biden campaign came from large donors (Watson 2020). Left-leaning critics suggested that Democratic candidates should follow Obama's successful example of not accepting money from PACs, which encouraged individuals to donate small amounts ($250 or less). Watson (2020) criticized Democrats who defended the use of Super PACS and "the general practice of sweet-talking rich people for cash" as necessary to keep up with Republican fundraising.

Public opinion polls show that Democratic respondents hold the same view as the party in their support for implementing limits on campaign funding and overturning *Citizens United*. In a 2018 Pew poll, 85 percent of Democrats supported a constitutional amendment to overturn *Citizens United* (Balcerzak 2018). The same percentage of Democrats and those who leaned Democratic favored campaign spending limits (Jones 2018). In 2020, the Democrats included this statement of widespread party sentiment as part of its official platform:

> Democrats believe that the interests and the voices of the American people should determine our elections. Money is not speech, and corporations are not people. Democrats will fight to pass a Constitutional amendment that will go beyond merely overturning *Citizens United* and related decisions like *Buckley v. Valeo* by eliminating all private financing from federal elections. In the meantime, Democrats will work with Congress on legislation to strengthen the public funding system by matching small-dollar donations for all federal candidates, crack down on foreign nationals who try to influence elections, and ensure that super PACs are wholly independent of campaigns and political parties. We will bring an end to "dark money" by requiring full disclosure of contributors to any group that advocates for or against candidates, and bar 501(c)(4) organizations from spending money on elections. Democrats will

Democrats Support Campaign Finance Reform Amendment

In 2014, Democrats introduced a constitutional amendment to institute campaign finance limits that had been overturned by the U.S. Supreme Court. In this excerpt from his testimony before the Senate Judiciary Committee, Democratic Senate Majority Leader Harry Reid argues that campaign finance reform is needed to protect the integrity of elections.

Mr. Chairman, Members of the Committee, I am here because the flood of dark money into our Nation's political system poses the greatest threat to our democracy that I have witnessed during my tenure in public service. The decisions by the Supreme Court have left the American people with a status quo in which one side's billionaires are pitted against the other side's billionaires.

So we sit here today with a simple choice: We can keep the status quo and argue all day and all night, weekends, forever, about whose billionaires are right and whose billionaires are wrong; or we can work together to change the system, to get this shady money out of our democracy and restore the basic principle of one American, one vote . . .

The *Citizens United* case and the other decisions the Supreme Court has made only made it worse. During the 2012 Presidential campaign, outside groups spent more than $1 billion. That is a conservative estimate. That is about as much money as was spent in the previous 12 elections. But this spike in the amount of shadowy money being pumped into elections is not surprising. Recent decisions rendered by the U.S. Supreme Court—I have mentioned Citizens United and McCutcheon—have eviscerated our campaign finance laws and opened the floodgates for special interests.

The cynics may scoff at the idea of us working together on an issue as critical as good government, but it was not all that long ago that the issue of campaign finance reform enjoyed support from both Democrats and Republicans. Campaign finance reform has been proposed a number of times before—even by my friend, the Republican Leader, Senator McConnell.

Source

Congress.gov. "S.Hrg. 113-889—Examining a Constitutional Amendment to Restore Democracy to the American People." Accessed January 19, 2023. https://www.congress.gov/event/113th-congress/senate-event/LC63201/text.

ban corporate PACs from donating to candidates and bar lobbyists from donating, fundraising, or bundling for anyone they lobby.

Internet Speech

During the 2020 election campaign, Democrats were at odds as to whether Section 230 should be revoked or reformed. The Democratic nominee, former vice president Joe Biden, argued that it should be revoked, while other Democrats argued that the law should be revised since the internet had changed significantly since its enactment.

Joe Biden argued that Section 230 should be revoked because big-tech companies, such as Facebook, are publishers of content and should not be exempted from civil liability from third-party posts. In an interview with the *New York Times* prior to the 2020 election, Biden noted that the *Times* could not knowingly publish false information and that he believed Facebook CEO Mark Zuckerberg should be held to the same standard. The Biden campaign had requested that Facebook remove an ad paid for by a PAC that falsely asserted that Biden had blackmailed Ukrainian government officials to prevent the release of information about his son, Hunter. The campaign had also asked Facebook to take down an ad with similar false accusations run by the Trump campaign; Facebook refused to remove the Trump ad because it was from a political leader.

Other Democrats have proposed reforming Section 230 rather than repealing it. The Protecting Americans from Dangerous Algorithms Act introduced by Congresswoman Anna Eshoo (2020), for example, proposed to limit the scope of Section 230 by limiting a company's liability if it employed "algorithmic amplification of harmful, radicalizing content that leads to offline violence." More specifically, it would remove liability for companies that used algorithms directly related to cases involving violations of civil rights and acts of terrorism. The bill applied to platforms with fifty million or more users. A 2021 Pew Research Center poll found that Democrats in the electorate were divided on the issue with 52 percent opposing lawsuits against social media companies for third-party content, while 45 percent said those types of lawsuits should be allowed (McClain 2021).

Republicans

Campaign Finance Reform

The FECA of 1971 and its 1974 amendments were enacted due to Republican president Richard Nixon's fundraising abuses. Since then, the party has advocated for some reforms but has become more adamant in its opposition to limits on campaign contributions and expenditures as violations of freedom of speech since the 2012 presidential election. The Republican Party has consistently opposed the use of union dues to help fund political campaigns.

Republican Party platforms provide an overview of the party's views on campaign finance reform. The 1976 Republican Party platform supported "improved lobby disclosure legislation so that people will know how much money is being spent to influence public officials." However, in 1980, the party adopted its current stance of opposing policies that limit campaign spending. The 1980 platform advocated repealing "restrictive campaign spending limitations that tend to create obstacles to local grass roots participation in federal elections." The party also opposed public financing of congressional elections labeling it "an effort by the Democratic Party to protect its incumbent Members of Congress with a tax subsidy." By 1984, the party specifically couched its opposition to campaign finance reform in terms of freedom of speech stating that "[e]ven well-intentioned restrictions on campaign activity stifle free speech and have a chilling effect on spontaneous political involvement by our citizens." In 1988, the party did not specifically mention campaign finance but advocated for greater political participation and for limits on "government controls that make it harder for average citizens to be politically active. We especially condemn the congressional Democrats' scheme to force taxpayer funding of campaigns."

In 1992, President George H. W. Bush vetoed a bill that would have provided partial public funding for congressional candidates. This action was touted in the party's 1992 platform, which criticized the Democrats for supporting a bill that "would have given $1 billion, over six years, in subsidies to candidates. . . . Campaign financing does need reform. It does not need a hand in the public's pocketbook." The platform also articulated the party's support for several areas of reform, including limiting congressional candidates to fundraising in their districts to reduce the amount of money spent on elections, prohibiting incumbents from keeping their unspent campaign contributions (i.e., their "war chests") to use in the next election cycle, eliminating PACs supported by corporations, unions, or trade associations, and restricting "bundling," a form of campaign fundraising that allows a supporter to solicit simultaneous contributions from a group of donors.

In 1996, the platform pledged to "eliminate made-in-Washington schemes to rig the election process under the guise of campaign reform. True reform is indeed needed: ending taxpayer subsidies for campaigns, strengthening party structures to guard against rogue operations, requiring full and immediate disclosure of all contributions, and cracking down on the indirect support, or 'soft money,' by which special interest groups underwrite their favored candidates." Despite the pledge of "cracking down" on soft money, the Republican Party, like the Democratic Party, received a record amount of soft money during the campaign.

Senator John McCain was a contender for the 2000 Republican nomination and made reforming campaign funding a signature issue. He held a town hall with prospective Democratic nominee, Bill Bradley, on that issue and pledged not to take any soft money if he were chosen as the party's nominee. During a debate among Republican presidential hopefuls, the eventual Republican nominee, Governor George W. Bush, stated that campaign finance reform "is bad for Republicans and it's bad for the conservative cause" because it would hurt their chances of winning elections. In 2002, Bush signed the McCain-Feingold Act while his critics accused him of "flip-flopping" on the issue. In a statement, he explained that the bill "improves the current system of financing for Federal campaigns" and specifically noted his approval of soft money limits, the increase in individual contributions, and disclosure requirements, but he also argued that it contained "flaws." Bush was critical of both the soft money ban as it applied to individuals and the limits on electioneering ads because of his concerns that they violated the First Amendment's Free Speech Clause (Bush 2002).

As the party's 2008 presidential nominee, McCain's support for campaign finance reform often put him at odds with members of his own party. The 2008 Republican platform, unlike previous platforms, did not specifically mention campaign finance reform. Instead, there was a more general statement that "[t]he rights of citizenship do not stop at the ballot box. They include the free-speech right to devote one's resources to whatever cause or candidate one supports. We oppose any restrictions or conditions upon those activities that would discourage Americans from exercising their constitutional right to enter the political fray or limit their commitment to their ideals." McCain highlighted his role as a reformer to appeal to independent voters. He also chose to abide by spending limits, unlike his Democratic opponent Barack Obama, to demonstrate his commitment to reform.

After the Court's ruling in *Citizens United*, Republicans began to more consistently argue that campaign spending limits violated freedom of speech. Many Republicans applauded *Citizens United*, including Senate Minority Leader Mitch McConnell who stated, "With today's monumental decision, the Supreme Court took an important step in the direction of restoring the First Amendment rights of these groups by ruling that the Constitution protects their right to express themselves about political candidates and issues up until Election Day" (O'Brien 2010). After Democrats introduced the DISCLOSE Act in 2010, McConnell stated that the goal of the legislation was to "protect unpopular Democrat politicians by silencing their critics and exempting their campaign supporters from an all out attack on the First Amendment" (Associated Press 2015). Republicans also opposed the release of donors' names arguing that if the names were public, it would have a "chilling effect" on their speech and might prevent them from donating to campaigns. The DISCLOSE Act died after Republicans filibustered the bill.

In the 2012 platform, the party reiterated its stance from 2008 but issued a stronger statement attacking campaign finance reform as a violation of the First Amendment. Indeed, the party supported repealing the remaining provisions of McCain-Feingold and increasing or eliminating individual campaign contribution limits. The platform also opposed Democratic efforts to overturn Supreme Court campaign finance rulings, including *Citizens United*. Republican nominee Mitt Romney agreed with the platform but was criticized for suggesting that teachers' unions should be prohibited from making campaign contributions because "[w]e simply can't have a setup where the teachers unions can contribute tens of millions of dollars to the campaigns of politicians and then those politicians, when elected, stand across from them at the bargaining table, supposedly to represent the interests of the kids. I think it's a mistake. I think we've got to get the money out of the teachers unions going into campaigns" (Reilly 2012).

In the 2016 campaign, Trump expressed support for the idea of campaign finance reform but was criticized by commentators for not outlining a specific plan to address it. He blasted his fellow Republicans and Democrats Hillary Clinton and Bernie Sanders for taking money from Super PACs; ultimately, Trump followed suit in May 2016. Although he had help from Super PACs, Trump had unprecedented success raising money from small donors. Indeed, he raised more from small donations than from any other candidate for the presidency. Trump stated numerous

Republicans Oppose Campaign Finance Reform Amendment

In this excerpt from his testimony before the Senate Judiciary Committee in 2014, Republican Senate Minority Leader Mitch McConnell argues that a proposed constitutional amendment to overturn Supreme Court rulings eliminating many restrictions on campaign contributions is counter to free speech.

. . . Americans from all walks of life understand how extraordinarily special the First Amendment is. Like the Founders, they know that the free exchange of ideas and the ability to criticize their Government are necessary for our democracy to survive . . .

Now, I understand that no politician likes to be criticized. And some of us are criticized more often than the rest of us. But the recourse to being criticized is not to shut up your fellow citizens, which, believe me, this is designed to do, to give us the power to pick winners and losers in the political discussion in this country. That is what this amendment is all about. It is to defend your—the solution to this is to defend your ideas, to defend your ideas more ably in the political marketplace, to paraphrase Justice Holmes, or simply to come up with better ideas.

The First Amendment is purposefully neutral when it comes to speech. It respects the right of every person to be heard without fear or favor, whether or not their views happen to be popular with the Government at any given moment. The First Amendment is also unequivocal. It provides that "Congress shall make no law"—"Congress shall make no law . . . abridging the freedom of speech." The First Amendment is about empowering the people, not the Government. The proposed amendment has it exactly backward. It says that Congress and the States can pass whatever law they want abridging political speech—the speech that is at the very core of the First Amendment.

Source

Congress.gov. "S.Hrg. 113-889—Examining a Constitutional Amendment to Restore Democracy to the American People." Accessed January 19, 2023. https://www.congress.gov/event/113th-congress/senate-event/LC63201/text.

times during the campaign that he was willing to spend $100 million of his own money as evidence of his commitment to win. While he spent $66.1 million of his own money, Trump also received $239 million from individual contributions of $200 or less late in the campaign (The Campaign Finance Institute 2017). This amount constituted 69 percent of the individual donations contributed to the campaign. By contrast, Barack Obama raised $218.8 million from individuals contributing $200 or less, but that amount was just 24 percent of the overall individual contributions (The Campaign Finance Institute 2017).

According to Fred Wertheimer (2015), a campaign finance attorney and founder of a nonpartisan organization, Democracy 21, that promotes transparency and accountability in government, "Trump himself is evidence of one of the big problems with our current campaign finance system—the ability of a billionaire to spend huge amounts of his personal wealth to seek public office. This kind of huge financial advantage that a billionaire like Trump has in running for office is unhealthy and wrong for our democracy."

While the Republican Party has supported *Citizens United* and opposed campaign finance reform, public opinion polls show that ordinary Republican voters feel differently. Indeed, a 2018 survey showed that 66 percent of Republicans favored a constitutional amendment to overturn *Citizens United* (Balcerzak 2018). A 2018 Pew poll indicated that 71 percent of Republicans and Republican-leaning independents support limits on campaign spending (Jones 2018).

Nonetheless, Republican leaders have firmly rejected the wishes of their voters on the issue, declaring in both the 2016 and 2020 GOP platforms that

> The rights of citizenship do not stop at the ballot box. Freedom of speech includes the right to devote resources to whatever cause or candidate one supports. We oppose any restrictions or conditions that would discourage citizens from participating in the public square or limit their ability to promote their ideas, such as requiring private organizations to publicly disclose their donors to the government. Limits on political speech serve only to protect the powerful and insulate incumbent officeholders. We support repeal of federal restrictions on political parties in McCain-Feingold, raising or repealing contribution limits, protecting the political speech of advocacy groups, corporations, and labor unions, and protecting political speech on the internet. We likewise call for an end to the so-called Fairness Doctrine, and support free-market approaches to free speech unregulated by government. (Republican Party Platform 2016, 2020)

Internet Speech

Republicans, like Democrats, supported legislation to prevent minors from accessing inappropriate or harmful materials online. After the 2016 presidential election, many Republicans argued that Section 230 of the CDA needed to be modified because it allowed websites, including social media sites, to permit criticism of conservatives to go unchecked.

Donald Trump has been referred to as the "Twitter President" because he consistently utilized the social media platform to communicate with his twenty million followers. Section 230 of the CDA drew the ire of President Trump during the 2020 presidential campaign after he tweeted false information about mail-in voting. Twitter added the following statement to the tweet, "Get the facts about mail-in ballots" along with a link to accurate voting information. Trump responded that Twitter was interfering with the election and "completely stifling FREE SPEECH." He also issued Executive Order 13925 entitled "Preventing Online Censorship" to limit Section 230. Specifically, the order rescinded liability protection when tech companies employed the "good faith" provision of the law to remove content.

In September 2020, Trump tweeted "repeal Section 230, immediately." Shortly thereafter, Republican senators Roger Wicker, Lindsay Graham, and Marsha

Blackburn introduced the Online Freedom and Viewpoint Diversity Act to modify several parts of Section 230. Senator Wicker stated that "[f]or too long, social media platforms have hidden behind Section 230 protections to censor content that deviates from their beliefs. These practices should not receive special protections in our society where freedom of speech is at the core of our nation's values" (United States Senate Commerce Committee 2020). The bill gave companies less discretion in removing content by protecting them from liability only when they could demonstrate that they used an "objective reasonableness standard" when removing content related to specific categories, including material that "promoted terrorism" or "self-harm." In December 2020, Senator Graham and Senate Majority Leader Mitch McConnell introduced separate bills to repeal Section 230 in its entirety.

Trump's calls for the repeal of Section 230 were criticized by Democratic senator Ron Wyden, one of the original cosponsors of Section 230. He argued that Trump's actions, not Twitter's, threatened free speech. If the company were held to a higher standard of liability, it would restrict speech for fear of being sued, rather than allow more speech. Wyden (2020) stated that "Americans don't want to be at the mercy of speech police, online or anywhere else. Section 230 gives sites, speakers and readers choices, and ensures that those choices will survive the hostility of those with power. It would be a terrible mistake to do away with it, especially now."

Despite the party's position on this issue, 60 percent of Republicans in a 2021 survey indicated that they did not believe that social media companies should be sued for third-party content. The percentage for conservative Republicans was lower than for those claiming to be moderate to liberal Republicans by a margin of 57–65 percent (McClain 2021).

Further Reading

Associated Press. 2015. "Obama Urges Republicans to Clear Way for Campaign Finance Bill Vote." *Fox News*, December 23. Accessed July 13, 2021. https://www.foxnews.com/politics/obama-urges-republicans-to-clear-way-for-campaign-finance-bill-vote.

Balcerzak, Ashley. 2018. "Study: Most Americans Want to Kill 'Citizens United' with Constitutional Amendment." Center for Public Integrity, May 10. Accessed July 23, 2021. https://www.pri.org/stories/2018-05-10/study-most-americans-want-kill-citizens-united-constitutional-amendment.

Biden, Joe. 2019. "Plan for a Government That Works for the People." Joe Biden for President. Accessed February 5, 2021. https://joebiden.com/governmentreform/.

Bush, George W. 2002. "Statement: President Signs Campaign Finance Reform Act." The White House, March 27. Accessed February 5, 2021. https://georgewbush-whitehouse.archives.gov/news/releases/2002/03/20020327.html.

The Campaign Finance Institute. 2017. "President Trump, with RNC Help, Raised More Small Donor Money Than President Obama; as Much as Clinton and Sanders Combined." February 21. Accessed September 5, 2022. http://www.cfinst.org/Press

/PReleases/17-02-21/President_Trump_with_RNC_Help_Raised_More_Small
_Donor_Money_than_President_Obama_As_Much_As_Clinton_and_Sanders
_Combined.aspx.

Democratic Party Platform. 1976–2016. American Presidency Project. Accessed November 22, 2022. https://www.presidency.ucsb.edu.

Democratic Party Platform. 2020. Accessed November 22, 2022. https://democrats.org/wp-content/uploads/sites/2/2020/08/2020-Democratic-Party-Platform.pdf.

Eshoo, Anna G. 2020. "Press Release from Congresswoman Anna G. Eshoo." Congresswoman Anna Eshoo, October 20. Accessed December 3, 2021. https://eshoo.house.gov/media/press-releases/reps-eshoo-and-malinowski-introduce-bill-hold-tech-platforms-liable-algorithmic.

Gilbert, Lisa. 2015. "Obama's Legacy on Campaign Finance Can Be More Than Just Rhetoric." The Hill, October 16. Accessed December 5, 2021. https://thehill.com/blogs/pundits-blog/the-administration/257112-obamas-not-yet-fulfilled-legacy-on-money-in-politics?rl=1.

Gore, Albert, Jr. 2000. "Remarks at Marquette University in Milwaukee, Wisconsin." The American Presidency Project, March 28. Accessed December 7, 2021. https://www.presidency.ucsb.edu/documents/remarks-marquette-university-milwaukee-wisconsin.

Jones, Bradley. 2018. "Most Americans Want to Limit Campaign Spending, Say Big Donors Have Greater Political Influence." Pew Research Center, May 8. Accessed December 9, 2021. https://www.pewresearch.org/fact-tank/2018/05/08/most-americans-want-to-limit-campaign-spending-say-big-donors-have-greater-political-influence/.

Lau, Tim. 2019. "Citizens United Explained." Brennan Center for Justice, December 12. Accessed December 13, 2021. https://www.brennancenter.org/our-work/research-reports/citizens-united-explained.

McCain, John, and Russ Feingold. 1996. "A Better Way to Fix Campaign Financing." Washington Post, February 20. Accessed December 14, 2021. https://www.washingtonpost.com/opinions/a-better-way-to-fix-campaign-financing/2018/08/26/b45ede68-a935-11e8-a8d7-0f63ab8b1370_story.html.

McClain, Colleen. 2021. "56% of Americans Oppose the Right to Sue Social Media Companies for What Users Post." Pew Research Center, July 1. Accessed December 16, 2021. https://www.pewresearch.org/fact-tank/2021/07/01/56-of-americans-oppose-the-right-to-sue-social-media-companies-for-what-users-post/.

Miers, Jesse. 2020. "A Primer on Section 230 and Trump's Executive Order." Brookings Institute, June 8. Accessed December 17, 2021. https://www.brookings.edu/blog/techtank/2020/06/08/a-primer-on-section-230-and-trumps-executive-order/.

Obama, Barack. 2010. "Remarks by the President in State of the Union Address." The White House, January 27. Accessed December 19, 2021. https://obamawhitehouse.archives.gov/the-press-office/remarks-president-state-union-address.

O'Brien, Michael. 2010. "McConnell: Court's Campaign Finance Ruling a Free Speech Victory." The Hill, January 21. Accessed December 22, 2021. https://thehill.com/blogs/blog-briefing-room/news/77281-mcconnell-courts-campaign-finance-ruling-a-free-speech-victory.

Ornitz, Jill, and Ryan Struyk. 2015. "Donald Trump's Surprisingly Honest Lessons about Big Money in Politics." ABC News, August 11. Accessed December 22, 2021. https://abcnews.go.com/Politics/donald-trumps-surprisingly-honest-lessons-big-money-politics/story?id=32993736.

"Pelosi Remarks at Press Event to Unveil a Better Deal for Our Democracy." 2018. Speaker Nancy Pelosi, May 21. Accessed December 15, 2022. https://www.speaker.gov /newsroom/52118-4.

Pildes, Richard. 2016. "What Are Donald Trump's Views on Campaign Finance Regulation?" Election Law Blog, March 23. Accessed May 2, 2021. https://electionlawblog .org/?p=81159.

Reilly, Mollie. 2012. "Mitt Romney: Teachers Unions' Contributions to Political Campaigns Should Be Limited." *HuffPost*, September 26. Accessed May 2, 2021. https://www .huffpost.com/entry/mitt-romney-teachers_n_1914968.

Republican Party Platform. 1976–2020. American Presidency Project. Accessed May 3, 2021. https://www.presidency.ucsb.edu/documents/presidential-documents-archive -guidebook/party-platforms-and-nominating-conventions-3.

Suro, Robert. 1998. "Clinton Faces New Campaign Probe." *Washington Post*, September 3. Accessed August 1, 2021. https://www.washingtonpost.com/wp-srv/politics/special /campfin/stories/clinton090398.htm.

United States Senate Commerce Committee. 2020. "Wicker, Graham, Blackburn Introduce Bill to Modify Section 230 and Empower Consumers Online." September 8. Accessed August 2, 2021. https://www.commerce.senate.gov/2020/9/wicker-graham-blackburn -introduce-bill-to-modify-section-230-and-empower-consumers-online.

Vogel, Kenneth P. 2008. "John McCain: The Return of the Reformer." *Politico*, July 15. Accessed August 4, 2021. https://www.politico.com/story/2008/07/john-mccain-the -return-of-the-reformer-011783.

Wachob, Luke. 2017. "Obama Was No One's Hero When It Came to Money in Politics." *The Hill*, February 8. Accessed August 7, 2021. https://thehill.com/blogs/pundits-blog /finance/318387-obamas-legacy-on-money-in-politics-is-not-what-progressives -hoped?rl=1.

Watson, Libby. 2020. "The Democrats Aren't Serious about Campaign Finance Reform." *New Republic*, October 16. Accessed August 10, 2021. https://newrepublic.com/article /159813/democrats-campaign-finance-reform-hr-1.

Weiner, Daniel. 2021. "GOP Resistance to Campaign Finance Reforms Shows Disregard for US Voters." *The Hill*, May 17. Accessed August 13, 2021. https://thehill.com/opinion /campaign/553835-gop-resistance-to-election-reforms-shows-disregard-for-us-voters.

Wertheimer, Fred. 2015. ""Donald Trump and Campaign Finance Reform." Democracy 21, September 1. Accessed December 15, 2022. https://democracy21.org/news-press/op-eds /fred-wertheimer-for-huffington-post-donald-trump-and-campaign-finance-reform

Wyden, Ron. 2020. "I Wrote This Law to Protect Free Speech: Now Trump Wants to Revoke It." *CNN Business: Perspectives*, June 9. Accessed August 13, 2021. https://www.cnn .com/2020/06/09/perspectives/ron-wyden-section-230/index.html.

Zhou, Li, Nancy Scola, and Ashley Gold. 2017. "Senators to Facebook, Google, Twitter: Wake Up to Russian Threat." *Politico*, November 1. Accessed August 21, 2021. https://www .politico.com/story/2017/11/01/google-facebook-twitter-russia-meddling-244412.

Government Surveillance

At a Glance

The federal government has a long history of using surveillance methods on U.S. citizens. After September 11, 2001, the passage of the USA Patriot Act and the creation of the Presidential Surveillance Program under President George W. Bush led to a new era of government surveillance, largely driven by the mass collection of metadata by the National Security Agency (NSA) related to technology (phone, email, and website records). Government surveillance of U.S. citizens has occurred under both Democratic and Republican administrations and has been supported by both parties in Congress at times. More liberal members of the Democratic Party and more libertarian members of the Republican Party have raised concerns over the extent and legality of government surveillance.

The issue became significantly more controversial in 2013 when Edward Snowden, an intelligence contractor working for the NSA, released a cache of documents that revealed to the public the extent of the surveillance being collected and analyzed by the NSA. While in the earliest years of its creation Democrats were the most critical of the surveillance program, recently the program has drawn more fire from Republicans since it was criticized by Donald Trump. The practice continues into 2022 with a looming expiration date for the Patriot Act in 2024. The future of government surveillance is very much up in the air. On one hand, technological advances allow for greater and more expansive surveillance than ever before. On the other hand, political support for the surveillance program is at an all-time low among both Democrats and Republicans.

According to many Republicans . . .

- The surveillance program and the Patriot Act are critical to national security and should be extended.
- Limiting the powers of the surveillance program or increasing the difficulty for the government to access records would make the nation less secure.

- The surveillance program represents government overreach and abuse of power, especially with regard to its use against the Donald Trump campaign for president in 2016.

According to many Democrats . . .

- The surveillance program and the Patriot Act are critical to national security and should be extended.
- Limiting the powers of the surveillance program is necessary to ensure that the civil liberties and privacy of Americans are maintained.
- The surveillance program represents government overreach and abuse of power and should be ended or greatly reduced in size and scope.

Overview

The history of the surveillance of U.S. citizens by the U.S. government goes back to at least the World War II and the creation of the Office of Censorship by President Franklin D. Roosevelt on December 19, 1941, ten days after the Japanese surprise attack on Pearl Harbor. On behalf of the U.S. government, employees at the Office of Censorship opened all international mail that traveled to or from the United States between the day he signed the order and August 1945, when World War II came to an end (Fiset 2001). Though the Office of Censorship was short-lived and escaped being challenged in the courts, it was only the beginning of the mass surveillance of civilian communications in the United States and a harbinger of the types of both legal and illegal tactics the government would bring to bear.

The onset of the Cold War spurred the creation of a number of government surveillance programs that operated largely in secret for several decades. Christopher Pyle, a captain in the Army Intelligence Command during the 1960s, revealed to the public one such program after he was discharged. According to an interview Pyle gave in 2005, one such Army Intelligence program involved over a thousand plainclothes agents who physically watched every significant protest or demonstration that took place inside the United States, then housed the intelligence they gathered in a large warehouse in Baltimore, Maryland (*Democracy Now!* 2005). Pyle's claims are corroborated by a series of U.S. Senate reports on Army spying that occurred in the 1960s, written by the Subcommittee on Constitutional Rights, part of the U.S. Senate Judiciary Committee (U.S. Senate 1972, 1973).

Efforts to Rein in Government Spying on American Citizens

In the 1970s, news of these secret operations by Army Intelligence and other government agencies came to light—combined with the troubling revelations of the Watergate investigation into President Nixon, his administration, and his 1972 campaign—resulted in the formation of a U.S. Senate Select Committee to Study Governmental Operations (widely known as the Church Committee, named for its chair, the Democratic senator from Idaho Frank Church) in 1975. The Church Committee investigation found some startling abuses of power by the U.S. government, including efforts to surveil U.S. citizens and their communications without warrants. Operation Shamrock and Operation Minaret, for example, involved the mass collection and analysis of telegrams that entered or exited the United States without any court orders or warrants being obtained.

The Church Committee produced a report in 1976 that outlined the extent of the surveillance conducted under Operation Shamrock: "From August 1945 until May 1975, NSA [National Security Agency] received copies of millions of international telegrams sent to, from, or transiting the United States. Codenamed Operation SHAMROCK, this was the largest governmental interception program affecting Americans . . . it is estimated that in later years approximately 150,000 per month were reviewed by NSA analysts" (U.S. Senate 1976a). This mass surveillance by the government of U.S. communications also involved the cooperation of the major telegram services themselves, a harbinger of the cooperation between private communications companies and the government that exists today.

Rather infamously, the Federal Bureau of Investigation (FBI) also used surveillance against individuals and groups it deemed subversive, including civil rights icon Martin Luther King, Jr. This FBI program, known as COINTELPRO, used wiretaps and hidden microphones to surveil Dr. King over a period of several years. According to the Church Committee investigation, COINTELPRO was employed against King and others around him, using "nearly every intelligence gathering technique at the Bureau's disposal" in an attempt to discredit him and the Civil Rights Movement (U.S. Senate 1976b).

For example, the U.S. government repeatedly and continuously engaged in mail opening (which according to the Church Committee was carried out by the FBI and CIA well after the disbanding of the Office of Censorship), telegram reading, and the wiretapping of phones. Many of these surveillance activities were taken without the use or obtainment of warrants. The Church Committee, as well as the Senate Judiciary Subcommittee on Constitutional Rights led by Democratic senator Sam Irvin (NC), pushed the federal government to reform its practices around data collection and surveillance of U.S. citizens.

The Foreign Intelligence Surveillance Act

In 1978, Congress passed the Foreign Intelligence Surveillance Act (known as FISA), which reformed the procedures for both electronic and physical surveillance conducted by the government. The purpose of the law was to create some oversight of government surveillance, in the form of the Foreign Intelligence Surveillance Court (FISC), which would be tasked with overseeing and approving all government requests for surveillance warrants. Despite the Church Committee's exposure of government abuse and the subsequent passing of FISA, government surveillance in the United States would only grow in the years to come, in partic-ular after the events of September 11, 2001.

The aftermath and government response to the terrorist attacks on September 11, 2001, led directly to the exponential growth of the mass surveillance efforts of the U.S. intelligence communities. Title II of the USA Patriot Act, enacted on Octo-ber 26, 2001, vastly expanded the U.S. government's legal authority to conduct surveillance—including electronic surveillance—on U.S. citizens. Included in the Patriot Act are provisions that expand the scope and ease of wiretapping orders and that allow the government to search and obtain stored voicemails more easily and to access the customer records from cable companies (U.S. Congress 2001). While the Patriot Act was passed under Republican president George W. Bush, it received broad bipartisan support in Congress, where it was passed 98–1 in the U.S. Senate (the lone "nay" vote was cast by Democratic senator Russell Feingold of Wisconsin) and 357–66 in the House of Representatives. Republicans in the House were nearly unanimous in their support of the law (211–3), while House Democrats were still supportive but more divided (145–62).

The passage of the Patriot Act amended sections of FISA, resulting in the gov-ernment having an easier time gaining access to surveillance material on U.S. cit-izens during criminal investigation—a significant change. Prior to the passing of the Patriot Act, FISC could only grant approval of surveillance warrants if the primary purpose of the investigation was *intelligence*, that is, to investigate the actions of foreign governments and actors. The Patriot Act, however, amends FISA rules by changing the phrase "the purpose" to "a significant purpose" (U.S. Con-gress 2001). In practice, this meant that the government could get a surveillance warrant by claiming that intelligence was simply part of the investigation, even if the primary purpose of the investigation was criminal in nature. This expansion of the government's ability to legally acquire surveillance on U.S. citizens proved to be extraordinarily important.

In 2013, leaked documents that were stolen from the NSA by one of its contractors—Edward Snowden—revealed to the world just how far the NSA had taken the authority granted to it in the Patriot Act. An article published in the *Guardian* on June 6, 2013, revealed that the NSA was collecting on an "ongoing, daily basis" the telephone records—including the associated numbers, location, duration, and time of each call—for millions of Verizon customers through a secret court order granted through the FISC (Greenwald 2013). Subsequent revelations showed that many more private companies, including Google, Apple, Facebook, Microsoft, and Yahoo, were partners to the global surveillance efforts conducted by the NSA (Greenwald and MacAskill 2013). As a result of these disclosures, the 2015 USA Freedom Act banned the bulk collection of telephone metadata; however, cell phone providers are required to continue to store this data, and the government is still allowed to access it on a case-by-case basis, subject to approval through FISC (U.S. Congress 2014). New camera technology has also allowed for old-fashioned physical surveillance to become much more efficient. By placing high-resolution cameras in planes, the FBI and the Department of Homeland Security can surveil an entire city from above—a practice that has been commonplace since at least 2016 (Aldhous and Seife 2016). In November 2020, it was reported by the *New York Times* that the U.S. military had been purchasing the location data of U.S. citizens, collected using cell phone applications (Ovide 2020). The location data is more typically used for marketing and is publicly available to purchase. Earlier reporting in 2020 suggested that the Department of Homeland Security was using similarly purchased data to track and find undocumented immigrants (Tau and Hackman 2020).

For now, the vast program of government surveillance continues to exist and is likely expanding behind closed doors. A February 2022 press release by Democratic senators Ron Wyden (Oregon) and Martin Heinrich (New Mexico) makes clear that bulk data collection by the CIA is still ongoing and operating "entirely outside the statutory framework that Congress and public believe govern this collection, and without any of the judicial, congressional or even executive branch oversight that comes from [FISA] collection" (Wyden 2022). Unlike in the past, U.S. citizens today routinely interact with devices that track and log their location and use. The rise of social media has led to most people having an online persona that can easily be accessed by anyone, including the government. The technological renaissance that has unfolded over the past two decades has also brought us to a new era of government surveillance. The government now has more potential avenues to surveil the American public than ever before. The public debate on the topic, however, is one of the least contentious in the modern era of hyper-partisan, polarized politics. Republican and Democratic presidents have continued to carry out these programs, and politicians of both parties largely continue to vote for measures that maintain the surveillance status quo. Nevertheless, there are some notable exceptions to the bipartisan consensus, and in general some Democratic politicians seem to be more skeptical of mass government surveillance.

Republicans

The modern debate over government surveillance began under the Republican administration of George W. Bush, after the events of September 11, 2001, during his first year in office led to the creation of the Department of Homeland Security and the passage of the USA Patriot Act. In 2005, it was revealed by a source within the government (later revealed to be NSA employee Thomas Tamm) to the *New York Times* that the Bush administration had created a program to spy on "the international telephone calls and international email messages of hundreds, perhaps thousands, of people inside the United States without warrants over the past three years" (Risen and Lichtblau 2005). Later leaks showed that the scope of the surveillance happening under the Bush administration was dramatically underestimated.

One report by *USA Today* in May 2006 included an anonymous source who alleged that the government was using data provided by three major telecom service providers—AT&T, Verizon, and BellSouth—to create "the largest database ever assembled in the world . . . a database of every call ever made" (Cauley 2006). These programs, known as the President's Surveillance Program and created by the Bush administration shortly after September 11, 2001, were continuously reauthorized every forty-five days by the president (Offices of Inspectors General 2009).

For the most part, Republicans in Congress during the two terms of Bush's presidency were willing to go along with the president's desire to continue these surveillance programs. The 2001 USA Patriot Act received every Republican vote in the Senate (and all but one Democratic vote), as well as 211/214 Republican votes in the House. The 2005 bill to reauthorize and make permanent much of the Patriot Act (though not the provisions allowing for warrantless surveillance) again passed the Senate with every Republican vote and passed the House with 207/225 Republican votes. A second reauthorization and amendment to the Patriot Act passed Congress in 2006 with similar margins for Republicans. What criticism existed of the Patriot Act, and the government's surveillance program between 2001 and 2008, was largely pushed by the Democratic Party while Republicans remained behind the president on this issue.

The majority of Republicans in Congress during the Obama administration continued to support the surveillance programs. In 2013, the Republican representative from Ohio and Speaker of the House John Boehner defended the Obama administration even as the Democratic president faced intense scrutiny over the surveillance program: "Transparency is important, but we expect the White House to insist that no reform will compromise the operational integrity of the program" (Savage and Shear 2013). Republican leadership in the House was also essential to defeating July 2013 legislation that would have sharply curtailed the NSA program (Weisman 2013). In an odd display of bipartisanship, conservative and more libertarian-leaning Republicans joined forces with more liberal members of the House to press the issue, only to narrowly fail as more moderate Democrats and Republicans joined together to support the Obama administration and the government's continued ability to carry out mass surveillance. The final vote on the Amash–Conyers amendment shows the deep divisions in the Republican Party over the issue in 2013, with Republicans ultimately voting to continue the surveillance program 134-94.

After the Snowden revelations in 2013, more Congressional conservatives began to speak out against the massive and ongoing government surveillance program. While most Republicans, including party leaders and important committee chairs in Congress, continued to support the program, some of the more libertarian-leaning representatives were much more vocal in their criticism after the 2013 revelations triggered by the Snowden leaks. Republican senator from Kentucky Rand Paul was one of the more outspoken critics on the Republican side of the aisle, even going so far as to file a lawsuit in 2014 in federal court alleging that the NSA's mass surveillance and data collection was illegal. In a statement at the time, Senator Paul outlined his key critique of the program's legality: "Today we ask the question for every phone user in America: can a single warrant allow the government to collect all your records, all the time? I don't think so" (Savage 2014). Senator Paul would go on to make ending government surveillance part of his unsuccessful bid for the Republican nomination for president in the 2016 Republican Primary.

Republican (and later Libertarian) representative from Michigan Justin Amash was another of the outspoken critics on the conservative side of the aisle. Amash, a member of the rising Tea Party faction of Republicans, was particularly willing to buck the establishment Republican orthodoxy and advocate for things such as ending the NSA surveillance program. The aforementioned Amash–Conyers amendment, which Representative Amash cowrote, would have ended the NSA's "authority for the blanket collection of records under the PATRIOT ACT" (Amash 2013). While the amendment would have faced greater obstacles to passing in the senate, it was nevertheless a sign of the growing Republican tensions during the Obama administration as more Tea Party movement representatives were elected who were willing to go against the party's leadership.

By 2015, it had become clear that something would need to be done to appease the growing appetite in Congress for reform. As even more Republicans supported reforming the laws governing the mass surveillance programs put in place during the Bush administration, the Obama administration eventually settled on a compromise with Congress that would restrict the ability of the government to access the cell phone data being mass collected. The legislation in question would shift the data collection of cell phone records to the telephone companies and require the government to acquire a warrant from the FISC to get access to the data. Many Republicans, including Speaker of the House John Boehner, supported the proposed changes. However, not all Republicans agreed. Reforms to the program in 2015 were opposed by the Republican senator from Kentucky and senate majority leader Mitch McConnell. A spokesman for McConnell at the time indicated that the Republican majority leader would prefer to keep the program in place as it was (Davis 2015). The fight over the reform package, a bill known as the USA Freedom Act, led to a rare moment of Republican criticism of Mitch McConnell. Republican representative of Utah Jason Chaffetz said at the time, "I don't think he's listening to America. The seminal question is how much liberty are we going to give up for security? People are on the brink. They're scared out of their wits" (Weisman and Steinhauer 2015). After a brief period where the provisions of the Patriot Act allowing for the surveillance were allowed to expire, Congress passed the reform bill and reauthorization on a bipartisan (although far from unanimous) basis.

The election of Donald Trump as president in 2016 once again changed the course of the debate on surveillance for Republicans. On the one hand, in 2018, the Republican-controlled Congress voted to extend the NSA's warrantless surveillance program for an additional six years. The decisive senate vote passed with Republicans voting 43-7 in favor, underscoring the program's continued support with the party. Senate Majority Leader McConnell summed up the prevailing Republican position at the time: "We need our armed forces and intelligence community to protect us, and they need us to give them the tools to do it" (Savage 2018). On the other hand, at the exact same time this reauthorization was occurring in January of 2018, Republicans were also accusing the government of abusing its power by having issued a warrant targeting a member of President Trump's campaign team (Savage and LaFraniere 2018). The president's concerns stemmed from the FBI's issuing of a surveillance warrant in 2014 on Carter Page, who later became an adviser to the Trump campaign in 2015–2016. In 2013, Page served as an adviser to "the staff of the Kremlin in preparation for their Presidency of the G-20 Summit" and was the target of Russian intelligence, who wanted to recruit him as an asset (Calabresi and Abramson 2018; Zengerle 2017). The ongoing investigation and surveillance of Page continued to his time as a member of the Trump campaign and was one of the critical links in the "Trump-Russia scandal" that dogged the president during his time in office.

The disconnect between the two stances of the party voting days apart to reauthorize the program without any revisions or reforms and also criticizing it for its role in the "Trump-Russia scandal" highlights the increasingly politicized nature of the issue. In reality, Republicans were largely for continuing the government's ability to use the secret FISCs to surveil whomever they chose, but in public they also needed to conform to the president's repeated opposition to having that power used against his campaign staff. As reported by the *New York Times*, President Trump's own communications from January 2018 highlight the double-edged nature of the issue for Republicans at the time; on the President's public Twitter account, he "expressed skepticism about government surveillance—even though a White House statement [issued the previous day] urged Congress to block significant new constraints on the NSA program" (Savage, Sullivan, and Fandos 2018).

By 2020, it was clear that President Trump was still wary of new reauthorizations of the surveillance program and had not gotten over the FBI's issuance of a warrant against campaign adviser Carter Page as part of that program. After his impeachment and acquittal in early 2020, in March, the president met with Republicans and seemed to be favoring sweeping reforms to the surveillance program. In May, the president scuttled the bipartisan talks that would have reauthorized the FBI's part of the program when he told the Republican caucus in the House to vote "no" on the measure in a series of statements made from his public Twitter account (Nakashima and DeBonis 2020). In August, the bill was allowed to quietly die in the senate, despite Senate Majority Leader McConnell's support (Savage 2020a). Finally, the Justice Department in September 2020 issued guidance that political figures and their aides and advisers should be warned that they may be the targets of FISA investigations before a warrant could be issued (Benner 2020). The guidance capped a run in the late stages of the Trump presidency of weakening the surveillance program. Overall, the Trump era saw a reversal among many Republicans who had previously supported the surveillance program. Largely as a result of the president's continued attacks on the program, by 2020, Republicans in Congress would no longer vote to maintain the expiring provisions of the law that allowed the FBI to participate in and petition the FISC, a stark difference from 2018 when the NSA program was reauthorized easily under a Republican-controlled Congress and signed into law by President Trump.

After the election of Joe Biden as president, Republicans have continued to express concerns over the intelligence community's data collection on American citizens. In April 2021, House Intelligence Committee meeting, for example, covered an intelligence community report on domestic violent extremism. In it, Republican representative Chris Stewart, while questioning Director of National Intelligence Avril Hanes, asked, "Do you think the CIA should be spying on American citizens?" (Barnes 2021). The future of Republican support for warrantless surveillance by the U.S. government is very much still up for debate. While other issues have thus far been at the forefront of the political world through 2021, it is possible that when the reauthorization of the Patriot Act provisions extended in 2018 come up again for reauthorization in 2024, Republicans will ultimately oppose them. Of course, this perhaps depends on the national political environment at the time, and whether or not former President Trump is the 2024 presidential nominee for the Republican Party. If Mr. Trump were to win the 2024 Republican primary, it is likely that many in his party would continue to oppose extensions of the Patriot Act. However, the makeup of Congress after the 2022 midterms will also play a role. If Republicans are able to regain control of one or both Houses of Congress, they may feel more at ease with the program under their oversight and leadership. Only time will tell where the party will land on this issue going forward.

Democrats

The Democratic Party has long been more skeptical of government surveillance than their Republican counterparts. The lone voice in the senate to oppose the initial passage of the Patriot Act in 2001, for example, was Democratic senator from Wisconsin Russell Feingold. Senator Feingold, at the time just days after the events of September 11, 2001, spoke against the Patriot Act on the floor of the senate: "This is an enormous expansion of authority, under a law that provides only minimal judicial supervision. . . . The debate on a bill that may have the most far-reaching consequences on the civil liberties of the American people in a generation was a non-debate . . . Congress will fulfill its duty only when it protects *both* the American people and the freedoms at the foundation of American society [emphasis original]" (Feingold 2001). In contrast to the 211-3 Republican vote in the House of Representatives for the USA Patriot Act, the Democrats in the House voted for the measure more narrowly, 145-62.

The following years would see Democratic opposition to the Bush administration, and the Patriot Act in particular, increase. Along with the invasion of Iraq, the Patriot Act and its threat to Americans' civil liberties were set to be a major campaign issue for the Democrats to pursue in the 2004 presidential election (Nagourney 2003). Many of the leading Democratic candidates for president were highly critical of Republican attorney general and Patriot Act author John Ashcroft, perhaps partially to deflect from their own votes in favor of the law in 2001 (Nagourney 2003). By the time the Patriot Act reauthorization was moving through Congress in 2005–2006, the sentiment in the Democratic Party in support of the law had completely reversed from the 2001 vote. Where the initial Patriot Act was passed in the House with Democrats voting 145-62, the 2005 Patriot Act reauthorization passed with only 44 Democratic votes and 155 Democrats voting against the measure. However, despite the growing opposition in the public and among the most liberal Democrats, not all Democrats were in full opposition to the law. A *New York Times* article from early 2006, for example, highlighted the need for Democrats to strike a delicate balance ahead of the 2006 midterm elections by both appearing tough on national security issues and criticizing the Bush administration and the domestic wiretapping program (Stolberg 2006).

The Obama presidency brought the debate around government surveillance into a new dynamic as for the first time the program was being administered by a Democratic president. While a vocal critic of the Bush administration and the policy of domestic wiretapping, President Obama himself voted in the Senate to reauthorize the Patriot Act in 2005. After assuming office in 2009, a spokesperson for the Obama administration said in April of that year that "[the administration] had taken comprehensive steps to bring the [NSA] into compliance with the law after a periodic review turned up problems with the 'overcollection' of domestic communications" (Risen and Lichtblau 2009). By 2013, however, it became clear to the American public after the Edward Snowden revelations that the NSA surveillance program was far larger and more widespread than had been previously believed. The Obama administration, instead of ending the contentious program of surveillance that began under President Bush, expanded it further as cell phones became more widespread—thus allowing for the collection of far more data than ever before.

The 2013 summer fight over the Amash–Conyers amendment, which would have ended the NSA's surveillance program, divided Democrats just as it did Republicans. The Obama administration ultimately made common cause with Republican Party leadership in the House to defeat the amendment (Weisman 2013). The amendment was defeated, but Democrats in the House (although not the leadership) supported it 111-83. Later that year, a panel of outside advisers put together a recommendation (publicly released by the Obama administration) that suggested forty-six changes to the existing surveillance program and the rules related to how and when the government could collect information (Clarke et al. 2013). The issue would remain controversial through the rest of the Obama presidency, ultimately resulting in a significant package of reforms put forward in 2015 that put in place some of the reforms suggested by the 2013 panel.

In June 2015, the most significant scaling back of the NSA's ability to warrant-lessly collect data on American citizens was passed into law under the USA Free-dom Act (U.S. Congress 2014; Steinhauer and Weisman 2015). The bill imposed limits on the ability of the government to collect data in bulk, instead shifting that burden to the telephone companies themselves and allowing the government to access the data on a much more limited basis when they could acquire a warrant through the FISC process. The bill also created an independent advocate for the constitutionality of individual cases that appeared before the FISC and included some provisions to improve transparency around the historically secretive FISC. The vote on the USA Freedom Act received all but 2 Democratic votes in the Senate (including Vermont Senator Bernie Sanders, an Independent who caucuses with the Democrats) but was much more controversial for Republicans led by Mitch McConnell, who did not want the surveillance powers to be limited at the time. The legislation was more controversial among Democrats in the House, where it passed with Democrats voting 142-41 in favor of the law.

The Trump era, beginning in 2017, continued to see Democrats split over the issue of government surveillance. The January 2018 reauthorization of the Patriot Act was passed in both Houses of Congress with a majority of Democrats voting against the bill (the senate was 21 for and 27 against, while in the House the split was 65-119). Had the Democrats been more unified in their opposition, it is likely they could have stopped the reauthorization, given that Republicans were also somewhat split on the measure and President Trump at the time was publicly denouncing the surveillance used against one of his campaign advisers, Carter Page (Savage, Sullivan, and Fandos 2018). The central tension in the Democratic Party displayed here is largely between House leadership and more "establish-ment" Democrats who mostly support the government's surveillance program, and the more progressive and liberal Democrats who want to significantly curtail or even end the program entirely.

The division in the Democratic Party over the issue continued into 2020. In late February of that year, Democrats (who controlled the U.S. House of Representa-tives) abruptly scuttled a committee vote on a bill to reauthorize Section 215 of the Patriot Act—a section that allows the FBI to access the collected data through the FISC—over some members' objections that the bill did not do enough to limit the government's surveillance powers. Democratic representative from California Zoe Lofgren planned to offer amendments banning the use of business-collected records and requiring a "friend of the court" to critique the government's argument in every FISC hearing for the approval of wiretapping an American (Fandos and Savage 2020). According to Lofgren, "We have the opportunity to reform the sys-tem. We should take that opportunity" (Fandos and Savage 2020).

President Obama Addresses the Issue of Government Surveillance

In this 2014 Speech, President Obama discusses the history and philosophy of government surveillance in the United States. The speech was given to address public concerns raised by many after the leaked documents provided by Edward Snowden ignited a political firestorm in 2013.

I believe critics are right to point out that without proper safeguards, this type of [surveillance] program could be used to yield information about our private lives, and open the door to more intrusive bulk collection programs in the future. They're also right to point out that . . . [the program] has never been subject to vigorous public debate.

For all these reasons, I believe we need a new approach. . . . Now, the reforms I'm proposing today should give the American people greater confidence that their rights are being protected, even as our intelligence and law enforcement agencies maintain the tools they need to keep us safe.

One thing I'm certain of: This debate will make us stronger. And I also know that in this time of change, the United States of America will have to lead. It may seem sometimes that America is being held to a different standard. And I'll admit to the readiness of some to assume the worst motives by our government can be frustrating. . . . But let's remember: We are held to a different standard precisely because we have been at the forefront of defending personal privacy and human dignity. . . . Those values make us who we are. And because of the strength of our own democracy, we should not shy away from high expectations.

Source

"Remarks by the President on Review of Signals Intelligence." 2014. The White House, January 17. Accessed November 23, 2022. https://obamawhitehouse.archives.gov/the-press-office/2014/01/17/remarks-president-review-signals-intelligence.

Despite the objections of Lofgren and other more progressive Democrats, the USA Freedom Reauthorization Act of 2020 ultimately passed the House of Representatives in March 2020 with Democrats voting 152-75 in favor of the bill. The politics of the bill, however, would quickly turn. After an amended version of the USA Freedom Reauthorization Act passed the senate, the efforts of Congress to produce a reconciled version of the bill stalled in August 2020 after Republican senator from Kentucky and senate majority leader Mitch McConnell never appointed any senators to the reconciliation committee (Savage 2020a). The larger events and context of 2020 and early 2021, including the global COVID-19 pandemic, the 2020 U.S. presidential election (which was protested by President Trump after his bid for reelection failed), and the second impeachment trial of President Trump, led to the further stalling of the reauthorization legislation.

While the Patriot Act and its subsidiaries, including the USA Freedom Act and the attempted reauthorization, received the most attention from Congress in 2020, other issues of government surveillance surfaced as well during the nationwide protests over the death of George Floyd and police conduct. According to one report in the *New York Times*, the Department of Homeland Security deployed a combination of helicopters, airplanes, and drones to fifteen U.S. cities where demonstrations were taking place (Kanno-Youngs 2020). A handful of House Democrats, including Representatives Carolyn Maloney and Alexandria Ocasio-Cortez (New York), Stephen Lynch and Ayanna Pressley (Massachusetts), and Jamie Raskin (Maryland), sent a letter to Acting Secretary of Homeland Security Chad Wolf over the matter. In the letter, the group of Representatives accused the Trump administration and the Department of Homeland Security of "undermin[ing] the First Amendment freedoms of American of all races who are rightfully protesting George Floyd's killing. The deployment of drones and officers to surveil protests is a gross abuse of authority and is particularly chilling when used against Americans who are protesting law enforcement brutality" (Maloney et al. 2020). The surveillance of protests in this case echoes that of the 1960s, in which anti-war and civil rights protestors were surveilled by undercover officers of the U.S. Army Intelligence Command. In *Leaders of a Beautiful Struggle v. Baltimore Police Department*, a federal appeals court in June 2021 found that such surveillance by government aircraft violated the Fourth Amendment rights of the citizens of Baltimore (Lavoie 2021). While the case has yet to be tested in the Supreme Court at the time of writing, it could be a harbinger of the types of government surveillance debates that are to come.

During the early days of the Biden era, however, it remains to be seen what will happen with regard to government surveillance going forward. Democratic majorities in the House and senate have so far chosen not to act on this issue, prioritizing COVID-19 relief, infrastructure, and voting rights legislation that are high priorities for the Biden administration. However, issues of citizen privacy in the face of government surveillance remain unsettled and could be taken up at any time. Congress has yet to act officially on programs such as aerial surveillance or the collection of visitor logs for websites, a practice that was recently revealed (Savage 2020b). As for what Democrats might do in the future, it seems likely that many will continue to oppose the Patriot Act, potentially meaning that its reauthorization in 2024 will be in jeopardy. A lot will probably depend on the makeup of Congress at the time and on whether or not President Biden is able to cooperate with a Congress partially or completely controlled by Republicans. Further complicating the matter is that while government surveillance is important to many in Congress, its importance to average Americans remains mixed (Geiger 2018). The upcoming political debate over the renewal of the Patriot Act in 2024 will likely determine a lot about the future of government surveillance in the United States and whether the modern era of mass warrantless surveillance is finally coming to an end or will continue on into its fourth decade of existence.

Stephen Joiner

Further Reading

Aldhous, Peter, and Charles Seife. 2016. "Spies in the Skies." *Buzzfeed News*, April 6. Accessed July 3, 2021. https://www.buzzfeednews.com/article/peteraldhous/spies-in-the-skies.

Amash, Justin. 2013. "House Amendment 413 to HR 2397." 113th Congress, offered July 24, 2013. Accessed July 3, 2021. https://www.congress.gov/amendment/113th-congress/house-amendment/413.

Barnes, Julian E. 2021. "Republicans Question Spy Agencies' Work on Domestic Extremism." *New York Times*, April 15, 2021. Accessed July 5, 2021. https://www.nytimes.com/2021/04/15/us/politics/intelligence-agencies-domestic-extremism.html?searchResultPosition=24.

Benner, Katie. 2020. "Barr Imposes Limits on F.B.I. Surveillance of Political Candidates." *New York Times*, September 1, 2020. Accessed July 5, 2021. https://www.nytimes.com/2020/09/01/us/politics/barr-elections-fbi-surveillance.html?searchResultPosition=6.

Calabresi, Massimo, and Alana Abramson. 2018. "Carter Page Touted Kremlin Contacts in 2013 Letter." *Time*, February 3, 2018. Accessed July 3, 2021. https://time.com/5132126/carter-page-russia-2013-letter/.

Cauley, Leslie. 2006. "NSA Has Massive Database of Americans' Phone Calls." *USA Today*, May 10. Accessed July 1, 2021. https://usatoday30.usatoday.com/news/washington/2006-05-10-nsa_x.htm.

Clarke, Richard A., Michael J. Morell, Geoffrey R. Stone, Cass R. Sunstein, and Peter Swire. 2013. "Liberty and Security in a Changing World." Obama White House, December 12. Accessed July 2, 2021. https://obamawhitehouse.archives.gov/sites/default/files/docs/2013-12-12_rg_final_report.pdf.

Davis, Julie Hirschfeld. 2015. "Obama Warns the Senate to Pass Surveillance Law." *New York Times*, May 29. Accessed July 1, 2021. https://www.nytimes.com/2015/05/30/us/politics/obama-warns-the-senate-to-pass-surveillance-law.html?searchResultPosition=7.

Democracy Now! 2005. "An Impeachable Offense? Bush Admits Authorizing NSA to Eavesdrop on Americans Without Court Approval." Episode aired originally on December 19. Transcript accessed July 1, 2021. https://www.democracynow.org/2005/12/19/an_impeachable_offense_bush_admits_authorizing.

Fandos, Nicholas, and Charlie Savage. 2020. "Push for More Privacy Protections Throws Surveillance Bill Talks into Disarray." *New York Times*, February 26. Accessed July 3, 2021. https://www.nytimes.com/2020/02/26/us/politics/congress-surveillance-bill-expiring.html?searchResultPosition=2.

Feingold, Russell. 2001. "On Opposing the U.S.A. PATRIOT ACT." Address given to the Associated Press Managing Editors Conference, October 12. Accessed July 1, 2021. http://www.archipelago.org/vol6-2/feingold.htm.

Fiset, Louis. 2001. "U.S. Censorship of Enemy Alien Mail in World War II." *Prologue Magazine*, Spring, vol. 33, no. 1. Accessed July 1, 2021. https://www.archives.gov/publications/prologue/2001/spring/mail-censorship-in-world-war-two-1.html.

Geiger, A. W. 2018. "How Americans Have Viewed Government Surveillance and Privacy Since Snowden Leaks." Pew Research Center, June 4. Accessed July 14, 2021. https://www.pewresearch.org/fact-tank/2018/06/04/how-americans-have-viewed-government-surveillance-and-privacy-since-snowden-leaks/.

Greenwald, Glenn. 2013. "NSA Collecting Phone Records of Millions of Verizon Customers Daily." *The Guardian*, June 6. Accessed July 2, 2021. https://www.theguardian.com /world/2013/jun/06/nsa-phone-records-verizon-court-order.

Greenwald, Glenn, and Ewen MacAskill. 2013. "NSA Prism Program Taps in to User Data of Apple, Google, and Others." *The Guardian*, June 7. Accessed July 2, 2021. https:// www.theguardian.com/world/2013/jun/06/us-tech-giants-nsa-data.

Kanno-Youngs, Zolan. 2020. "U.S. Watched George Floyd Protests in 15 Cities Using Aerial Surveillance." *New York Times*, June 19. Accessed July 4, 2021. https://www .nytimes.com/2020/06/19/us/politics/george-floyd-protests-surveillance.html? searchResultPosition=1.

Lavoie, Denise. 2021. "Court Finds Baltimore Aerial Surveillance Unconstitu- tional." *AP News*, June 24. Accessed July 4, 2021. https://apnews.com/article /baltimore-courts-503b2eb629abf94c25edf4111baf64bd.

Maloney Carolyn, Raskin Jaime, Lynch Stephen, Ocasio-Cortez Alexandria, and Ayanna Pressley. 2020. "Letter to Acting Secretary of Homeland Security Chad Wolf." June 5. Accessed July 2, 2021. https://oversight.house.gov/sites/democrats.oversight.house .gov/files/2020-06-05.CBM%20et.%20al%20to%20Wolf-%20DHS%20re%20Peaceful %20Protestors_0.pdf.

Nagourney, Adam. 2003. "For Democrats Challenging Bush, Ashcroft Is Exhibit A." *New York Times*, July 13. Accessed July 1, 2021. https://www.nytimes.com/2003/07/13/us /for-democrats-challenging-bush-ashcroft-is-exhibit-a.html?searchResultPosition=9.

Nakashima, Ellen, and Mike DeBonis. 2020. "House Effort to Pass Surveillance Overhaul Collapses after Trump Tweets and Pushback from DOJ." *Washington Post*, May 28. Accessed July 3, 2021. https://www.washingtonpost.com/national-security/house -effort-to-pass-surveillance-overhaul-collapses-after-trump-tweets-and-pushback -from-doj/2020/05/27/a3f224f8-a047-11ea-81bb-c2f70f01034b_story.html.

Offices of Inspectors General. 2009. "Unclassified Report on the President's Surveillance Program." July 10. Accessed July 1, 2021. https://fas.org/irp/eprint/psp.pdf.

Ovide, Shira. 2020. "Government Surveillance by Data." *New York Times*, November 18. Updated June 14, 2021. Accessed July 2, 2021. https://www.nytimes.com/2020/11/18 /technology/government-surveillance-by-data.html?searchResultPosition=41.

Risen, James, and Eric Lichtblau. 2005. "Bush Lets U.S. Spy on Callers Without Courts." *New York Times*, December 16. Accessed July 1, 2021. https://www.nytimes.com/2005 /12/16/politics/bush-lets-us-spy-on-callers-without-courts.html.

Risen, James, and Eric Lichtblau. 2009. "E-Mail Surveillance Renews Concerns in Con- gress." *New York Times*, June 16. Accessed July 2, 2021. https://www.nytimes.com/2009 /06/17/us/17nsa.html?searchResultPosition=9.

Roosevelt, Franklin. 1941. "Executive Order 8985 Establishing the Office of Censor- ship." Accessed July 1, 2021. https://www.presidency.ucsb.edu/documents/executive -order-8985-establishing-the-office-censorship.

Savage, Charlie. 2014. "Rand Paul Files Lawsuit Over N.S.A. Call Surveillance." *New York Times*, February 12. Accessed July 2, 2021. https://www.nytimes.com/2014/02/13 /us/politics/rand-paul-files-lawsuit-over-nsa-call-surveillance.html?searchResult Position=2.

Savage, Charlie. 2018. "Congress Approves Six-Year Extension of Surveillance Law." *New York Times*, January 18. Accessed July 4, 2021. https://www.nytimes.com/2018/01/18 /us/politics/surveillance-congress-snowden-privacy.html?searchResultPosition=2.

Savage, Charlie. 2020a. "McConnell Appears Set to Quietly Suffocate Long-Debated F.B.I. Surveillance Bill." *New York Times*, August 14. Accessed July 1, 2021. https://www.nytimes.com/2020/08/14/us/politics/mcconnell-fisa-bill.html?searchResultPosition=8.

Savage, Charlie. 2020b. "U.S. Used Patriot Act to Gather Logs of Website Visitors." *New York Times*, December 3. Accessed July 2, 2021. https://www.nytimes.com/2020/12/03/us/politics/section-215-patriot-act.html?searchResultPosition=28.

Savage, Charlie, and Sharon LaFraniere. 2018. "Republicans Claim Surveillance Power Abuses in Russia Inquiry." *New York Times*, January 19. Accessed July 3, 2021. https://www.nytimes.com/2018/01/19/us/politics/republicans-surveillance-trump-russia-inquiry.html?searchResultPosition=6.

Savage, Charlie, and Michael Shear. 2013. "President Moves to Ease Worries on Surveillance." *New York Times*, August 9. Accessed July 3, 2021. https://www.nytimes.com/2013/08/10/us/politics/obama-news-conference.html?searchResultPosition=4.

Savage, Charlie, Eileen Sullivan, and Nicholas Fandos. 2018. "House Extends Surveillance Law, Rejecting New Privacy Safeguards." *New York Times*, January 11. Accessed July 1, 2021. https://www.nytimes.com/2018/01/11/us/politics/fisa-surveillance-congress-trump.html?searchResultPosition=4.

Steinhauer, Jennifer, and Jonathan Weisman. 2015. "U.S. Surveillance in Place Since 9/11 Is Sharply Limited." *New York Times*, June 2. Accessed July 1, 2021. https://www.nytimes.com/2015/06/03/us/politics/senate-surveillance-bill-passes-hurdle-but-showdown-looms.html?searchResultPosition=13.

Stolberg, Sheryl Gay. 2006. "Domestic Surveillance: The Democrats; Balancing Act by Democrats at Hearing." *New York Times*, February 7. Accessed July 4, 2021. https://www.nytimes.com/2006/02/07/us/domestic-surveillance-the-democrats-balancing-act-by-democrats-at.html?searchResultPosition=4.

Tau, Byron, and Michelle Hackman. 2020. "Federal Agencies Use Cellphone Location Data for Immigration Enforcement." *Wall Street Journal*, February 7. Accessed July 1, 2021. https://www.wsj.com/articles/federal-agencies-use-cellphone-location-data-for-immigration-enforcement-11581078600.

U.S. Congress. 2001. "United and Strengthening America by Providing Appropriate Tools Required to Intercept and Obstruct Terrorism (USA Patriot Act) Act of 2001." HR 3162. 107th Cong., 1st sess., introduced in House October 23, 2001. Accessed July 1, 2021. https://www.congress.gov/107/plaws/publ56/PLAW-107publ56.pdf.

U.S. Congress. 2014. "USA Freedom Act." HR 3361. 113th Cong., 2nd sess., passed May 15, 2014. Accessed July 2, 2021. https://www.congress.gov/113/crpt/hrpt452/CRPT-113hrpt452-pt1.pdf.

U.S. Senate. 1972. "Army Surveillance of Civilians: A Documentary Analysis." Subcommittee on Constitutional Rights, Committee on the Judiciary, U.S. Senate. Accessed October 6, 2022. https://archive.org/details/Army-Surveillance-Civilians-1972/mode/2up.

U.S. Senate. 1973. "Military Surveillance of Civilian Politics." Subcommittee on Constitutional Rights, Committee on the Judiciary, U.S. Senate. Accessed October 6, 2022. https://archive.org/details/Military-Surveillance-Civilian-Politics-1973.

U.S. Senate. 1976a. "Final Report of the Select Committee to Study Governmental Operations with Respect to Intelligence Activities. Book III. Supplementary Detailed Staff Reports on Intelligence Activities and the Rights of Americans." April 23. Accessed July 2, 2021. https://web.archive.org/web/20130113101946/http://www.icdc.com/~paulwolf/cointelpro/churchfinalreportIIIj.htm.

U.S. Senate. 1976b. "Final Report of the Select Committee to Study Governmental Operations with Respect to Intelligence Activities. Book II. Intelligence Activities and the Rights of Americans." April 26. Accessed July 2, 2021. https://www.intelligence.senate.gov/sites/default/files/94755_II.pdf.

Weisman, Jonathan. 2013. "House Defeats Effort to Rein in N.S.A. Data Gathering." *New York Times*, July 24. Accessed July 3, 2021. https://www.nytimes.com/2013/07/25/us/politics/house-defeats-effort-to-rein-in-nsa-data-gathering.html.

Weisman, Jonathan, and Jennifer Steinhauer. 2015. "Patriot Act Faces Revisions Backed by Both Parties." *New York Times*, April 30. Accessed July 1, 2021. https://www.nytimes.com/2015/05/01/us/politics/patriot-act-faces-revisions-backed-by-both-parties.html?searchResultPosition=4.

Wyden, Ron. 2022. "Wyden and Heinrich: Newly Declassified Documents Reveal Previously Secret CIA Bulk Collection, Problems with CIA Handling of Americans' Information." U.S. Senator Ron Wyden, February 10. Accessed February 13, 2022. https://www.wyden.senate.gov/news/press-releases/wyden-and-heinrich-newly-declassified-documents-reveal-previously-secret-cia-bulk-collection-problems-with-cia-handling-of-americans-information.

Zengerle, Jason. 2017. "What (If Anything) Does Carter Page Know?" *New York Times*, December 18. Accessed July 3, 2021. https://www.nytimes.com/2017/12/18/magazine/what-if-anything-does-carter-page-know.html.

Gun Control

At a Glance

The political debate over gun control involves two conflicting interests: an individual's constitutional right to keep and bear arms versus the government's responsibility to protect its citizens from violence. Gun control laws have existed throughout U.S. history, primarily at the state level. The Gun Control Act of 1968 contributed to a national debate on gun regulations that has permeated American politics ever since its passage. While public opinion polls show that most Americans favor some types of gun control, the gun lobby has played a significant role in limiting gun control policies. Recent U.S. Supreme Court rulings have prioritized the Second Amendment's right to keep and bear arms over restrictive gun legislation. Despite the gun lobby's efforts and the Court's rulings, in 2022, Democratic president Joe Biden signed the first bipartisan gun control law to be enacted since 1994. Democrats have been more supportive of government restrictions on firearms, while Republicans have been more supportive of gun rights.

According to many Democrats . . .

- Gun control is necessary to protect society from gun violence.
- Second Amendment rights should be respected but should also be subject to reasonable regulations to protect public health and safety.

According to many Republicans . . .

- Gun ownership allows Americans to protect their homes and communities.
- The Second Amendment right to keep and bear arms is an important constitutional guarantee to protect citizens from an oppressive government.

———————

Overview

The Second Amendment provides that "[a] well regulated Militia, being necessary to the security of a free State, the right of the people to keep and bear Arms, shall not be infringed." Although this amendment was ratified in 1791 as part of the Bill of Rights, the debate over its meaning was fairly low-key until the 1970s, when it intensified dramatically, and has had a continued impact on American politics.

From the colonial era until the early twentieth century, restrictions on guns and other weapons were enacted by states. President Franklin Roosevelt's efforts to expand the power of the federal government during the Great Depression included a "New Deal on Crime." The National Firearms Act of 1934, the first federal law restricting guns, was part of this initiative. The Roosevelt administration believed this federal law was needed because states lacked adequate financial resources to stop the highly publicized criminal activity of gangsters, such as Al Capone and Bonnie and Clyde, who earned notoriety during Prohibition and the Great Depression. The law imposed a tax on the manufacture or sale of gangster-style weapons such as machine guns and sawed-off shotguns and required those sales to be registered. This was followed by the National Firearms Act of 1938, which required interstate gun dealers to be licensed and to record their sales. It also prohibited the sale of firearms to individuals who had been indicted or convicted of violent crimes.

Federal gun control legislation reemerged as a national issue in the 1960s after the assassination of President John F. Kennedy, riots in multiple American cities, images of the Black Panther Party openly carrying guns, and the 1968 assassinations of civil rights leader Dr. Martin Luther King, Jr. and Democratic presidential hopeful Senator Robert F. Kennedy. The Gun Control Act of 1968 amended the National Firearms Act of 1934 by prohibiting (1) the interstate sale of firearms through the mail, (2) the interstate sales of handguns, and (3) the sale of firearms to felons and the mentally ill. The law also raised the legal age to purchase a weapon to twenty-one, required individuals involved in manufacturing, importing, or selling firearms as a business to obtain a federal license, and required gun dealers to maintain records of their sales.

The National Rifle Association (NRA) has played a pivotal role in the gun control debate. When the organization was founded in 1871 to promote rifle shooting, it supported early state legislative efforts to limit access to firearms. The NRA even supported the National Firearms Act of 1934, although it successfully lobbied against a provision that would have taxed the sale of handguns. As the gun control issue became increasingly politicized in the 1960s and 1970s, though, NRA hardliners who were opposed to increased government restrictions on guns seized control of the organization at its annual meeting in 1977. In 1980, the organization made its first-ever presidential endorsement when it announced its support for Republican nominee Ronald Reagan. The NRA has been a staunch ally of the Republican Party ever since.

In 1981, a mentally ill gunman, John Hinckley Jr., shot President Reagan, White House Press Secretary James Brady (who was permanently disabled in the attack), and two law enforcement officers with a cheap handgun known as a Saturday night special. Unswayed by the attack, Reagan continued to support gun rights. He signed the GOP-supported Firearm Owner Protection Act of 1986, which amended the Gun Control Act of 1968. This law limited the Bureau of Alcohol, Tobacco, and Firearms (ATF) to inspecting licensed gun dealers once per year—a response to NRA complaints that ATF agents were harassing dealers with multiple inspections.

The law also prohibited the federal government from maintaining a national gun registry. Republicans argue that such a registry violates gun owners' privacy rights because it gives the government information that could be used to seize weapons. The Firearm Owners Protection Act also authorized gun owners to transport firearms through states where they were banned and permitted ammunition shipments through mail. The law prohibited civilian transfer or possession of machine guns. This was a minor provision that had limited impact since machine guns had been prohibited since 1934.

While Reagan maintained his support for gun rights even after the assassination attempt, James Brady, who was paralyzed after being shot in the head, joined with his wife Sarah to become vocal and influential proponents of gun control. The Brady Handgun Violence Prevention Act was introduced in Congress several times but was opposed by Congressional Republicans, the NRA, and President George H. W. Bush, an NRA member. In 1993, however, Democrats controlled both chambers of Congress and the White House, and the bill finally passed through Congress and went to Democrat Bill Clinton's desk for his signature. The law requires federally licensed gun dealers to conduct background checks on gun purchasers to prevent potentially dangerous individuals from obtaining weapons. Because the law does not apply to private sales, it is possible to buy a handgun without a background check. Private sales often occur at gun shows where vendors sell weapons resulting in a gun show loophole.

In 1994, Clinton signed the Public Safety and Recreational Firearms Use Protection Act, also known as the Assault Weapons Ban, which prohibited the manufacture, transfer, or possession of semiautomatic weapons. It also prohibited the manufacture of large capacity ammunition feeding devices that could accommodate ten or more rounds. The law included a grandfather clause allowing individuals who owned or possessed such weapons or ammunition prior to the law's enactment to keep them without penalty.

The Assault Weapons Ban passed the House in 1994 by a vote of 216-214: 177 Democrats, 38 Republicans, and 1 Independent voted for the bill. Former presidents Jimmy Carter, Gerald Ford, and Ronald Reagan wrote a letter to the House of Representatives supporting the bill, in which they noted that 77 percent of Americans supported such a ban. Reagan also wrote to individual Republicans to ask for their vote. The bill narrowly passed in the Senate by a vote of 52-48. The law contained a sunset provision meaning that it would expire after ten years unless Congress voted to renew it—which it did not; as a result, the law disappeared off the books in 2004. Democratic senator Dianne Feinstein, the author of the original bill, attempted to renew the ban several times, most notably in 2013 after the mass killing at Sandy Hook Elementary School, but she was unsuccessful.

Although the NRA was unable to stop the Brady Law and the Assault Weapons Ban from being enacted, it soared in political influence in the late 1990s. In the 2000s, the NRA supported the Protection of Lawful Commerce in Arms Act of 2005, which protected gun manufacturers, distributors, and dealers from civil liability when their products were used in a criminal act. The organization was concerned that Second Amendment rights would be indirectly denied if gun manufacturers were held responsible for gun violence. Republican president George W. Bush signed the law, which had bipartisan support in Congress.

The political debate over gun control included arguments about the Second Amendment's protection of an individual's right to keep and bear arms. The U.S. Supreme Court had rarely addressed the Second Amendment before its ruling in *District of Columbia v. Heller* (2008). In a 5-4 ruling, the Court invalidated DC gun regulations, which banned the possession of handguns (except those purchased prior to 1975) in the home and required other firearms in the home to be kept unloaded and disassembled or equipped with a trigger lock. The majority held that the Second Amendment protected an individual's right to own firearms for self-defense in the home and that DC's policies violated that right. The dissenting justices argued that the amendment protected a collective right for members of a militia to possess weapons to protect the state. Since *Heller* involved the District of Columbia, which is not a state, the Court could not require states to follow its interpretation of the amendment until *McDonald v. City of Chicago* (2010). Here, a five-member majority of the Court invalidated Chicago laws that effectively banned the possession of handguns. The majority, relying on its decision in *Heller*, emphasized that policies preventing gun ownership for self-defense in the home violated the Second Amendment. The dissenting justices renewed the critique of *Heller*'s historical underpinnings arguing that it was flawed and that there was little evidence that the Second Amendment protected an individual's right to keep and bear arms.

After these rulings, commentators speculated about the constitutionality of state gun regulations that applied outside the home. In *New York State Rifle & Pistol Association v. Bruen* (2022), the Court invalidated concealed carry restrictions in six states. These regulations required individuals to demonstrate a need to carry a concealed weapon before they could obtain a permit to carry. In a 6-3 ruling, the Court held that the laws interfered with an individual's right to keep and bear arms. It held that the right to have a gun for self-defense was not limited to the home and that the state regulations prevented individuals from carrying a firearm for that purpose. The dissenting justices argued that the ruling wrongly interfered with the state's ability to prevent its citizens from the substantial threat of gun violence.

Public opinion polls indicate that Americans in both parties support several gun control policies. According to a 2018 Pew Research Center poll, 89 percent of Republicans (including independent-leaning Republican) and 89 percent of

Democrats (including independent-leaning Democrat) believe that mentally ill people should be prohibited from purchasing weapons. Moreover, 86 percent of Democrats and 83 percent of Republicans favor denying gun sales to individuals on federal no-fly or watch lists. Similarly, significant majorities in each party favor background checks for private sales and at gun shows (91 percent of Democrats and 79 percent of Republicans). The greatest partisan differences are on the issues of allowing K–12 teachers to carry guns in school—69 percent of Republicans support these policies compared with only 22 percent of Democrats. The numbers are similar for expanding concealed carry policies, which are supported by 68 percent of Republicans and 26 percent of Democrats. Overall, 57 percent of Americans indicated that gun laws should be stricter (Pew Research Center 2018).

After high-profile shootings in a Buffalo, New York, grocery store and a Uvalde, Texas, elementary school, a group of twenty senators, ten Democrats and ten Republicans, created a working group to develop bipartisan gun control legislation. The Safer Communities Act of 2022 passed the Senate by a vote of 65-33 and the House by a vote of 234-193. In each chamber, fifteen Republicans joined with every Democrat to pass the legislation. The law expands background checks for gun buyers under age twenty-one so that authorities could examine their juvenile and mental health records. It contains a provision preventing "straw purchases" making it illegal to purchase a firearm for someone who is not legally allowed to own one. It also allocates federal money for mental health resources, school safety, and crisis intervention programs. The latter may include red flag laws, which allow judges to take guns from individuals who pose a danger to themselves or others.

Public opinion polls taken after the law was passed demonstrated that while 64 percent of Americans supported the law, 78 percent believed it would do little or nothing to reduce gun violence. There was a stark difference among Republicans and Democrats who were surveyed concerning the enactment of additional gun control laws. Democrats supported the proposal (89 percent) while Republicans did not (66 percent) (Pew Research Center 2022). The political parties have addressed gun control policies since their 1968 platforms. While most Americans support some form of gun control, the gun lobby has exerted a considerable amount of influence on the political process since the 1980 presidential election. The salience of gun control has varied by election. The Republicans Party addressed gun rights prominently in the 2000s and especially since 2012. Democrats emphasized gun control policies in the 1990s and since 2016. Republicans have been more supportive of gun rights, while Democrats have been more supportive of government regulations.

Republicans

In the late 1960s, Republicans supported limiting criminal access to handguns and emphasized support for the right to keep and bear arms. The party opposed the Brady Bill and the Assault Weapons Ban in the 1990s. While Republicans have since embraced background checks, the party has opposed mandatory federal registration of firearms, lawsuits against gun manufacturers, restrictions on assault weapons and large ammunition clips, and extending the background check system.

The party platforms from 1968 to 1988 contained brief statements on gun control. The 1968 and 1972 platforms emphasized that states should be primarily responsible for implementing restrictions on firearms. The 1972 platform also pledged to "intensify efforts to prevent criminal access to all weapons," especially handguns. The language of the 1976 platform differed by stating that the party supported the right of citizens to keep and bear arms. In 1980, the party stated that it opposed federal registration of firearms and criticized provisions of the Gun Control Act of 1968 that restrained "the law-abiding citizen in his legitimate use of firearms." The 1984 and 1988 platforms continued support for the right to keep and bear arms and for stiff, mandatory penalties for criminals who violate gun laws.

President Reagan echoed this language two years after he was shot in a failed assassination attempt. In a 1983 address to the annual meeting of the NRA, he stated that "[g]uns don't make criminals. Hard-core criminals use guns. And locking them up, the hard-core criminals up, and throwing away the key is the best gun-control law we could ever have." He argued that gun control laws only harm law-abiding citizens. "It's a nasty truth, but those who seek to inflict harm are not fazed by gun control laws. I happen to know this from personal experience" (Hoffman 1983).

In 1989, President George H. W. Bush issued an executive order implementing a permanent ban on importing most foreign-made semiautomatic assault weapons because criminals frequently used them in drug-related crimes. The ban was criticized by the NRA, which pledged to "fight this decision in the courts, on Capitol Hill, and at the ballot box" (Rasky 1989). Bush, however, opposed the Brady Bill despite overwhelming public support for it. Even former president Ronald Reagan offered his support for the Brady Bill in a 1991 speech, ten years after the assassination attempt. He stated that "I want to tell all of you here today something that I'm not sure you know. You do know that I'm a member of the NRA. My position on the right to bear arms is well known. But I want you to know something else. And I'm going to say it in clear unmistakable language. I support the Brady bill and I urge the Congress to enact it" (Morganthau 1991).

In the 1992 platform, Republicans continued to defend the right to keep and bear arms and support stiff mandatory sentences for those who use firearms in a crime. Notably, the NRA refused to endorse George H. W. Bush during this campaign due to his ban on importing semiautomatic assault weapons. In 1995, Bush publicly resigned his lifetime NRA membership because the organization refused to apologize for remarks made by its president, Wayne LaPierre, in a fundraising letter to NRA members. LaPierre described federal law enforcement agents as "jack-booted thugs," and Bush responded, "To attack . . . any government law enforcement people as 'wearing Nazi bucket helmets and black storm trooper uni-forms' wanting to 'attack law abiding citizens' is a vicious slander on good people."

In 1995, prior to announcing his candidacy for the Republican presidential nomination, Senate Majority Leader Bob Dole assured the NRA that repealing the Assault Weapons Ban was a legislative priority. In a letter to the organization, Dole stated, "As long as I am Senate majority leader, I will continue to do everything to prevent passage of anti-Second Amendment legislation in the Senate" (Gray 1995). However, his unwillingness to schedule a vote on the issue when he was majority leader concerned NRA members. The 1996 platform, in addition to statements that the party would defend the right to bear arms and keep guns from criminals, pledged that the party would "promote training in the safe usage of firearms, espe-cially in programs for women and the elderly."

In the 2000s, platforms more specifically emphasized the party's commitment to protecting Second Amendment rights than in previous platforms. The 2000 platform characterized self-defense as a "basic human right" and supported gun training programs in that context. It also stated that it was an individual's respon-sibility to safely use and store firearms. The party pledged to vigorously enforce existing gun laws. The NRA endorsed Republican nominee George W. Bush in the 2000 campaign. However, the organization limited its campaign on behalf of Bush due to the unpopularity of their views among the general public.

The 2004 platform praised President Bush and Congressional Republicans for their efforts in protecting the Second Amendment. Specifically, it noted the Bush administration's efforts in expanding opportunities for hunters and the passage of the Law Enforcement Officers Safety Act, allowing active and retired law enforce-ment officers to carry concealed weapons in public while they are off duty. Addi-tionally, the platform highlighted the role of Congressional Republicans in "seeking to stop frivolous lawsuits against firearms manufacturers, which is a transparent attempt to deprive citizens of their Second Amendment rights."

The 2008 platform, in addition to reiterating many of the provisions from 2004, applauded the U.S. Supreme Court's *Heller* decision and called on the next pres-ident to appoint judges who would respect the Constitution. It also stated that policies such as national registration and federal licensing requirements penalize law-abiding citizens and do not reduce violent crime. Prior to his 2008 presidential campaign, Republican nominee Senator John McCain had supported closing the gun show loophole by requiring background checks on gun sales at gun shows. In a campaign speech given to the NRA, McCain conceded that he had past differences with the organization, which had labeled him as "one of the premier flag-carriers for enemies of the Second Amendment." McCain highlighted his record "opposing efforts to ban guns, ban ammunition, ban magazines, and dismiss gun owners as some kind of fringe group unwelcome in modern in America."

In the 2012 platform, the party expanded its definition of Second Amendment rights to include the right to obtain and store ammunition without registration.

Additionally, it opposed legislation limiting the capacity of clips or magazines. While previous platforms limited self-defense rights to the home, the 2012 platform supported the "fundamental right" to self-defense anywhere a law-abiding citizen had a legal right to be, along with federal legislation that would allow individuals with carry permits to carry firearms in any state that issued them. Former Massachusetts governor Mitt Romney, the party's 2012 nominee, had supported gun control at various points in his career. In a 1994 U.S. Senate bid, he stated that his views did not "line up" with those of the NRA. As Massachusetts governor, Romney signed legislation banning assault weapons. Just before his first presidential campaign, Romney became an NRA member, and during both the 2008 and 2012 campaigns, he asserted his support for gun rights.

In 2016, the party platform was very similar to the 2012 platform. As the Republican nominee and as president, Donald Trump advocated a wide range of gun control policies. Before he was a politician, Trump supported the 1994 Assault Weapons Ban, but in a March 2016 Republican debate, he stated that he no longer supported it.

In 2018, Trump "stunned" Republicans on live television by backing several gun control measures, including closing the gun show loophole and preventing mentally ill individuals and dangerous individuals from owning guns by extending background checks. Regarding mentally ill individuals, Trump stated, "I like taking the guns early. Take the guns first, go through due process second." Trump was criticized in a *USA Today* editorial for his shifting rhetoric on gun control laws. After a weekend in which thirty-one individuals were shot and killed in two separate incidents, Trump suggested several proposals to address gun violence, including extending background checks and promoting red flag laws that allow judges to take guns from individuals who pose a danger to themselves or others. According to the editorial, "After pushback from gun rights supporters, Trump put the issue on ice." Indeed, he threatened to veto Democratic bills that would have extended background checks claiming that they would interfere with Second Amendment rights. Trump did, however, issue an executive order imposing a ban on bump stocks after the worst mass shooting in modern U.S. history. In Las Vegas, Nevada, a gunman opened fire on concertgoers killing sixty and injuring more than five hundred with a rifle equipped with a bump stock. Bump stocks are added to rifles to significantly increase their firepower.

After the Court's ruling in *Bruen*, many Republicans indicated that they supported the decision. House Minority Leader Kevin McCarthy characterized the New York regulations as "burdensome" and applauded the ruling, which "rightfully ensures the right of all law-abiding Americans to defend themselves without unnecessary government interference."

In 2022, although enough Congressional Republicans joined with Democrats to pass the Safer Communities Act, most opposed the legislation. Republican congressman and minority whip Steve Scalise urged his fellow House Republicans

Republicans Emphasize Individual Factors Rather than Regulations to Address Gun Violence

On August 5, 2019, President Donald Trump delivered a speech after two mass shootings over one weekend in El Paso, Texas, and Dayton, Ohio, killing thirty-one people. Trump emphasized individual factors, such as violent video games and mental health issues, over stricter gun regulations.

In the two decades since Columbine, our nation has watched with rising horror and dread as one mass shooting has followed another.

We cannot allow ourselves to feel powerless. . . . We must seek real, bipartisan solutions.

First, we must do a better job of identifying and acting on early warning signs. I am directing the Department of Justice to work in partisan—partnership with local, state, and federal agencies, as well as social media companies, to develop tools that can detect mass shooters before they strike.

As an example, the monster in the Parkland high school in Florida had many red flags against him, and yet nobody took decisive action. Nobody did anything. Why not?

Second, we must stop the glorification of violence in our society. This includes the gruesome and grisly video games that are now commonplace. It is too easy today for troubled youth to surround themselves with a culture that celebrates violence.

Third, we must reform our mental health laws to better identify mentally disturbed individuals who may commit acts of violence and make sure those people not only get treatment, but, when necessary, involuntary confinement. Mental illness and hatred pulls the trigger, not the gun.

Fourth, we must make sure that those judged to pose a grave risk to public safety do not have access to firearms, and that, if they do, those firearms can be taken through rapid due process. That is why I have called for red flag laws, also known as extreme risk protection orders.

Today, I am also directing the Department of Justice to propose legislation ensuring that those who commit hate crimes and mass murders face the death penalty.

I am open and ready to listen and discuss all ideas that will actually work and make a very big difference.

Source

"Remarks by President Trump on the Mass Shootings in Texas and Ohio—the White House." n.d. The White House. Accessed November 23, 2022. https://trumpwhitehouse.archives .gov/briefings-statements/remarks-president-trump-mass-shootings-texas-ohio/.

to oppose the law. He stated that the "legislation takes the wrong approach in attempting to curb violent crimes." And that "House Republicans are committed to identifying and solving the root causes of violent crimes, but doing so must not infringe upon" Second Amendment freedoms (Shabad, Wong, and Stewart 2022). Senate Minority Leader Mitch McConnell, however, supported the legislation. He argued that the law imposed necessary regulations that would make schools and communities safer without infringing on Second Amendment rights. He noted that the law "contains zero new restrictions, zero new waiting periods, zero mandates and zero bans of any kind for law-abiding gun owners" (Watkins 2022).

Republicans have sought to protect Second Amendment rights by opposing gun regulations, including bans on assault weapons and large capacity magazines. The NRA has played a significant role in the party's stance on this issue although its influence appears to be waning in the wake of mass shootings at elementary schools. More recently, the party has forcefully asserted that Americans have a right to own and carry guns for personal protection.

Democrats

The Democratic Party's early gun control stance emphasized handgun regulations, strict sentences for individuals who violate gun laws, and protection for hunters and sportsmen. After de-emphasizing gun control in the 1980s, Democrats were instrumental in enacting the Brady Law and the Assault Weapons Ban in the 1990s. More recently, the party has sought to balance the protection of gun owners' Second Amendment rights with "commonsense" gun control measures. It supports reinstating the Assault Weapons Ban, closing the gun show loophole, and improving and expanding the background check system.

During the 1968 presidential campaign, Democrats touted the party's role in passing the Gun Control Act of 1968 as "a step toward putting the weapons of wanton violence beyond the reach of criminal and irresponsible hands." The platform pledged to promote and enforce gun control legislation at the federal, state, and local levels of government. The Democratic nominee, Vice President Hubert Humphrey, advocated stricter gun control legislation than President Johnson by supporting national gun registration.

During the 1970s, the party consistently focused on handgun regulation. The 1972 platform noted that three out of four killings of police officers were with handguns, and that those weapons were used to assassinate one presidential candidate, Bobby Kennedy, and wound another, George Wallace. The platform specifically supported banning Saturday night specials. In 1976, the party also supported mandatory sentencing for individuals who committed a felony with a gun, and the right of sportsmen to have guns for hunting and target-shooting purposes. The 1980 platform reiterated the position expressed in 1976 but did not address mandatory sentencing.

In 1984, the party's stance on gun control consisted of a single statement: "We support tough restraints on the manufacture, transportation, and sale of snub-nosed handguns, which have no legitimate sporting use and are used in a high proportion of violent crimes." The 1988 platform only sought to "enforce a ban on 'cop killer' bullets that had no purpose other than the killing and maiming of law enforcement officers." The 1988 Democratic nominee, Massachusetts governor

Michael Dukakis, backed a seven-day waiting period for pistols and a ban on Saturday night specials. Dukakis opposed restrictions on guns used for hunting and target sports and to protect homes or businesses.

To combat the perception that Democrats were "soft" on crime, the 1992 and 1996 platforms and campaigns emphasized gun control legislation. In 1992, the platform supported the provisions of the Brady Bill and a ban on assault weapons. The party also pledged to implement stronger sentences for criminals who use guns and on people who sell guns to children. While campaigning in 1992, Bill Clinton criticized President George H. W. Bush for refusing to sign the Brady Bill. At a press conference attended by police officers in Dallas, Texas, Clinton argued that by failing to sign the bill, Bush endangered the lives of law enforcement officers. The 1996 platform contained the most extensive gun control plank to date. It was critical of Republicans for holding the Brady Bill "hostage" for the gun lobby until President Clinton signed it. The platform asserted that the law stopped more than sixty thousand "felons, fugitives, and stalkers" from purchasing guns. It also highlighted the passage of the Assault Weapons Ban while acknowledging that many Democrats lost their seats in Congress due to their defiance of the gun lobby. Indeed, Democrats suffered significant defeats in the 1994 midterm elections, losing their majorities in both Houses of Congress. The party lost control of the House of Representatives for the first time in forty years as Republicans gained fifty-four House seats and eight Senate seats. The party's gun control stance was a significant factor in these losses.

Despite those losses, the 2000 platform praised Bill Clinton and Al Gore for "standing up to the gun lobby" and highlighted statistics showing declines in the rates of gun crimes. The platform supported "the rights of hunters, sportsmen, and legitimate gun owners" but criticized Republicans for their lack of response to the Columbine school shooting in 1999. The platform specified a list of proposals, including mandatory child safety locks and new restrictions on handgun purchases such as "a photo license I.D., a full background check, and a gun safety test." In addition, Gore pledged to veto any law that would prohibit lawsuits against gun manufacturers.

Compared with the 1996 and 2000 platforms, the 2004 platform was very brief. In one sentence, the party pledged to "protect Americans' Second Amendment right to own firearms, and [to] keep guns out of the hands of criminals and terrorists by fighting gun crime, reauthorizing the Assault Weapons Ban, and closing the gun show loophole, as President Bush proposed and failed to do." It was the party's first specific acknowledgment of the Second Amendment in a platform and an indicator that its previous stance supporting strict gun control initiatives had negative electoral consequences. According to Second Amendment scholar Adam Winkler (2012), "Democrats came to believe that even talking about gun control was a sure ticket home come Election Day." During the 2004 campaign, Democratic nominee Senator John Kerry, an avid hunter who had supported the Brady

Law, the Assault Weapons Ban, legislation to close the gun show loophole, and mandatory gunlocks, emphasized his support for the Second Amendment. Kerry had long supported the right of hunters and sportsmen to own weapons appropriate for those activities but drew the line at assault weapons.

The Democratic strategy, as evidenced by specific proposals in platforms and by their presidential candidates, has emphasized a move from advocating strict gun control policies to endorsing a balance between the rights of law-abiding gun owners and the safety of communities. The 2008 platform reiterated the party's support for the Second Amendment but stated that reasonable regulations based on local needs were important. The platform advocated "commonsense" gun laws and provided several examples, including closing the gun show loophole, improving the background check system, and reinstating the Assault Weapons Ban. The 2012 platform reinforced the party's support for the Second Amendment and pledged to "preserve Americans' . . . right to own and use firearms" subject to reasonable regulation. It also emphasized, as had the 2008 platform, that there was a need for commonsense regulations, such as the Assault Weapons Ban and closing the gun show loophole, to prevent criminals from obtaining guns.

As president, Barack Obama signed legislation allowing loaded guns in national parks but did not pursue an aggressive gun control agenda. Nevertheless, NRA executive vice president Wayne LaPierre criticized the president's passive record on gun control as "a massive Obama conspiracy to deceive voters and hide his true intentions to destroy the Second Amendment." In 2013, after the defeat of a bipartisan bill to expand background checks, Obama claimed that the NRA "willfully lied" about a bill to expand background checks claiming that it would create a federal gun registry even though that was specifically prohibited in the bill. Obama pled for "meaningful action" on gun control in an emotional press conference in 2016 (Koren 2016). He proposed eliminating the gun show loophole, expending more resources to improve the effectiveness of the background check system, and more research on smart gun technology to improve firearm safety. He also proposed stronger enforcement of existing gun laws, additional resources for mental health treatment, and including information about an individual's mental health in the background check database.

Unlike the more recent platforms, the 2016 platform did not mention the Second Amendment but rather suggested that the party "must finally take sensible action to address gun violence" while also respecting the rights of responsible gun owners. The platform specifically addressed expanding background checks, closing "dangerous loopholes," repealing the Protection of Lawful Commerce in Arms Act (PLCAA), and banning assault weapons and large capacity ammunition magazines. It also pledged to keep guns out of "the hands of terrorists, intimate partner abusers, other violent criminals, and those with severe mental health issues." During the 2016 campaign, Democratic nominee Hillary Clinton frequently addressed gun control and articulated stances consistent with the platform. As

Biden Argues Gun Violence Is Motivated by Racism

Then Democratic presidential candidate, and former vice president, Joe Biden responded to President Trump's comments on gun control in an August 7, 2019, speech in Iowa. Biden criticized Trump for a "lack moral leadership" by refusing to acknowledge that racism was a cause of gun violence.

We have a problem with this rising tide of white supremacy in America, and we have a president who encourages and emboldens it.

His own FBI director recently testified to Congress that extreme right-wing groups, white nationalists posed the greatest threat to racially motivated domestic terrorism. And what has Trump done? He's poured fuel on the fire. He's retweeted postings from extremists and white nationalists. He's cutting funding, and in some cases, completely eliminated funding initiated by Barak, by the president and I, in our administration to counter violent extremism at home. Trump readily, eagerly attacks Islamic terrorism, but can barely bring himself to use the words white supremacy. Even when he says it, he doesn't appear to believe it. He seems more concerned about losing their votes than beating back this hateful ideology. He says guns are not the problem in mass shootings. The issue is mental health. It's a dodge. Hatred isn't a mental health issue. I can tell you as the guy along with Senator Dianne Feinstein, got the assault weapons banned and the high capacity magazines banned in this country for 10 years, if elected presidents, we will do it again. We will do it again.

A hundred rounds date, 30 round clips in El Paso. They'll be banned. And when we do it, we will put in place a buy back program to get as many as these military style weapons of war as possible off the street, and we need a domestic terrorism law. We can do it without infringing on anyone's free speech, without tampering with anybody's liberties. Quite simply, we have to make the same commitment as a nation to root out domestic terrorism that we have stopping international terrorism.

Source

"Joe Biden Iowa Trump Rebuke Speech Transcript August 7, 2019." 2019. Rev, August 7. Accessed November 23, 2022. https://www.rev.com/blog/transcripts/joe-biden-iowa -trump-rebuke-speech-transcript-august-7.

a senator, Clinton had supported gun control bills. However, her views changed when she ran for president in 2008 and supported "sensible regulation . . . consistent with the constitutional right to keep and bear arms." Republican nominee Donald Trump claimed that Clinton wanted to abolish the Second Amendment; however, she insisted that she was not seeking to repeal the amendment but rather to "keep guns out of the wrong hands."

The 2020 Democratic platform neither addressed the Second Amendment nor mentioned responsible gun ownership. Rather, it emphasized gun violence as a public health issue and pledged to "make gun violence a thing of the past." As in 2016, it vowed to ban assault weapons and large capacity magazines while also

preventing certain classes of people, including domestic abusers, hate crime perpetrators, and those who pose a danger to themselves or others, from obtaining
a gun. The campaign website of the 2020 Democratic nominee, former senator
and vice president Joe Biden, highlighted the candidate's record opposing the
NRA. Specifically, it noted his leadership in getting the Brady Law and Assault
Weapons Ban enacted. It also stated that Biden would respect the Second Amendment, which was limited. He advocated all the policies outlined in the platform
and echoed support for Obama's policies outlined in his 2016 press conference
(joebiden.com). After mass shootings in 2022, including one at an elementary
school, Biden and Congressional Democrats advocated for more gun regulations.
When Biden signed the Safer Communities Act, he noted that the law did not
impose as many regulations as he would have liked. He later offered several additional gun control proposals in his Safer America Plan. The proposals included
increased funding for the Bureau of Alcohol Tobacco and Firearms (ATF) to help
prevent gun trafficking, a ban on assault weapons and high capacity magazines,
and a stronger background check program that would require background checks
for almost all gun purchases (The White House 2022).

The Democratic Party has consistently advocated for gun regulations. Democrats passed significant gun regulations in the 1990s but paid a price for those laws
at the ballot box. The party and its presidential candidates softened their language
in the 2000s, but with an increase in the number of mass shootings, they support
more restrictions as a public health and safety measure.

Further Reading

Bruni, Frank. 2000. "Gore and Bush Clash Further on Firearms." *New York Times*, May 6.
    Accessed November 23, 2022. https://www.nytimes.com/2000/05/06/us/the-2000
    -campaign-the-gun-issue-gore-and-bush-clash-further-on-firearms.html.
Corasaniti, Nick. 2016. "Gun Control Group Backs Hillary Clinton and Pledges Help with
    Primary." *New York Times*, June 3. Accessed November 23, 2022. https://www.nytimes
    .com/2016/06/04/us/politics/hillary-clinton-gun-control.html?auth=login-email.
Dao, James. 2004. "N.R.A. Opens an All-Out Drive for Bush and Its Views." *New York
    Times*, April 16. Accessed November 23, 2022. https://www.nytimes.com/2004/04/16
    /us/2004-campaign-gun-group-nra-opens-all-drive-for-bush-its-views.html.
Democratic Party Platform. 1968–2020. American Presidency Project. Accessed November
    23, 2022.https://www.presidency.ucsb.edu/documents/presidential-documents-archive
    -guidebook/party-platforms-and-nominating-conventions-3.
Editorial Board of *USA Today*. 2019. "Trump on Gun Laws Is All Talk, No Action and More
    Deaths." *USA Today*, November 18. Accessed January 2, 2020. https://www.usatoday
    .com/story/opinion/2019/11/18/donald-trump-gun-laws-all-talk-no-action-editorials
    -debates/4224132002/.
Editors of the *National Review*. 2019. "Against Universal Background Checks." *National
    Review*, August 10. Accessed January 2, 2020. https://www.nationalreview.com/2019
    /08/against-universal-background-checks/.

Gray, Jerry. 1995. "Dole, in a 2d Nod to Right, Pledges to Fight Gun Ban." *New York Times*, March 18. Accessed January 3, 2020. https://www.nytimes.com/1995/03/18/us/dole -in-a-2d-nod-to-right-pledges-to-fight-gun-ban.html.

"Gun-Control Group Backs Clinton: Will It Make a Difference in 2016 Race?" 2006. *Christian Science Monitor*, June 4. Accessed January 6, 2020. https://www.csmonitor .com/USA/Politics/2016/0604/Gun-control-group-backs-Clinton-Will-it-make-a -difference-in-2016-race.

Haberman, Clyde. 2018. "Do Stronger Gun Laws Stand a Chance? It's Been an Uphill Battle." *New York Times*, April 30. Accessed December 11, 2019. https://www.nytimes .com/2018/04/29/us/gun-control-laws-retro-report.html.

Hoffman, David. 1983. "Reagan Denounces Gun Control Laws." *Washington Post*, May 7. Accessed January 6, 2020. https://www.washingtonpost.com/archive/politics /1983/05/07/reagan-denounces-gun-control-laws/c935ce47-4473-4203-aad8 -bde8d354cdc7/.

Koren, Marina. 2016. "President Obama's Emotional Speech on Gun Control." *The Atlantic*, January 5. Accessed October 26, 2019. https://www.theatlantic.com/politics/archive /2016/01/obama-executive-action-gun-control/422661/.

McCarthy, Kevin. 2022. "Leader McCarthy's Statement on the Supreme Court's Decision Regarding the Second Amendment." House Republican Leader, June 23. Accessed September 23, 2022. https://www.republicanleader.gov/leader-mccarthys-statement-on -the-supreme-courts-decision-regarding-the-second-amendment/.

"McCarthy Leads Renewed Gun Control Effort." 2008. *Newsday* [Melville, NY], January 8. *Gale OneFile: News*. Accessed November 23, 2022. https://link.gale.com/apps /doc/A173172902/STND?u=tel_a_carsonnc&sid=STND&xid=03bbe9ce.

Morganthau, Tony. 1991. "A Boost for Brady." *Newsweek*, April 7. Accessed January 3, 2020. https://www.newsweek.com/boost-brady-202258.

"Obama, Gun Control, and the Lesson He's Teaching Republicans." 2016. *Christian Science Monitor*, January 5. Accessed December 13, 2019. https://www.csmonitor.com/USA /Politics/2016/0105/Obama-gun-control-and-the-lesson-he-s-teaching-Republicans.

O'Keefe, Ed, and Karoun Demirjian. 2016. "In Wake of Orlando Shootings, Gun Control Getting a Fresh Look from GOP." *Washington Post*, June 15. Accessed December 12, 2019. https://www.washingtonpost.com/politics/in-wake-of-orlando-shootings-gun -control-plans-getting-a-fresh-look-from-gop/2016/06/15/e25e3b2a-3311-11e6-8758 -d58e76e11b12_story.html.

Palmer, Ewan. 2022. "What Donald Trump Has Said About Gun Control as He Heads to NRA Convention." *Newsweek*, May 27. Accessed September 20, 2022. https://www .newsweek.com/trump-gun-control-nra-texas-school-shooting-1710794.

Pew Research Center. 2018. "Gun Policy Remains Divisive, but Several Proposals Still Draw Bipartisan Support." May 30. Accessed January 2, 2020. https://www.pewresearch .org/politics/2018/10/18/gun-policy-remains-divisive-but-several-proposals-still -draw-bipartisan-support/.

Pew Research Center. 2022. "Broad Public Approval of New Gun Law, but Few Say It Will Do a Lot to Stem Gun Violence." July 11. Accessed September 1, 2022. https://www .pewresearch.org/politics/2022/07/11/broad-public-approval-of-new-gun-law-but -few-say-it-will-do-a-lot-to-stem-gun-violence/.

Porter, Tom. 2018. "Trump Moves to Ban Bump Stocks as Pressure on White House Over Gun Laws Intensifies after Florida Shooting." *Newsweek*, February 21. Accessed

September 20, 2022. https://www.newsweek.com/trump-moves-ban-bump-stocks
-pressure-white-house-over-gun-laws-intensifies-813986.

Rasky, Susan F. 1989. "Import Ban on Assault Rifles Becomes Permanent." *New York Times*,
July 8. Accessed November 8, 2019. https://www.nytimes.com/1989/07/08/us/import
-ban-on-assault-rifles-becomes-permanent.html.

Republican Party Platform. 1968–2012. American Presidency Project. Accessed November 23, 2022. https://www.presidency.ucsb.edu/documents/presidential-documents
-archive-guidebook/party-platforms-and-nominating-conventions-3.

Republican Party Platform. 2016. American Presidency Project. Accessed November 23, 2022.https://www.presidency.ucsb.edu/documents/presidential-documents-archive
-guidebook/party-platforms-and-nominating-conventions-3.

Shabad, Rebecca, Scott Wong, and Kyle Stewart. 2022. "House Republican Leaders to
Work in Opposition to Senate Gun Deal." *NBC News*, June 22. Accessed September
23, 2022. https://www.nbcnews.com/politics/congress/house-gop-whip-bipartisan
-gun-violence-prevention-bill-rcna34751.

Watkins, Morgan. 2022. "How Mitch McConnell, Rand Paul Voted on the Biggest Gun
Reform Bill in Decades—And Why." *Louisville Courier Journal*, June 24. Accessed
September 23, 2022. https://www.courier-journal.com/story/news/politics/mitch
-mcconnell/2022/06/24/why-did-mitch-mcconnell-vote-biggest-gun-reform-bill-in
-decades/7711139001/.

Weiner, Rachel. 2012. "Where Obama and Romney Stand on Gun Control." *Washington
Post*, July 20. Accessed December 12, 2019. https://www.washingtonpost.com/blogs
/the-fix/post/where-obama-and-romney-stand-on-gun-control/2012/07/20/gJQAw
MpNyW_blog.html.

The White House. 2022. "Fact Sheet: President Biden's Safer America Plan." August 1.
Accessed September 23, 2022. https://www.whitehouse.gov/briefing-room/statements
-releases/2022/08/01/fact-sheet-president-bidens-safer-america-plan-2/.

Winkler, Adam 2012. "Franklin Roosevelt: The Father of Gun Control." *New Republic*,
December 19. Accessed December 12, 2019. https://newrepublic.com/article/111266
/franklin-roosevelt-father-gun-control.

Health Care

At a Glance

Democrats and Republicans disagree over the extent to which the federal government should regulate health care. Democrats enacted the Patient Protection and Affordable Care Act (also referred to as the Affordable Care Act [ACA] or "Obamacare") in 2010 to decrease costs and increase access to health care. Republicans argue that the law is an inappropriate expansion of federal power and that it should be repealed. The parties have disagreed over the applicability of nondiscrimination provisions of the law to LGBT persons and over women's access to family planning services. The parties have also disagreed over the role of the federal government in addressing the COVID-19 pandemic with Democrats favoring vaccine mandates and Republicans arguing such mandates interfere with individual liberties.

According to many Democrats . . .

- The ACA should be expanded to increase access to health care.
- The ACA's nondiscrimination provisions apply to LGBT persons.
- The federal government should fund Planned Parenthood and other family planning organizations that provide various health-care services to women.
- The federal government should require businesses to adopt COVID-19 vaccine-or-test requirements to protect public health.

According to many Republicans . . .

- The ACA should be repealed.
- The ACA's nondiscrimination provision only applies to biological sex and not sexual orientation or gender identity.
- The federal government should defund Planned Parenthood and any organization that provides family planning and abortion services.
- The federal government should not require businesses to adopt COVID-19 vaccine-or-test mandates, because it limits individual freedom of choice.

———————

Overview

The political debate over U.S. health-care policy involves two interrelated issues: access and cost. The United States differs from other major industrialized nations by not offering national health insurance for its citizens. Since the mid-twentieth century, most insured Americans have obtained health insurance from their employers—which left millions of Americans uninsured. Although comprehensive health insurance reform had been proposed since Medicare and Medicaid were passed in the 1960s, it was not enacted until the ACA was passed in 2010.

Passage of this law, which sought to increase access and decrease costs of health care, was a partisan slugfest between Democrats who support more federal involvement in health care to achieve those goals, while Republicans favor a limited federal role arguing that leaving health care to the private sector results in lower costs and higher quality due to competition among health-care providers. Section 1557 of the ACA prohibits discrimination on the basis of "race, color, national origin, sex, age or disability in certain health programs and activities." Democrats argue that "sex" includes sexual orientation and gender identity, while Republicans argue that it does not. The ACA was controversial for many reasons, including coverage for certain aspects of women's health care. The law required insurance companies to cover essential health benefits, which was interpreted by the Department of Health and Human Services (HHS) to include contraceptives for women. Some businesses argued that the mandate forced them to subsidize certain contraceptives to their employees against their religious beliefs. Democrats support women's access to contraceptives, while Republicans prioritize religious liberty interests. Democrats support federal vaccine-or-test mandates, while Republicans argue that such mandates limit individual freedom.

Health-Care Access
Several U.S. presidents have attempted to increase access to health care since health-care costs began to soar in the early twentieth century with advances in medicine and medical technology. Democratic president Franklin Roosevelt considered including universal health care as part of the 1935 Social Security Act and Democratic president Harry Truman advocated for universal health care in the 1940s. While these efforts failed, Democratic president Lyndon Johnson worked with Congress to enact Medicare and Medicaid in 1965. These programs expanded health-care access to millions of Americans. Medicare is a federal government health-care program available to Americans over the age of sixty-five, the disabled, and individuals suffering from end-stage renal disease. Medicaid is an insurance program jointly administered by the federal government and the states primarily for low-income individuals. Republican president Richard Nixon also supported universal health care by mandating employer coverage, expanding Medicare, and replacing Medicaid with a federal program to provide

coverage for individuals who were not part of the first two groups. Nixon made this proposal during the Watergate scandal, which embattled and then ultimately ended his presidency. He also faced opposition from Democratic senator Ted Kennedy and other progressive Democrats, who hoped to expand Medicare to every American.

In 1993, universal health care was a high priority for Democratic president Bill Clinton and many members of his party. Convinced that the public would support an ambitious plan to expand health care to all Americans, including millions without insurance, he appointed First Lady Hillary Clinton to chair the Task Force on National Health Reform after only five days in office. The 1342-page bill produced by Clinton's task force proposed sweeping changes to health care, including the creation of a national health board, which would have oversight of the health-care system; regional health alliances from which every American would be required to obtain insurance if they did not have it through their employers; and spending caps for public and private insurance spending and for doctors' fees. The plan, however, was never voted on due to opposition from Republicans, insurance companies, and other sectors of the health-care industry.

The Battle over Obamacare

The ACA is the most significant health-care law to be passed since Medicare and Medicaid were enacted. Health-care reform was an important issue in the 2008 presidential election. When Democrat Barack Obama was elected in 2008, Democrats controlled Congress. In February 2009, just over a month into his presidency, Obama announced that reform was necessary due to the high costs of medical care and health insurance for millions of Americans.

In November 2009, the Democratic-controlled House of Representatives passed a health-care bill by a vote of 220–215, with one Republican voting for it and thirty-nine Democrats voting against it. In the Senate, Republicans threatened to filibuster a health-care reform bill, which forced Democrats to create a bill that would garner all 60 votes of their members. In December 2009, the bill passed the Senate 60–39 with no Republican votes. Because there were significant differences between the House and Senate versions of the bill, creating a compromise version of the bill that would appease conservative Senate Democrats and liberal House Democrats posed a major hurdle to the bill's passage.

Further complicating matters for the Democrats in their efforts to craft a compromise bill to send for Obama's signature was the loss of Senator Ted Kennedy, a champion of health-care reform, to brain cancer. A Republican won a special election to fill his seat in Massachusetts, reducing the number of Democrats to fifty-nine and costing the party its filibuster-proof majority. Democrats decided that the House would pass the Senate version of the bill and that any differences between the two would be dealt with in subsequent legislation passed through the budget reconciliation process, which only requires a majority vote in the Senate.

Ultimately, the bill passed without any Republican votes. President Obama signed the law in 2010.

The nine-hundred-odd-page legislation contains several major provisions. The individual mandate, also referred to as the minimum coverage requirement, requires individuals to purchase insurance for themselves and their dependents if they are not insured through their employers. Individuals who do not purchase insurance are required to pay a fee to the Internal Revenue Service (IRS). This provision was intended to lower insurance costs by spreading them throughout the population. The ACA also expanded Medicaid by increasing the number of individuals eligible for the program and the types of services provided. Because the program is jointly administered by the state and federal governments, this would have increased costs to the states. Congress funded the initial expansion of the program; however, states that refused to participate in the expansion would lose all federal Medicaid funding. The law also established state health-care exchanges from which uninsured individuals could purchase health insurance and required employers with over fifty employees to provide affordable health insurance to their employees or pay a fine.

Additional provisions of the law allowed young adults to remain on their parents' health insurance until they were twenty-six, required insurance companies to cover individuals who had preexisting medical conditions, prohibited insurance companies from denying coverage, eliminated lifetime limits on essential health-care services, such as hospitalization, and imposed regulations on annual dollar limits set by insurance companies for essential services. The law encouraged preventive health-care services by requiring insurance companies to cover health screenings, such as blood pressure and cholesterol, without out-of-pocket payments. These screenings allow health-care providers to find problems before they become more costly to treat. The law was estimated to expand health-care access to approximately thirty-two million of the forty-five million uninsured Americans.

Several provisions of the law were immediately challenged in court. In *National Federation of Independent Business v. Sebelius* (2012), the U.S. Supreme Court upheld the individual mandate by a 5–4 vote as a valid exercise of Congress' power to tax; however, it invalidated the Medicaid expansion provisions by a 7–2 vote. The Court found that because the federal government threatened to withhold Medicaid funding, the states were being unconstitutionally coerced into expanding the program. This ruling allowed states to choose whether to expand Medicaid coverage. By early 2022, thirty-eight states and the District of Columbia expanded Medicaid coverage. States that declined to expand the coverage were primarily located in the South where Republican governors opposed what they considered the overreach of federal power. The ACA has led to significant increases in the number of Americans who have health insurance. According to HHS, in early 2022, the number of uninsured fell to the lowest level in U.S. history. The ACA reduced the number of uninsured from almost 18 percent of the population in 2015 to 8 percent of the population in 2022 (Department of Health and Human Services 2022). Insurance rates rose at a lower rate than before the ACA's enactment. In the decade prior to the ACA, health insurance premiums rose by 7.9 percent for single coverage and 8.2 percent for family coverage. After the ACA, those percentages dropped to 4.0 percent and 4.6 percent, respectively (Patton 2020). The Inflation Reduction Act of 2022 expanded the ACA by lowering premiums for working families and extending coverage to three million more Americans (The White House 2022).

Health-Care Discrimination

After slavery was abolished, Black Americans were denied access to quality health care due to segregationist Jim Crow laws. Although the Civil Rights Act of 1964 prohibits discrimination on the basis of race color, or national origin in programs and activities that receive federal financial assistance, the law had a limited impact on Black health care, as it could not address issues related to access, such as the location of doctors' offices, hospitals, and lower quality of care (Newkirk 2017). The law also did little to desegregate medical facilities until Medicare and Medicaid were passed and medical facilities receiving those funds were required to integrate. In 1985, the Secretary of Health and Human Services, Margaret Heckler, issued the findings of a Task Force on Black and Minority Health, which recommended a national agenda for improving minority health.

The ACA—or Obamacare, as both opponents and supporters of the law often called it—was intended to reduce racial disparities in health care. Indeed, as Professor Jamila Michener stated in an analysis of race and the ACA, "The original bill contained 34 references to 'disparities,' 28 references to either 'discrimination' or 'non-discrimination,' 33 instances using either the word racial or race, and 35 instances using either the word ethnicity or ethnic. Though Barack Obama's approach to advancing his policy goals was often deracialized, the explicit emphasis on race in the ACA reveals a pronounced goal of diminishing racial disparities" in access and quality of health care in the United States (Michener 2020). The ACA reduced disparities in health insurance coverage, access to care, and utilization of health-care services (Michener 2020). Despite these gains, "health insurance inequities persist and are even greater in states that have not expanded Medicaid" (Ortega and Roby 2021). In an issue of the *Journal of the American Medical Association* dedicated to inequities in health care, public health professors Alexander Ortega and Dylan Roby argued that expanding health insurance is inadequate to combat structural racism in health-care delivery. They noted, for example, that even with free COVID-19 vaccines, there were racial inequities in vaccination rates, which led to disparities in COVID-19-related health issues.

Section 1557 of the ACA prohibits discrimination on the basis of "race, color, national origin, sex, age or disability in certain health programs and activities." In 2016, the Office of Civil Rights (OCR) in HHS issued a rule equating sex discrimination with gender identity discrimination. The rule was reversed by OCR under President Trump in 2019 and restored under President Biden in 2021. Democrats argue that the term "sex" is broad enough to include sexual orientation and gender identity, while Republicans argue that it only applies to biological sex.

Women's Reproductive Health

The ACA required that insurance companies cover preventive care and screenings for women without any cost-sharing requirement. Congress did not define what medical services constituted preventive care but rather left that determination to HHS. HHS issued a rule in 2010 that required insurance companies to cover contraceptives approved by the Food and Drug Administration (FDA); however, religious employers, such as churches, and religious nonprofit organizations who objected were exempt from this rule. Several employers argued that the rule violated the Religious Freedom Restoration Act (RFRA). In *Burwell v. Hobby Lobby* (2014), the U.S. Supreme Court ruled that closely held for-profit corporations had free exercise rights protected by RFRA. Hobby Lobby and two other family-owned businesses argued that providing access to four of the eighteen types of FDA-approved contraceptives violated their religious beliefs because they were more like abortions than contraceptives. In a 5–4 ruling, the Court held that these businesses could not be forced to provide coverage against their religious beliefs. Under Republican president Donald Trump, HHS implemented a rule allowing any employer with a religious or moral objection to opt out of providing contraceptives to their employees under the ACA. This rule was upheld by the U.S. Supreme Court by a 7–2 margin. In *Little Sisters of the Poor Saints Peter and Paul Home v. Pennsylvania* (2020), the Court held that the law was broad enough to allow for employer exemptions based on religious beliefs.

In addition to the ACA, other federal legislation addresses women's reproductive health. Title X of the Public Health Service Act of 1970 provides federal funding for family planning services primarily to low-income patients; however, the law prohibits the use of Title X funds for abortions. The Planned Parenthood Federation is an umbrella organization for the independent Planned Parenthood clinics, which receive Title X funds and Medicaid funds to provide a variety of health services to women. These services include testing and treating for sexually transmitted diseases, access to and information about contraceptives, and cancer screenings. Planned Parenthood provides access to abortion but cannot use federal funds to pay for the procedure. Republicans have argued that Planned Parenthood should be defunded because their clinics provide abortions. Democrats, conversely, argue that federal funds pay for women's health services, not abortions, and that the organization should continue to receive federal money.

In 2019, HHS fulfilled a campaign pledge by Donald Trump by implementing a rule prohibiting a health-care provider that received Title X funds from discussing abortion as an option to patients. The rule also applied when patients requested a referral to a clinic that could provide the service. The rule required Title X recipients to be physically separate from abortion providers, which meant that agencies providing abortion and other Title X services had to be in different offices. According to the Kaiser Family Foundation, 26 percent of Title X providers left the network including all Planned Parenthood clinics, and 3.1 million fewer individuals received care as a result (Long et al. 2020). In November 2021, the Biden administration revoked the rule.

In 2022, the U.S. Supreme Court overturned *Roe v. Wade* in a controversial 6–3 decision. Justice Samuel Alito wrote the majority opinion in *Dobbs v. Jackson Women's Health Organization*, holding that there was no constitutional right to privacy that allowed a woman to choose to terminate her pregnancy. The ruling allowed states to ban abortion. The three dissenting justices, appointed by Democratic presidents, argued that abortion bans create significant health-care problems for women. Justice Elena Kagan stated that "[e]xperts estimate that a ban on abortions increases maternal mortality by 21 percent, with white women facing a 13 percent increase in maternal mortality while black women face a 33 percent increase. Pregnancy and childbirth may also impose large-scale financial costs," and many women "still do not have adequate healthcare coverage before and after pregnancy; and, even when insurance coverage is available, healthcare services may be far away."

A draft of the *Dobbs* ruling was leaked before the Court formally released the opinion. In response to the draft, the American Medical Association (AMA) issued a press release that expressed the concern that *Dobbs* would allow the government to interfere with the doctor-patient relationship and that "[a]llowing the lawmakers of Mississippi or any other state to substitute their own views for a physician's expert medical judgment puts patients at risk and is antithetical to public health and sound medical practice" (Harmon 2022). Democrats vehemently opposed the Court's ruling for many reasons, including the impact on women's health care. Republicans supported the Court's ruling, choosing to prioritize the life and health of the fetus.

COVID-19 Vaccine Mandate

In March 2020, a global pandemic reached the United States and an intense political debate about the role of government in public health ensued. Virus mitigation measures became politicized particularly when vaccines became available in early 2021. Indeed, "[a]s of mid-September [2021], 90 percent of adult Democrats had been vaccinated, compared with 58 percent of adult Republicans" (Weisman 2021). According to data from Johns Hopkins University, the country's most Republican counties had a death rate "nearly six times as high as the death rate in the [most] Democratic counties" (Weisman 2021). COVID-19 infections declined in the early summer of 2021 but began to increase due to a new variant in the late summer and fall of 2021. In September 2021, President Biden announced that the Occupational Health and Safety Administration (OSHA) would issue an emergency temporary standard (ETS) requiring businesses with over one hundred employees to adopt vaccine-or-test requirements. The ETS required employers to adopt and enforce a mandatory vaccination policy or to adopt and implement a weekly testing and face-covering policy. Businesses that did not comply faced a significant fine. The government estimated that the rule would "save thousands of lives and prevent over 250,000 hospitalizations during the six months after imple-mentation" (Gangitano 2021). The ETS was characterized as a vaccine mandate, even though it did not require vaccinations. It was also immediately criticized by Republican governors, many of whom sought to ban employers in their states from mandating vaccines. Congressional Republicans also attempted to thwart the implementation of the ETS by withholding funding. After the U.S. Supreme Court held that the rule was an overreach of federal authority, the Biden administration withdrew the ETS in 2022.

Democrats

The Democratic Party has consistently supported expanding health insurance cov-erage. Party members have disagreed, however, on the extent to which health-care coverage should rely on private insurance or the federal government. During the 2020 presidential campaign, party members differed in terms of whether the ACA should be expanded or whether Medicare should offer universal health-care cov-erage. Democrats have interpreted prohibitions of sex discrimination in the ACA to include LGBT persons. Democrats have also consistently supported funding for Planned Parenthood and access to contraceptives for women. During the COVID-19 pandemic, Democrats supported a stronger role for the government in requiring vac-cinations or weekly testing to mitigate the spread and reduce the harm of the virus.

Health-Care Access
In the twentieth century, Democratic presidents Franklin Roosevelt, Harry Truman, John F. Kennedy, Lyndon Johnson, and Bill Clinton supported expanding health-care access; however, only Johnson was successful with the passage of Medicare and Medicaid. In 2009, President Obama discussed the necessity of health-care reform in a speech to a joint session of Congress. He stated that "we can no longer afford to put healthcare reform on hold," because rising health-care costs "causes a bankruptcy every thirty seconds. By the end of the year, it could cost 1.5 million Americans to lose their homes. . . . It is one of the major reasons why small busi-nesses close their doors and corporations ship jobs overseas. And it's one of the largest and fastest growing parts of our budget" (Remarks of President Obama—Address to a Joint Session of Congress 2009).

After the ACA was enacted to address these issues, Democrats have continued to support the law. In 2020, for example, the party's official platform stated:

> Democrats have fought to achieve universal health care for a century. We are proud to be the party of Medicare, Medicaid, and the Affordable Care Act. Because of the Obama-Biden Administration and the Affordable Care Act, more than 100 million Americans with pre-existing conditions, from heart disease to asthma, are secure in the knowledge that insurance companies can no longer discriminate against them. Women can no longer be charged more than men just because of their gender. And more Americans are able to get health coverage than ever before.
>
> Democrats will keep up the fight until all Americans can access secure, affordable, high-quality health insurance—because as Democrats, we fundamentally believe health care is a right for all, not a privilege for the few.
>
> Unfortunately, at every turn, Democrats' efforts to guarantee health coverage have been met by obstruction and opposition from the Republican Party. It has been Republicans who have embraced junk plans that undermine protections for pre-existing conditions. It was Republican state attorneys general who sued to block Medicaid expansion and Republican governors who refused to extend Medicaid coverage to their citizens, leaving millions of low-income Americans, disproportionately people of color, unable to access health coverage. And in the midst of the worst global pandemic in generations—one that has left more than 150,000 Americans dead and counting—the Trump Administration is fighting in court to invalidate the entirety of the Affordable Care Act and eliminate insurance for tens of millions of people. Overturning the Affordable Care Act remains a central plank of the Republican Party platform. The difference in values between the two parties on this life-or-death issue could not be more stark. (Democratic Party Platform 2020)

However, during the 2020 presidential campaign, Democrats were divided over whether to expand the ACA to increase access to health care or whether to expand Medicare, a plan known as Medicare for All. According to a 2020 Pew Research Center poll, 54 percent of Democrats and Democratic leaders favor a single national government health insurance program, such as Medicare for All, up from 44 percent the previous year (Jones 2020).

Joe Biden was opposed to Medicare for All and instead favored ACA expansion. The Biden administration has attempted to increase the law's coverage. In November 2021, the Democratic-controlled House passed the Build Back Better Act, a wide-ranging bill, without any Republican support. This bill contains several provisions related to health care that would supplement the ACA. For example, it would offer insurance through Medicaid to individuals in states that have not expanded Medicaid, expand Medicare benefits to include coverage for hearing, but not vision or dental, services, increasing subsidies for those who purchase their insurance through one of the ACA's exchanges, and capping the amount Medicare recipients spend on prescription drugs (Abelson et al. 2021).

Some Democrats have advocated for universal health-care coverage through Medicare expansion. Representative John Conyers was the first Democrat to introduce this type of legislation in Congress. Although the bill garnered little attention, Conyers introduced it in every term from 2003 until his retirement in 2017. In 2008, presidential candidate Dennis Kucinich was the lone Democratic candidate to support Medicare expansion, while the other candidates, including Barack Obama and Hillary Clinton, supported reform of private insurance. Senator Bernie Sanders, who ran for the Democratic presidential nomination in 2016 and 2020, has been a vocal advocate of Medicare for All and introduced legislation in the Senate in 2013. While that legislation had no cosponsors, the issue received a significant amount of attention during the 2020 contest for the Democratic nomination.

The central argument of Medicare for All advocates is that health care is a human right and that the profit motive of insurance companies and the medical establishment interferes with access to care. They argue that a national health-care system would eliminate the profit motive and guarantee care to all Americans, regardless of their ability to pay. Medicare for All proposals that have been introduced in Congress by Sanders and Democratic Representative Pramila Jayapal eliminate the private insurance industry. They also eliminate co-pays and deductibles ordinarily charged by insurance companies and expand health coverage to include vision and dental benefits and long-term nursing home care. Medical service providers, including doctors in private practice, would be paid based on a national scale and would likely make less money than with private insurance. Critics of Medicare for

---

Senator Sanders Proposes Medicare-for-All Bill

Congressional Democrats disagreed over whether to extend the ACA or to create a Medicare-for-All program. In 2022, Senator Bernie Sanders and fourteen Democratic Senators introduced the Medicare-for-All 2022 Act. The following is a statement from Senator Sanders offering a justification for the bill.

> The American people understand, as I do, that health care is a human right, not a privilege and that we must end the international embarrassment of the United States being the only major country on earth that does not guarantee health care to all of its citizens. It is not acceptable to me, nor to the American people, that over 70 million people today are either uninsured or underinsured. As we speak, there are millions of people who would like to go to a doctor but cannot afford to do so. This is an outrage. In America, your health and your longevity should not be dependent on your wealth. Health care is a human right that all Americans, regardless of income, are entitled to and they deserve the best health care that our country can provide.

Source
"NEWS: Sanders Introduces Medicare for All with 14 Colleagues in the Senate." 2022. Senator Bernie Sanders, May 12. Accessed February 12, 2023. https://www.sanders.senate.gov/press-releases/news-sanders-introduces-medicare-for-all-with-14-colleagues-in-the-senate/.

All, including Joe Biden, argue that the plan is too expensive with estimates suggesting it would cost between $30 and $40 trillion over a ten-year period (Higgins 2020), which would require tax increases to fund. Critics also note that physicians would earn significantly less income and that one hundred million jobs would be lost with the elimination of health insurance companies (Eichhorn and Hutchinson 2019).

Sex Discrimination
Sexual Orientation and Transgender Status
In 2016, HHS interpreted Section 1557's prohibition of sex discrimination to include discrimination on the basis of pregnancy, sex stereotyping, and gender identity. HHS secretary Sylvia Burwell stated that "[a] central goal of the Affordable Care Act is to help all Americans access quality, affordable health care. Today's announcement is a key step toward realizing equity within our health care system and reaffirms this Administration's commitment to giving every American access to the health care they deserve." Proponents of the rule, such as the Human Rights Campaign, argue that "fear of discrimination causes many LGBTQ people to avoid seeking medical care. The group cites studies that show that 70 percent of transgender patients say they have experienced discrimination in a health care setting" (Kodjak and Wroth 2019) as justification for the policy. The rule did not require insurance companies to cover specific procedures relating to individuals in those categories, but rather it required that if a service, such as hormone therapy, was offered to other patients, it could not be denied to those individuals (Young 2016). The rule was not fully implemented due to legal challenges. It was rescinded by the Trump administration in favor of an interpretation of "sex" referring to biological sex. After Joe Biden was elected, HHS issued a new rule based on the U.S. Supreme Court's ruling in *Bostock v. Clayton County* (2020) in which the Court held that the Civil Rights Act of 1964's Title VII prohibition of sex discrimination also applied to LGBT persons. The HHS notice specified that under Section 1557 of the ACA, discrimination based on sexual orientation or transgender status was prohibited.

Critics of the rule included the former head of OCR at HHS during the Trump administration, Roger Severino. He stated that "[m]any people of good will who are scientists and doctors believe sex is a biological reality. This action is attempting to impose a contrary view" (Shear and Sanger-Katz 2021). Some religious advocacy groups also opposed the action. According to Brian Burch, president of Catholic-Vote, the administration's policy "turns back the clock on medical sanity" (Shear and Sanger-Katz 2021).

Women's Reproductive Health
Senate Democrats proposed legislation to overturn the Supreme Court's ruling in *Burwell v. Hobby Lobby*. Senators Patty Murray and Mark Udall introduced the

Protect Women's Health from Corporate Interference Act, also referred to as the Not My Boss's Business Act. This bill would restore the ACA's contraceptive coverage requirement. Murray characterized the Court's ruling as "misguided" (Murray 2014), while Democratic Senate majority leader Harry Reid stated that it was "outrageous" (Pear 2014). Reid also stated that Democrats would "ensure that women's lives are not determined by virtue of five white men" referring to the five Supreme Court Justices who voted in the majority (Pear 2014). The party was unable to pass the legislation.

Congressional Democrats also opposed HHS changes to Title X that imposed a gag rule on abortion services for recipients of Title X funds. A 2018 letter to HHS secretary Alex Azar, signed by over two hundred House Democrats, outlined the party's strong opposition to the Trump administration's proposal to reinstate the "gag rule" on abortion. The letter noted that Title X provided services to approximately four million women, men, and adolescents. By providing basic medical care to "low-income, uninsured, and underinsured individuals, Title X yields critical cost savings to the American healthcare system. Every dollar invested in Title X yields a saves more than seven dollars in Medicaid-related costs" (Rewire News Group 2018). Additionally, the letter argued that the proposed gag rule would have a "devastating impact on the entire Title X network" that would "disproportionately impact communities of color, the uninsured, and low-income individuals, and it could reverse progress made in critical areas" (Rewire News Group 2018). These areas included a decline in unintended pregnancies. The letter pointed out that Title X contraceptive services had prevented 822,000 unwanted pregnancies, which would have led to 387,000 unplanned births and 278,000 abortions" (Rewire News Group 2018).

In a 2021 memorandum directing HHS to review the rule, President Biden noted that the Trump policy "puts women's health at risk by making it harder for women to receive complete medical information" (The White House 2021). HHS revoked the Trump rule and reinstated the previous rule. Ruth Dawson of the Guttmacher Institute, an organization committed to advancing sexual and reproductive health, argued that the Biden rule should have included protection for Title X recipients. Specifically, she argued that in situations where Title X grant money is awarded to states, which in turn disperse funds to providers, providers are at risk if states have restrictive laws on fund disbursement. She suggested that the rule should have provided that an entity receiving Title X grant money be prohibited from discriminating against recipients of those funds for political reasons (Dawson 2021).

Abortion

The Democratic Party first linked abortion rights with health care in its 2016 party platform. The party pledged that "every woman should have access to quality reproductive health-care services, including safe and legal abortion—regardless of where she lives, how much money she makes, or how she is insured." The 2016

Democratic nominee, former senator and former secretary of state, Hillary Rodham Clinton, unequivocally supported *Roe v. Wade* and "women's rights to make their own healthcare decisions." Her stance differed from previous Democratic candidates who conceded that they supported some limits on abortion. Clinton supported limits on late-term abortions unless the mother's life was in danger. The 2020 platform language also emphasized abortion as part of women's reproductive health care.

With the *Dobbs* ruling looming, Democrats proposed legislation to protect abortion rights and women's health. The Women's Health Protection Act passed the House in 2022 along party lines with all Democrats voting for it and all Republicans plus one Democrat voting against it. The bill would have codified Roe and limited the states' ability to restrict abortion. It also prohibited governments from limiting health-care providers "from prescribe certain drugs, offer abortion services via telemedicine, or immediately provide abortion services when the provider determines a delay risks the patient's health" (GovTrack 2022). Senate Republicans prevented a vote on the bill.

In his remarks after the Court's ruling in *Dobbs*, President Joe Biden argued that the ruling negatively affected women's health care. He stated that "[n]ow, with *Roe* gone, let's be very clear: The health and life of women in this nation are now at risk" and that "state laws banning abortion are automatically taking effect today, jeopardizing the health of millions of women, some without exceptions" ("Remarks by President Biden on the Supreme Court Decision to Overturn Roe v. Wade" 2022).

In 2022, the House Oversight and Reform Committee held hearings on the impact of *Dobbs*. In her opening statement, Democratic Chairperson Carolyn B. Mahoney stated that "[w]hile Republicans are pushing to criminalize abortion nationwide, Democrats are fighting to protect the freedom of every person to make their own medical decisions—without interference from the state—and to protect the doctor-patient relationship."

COVID-19 Vaccine Mandate

In 2021, President Biden's vaccine or testing requirement for businesses with at least 100 employees was strongly supported by Democrats. A September 2021 Gallup Poll indicated that six in ten Americans approved of Biden's requirement, including 93 percent of Democrats (Jones 2021). Additionally, 94 percent of Democrats supported vaccine mandates for federal workers, hospital workers in hospitals that receive Medicare or Medicaid funds, and paid leave to get a vaccine or to recover from COVID-19 (Jones 2021). Writing in the *National Review*, Jason Richwine argued that there is "little justification for broad-based mandates that treat all unvaccinated people as second-class citizens" (Richwine 2021). He suggested that mandates violate individual autonomy and cause psychological distress and that mandates have not stopped the spread of COVID-19 in countries with high vaccination rates.

Republicans

Republicans oppose the involvement of the federal government in regulating health care and support the repeal of the ACA. Republicans disagree with the Obama and Biden administration's interpretation of Section 1557 to prohibit LGBT discrimination arguing that the law only prevented sex discrimination. Republicans also oppose the ACA's contraceptive coverage and funding for Planned Parenthood. Republicans have opposed President Biden's vaccine requirement because it infringes on individual liberty.

Republicans have advocated repealing the ACA since the day it was enacted when Republican senator Jim DeMint filed a bill consisting of one sentence: "The Patient Protection and Affordable Care Act, and the amendments made by that Act, are repealed." While the Republican Party's mantra with regard to the ACA, which they refer to as Obamacare, became "repeal and replace," it has not been able to do either. The party, and particularly President Trump, has been criticized for not developing an alternative comprehensive health-care plan. Repealing Obamacare has been criticized on the grounds that it would result in loss of access to health care primarily for minority and lower-income Americans.

Congressional Republicans passed the Restoring American's Healthcare Freedom Reconciliation Act in 2016 through the budget reconciliation process in the Senate, which would have repealed the ACA. President Obama vetoed the bill. Despite this action, Republicans considered the passage of an ACA repeal bill a victory. As Republican House Speaker Paul Ryan stated, "We have now shown that there is a clear path to repealing Obamacare without 60 votes in the Senate. So, next year, if we're sending this bill to a Republican president, it will get signed into law. Obamacare will be gone" (Harris 2016).

During the 2016 presidential campaign, Republican presidential nominee Donald Trump proposed eliminating the ACA except for the requirement that insurance companies cover preexisting conditions. After he was elected, Trump and Congressional Republicans, who controlled both chambers of Congress, attempted to repeal and replace Obamacare. In 2017, the House passed the American Health Care Act, which proposed reducing the federal role in health care by giving more authority to the states; specifically, the bill would have repealed Obamacare, eliminated the Medicaid expansion and subsidies for health-care exchanges, and directed most of those funds to the states to create health insurance plans. Senate Republicans introduced the Health Care Freedom Act, referred to as a "skinny" repeal of Obamacare because it eliminated a few key provisions of the law. The bill eliminated the individual mandate and the penalty for employers who did not provide affordable health insurance. It also allowed states flexibility in complying with parts of the law requiring the coverage of preexisting conditions and essential health benefits. The skinny repeal failed by a vote of 51–49, with three Republicans, Susan Collins, John McCain, and Lisa Murkowski, voting with Senate Democrats to defeat the bill. While these larger efforts were unsuccessful, Republicans enacted the Tax Cuts and Jobs Act in 2017, which eliminated the penalty for non-compliance with the individual mandate.

Although Congressional Republicans were unable to repeal the ACA, President Trump took several steps to limit the law's impact. He reduced outreach and opportunities for enrollment in the ACA's insurance exchanges, cut subsidies to insurance companies offering coverage on the exchanges, allowed exchanges to offer cheaper, lower-quality insurance, and approved waivers for states that imposed work requirements and administrative burdens on nonelderly Medicaid recipients. He also discouraged legal aliens from enrolling in Medicaid through the Department of Homeland Security's policy of treating Medicaid enrollment as a negative factor when considering legal aliens' requests to extend their stay or change their status (Thompson 2020).

Republicans Oppose Democratic Health Care Plans

In 2021, Senate Minority Leader Mitch McConnell delivered a speech on the Senate floor in which he criticized many aspects of the Democratic Party's health care plans. This excerpt provides some insight into Republican criticism of Democratic health care proposals.

. . . Democrats want to axe the private insurance plans that millions of Americans have chosen and prefer. They want to build new federal health programs and expand the ones that exist today, heaping more than $550 billion in new expenses on taxpayers to insure less than 4 million more people.

Here's the truth: the overwhelming majority of Americans today have access to healthcare. Democrats just don't like the private plans that most Americans choose.

Then, there's the plan to heap hundreds of billions of dollars in new programs and huge pools of additional people into a Medicare system that experts say is already dangerously close to insolvency. A huge, risky leap toward Medicare-for-All, at the expense of the stability and the security of the actual Medicare system that millions of seniors rely on right now.

Democrats want to pour cold water on America's world-leading medical innovation sector by imposing socialist price caps on prescription medicines. In another example of Democrats' magic math, the rationale here is apparently that calling something cheaper makes it so!

In reality, research tells us this would mean fewer new treatments and cures. By one analysis, these price controls could cause up to 20 times as much lost life over a decade as the once-in-a-century COVID pandemic already has. Suppressing innovation through drug socialism would literally cost American lives.

Source

"Democrats' Steps toward Socialized Medicine Would Cost Some Americans Their Coverage, Others Their Lives." 2021. U.S. Senator Mitch McConnell, October 21. Accessed February 13, 2023. https://www.mcconnell.senate.gov/public/index.cfm/2021/10/democrats-steps -toward-socialized-medicine-would-cost-some-americans-their-coverage-others-their-lives.

Writing in *The Atlantic*, Jonathan Cohn argued that the Republican Party's inability to develop a replacement for the ACA did not hurt Republicans until 2017. He suggested that unlike Democrats, who had been working on health-care policy since the Clinton administration, Republicans had not worked with insurance companies and other constituencies to gather information needed to develop policies. Additionally, there was no Republican consensus on what policies would replace the ACA. "Some Republicans wanted mainly to downsize the Affordable Care Act, others to undertake a radical transformation in ways they said would create more of an open, competitive market. Still others just wanted to get rid of Obama's law and didn't especially care what, if anything, took its place" (Cohn 2021).

Critics of repealing the ACA, such as the American Civil Liberties Union (ACLU), argued that it would severely harm minorities, disabled persons, and low-income individuals (Melling 2020) because they had gained access to insurance coverage and services through the law. The law has also been difficult to repeal because many of its provisions are popular even among Republican voters. A 2016 Pew Research Center poll showed that while most Republicans (85 percent) favored repealing Obamacare, it also indicated that Republicans hold a favorable opinion about several aspects of the law, including allowing young adults to remain on their parents' insurance until age twenty-six (82 percent), eliminating out-of-pocket costs for preventive care (77 percent), health-care exchanges (72 percent), and requiring insurance companies to cover preexisting conditions (63 percent) (Bialik and Geiger 2016).

Sex Discrimination
Sexual Orientation and Transgender Status

The Trump administration reversed the Obama-era rule that Section 1557's prohibition of sex discrimination included discrimination on the basis of pregnancy, sex stereotyping, and gender identity. Roger Severino, the director of the OCR in HHS, stated that "[w]hen Congress prohibited sex discrimination, it did so according to the plain meaning of the term, and we are making our regulations conform" (Kodjak and Wroth 2019). Some religious liberty organizations supported this rule, including Luke Goodrich, vice president of the Becket Fund for Religious Liberty, who argued that the rule "protects the doctor-patient relationship and ensures that no doctor will be forced to provide medical procedures in violation of his medical judgment and at risk of patients" (Kodjak and Wroth 2019).

This decision was criticized by LGBT groups and civil rights organizations. The Human Rights Campaign (HRC) filed suit to prevent the rule from going into effect. In a statement, HRC president Alphonso David stated that "LGBTQ people should not live in fear that they cannot get the care they need simply because of who they are. It is clear that this administration does not believe that LGBTQ people, or other marginalized communities, deserve equality under the law. But we have a reality check for them: we will not let this attack on our basic right to be free from discrimination in health care go unchallenged" (Padgett 2020).

Women's Reproductive Health

The debate over the ACA's contraceptive coverage became a significant issue in the 2012 presidential election and has continued since. During one of the 2012 presidential debates, Republican nominee, Mitt Romney, stated that "I don't believe that bureaucrats in Washington should tell someone whether they can use contraceptives or not, and I don't believe employers should tell someone whether they could have contraceptive care or not. Every woman in America should have access to contraceptives" (Rovner 2012). While Romney supported defunding Planned Parenthood, critics charged that he was "softening" his stance on contraceptives to appeal to female voters (Rovner 2012).

Republicans addressed contraceptive coverage and Planned Parenthood funding in the 2016 presidential campaign. According to the official GOP platform in both 2016 and 2020:

> Any honest agenda for improving healthcare must start with repeal of the dishonestly named Affordable Care Act of 2010: Obamacare. It weighs like the dead hand of the past upon American medicine. It imposed a Euro-style bureaucracy to manage its unworkable, budget-busting, conflicting provisions. It has driven up prices for all consumers. . . . We agree with the four dissenting judges of the Supreme Court: "In our view, the entire Act before us is invalid in its entirety." It must be removed and replaced with an approach based on genuine competition, patient choice, excellent care, wellness, and timely access to treatment. To that end, a Republican president, on the first day in office, will use legitimate waiver authority under the law to halt its advance and then, with the unanimous support of Congressional Republicans, will sign its repeal. The Supreme Court upheld Obamacare based on Congress' power to tax. It is time to repeal Obamacare and give America a much-needed tax cut.
>
> America's healthcare professionals should not be forced to choose between following their faith and practicing their profession. We respect the rights of conscience of healthcare professionals, doctors, nurses, pharmacists, and organizations, especially the faith-based groups which provide a major portion of care for the nation and the needy.
>
> We oppose the use of public funds to perform or promote abortion or to fund organizations, like Planned Parenthood, so long as they provide or refer for elective abortions or sell fetal body parts rather than provide healthcare. (Republican Party Platform 2016, 2020)

While campaigning for the Republican nomination in 2016, Donald Trump indicated that he supported some of Planned Parenthood's health-care services for women but opposed the organization's position on abortion. He stated that Planned Parenthood does "some very good work. Cervical cancer, lots of women's issue, women's health issues are taken care of." He added that "I'm not going to fund it if it's doing the abortion. I am not going to fund it" (Terkel 2016). Trump sent a letter to pro-life organizations when running for reelection in 2020 in which he specifically pledged to defund Planned Parenthood.

As president, Trump's changes to Title X were supported by conservatives. The Editorial Board of the *National Review* argued that "Democratic presidents have resisted proper enforcement and have allowed abortion-providing organizations such as Planned Parenthood ready access to Title X funds with minimal (and minimally effective) restrictions" (Editorial Board of the *National Review* 2018).

The Editorial Board of the *New York Times*, however, opposed the rules arguing that they "make clear that these politicians have always been trying to do more than prevent abortions. These are attacks on women's ability to control if and when they get pregnant. On their health and well-being. On some of the most vulnerable members of society" (Editorial Board of the *New York Times* 2019). Some pro-life groups criticized the president and Congressional Republicans for failing to defund Planned Parenthood. Kristan Hawkins, the president of the antiabortion group Students for Life, stated that "[t]hey had two years to defund Planned Parenthood, and they failed. . . . We worked so hard to elect supposedly these pro-life Republican officials, and we expected results" (Ollstein 2018).

In addition to the Title X rule change and the changes in the ACA contraceptive coverage, the Trump administration diverted Title X funds to crisis pregnancy centers, which do not provide contraception, and attempted to eliminate the Teen Pregnancy Prevention Program and direct the funding to abstinence-only education programs, which are ineffective in preventing teen pregnancy (Long, Ramaswamy, and Salganicoff 2020).

Abortion

The Republican Party applauded the Court's ruling in *Dobbs*. The party's 2016 and 2020 platforms (Republicans opted to reissue the 2016 platform for 2020 rather than create a new one), argued that "[t]hrough Obamacare, the current Administration has promoted the notion of abortion as healthcare. We, however, affirm the dignity of women by protecting the sanctity of human life. Numerous studies have shown that abortion endangers the health and well-being of women, and we stand firmly against it" (Republican Party Platform 2016).

Republicans opposed the Women's Health Protection Act passed by House Democrats. Senate minority leader Mitch McConnell stated that the law was extreme and criticized Democrats for holding a "show vote" on abortion when there were more important issues for Congress to address. He also charged that Democrats showed that "the radical left fringe runs today's Democratic Party" (Hulse 2022). Critics of the bill argued that it went far beyond *Roe*. Jeanne Mancini, the president of the pro-life organization March for Life, stated that "[t]he misnamed Women's Health Protection Act is the most radical abortion bill in United States history. It would enshrine into federal law abortion on demand until the moment of birth, and it would nullify state laws—new and existing—that protect unborn children and their mothers" (Hulse 2022).

COVID-19 Vaccine Mandate

Many Congressional Republicans opposed vaccine mandates to mitigate the spread and the threat of serious illness due to COVID-19. Republican senator Mike Braun, along with forty Republican senators, sought to have the Biden HHS vaccine-or-test mandate nullified under the Congressional Review Act. The act allows Congress to nullify executive branch rules through a joint resolution. Braun characterized the HHS emergency rule as a "highly inappropriate invasion of what should be a personal medical decision for every American" (Braun 2021). The resolution passed the Senate by a vote of 52–48, with two Democrats voting for it. Democrats criticized this action arguing that Republicans were "driving anti-vaccination sentiment in some parts of the country, undermining the country's response to the pandemic" (Clark and Tsirkin 2021). While a high percentage of Democrats support vaccine mandates, very low percentages of Republicans do. A September 2021 Gallup Poll showed that only 17 percent of Republicans supported Biden's proposed policy. Similarly, only 19 percent of Republicans agreed with mandating vaccines for federal workers, 25 percent agreed with required vaccinations for health-care workers in hospitals receiving funding from Medicare or Medicaid, and 33 percent agreed that workers should get paid leave to recover from vaccination or COVID-19 (Jones 2021).

Further Reading

Abelson, Reed, Sarah Kliff, Margot Sanger-Katz, and Sheryl Gay Stolberg. 2021. "Democrats' Bill Would Go Far toward 'Patching the Holes' in Health Coverage." *New York Times*, December 1. Accessed January 3, 2022. https://www.nytimes.com/2021/12/01/us/politics/build-back-better-act-health-coverage.html.

Bialik, Kristen, and A. W. Geiger. 2016. "Republicans, Democrats Find Common Ground on Many Provisions of Health Care Law." Pew Research Center, December 8. Accessed January 4, 2022. https://www.pewresearch.org/fact-tank/2016/12/08/partisans-on-affordable-care-act-provisions/.

Braun, Mike. 2021. "Braun Leads 40 Colleagues in Officially Challenging Biden's Vaccine Mandate." U.S. Senator Mike Braun, November 3. Accessed February 1, 2022. https://www.braun.senate.gov/braun-leads-40-colleagues-officially-challenging-bidens-vaccine-mandate.

Clark, Dartunorro, and Julie Tsirkin. 2021. "Senate Passes Resolution to Repeal Biden Vaccine Mandate, with Help of Two Democrats." *NBC News*, December 8. Accessed February 1, 2022. https://www.nbcnews.com/politics/congress/senate-passes-resolution-defund-repeal-biden-vaccine-mandate-n1285636.

Cohn, Jonathan. 2021. "The Real Reason Republicans Couldn't Kill Obamacare." *The Atlantic*, March 22. Accessed January 31, 2022. https://www.theatlantic.com/politics/archive/2021/03/why-trump-republicans-failed-repeal-obamacare/618337/.

Dawson, Ruth. 2021. "After Years of Havoc, the Biden-Harris Title X Rule Is Now in Effect: What You Need to Know." Guttmacher Institute, December 14. Accessed February 1, 2022. https://www.guttmacher.org/article/2021/12/after-years-havoc-biden-harris-title-x-rule-now-effect-what-you-need-know.

Democratic Party Platform. 2016–2022. American Presidency Project. Accessed February 6, 2023. https://www.presidency.ucsb.edu/people/other/democratic-party-platforms.

Department of Health and Human Services, Office of the Assistant Secretary for Planning and Evaluation. 2022. "National Uninsured Rate Reaches All-Time Low in Early 2022." August. Accessed September 23, 2022. https://aspe.hhs.gov/sites/default/files/documents/f2dedbf8a4274ae7065674758959567f/Uninsured-Q1-2022-Data-Point-HP-2022-23.pdf.

Editorial Board of the National Review. 2018. "Defunding Planned Parenthood: Donald Trump's Good Start." National Review, May 18. Accessed January 3, 2022. https://www.nationalreview.com/2018/05/trump-planned-parenthood-decision-good-start-towards-defunding/.

Editorial Board of the New York Times. 2019. "It Just Got Harder to Get Birth Control in America." New York Times, August 19. Accessed February 10, 2023. https://www.nytimes.com/2019/08/19/opinion/planned-parenthood-title-x.html.

Eichhorn, Edward, and Michael Hutchinson. 2019. "Why Medicare-for-All Is Not Good for America." U.S. News and World Report, April 26. Accessed January 3, 2022. https://www.usnews.com/news/healthcare-of-tomorrow/articles/2019-04-26/commentary-why-medicare-for-all-is-not-good-for-america.

Gangitano, Alex. 2021. "Vaccine Mandate for Businesses Published, Setting Jan. 4 Deadline." The Hill, November 4. Accessed January 31, 2022. https://thehill.com/homenews/administration/579986-biden-administration-published-vaccine-mandate-for-businesses-argues?rl=1.

GovTrack. 2022. "S. 4132: Women's Health Protection Act of 2022." May 3. Accessed September 23, 2022. https://www.govtrack.us/congress/bills/117/s4132/summary.

Harmon, Gerald E. 2022. "AMA Statement on Draft Supreme Court Opinion." American Medical Association, May 5. Accessed February 10, 2023. https://www.ama-assn.org/press-center/press-releases/ama-statement-draft-supreme-court-opinion.

Harris, Gardiner. 2016. "Obama Vetoes Bill to Repeal Health Law and End Planned Parenthood Funding." New York Times, January 8. Accessed January 31, 2022. https://www.nytimes.com/2016/01/09/us/politics/obama-vetoes-bill-to-repeal-health-law-and-end-planned-parenthood-funding.html.

Higgins, Tucker. 2020. "Biden Suggests He Would Veto 'Medicare for All' Over Its Price Tag." CNBC, March 10. Accessed January 31, 2022. https://www.cnbc.com/2020/03/10/biden-says-he-wouldd-veto-medicare-for-all-as-coronavirus-focuses-attention-on-health.html.

Hulse, Carl. 2022. "Republicans Block Abortion Rights Measure in Senate." New York Times, February 28.

Jones, Bradley. 2020. "Increasing Share of Americans Favor a Single Government Program to Provide Health Care Coverage." Pew Research Center, September 29. Accessed August 23, 2021. https://www.pewresearch.org/fact-tank/2020/09/29/increasing-share-of-americans-favor-a-single-government-program-to-provide-health-care-coverage/.

Jones, Jeffrey M. 2021. "Majority in U.S. Supports Biden COVID-19 Vaccine Mandates." Gallup, September 24. Accessed January 3, 2022. https://news.gallup.com/poll/354983/majority-supports-biden-covid-vaccine-mandates.aspx.

Kodjak, Alison, and Carmel Wroth. 2019. "Trump Administration Proposes Rule to Reverse Protections for Transgender Patients." National Public Radio, May 24. Accessed January 12, 2022. https://www.npr.org/sections/health-shots/2019/05/24/726552816/trump-administration-proposes-rule-to-reverse-protections-for-transgender-patien.

Long, Michelle, Amrutha Ramaswamy, and Alina Salganicoff. 2020. "The 2020 Presidential Election: Implications for Women's Health." Kaiser Family Foundation, October 15. Accessed July 30, 2021. https://www.kff.org/womens-health-policy/issue-brief/the -2020-presidential-election-implications-for-womens-health/.

Melling, Louise. 2020. "The Affordable Care Act—And With It, Our Civil Rights—Are Under Attack." American Civil Liberties Union, November 9. Accessed August 31, 2021. https://www.aclu.org/news/disability-rights/the-affordable-care-act-and-with-it -our-civil-rights-are-under-attack/.

Michener, Jamila. 2020. "Race, Politics, and the Affordable Care Act." *Journal of Health, Politics, Policy and Law* 45, no. 4: 547–566. https://doi.org/10.1215/03616878-8255481.

Murray, Patty. 2014. "HOBBY LOBBY: Murray, Udall Kickoff Debate on Not My Boss's Business Act." Senator Patty Murray. July 15. Accessed February 2, 2022. https://www.murray .senate.gov/hobby-lobby-murray-udall-kickoff-debate-on-not-my-bosss-business-act/.

Newkirk, Vann R., II. 2017. "The Fight for Health Care Has Always Been about Civil Rights." The Atlantic, June 27. Accessed February 9, 2023. https://www.theatlantic.com/politics /archive/2017/06/the-fight-for-health-care-is-really-all-about-civil-rights/531855/.

Nixon Foundation. 2009. "More on Ted Kennedy, Nixon, and Health Care." August 26. Accessed October 1, 2022. https://www.nixonfoundation.org/2009/08/more-on -ted-kennedy-nixon-and-health-care/.

Ollstein, Alice Miranda. 2018. "GOP Lawmakers' Reality: They Won't Cut Planned Parenthood." *Politico*, December 2. Accessed December 1, 2021. https://www.politico.com /story/2018/12/02/gop-congress-planned-parenthood-1036942.

Ortega, Alexander N., and Dylan H. Roby. 2021. "Ending Structural Racism in the US Health Care System to Eliminate Health Care Inequities." *Journal of the American Medical Association* 326, no. 7: 613–615.

Padgett, Donald. 2020. "Trump Administration Kills Trans Protections in Affordable Care Act." Advocate, June 12. Accessed February 3, 2022. https://www.advocate.com /transgender/2020/6/12/trump-administration-kills-trans-protections-affordable-care -act.

Patton, Mike. 2020. "Obamacare 10 Years Later: Success or Failure?" *Forbes*, November 11. Accessed September 22, 2022. https://www.forbes.com/sites/mikepatton/2020/11/11 /obamacare-10-years-later-success-or-failure/?sh=123691ad4844.

Pear, Robert. 2014. "Democrats Push Bill to Reverse Supreme Court Ruling on Contraceptives." *New York Times*, July 9. Accessed August 3, 2021. https://www.nytimes .com/2014/07/09/us/politics/democrats-draft-bill-to-override-contraception-ruling .html.

Republican Party Platform. 2016–2022. American Presidency Project. Accessed February 6, 2023. https://www.presidency.ucsb.edu/people/other/republican-party-platforms.

"Remarks by President Biden on the Supreme Court Decision to Overturn Roe v. Wade." 2022. The White House. June 24. Accessed February 10, 2023. https://www .whitehouse.gov/briefing-room/speeches-remarks/2022/06/24/remarks-by-president -biden-on-the-supreme-court-decision-to-overturn-roe-v-wade/.

"Remarks of President Obama—Address to a Joint Session of Congress." 2009. The White House, February 24. Accessed February 10, 2023. https://obamawhitehouse.archives .gov/the-press-office/remarks-president-barack-obama-address-joint-session-congress.

Rewire News Group. 2018. "Letter to HHS Opposing Domestic Gag on Title X." May 14. Accessed February 12, 2023. https://rewirenewsgroup.com/wp-content/uploads /2018/05/2018.05.14-Letter-to-HHS-Opposing-Domestic-Gag-on-Title-X2.pdf.

Richwine, Jason. 2021. "The Case against the Mandates." *National Review*, November 16. Accessed February 1, 2022. https://www.nationalreview.com/corner/the-case-against -the-mandates/.

Rovner, Julie. 2012. "Romney Tries to Soften Birth Control Message." National Public Radio, October 17. Accessed February 10, 2023. https://www.npr.org/sections /health-shots/2012/10/17/163113629/romney-tries-to-soften-birth-control-message.

Shear, Michael D., and Margaret Sanger-Katz. 2021. "Biden Administration Restores Rights for Transgender Patients." *New York Times*, May 10. Updated September 28, 2021. Accessed January 31, 2022. https://www.nytimes.com/2021/05/10/us/politics/biden -transgender-patient-protections.html.

Simmons-Duffin, Selena. 2020. "Transgender Health Protections Reversed by Trump Administration." National Public Radio, June 12. Accessed February 1, 2022. https://www.npr.org/sections/health-shots/2020/06/12/868073068/transgender -health-protections-reversed-by-trump-administration.

Terkel, Amanda. 2016. "Donald Trump Stands by Planned Parenthood—Except on Abortion." *Huffington Post*, February 21. Accessed February 1, 2022. https://www.huffpost .com/entry/donald-trump-planned-parenthood_n_56c9cff0e4b0928f5a6c3b38.

Thompson, Frank. 2020. "Six Ways Trump Has Sabotaged the Affordable Care Act." The Brookings Institute, October 9. Accessed January 3, 2022. https://www.brookings .edu/blog/fixgov/2020/10/09/six-ways-trump-has-sabotaged-the-affordable-care-act/.

Vakil, Caroline. 2022. "Biden Administration Withdraws Its Vaccine-or-Test Mandate for Businesses." *The Hill*, January 25. Accessed February 1, 2022. https://thehill.com /homenews/administration/591260-biden-administration-plans-to-withdraw-its -emergency-vaccine-or-test?rl=1.

Weisman, Jonathan. 2021. "G.O.P. Fights COVID Mandates, Then Blames Biden as Cases Rise." *New York Times*, November 24. Updated November 25, 2021. Accessed January 3, 2022. https://www.nytimes.com/2021/11/24/us/politics/republicans-biden -coronavirus.html.

The White House. 2021. "Memorandum on Protecting Women's Health at Home and Abroad." January 21. Accessed February 1, 2022. https://www.whitehouse.gov/briefing -room/presidential-actions/2021/01/28/memorandum-on-protecting-womens-health -at-home-and-abroad/.

The White House. 2022. "FACT Sheet: How the Inflation Reduction Act Builds a Better Future for Young Americans." August 16. Accessed October 1, 2022. https://www .whitehouse.gov/briefing-room/statements-releases/2022/08/16/fact-sheet-how-the -inflation-reduction-act-builds-a-better-future-for-young-americans/.

Young, Jeffrey. 2016. "Obama Makes Big Move for Transgender Rights in Health Care." *Huffington Post*, May 13. Accessed January 3, 2022. https://www.huffpost.com/entry /obama-transgender-health-care_n_5735f011e4b08f96c182f23b.

Housing Policy

At a Glance

President Franklin Roosevelt initiated the first federal housing policies to address the Great Depression in the 1930s. During the 1960s, civil rights leaders lobbied for legislation to outlaw housing discrimination, resulting in the passage of the Fair Housing Act (FHA) in 1968. However, critics argue that the law has not been meaningfully enforced. When Democratic president Barack Obama's administration instituted new housing rules to enforce the FHA, Republicans opposed them, arguing that the federal government lacked that authority. The Republican Trump administration rescinded the rules, but they were reinstated by the Biden administration.

Similarly, the Trump administration changed course on Obama's homelessness policy. The Obama administration had emphasized a "housing-first" approach, which seeks to house homeless individuals and then address the cause of their homelessness. Trump's approach emphasized personal accountability. The Biden administration has returned to a "housing-first" approach. The parties also disagree over how to make housing more affordable for lower-income Americans with Republicans arguing that regulations, such as building permits and environmental regulations, should be eliminated and Democrats arguing that government subsidies will help lower-income individuals and families find homes.

According to many Republicans . . .

- The federal government should emphasize prohibiting racial discrimination instead of pushing racial integration in enforcing the FHA.
- Individuals should address the root cause of their homelessness, such as drug addiction or mental health problems, prior to receiving any type of government housing.
- Eliminating government regulations will make housing more affordable.

According to many Democrats . . .

- The federal government should emphasize policies that promote racial integration rather than those that merely prohibit racial discrimination in enforcing the FHA.

- The government should provide housing and then support individuals with drug abuse or mental health services to address their homelessness.
- Government subsidies will help make housing more affordable.

Overview

In the late 1800s, in many Northern cities, small Black populations were interspersed with white neighborhoods. Blacks in the South often lived near the plantations on which they had been previously enslaved. Housing segregation increased as Southern Blacks migrated to the North or West and their numbers increased in those areas. During Industrialization, Black Americans' homes became concentrated in cities near factories that offered employment opportunities. As racial tensions increased over labor issues, Blacks self-segregated to protect themselves as law enforcement was unwilling to do so. Also at this time, many American cities engaged in public works projects that eliminated integrated areas and enacted zoning restrictions requiring racial segregation.

The federal government became involved in housing policy during the Great Depression. Democratic president Franklin Roosevelt launched several programs to improve the U.S. economy, including programs to help homeowners pay their mortgages. While these policies were intended to keep Americans from losing their homes during an unprecedented economic crisis, they primarily benefited white homeowners and led to residential segregation. The Federal Housing Administration (FHA) was created to insure private lenders who provide loans to homeowners; however, it only guaranteed loans made to white borrowers. Similarly, the Homeowners Loan Corporation (HOLC), created in 1935 to help homeowners who could no longer afford their mortgage payments, was prohibited from making loans to Black homeowners. HOLC used a color-coding system with green residential areas considered an acceptable risk for issuing a loan and red residential areas considered a high risk. This discriminatory system became known as redlining and resulted in lower property values for homes owned by Blacks, even if they were like white residential neighborhoods. Local housing policies also promoted residential segregation.

In *Plessy v. Ferguson* (1896), the U.S. Supreme Court held that state segregation policies did not violate the Equal Protection Clause of the Fourteenth Amendment. This infamous ruling led states to create "separate but equal" accommodations in many areas of public life, including housing. In *Buchanan v. Warley* (1917), the U.S. Supreme Court invalidated an ordinance passed by the city of Louisville, Kentucky that prevented homeowners of one race from living in an area occupied by a different racial majority. The Court held the policy was unconstitutional because it interfered with property rights protected by the Due Process Clause of the Fourteenth Amendment. The Court distinguished this ruling from *Plessy* arguing that while

Homer Plessy could lawfully be required to ride in a separate passenger car, he was not denied transportation. In this situation, however, whites and Blacks were both deprived of their right to sell property to buyers they chose.

As a result of this ruling, whites wishing to preserve racial segregation in their communities created racially restrictive covenants. Restrictive covenants are private agreements among white neighbors to sell their homes only to other white buyers. Some legal scholars argued that because these agreements were between individuals, they were beyond the reach of the Fourteenth Amendment, which only applies to government policies. In *Shelley v. Kraemer* (1948), however, the U.S. Supreme Court invalidated restrictive covenants. By a 6-0 vote, with three justices recusing themselves—not participating—because they lived in homes with racial covenants, the Court held that because those agreements were enforced by state courts, they were not private contracts. As Chief Justice Fred Vinson noted, "It is clear that but for the active intervention of the state courts, supported by the full panoply of state power, petitioners would have been free to occupy the properties in question without restraint."

Housing discrimination was not addressed again at the federal level until 1962, when Democratic president John F. Kennedy issued Executive Order 11063. This directive prohibited discrimination based on race, color, religion, or national origin in housing owned, operated, or assisted by the federal government. The order did little to combat housing discrimination, however, because it did not apply to the private sector, which comprised 99 percent of housing in the United States. After Kennedy's assassination in 1963, Democratic president Lyndon B. Johnson launched the Great Society program in which the federal government addressed critical social issues, including racial discrimination. The Civil Rights Act of 1964 and the Voting Rights Act of 1965 were significant milestones in the advancement of civil rights. By the late 1960s, however, growing Black anger and frustration with the pace of social and political change triggered violent unrest in many of America's urban centers, where many African American communities were based. Johnson appointed the bipartisan National Advisory Commission on Civil Disorders, better known as the Kerner Commission, in 1967 to study the cause of the riots.

Johnson's action was initially met with skepticism from civil rights leaders, but the commission's findings provided support for the movement, including its determination that housing segregation was inextricably linked to urban riots and school segregation. The commission's report argued that the United States was "moving toward two societies, one black, one white—separate and unequal" and concluded that a federal fair housing law was a necessary element of any meaningful effort to address and reduce racial polarization in America.

The FHA of 1968, spelled out in Title VII of the monumental Civil Rights Act of 1968, was enacted to address this concern. Johnson had attempted to persuade members of Congress to pass housing legislation several times since 1966; however, segregationist senators refused to consider such legislation. In 1968, FHA passed the Senate by a vote of 71-20 on March 11 but was stalled in the House of Representatives until the April 4 assassination of Dr. Martin Luther King, Jr. The next day, Johnson joined with Walter Mondale, a Democratic senator and coauthor of FHA (and future vice president in the Carter administration), to urge the House to pass the law as a memorial to the slain civil rights leader. The House voted to approve the bill by a vote of 250-172 on April 10.

The FHA initially prohibited housing discrimination based on race, color, religion, or national origin. It was amended in 1974 to outlaw sex-based discrimination and again in 1988 to forbid discrimination against physically or mentally incapacitated individuals and discrimination based on family status. The law applies to the sale or rental of housing, and financing and brokerage services to secure housing. It also specifies that the goal of the Department of Housing and Urban Development (HUD) is to "affirmatively further fair housing." From the outset, the party leaders disagreed over the scope of the law. Senator Mondale argued that its goal was the integration of American society; however, during the 1968 presidential campaign and during his presidency, Republican Richard Nixon argued that the law only required nondiscrimination; actual racial integration was not a part of the law's mandate. Nixon's position was designed to attract the support of white suburban voters, many of whom had fled cities to avoid school desegregation and rising crime levels in many American cities. Most presidents have followed Nixon's strategy and have not fully enforced FHA.

In considering whether an FHA violation has occurred, courts have not only determined that intentional acts of discrimination violate the law but also unintentional acts that have a discriminatory impact. Known as disparate impact discrimination, judges consider the discriminatory impact of a policy regardless of whether there was an intent to discriminate. In 2013, during the second term of Democratic president Barack Obama, HUD formalized the "disparate impact" rule so that judges nationwide would apply the same standard. The standard required defendants to justify discriminatory actions. The rule was enacted to prevent the use of policies, such as criminal background checks and the use of algorithms to predict creditworthiness, that appear neutral but have a disproportionate negative effect on people of color. The Obama administration also implemented a rule in 2015, known as the "Affirmatively Furthering Fair Housing" (AFFH) rule, requiring entities that received federal funds for any aspect of housing to assess whether there were fair housing issues, including segregation, in their jurisdictions, determine the cause of the issue, and develop a plan to address the problem.

Republican president Donald Trump's administration rescinded both policies. Some Republicans argue that the disparate impact standard holds providers, such as mortgage lenders, liable for discrimination they did not cause. Trump's secretary of housing and urban development, Dr. Ben Carson, argued that the 2015 rule was an impermissible overreach of federal power. HUD did not enforce the rule and replaced it with a rule giving localities more authority to determine what

Republicans Support Removing Regulations to Increase Affordable Housing

In a February 2020 speech given to a summit addressing homelessness in California, President Trump's secretary of housing and urban development, Dr. Ben Carson, argues that eliminating regulatory barriers will make housing more affordable.

During this "Driving Affordable Housing Across America" bus tour, I am visiting communities across the country and a wide range of stakeholders from the public, private and non-profit sectors to work together on eliminating regulatory barriers that put affordable housing out of reach.

Expert research confirms: our country's current lack of affordable housing is caused in large part by burdensome regulations on new construction and development.

Those costs can account for up to 42 percent of multifamily development costs—and as a result, the largest portion of most Americans' paychecks go to housing.

To encourage the growth of new homes, last summer, President Trump established the White House Council on Eliminating Regulatory Barriers to Affordable Housing.

This Council, which I have the privilege to chair, is working with local and state leaders to identify and remove regulatory barriers that artificially limit housing supply.

There is no shortage of regulatory barriers for our Council to confront.

Among them: restrictive zoning and growth management controls; maximum density allowances for multifamily developments; excessively high developer fees; outdated building and rehabilitation codes; and unwieldy, inefficient permitting procedures.

The American builder faces a whole host of excessive restrictions, fees, and delays—and we at HUD want to work with the American people to address these issues first-hand.

But as we learned a decade ago during the Financial Crisis—which was really a Housing Crisis—we can't just inflate our way out of problems or impose top-down solutions.

Answers need to come from the bottom-up, in collaboration with community and private sector leaders, such as those I have the honor to meet with in Southern California throughout this week.

Source

Carson, Ben. 2020. "'UnHoused': Addressing Homelessness in California Summit." Department of Housing and Urban Development, February 13. Accessed September 5, 2022. https://archives.hud.gov/remarks/carson/speeches/2020-02-13.cfm.

---

constituted a fair housing problem and how to solve it. During the 2020 presidential campaign, Democratic nominee Joe Biden pledged to restore the disparate impact standard and the Obama AFFH rule.

Homelessness

As with housing discrimination, the federal government first addressed homelessness during the Great Depression. Many of the New Deal organizations created by the Roosevelt administration for infrastructure projects included housing for workers. After the Depression ended, so did those programs. Rather than implement policies specifically addressing homelessness, the federal government initiated comprehensive anti-poverty programs instead. Scholars believe that the Mental Retardation Facilities and Community Mental Health Centers Construction Act of 1963 may have also unintentionally increased America's homeless population. This law, supported by President John F. Kennedy and mental health advocates, was a victory for individuals confined to mental institutions, giving them more rights and care options. But even though it authorized funding for local outpatient facilities, it had the unintended consequence of increasing homelessness as some patients who could not find outpatient treatment ended up on the street. Homelessness also increased during the early and mid-1980s when Republicans in Congress and the Reagan administration cut millions of dollars from the federal budget for low-income housing and homeless shelters.

The McKinney-Vento Homeless Assistance Act (1987) was the first comprehensive federal law to address homelessness. It passed the House by a vote of 264-121, with the votes of 221 Democrats and 43 Republicans; 113 Republicans and 8 Democrats voted against it. The law provided funding for homelessness assistance programs, four of which are administered by HUD. It also created the U.S. Interagency Council on Homelessness (USICH), which coordinates the efforts of nineteen federal agencies to address homelessness. USICH is responsible for evaluating the effectiveness of federal homeless programs and notifying state and local governments and organizations in the public and private sectors about those programs. It provides an annual report to Congress and the president on its efforts to combat homelessness.

The George W. Bush administration launched the most significant homelessness program after McKinney-Vento. The administration started a "housing-first" initiative to end chronic homelessness. Individuals were considered chronically homeless if they were mentally ill or otherwise disabled and had been without a residence for at least a year, or who had experienced homelessness several times over several years. Many factors contribute to homelessness—unemployment, mental illness, drug use, poverty, disability, and lack of affordable housing. "Housing-first" programs prioritize housing before addressing other needs, such as drug treatment or mental health counseling.

In 2009, Congress passed the Homeless Emergency Assistance and Rapid Transition to Housing (HEARTH) Act, which included sweeping changes to McKinney-Vento. It expanded the definition of "homeless" and required a national strategic plan to address homelessness. Based on that plan, the Obama administration created an initiative known as "Opening Doors." The program, which expanded the Bush administration's "housing-first" plan, sought to eliminate homelessness for families and veterans. The Trump administration argued that these programs were ineffective because they did not mandate that individuals seek treatment or obtain assistance for other issues. Instead, the administration proposed a system of accountability, sometimes referred to as Treatment First, placing requirements on homeless individuals prior to securing housing. The Biden administration created "House America," a "housing-first" program, which provided guidance and support to provide permanent housing for homeless individuals and build affordable housing for individuals close to experiencing homelessness. Both parties have also addressed a related issue: housing affordability. Republicans argue that decreasing regulations, such as certain types of building permits and environmental regulations, will reduce housing costs. Democrats support more federal subsidies for low-income individuals.

Republicans

Republican president Richard Nixon's interpretation of the FHA was that the law prohibited discrimination. George Romney, Nixon's HUD secretary, however, believed that the law required steps to ensure racial integration. Romney implemented an "Open Communities" program, which denied federal funds to local governments that had not revised their zoning policies to allow the construction of subsidized housing for lower-income Black families. After a considerable suburban backlash, Nixon forced Romney to rescind the policy and eventually forced him out of office.

Republicans responded similarly to Democratic president Barack Obama's 2015 AFFH rule. AFFH required local governments to assess residential housing patterns for evidence of discrimination and segregation and to report the results to HUD every three to five years. It also required them to determine the barriers to equal housing and implement plans to reduce them. Republicans opposed the rule and argued that it should be rescinded. One Republican candidate for the party's presidential nomination in 2016, Dr. Ben Carson, compared the rule to busing policies in the 1970s and 1980s, which desegregated schools, labeling them a failed "social experiment" (Carson 2015). He argued that the rule relies on a "tortured reading" of the FHA to facilitate a "government-engineered attempt to legislate racial equality." The 2016 Republican Party platform used similarly scornful language:

> We must scale back the federal role in the housing market, promote responsibility on the part of borrowers and lenders, and avoid future taxpayer bailouts. Reforms should provide clear and prudent underwriting standards and guidelines on predatory lending and acceptable lending practices. . . . Zoning decisions have always been, and must remain, under local control. The [Obama administration] is trying to seize control of the zoning process through its Affirmatively Furthering Fair Housing regulation. It threatens to undermine zoning laws in order to socially engineer every community in the country. While the federal government has a legitimate role in enforcing non-discrimination laws, this regulation has nothing to do with proven or

alleged discrimination and everything to do with hostility to the self-government of citizens.

In 2017, Senate Republicans introduced the Local Zoning Decisions Protection Act to prohibit the federal government from obtaining racial disparity data to enforce FHA. Specifically, the bill proposed eliminating federal funding for cities that gathered the necessary data for AFFH, thus nullifying the rule. It would also prohibit gathering data to be used for disparate impact cases. Republican Senator Mike Lee, one of the bill's sponsors, stated that gathering data for disparate impact cases was an attempt "to punish communities that are not as demographically diverse as the [Obama] administration would like." He also argued that "[e]very American should be free to choose where to live, and every community should be free to zone its neighborhoods and compete for new residents according to its distinct values" ("Lee Introduces Local Zoning Decisions Protection Act" 2017). Critics noted that HUD specifically stated in the rule that it "does not impose any land use decisions or zoning laws on any local government" ("Joint Statement of the Department of Justice and the Department of Housing and Urban Development" 2020).

Trump's HUD secretary, Ben Carson, proposed rescinding the rule in 2020 saying that it "proved to be complicated, costly and ineffective. We found it to be unworkable and ultimately a waste of time for localities to comply with, too often resulting in funds being steered away from communities that need them most" (Wilkie 2020). During the 2020 presidential campaign, Trump highlighted this decision and criticized Democratic presidential nominee Joe Biden, who pledged to restore the rule, by falsely claiming that Biden would "totally destroy the beautiful suburbs. Suburbia will be no longer as we know it. So they wanted to defund and abolish your police and law enforcement while at the same time destroying our great suburbs" (Samuels 2020). After HUD formally announced that it was rescinding the rule, Trump tweeted, "I am happy to inform all of the people living their Suburban Lifestyle Dream that you will no longer be bothered or financially hurt by having low income housing built in your neighborhood. . . . Your housing prices will go up based on the market, and crime will go down. I have rescinded the [Barack] Obama-[Joe] Biden AFFH Rule. Enjoy!" (Wilkie 2020). Trump's comments coincided with a decline in support among suburban voters. Critics contended that he was stoking racial fears with the comments. Shaun Donovan, Obama's second HUD secretary, characterized Trump's actions as "a blatantly racist appeal to and attempt to return us to an era when the federal government actively implemented racist policies based on the false notion that Black families moving to white communities brings down property values" (Fuchs 2020).

HUD replaced AFFH with "Preserving Community and Neighborhood Choice," which gave local governments more flexibility in addressing housing issues. The new rule emphasized increasing "fair housing choice" by increasing the supply of housing, which HUD contended would allow families to live where they wanted to instead of attempting to racially integrate communities (Jan 2020a). The new rule altered the definition of fair housing as "housing that, among other attributes, is affordable, safe, decent, free of unlawful discrimination, and accessible under civil rights laws" (U.S. Dept. of Housing and Urban Development 2020). It also changed the criteria by which a local government met the FHA requirement of AFFH to mean "any action rationally related to promoting any of the above attributes of fair housing" (U.S. Dept. of Housing and Urban Development 2020).

Civil rights organizations criticized these actions. The National Fair Housing Alliance, a consortium of over two hundred nonprofit fair housing organizations, state and local civil rights organizations, and concerned individuals, issued a press release condemning the repeal of AFFH and its replacement with "Preserving Community and Neighborhood Choice." The statement called the new rule "a sham" arguing that "it lacks substance, clarity, and accuracy in its definition of fair housing. To make matters worse, this rule is going into effect amid a global health pandemic and economic downturn that's disproportionately impacting under-resourced communities of color. It also ignores the growing public outcry for the country to dismantle structural racism and make true progress and equal opportunity a reality for all Americans" (National Fair Housing Alliance 2020).

Secretary Carson also eliminated the 2013 disparate impact rule and replaced it with a rule requiring plaintiffs filing disparate impact suits to meet a higher legal standard. Carson suggested that civil rights organizations sued him to prevent the rule from going into effect. They argued that the new rule "radically alters, and effectively eviscerates, well-settled disparate-impact doctrine." It also "makes it nearly impossible for plaintiffs to prevail in a disparate-impact case, thus undoing decades of hard-won fair housing and fair lending progress in cities and counties across the nation" (Jan 2020b). Federal courts blocked the new rule from going into effect, and the standard was reinstated by the Biden administration.

Homelessness

Ronald Reagan signed the McKinney-Vento bill into law in 1987, which Congressional Republicans opposed. George W. Bush initiated a "Housing-First" policy, which focused on ending chronic homelessness—an approach expanded by President Obama.

President Donald Trump, however, reversed this initiative and replaced it with a Treatment-First program, which prioritizes personal accountability for factors leading to homelessness. In a July 2019 Fox News interview, Trump falsely asserted that homelessness was "a phenomenon that started two years ago" (Shear 2019). He also argued that the "liberal establishment" was to blame for homelessness and linked the issue with sanctuary cities, which did not cooperate with federal authorities on immigration policies. When homelessness became a significant issue in California, a large state with a mild year-around climate, Trump criticized

California's Democratic governor, Gavin Newsom, for the situation and threatened federal intervention. The proposed solutions included a federal mass detention facility and razing tent camps; however, critics noted that the federal government lacked jurisdiction to address the issue (Stein et al. 2019). Oakland's mayor, Democrat Libby Schaaf, suggested that if the president were truly concerned about homelessness, then he would increase funding for mental health services and federal housing rather than criticize the state. "His track record of vilifying and harming the most vulnerable populations is clear. It is hard to believe that his interests in this is sincere or will be effective" (Wilson 2019). The mayor was alluding to an HUD proposal prohibiting federal housing for families if one member was an undocumented immigrant. Previously, illegal immigrants were allowed to live with their families in federally subsidized housing if one family member lawfully resided in the United States. Carson argued that the policy would prioritize Americans who needed housing. However, critics of the policy argued that it would displace lawful U.S. citizens or residents who wanted to remain with their families. It would also cost HUD an estimated $193 billion if it had to pay subsidies for each resident (Kanno-Youngs and Thrush 2019).

Trump issued an executive order in 2019 "Establishing a White House Council on Eliminating Regulatory Barriers to Affordable Housing." The order suggested that access to housing had become increasingly difficult due to rising costs caused by government regulations imposed by federal, state, local, and tribal governments. The order also stated that increased government funding for lower-income housing was ineffective in solving the problem and that the new council would work with state and local governments to remove cumbersome regulations to increase the supply of affordable housing, a significant factor in homelessness.

Additionally, Trump fired the executive director of USICH in 2019 and replaced him with Robert Marbut, Jr., who had been a homelessness consultant for several major U.S. cities. Marbut called his approach a "velvet hammer" as he advocated eliminating "goodies" such as allowing individuals or organizations to hand out food to homeless people while also arguing that arresting homeless people should be a last resort. In October 2019, USICH issued "Expanding the Toolbox: The Whole of Government Response to Homelessness" plan. The report stated that "housing-first" policies were ineffective because they did not "address the real root causes of homelessness" and because they offered a "one size fits all approach" to homelessness when a variety of approaches are necessary.

Ten leading national homelessness organizations were among Expanding the Toolbox's critics. The National Alliance to End Homelessness (NAEH) issued a statement condemning the plan for being "neither strategic, nor a plan, despite the urgency for both given the rising levels of homelessness during the Trump administration." The statement described the plan as "an extensive, inaccurate, and largely incomprehensible analysis of homelessness and the federal efforts to address it" (National Alliance to End Homelessness 2020). NAEH was also critical of the plan for not addressing the federal government's responsibility for developing and implementing plans to address homelessness.

Democrats

The Democratic Party was initially divided over landmark civil rights legislation enacted in the 1960s. President Lyndon Johnson and Northern Democrats supported these laws while Southern Democrats consistently opposed them. Although the FHA was signed into law in 1968, the Obama administration was the first since the Nixon administration to make a serious effort to enforce it. The administration codified the disparate impact standard and issued the AFFH rule. The Trump administration rescinded both rules; however, President Joe Biden restored them. Biden also undertook efforts to redress historic housing discrimination.

In 2013, HUD codified the disparate impact standard courts used to evaluate claims of racial discrimination in housing. HUD took this action to ensure that judges uniformly applied the legal standard. A 2015 U.S. Supreme Court ruling, *Texas Department of Community Affairs v. Inclusive Communities Project*, upheld the disparate impact standard but also emphasized that HUD and lower courts must determine that a particular policy caused the disparate impact for the plaintiff to prevail. The 5-4 ruling also advised lower courts to swiftly dispose of claims in which the plaintiff could not show causality.

The move by HUD to codify the disparate impact standard and the Supreme Court ruling spurred Congressional Republicans to eliminate it in 2015. They introduced the Protect Local Communities Act, which would have amended FHA to remove the standard, and proposed two amendments to House legislation, which would have prohibited HUD from using funds to enforce the standard; none of these efforts were successful.

In July 2015, Julián Castro, President Obama's first HUD secretary, announced that the AFFH rule had been finalized. This policy was characterized as "the most significant federal effort in a generation to address long-standing, pervasive residential segregation by race and to increase equality of access to place-based opportunities, such as high-performing schools or access to jobs" (Steil et al. 2021). HUD created the rule due to the persistence of racial discrimination in housing. Research has shown that housing discrimination has led to lower levels of socioeconomic mobility, regardless of race, in metropolitan areas and negative consequences for Black and Latinx children, "including wider gaps in educational attainment, employment, and earnings; negative health outcomes; and reduced political power" (Steil et al. 2021). The Trump administration rescinded this policy.

During the 2020 presidential campaign, Democratic nominee Joe Biden advocated ending "systemic housing discrimination and other contributors" to low homeownership rates among Blacks and Latinos (Biden 2020). He proposed investing $640 billion over ten years so that every American would have access to affordable, stable, safe, healthy, and energy-efficient housing that was accessible to individuals with disabilities and located near good schools with a reasonable commute to their jobs. Biden proposed a Homeowner and Renter Bill of Rights to address discrimination and unfair housing practices by mortgage lenders and landlords to accomplish those goals.

One of Biden's first actions as president was to issue an executive order to the HUD secretary to examine the disparate impact rule and AFFH rule implemented by the Trump administration. In "Redressing Our Nation's and the Federal Government's History of Discriminatory Housing Practices and Policies," Biden recounted the history of housing discrimination in the United States noting that the effects of those policies linger. He described the federal government's role in ending housing discrimination as "crucial" and stated that his administration would work to end housing discrimination in all stages of home-buying and renting, to provide remedies to those who had experienced discrimination, "to promote diverse and inclusive communities, to ensure sufficient physically accessible housing, and to secure equal access to housing opportunity for all" ("Memorandum on Redressing Our Nation's and the Federal Government's History of Discriminatory Housing Practices and Policies" 2021).

The Biden rule differs from the 2015 rule in that it provides more flexibility to local communities, which remedied one of Secretary Carson's criticisms of the policy. The Biden rule did not require local governments to go through the same compliance process outlined by the 2015 rule. Biden's HUD secretary, Marcia L. Fudge, wrote an op-ed in the *Washington Post* supporting the administration's emphasis on combating race discrimination in housing. She stated, "To put it directly: HUD has a legal mandate to proactively break down unjust barriers that block too many people from moving into neighborhoods with greater opportunities. Too often, our government failed to live up that mandate. That is not the case in the administration of President Biden" (Fudge 2021). She rebuffed the charges made by Republicans that the rule constituted "social engineering" by noting that cities had the flexibility to determine and develop policies that comply with FHA.

Homelessness

Democrats have supported a broader definition of "homeless" and more funding for Housing-First initiatives. In 2009, Obama signed the HEARTH Act. This law, attached to a larger housing bill, amended the McKinney-Vento law. It changed the definition of homeless. Previously, HUD defined "homelessness" as "[a]n individual or family who lacks a fixed, regular, and adequate nighttime residence." HEARTH expanded that definition to include "people at imminent risk of homelessness, previously homeless people temporarily in institutional settings, unaccompanied youth and families with persistent housing instability, and people fleeing or attempting to flee domestic violence" (Leopold 2019). The law also directed USICH to develop a comprehensive national strategy to end homelessness. The

2010 report, *Opening Doors: Federal Strategic Plan to Prevent and End Homelessness*, proposed to end chronic homelessness, homelessness among veterans, and family and youth homelessness within ten years.

After Trump rescinded the Obama homeless policy, Democratic representative Maxine Waters introduced the Ending Homelessness Act, which passed the House Financial Services Committee. Waters was a vocal critic of Trump's reversal of the Obama-era housing policies. This bill, which she first introduced in 2016, proposed spending $13.27 billion over five years to fight homelessness and housing shortages. It would also provide over 400,000 new, affordable homes for the lowest-income households. House Republicans on the Financial Services Committee opposed the bill. Ranking member Republican Patrick McHenry stated, "There's not one person on this committee that doesn't want to end homelessness, but authorizing $13 billion in mandatory spending over five years actually won't end homelessness. It feeds a broken system that will not yield results" (Ramirez 2019).

In 2020 the Democratic Party platform promised deep reforms to American housing policies if the party retook the White House in the November election:

> The United States is facing an unprecedented housing crisis as a result of the COVID-19 pandemic and President Trump's recession, with millions of families at risk of being evicted. We support state and local measures to freeze rent increases, evictions, utility shutoffs, and late fees for rent, to prevent families from becoming homeless and making the pandemic even worse.
>
> Housing in America should be stable, accessible, safe, healthy, energy efficient, and, above all, affordable. No one should have to spend more than 30 percent of their income on housing, so families have ample resources left to meet their other needs and save for retirement. Democrats believe the government should take aggressive steps to increase the supply of housing, especially affordable housing, and address long-standing economic and racial inequities in our housing markets.

The Biden administration launched *House America: An All-Hands-On-Deck Effort to Address the Nation's Homelessness Crisis*. The plan called on state, tribal, and local leaders to work with HUD and USICH to rehouse and build affordable housing through the American Rescue Plan, which provided $10 billion to end homelessness during the COVID-19 pandemic. House America offered significant funding to governments willing to partner with the federal government in two ways: (1) providing permanent housing for the homeless, and (2) providing affordable housing for those close to being homeless. The virus led to increased homelessness when individuals could no longer pay their rent or mortgage. The virus was also more likely to be contracted and spread by individuals without permanent housing.

The Biden administration's plans to increase affordable housing took on new significance due to a housing crisis caused by the COVID-19 pandemic. As many employees were initially forced and then chose to work remotely, workers began

Democrats Support Increasing the Supply of Affordable Housing

In 2022, Democratic president Joe Biden released a Housing Supply Action Plan to increase affordable housing. This excerpt provides an overview of the plan.

Today's rising housing costs are years in the making. Fewer new homes were built in the decade following the Great Recession than in any decade since the 1960s—constraining housing supply and failing to keep pace with demand and household formation. This mismatch between housing supply and housing demand grew during the pandemic. While estimates vary, Moody's Analytics estimates that the shortfall in the housing supply is more than 1.5 million homes nationwide. This shortfall burdens family budgets, drives up inflation, limits economic growth, maintains residential segregation, and exacerbates climate change. Rising housing costs have burdened families of all incomes, with a particular impact on low- and moderate-income families, and people and communities of color.

As his Action Plan reflects, President Biden believes the best thing we can do to ease the burden of housing costs is to boost the supply of quality housing. This means building more new homes and preserving existing federally-supported and market-rate affordable housing, ensuring that total new units do not merely replace converted or dilapidated units that get demolished.

The President continues to urge Congress to pass investments in housing production and preservation. One independent analysis of proposals in the House of Representatives-passed reconciliation bill found that the housing-related proposals would finance close to 1 million affordable homes. . . . The President's 2023 Budget includes investments in housing supply that would lead to the production or rehabilitation of another 500,000 homes.

Building on the actions the Administration announced last September to build and rehabilitate 100,000 homes over the next three years, these legislative proposals and the new administrative steps being launched—in partnership with state, local, for-profit, and non-profit partners—can put the economy on a path to closing the housing supply gap in the next five years.

Source

"President Biden Announces New Actions to Ease the Burden of Housing Costs." 2022. The White House, May 16. Accessed September 23, 2022. https://www.whitehouse.gov /briefing-room/statements-releases/2022/05/16/president-biden-announces-new-actions -to-ease-the-burden-of-housing-costs/.

moving out of cities to less densely populated areas. This situation caused housing prices and inflation to rise. Housing prices were up over 19 percent from February 2021 to February 2022. Rent prices also increased by 20 percent from 2020 to 2022. The administration and Congressional Democrats supported a massive $1.75 trillion infrastructure package, known as Build Back Better, which would have provided $170 billion for rental assistance, public housing, and affordable housing. Republicans opposed the bill due to its extremely high cost. In 2022, Biden included $10 billion in the budget to incentivize local governments to change their zoning ordinances and land-use policies to allow for the construction of housing for lower-income individuals.

While most scholars and policy analysts argue that housing-first is an effective approach to addressing homelessness, some disagree. Christopher Rufo, a former fellow with the conservative Heritage Foundation, for example, argues that home-lessness is not a housing problem but a human problem. He cites studies indicating that despite high rates of housing retention among participants in "housing-first programs," individuals "consistently do not demonstrate any improvement in overcoming substance abuse, reduced psychiatric symptoms, or improved general well-being—the 'human outcomes'" (Rufo 2020).

Further Reading

Benner, Katie, and Erica L. Green. 2021. "Justice Dept. Seeks to Pare Back Civil Rights Protections for Minorities." *New York Times*, January 5. Accessed June 24, 2022. https://www.nytimes.com/2021/01/05/us/politics/justice-department-disparate-impact.html.

Biden, Joe. 2020. "The Biden Plan for Investing in Our Communities through Housing." Joe Biden for President: Official Campaign Website. Accessed May 3, 2022. https://joebiden.com/housing/.

Capps, Kriston. 2019. "The Consultant Leading the White House Push against Home-lessness." *Bloomberg City Lab*, December 19. Accessed June 10, 2022. https://www.bloomberg.com/news/articles/2019-12-12/trump-s-homeless-policy-gets-a-controversial-boss.

Carson, Ben. 2015. "Obama's Housing Rules Try to Accomplish What Busing Could Not." *Washington Times*, July 23. Accessed May 20, 2022. https://www.washingtontimes.com/news/2015/jul/23/ben-carson-obamas-housing-rules-try-to-accomplish-/.

Driver, Justin. 2018. "The Report on Race That Shook America." *The Atlantic*. Accessed May 20, 2022. https://www.theatlantic.com/magazine/archive/2018/05/the-report-on-race-that-shook-america/556850/.

Fuchs, Hailey. 2020. "Trump Moves to Roll Back Obama Program Addressing Housing Dis-crimination." *New York Times*, July 23. Accessed June 11, 2022. https://www.nytimes.com/2020/07/23/us/politics/trump-housing-discrimination-suburbs.html.

Fudge, Marcia. 2021. "How the Biden Administration Is Pushing the Country Toward Fairer Housing." *Washington Post*, June 10. Accessed June 20, 2022. https://www.washingtonpost.com/opinions/2021/06/10/marcia-fudge-hud-fair-housing-act/.

Gillon, Stephen M. 2018. *Separate and Unequal: The Kerner Commission and the Unraveling of American Liberalism*. New York: Basic Books.

Jan, Tracy. 2020a. "HUD Releases Proposal, Further Weakening Enforcement of Fair Housing Laws." *Washington Post*, January 7. Accessed June 6, 2022. https://www.washingtonpost.com/business/2020/01/03/ben-carsons-latest-plan-weaken-fair-housing-enforcement/.

Jan, Tracy. 2020b. "New Federal Rule Will Make It Harder to Challenge Discrimination in the Housing Industry, Lawsuits Allege." *Washington Post*, October 22. Accessed December 20, 2022. https://www.washingtonpost.com/business/2020/10/22/housing-discrimination-lawsuit-hud/.

"Joint Statement of the Department of Justice and the Department of Housing and Urban Development." 2015. U.S. Department of Justice, August 6. Accessed December 20, 2020. https://www.justice.gov/crt/joint-statement-department-justice-and-department -housing-and-urban-development.

Jones, Athena. 2015. "Obama Administration Announces New Fair Housing Rules." *CNN*, July 8. Accessed June 1, 2022. https://www.cnn.com/2015/07/08/politics/fair-housing -rules-obama-administration/index.html.

Kanno-Youngs, Zolan, and Glenn Thrush. 2019. "HUD Says Its Proposed Limit on Public Housing Aid Could Displace 55,000 Children." *New York Times*, May 10. Accessed June 13, 2022. https://www.nytimes.com/2019/05/10/us/politics/hud-public-housing -immigrants.html.

Klein, Betsy. 2022. "Biden Administration Unveils Action Plan to Boost Affordable Housing." *CNN*, May 16. Accessed June 4, 2022. https://www.cnn.com/2022/05/16/politics /biden-administration-action-plan-affordable-housing/index.html.

Kurtzleben, Danielle. 2020. "Seeking Suburban Votes, Trump to Repeal Rule Combating Racial Bias in Housing." National Public Radio, July 20. Accessed June 4, 2022. https://www.npr.org/2020/07/21/893471887/seeking-suburban-votes-trump-targets -rule-to-combat-racial-bias-in-housing.

Lamb, Charles M. 2005. *Housing Segregation in Suburban America Since 1960: Presidential and Judicial Politics*. New York: Cambridge University Press.

"Lee Introduces Local Zoning Decisions Protection Act." 2017. Mike Lee US Senator for Utah, January 12. Accessed December 20, 2022. https://www.lee.senate.gov/2017/1 /lee-introduces-local-zoning-decisions-protection-act.

Leopold, Josh. 2019. "Five Ways the HEARTH Act Changed Homelessness Assistance." Urban Institute, May 19. Accessed June 10, 2022. https://www.urban.org/urban-wire /five-ways-hearth-act-changed-homelessness-assistance.

Locke, Taylor. 2021. "Build Back Better Includes $170 Billion for Affordable Housing— Here's Where It Would Go." *CNBC*, November 24. Accessed June 1, 2022. https:// www.cnbc.com/2021/11/24/build-back-better-includes-170-billion-for-housing.html.

Massey, Douglas S., and Nancy Denton. 1993. *American Apartheid: Segregation and the Making of the Underclass*. Cambridge, MA: Harvard University Press.

McGray, Douglas. 2004. "The Abolitionist." *The Atlantic*, June. Accessed May 23, 2022. https://www.theatlantic.com/magazine/archive/2004/06/the-abolitionist/302969/.

"Memorandum on Redressing Our Nation's and the Federal Government's History of Discriminatory Housing Practices and Policies." 2021. The White House, January 26. Accessed January 30, 2023. https://www.whitehouse.gov/briefing-room/presidential -actions/2021/01/26/memorandum-on-redressing-our-nations-and-the-federal -governments-history-of-discriminatory-housing-practices-and-policies/.

Murakami, Kery. 2022. "Biden Is Doubling Down on a Push to Roll Back Single-Family Zoning Laws." *Route Fifty*, April 12. Accessed May 21, 2022. https://www.route-fifty .com/infrastructure/2022/04/bidens-10-billion-proposal-ramps-equity-push-change -neighborhoods-cities/365581/.

National Alliance to End Homelessness. 2020. "Statement in Response to USICH's 'Expanding the Toolbox' Report." National Alliance to End Homelessness, October 20. Accessed May 20, 2022. https://endhomelessness.org/blog/statement-in-response -to-usichs-expanding-the-toolbox-report/.

National Fair Housing Alliance. 2020. "Press Release: Civil Rights Groups Strongly Oppose HUD's New 'Fair Housing' Rule and Call on the Agency to Reinstate the 2015 AFFH Regulation." National Fair Housing Alliance, September 8. Accessed May 22, 2022. https://nationalfairhousing.org/civil-rights-groups-strongly-oppose-huds -new-fair-housing-rule-and-call-on-the-agency-to-reinstate-the-2015-affh-regulation/.

Ramirez, Kelsey. 2019. "Housing Committee Passes Bill to End Homelessness." *HousingWire*, April 1. Accessed June 10, 2022. https://www.housingwire.com/articles /48683-house-committee-passes-bill-to-end-homelessness/.

Rothstein, Richard. 2017. *The Color of Law: A Forgotten History of How Our Government Segregated America.* New York: Liveright.

Rufo, Christopher. 2020. "The 'Housing First' Approach Has Failed: Time to Reform Federal Policy and Make It Work for Homeless Americans." The Heritage Foundation, August 4. Accessed May 20, 2022. https://www.heritage.org/housing/report /the-housing-first-approach-has-failed-time-reform-federal-policy-and-make-it-work.

Samuels, Brett. 2020. "Trump Administration Ends Obama Fair Housing Rule." *The Hill*, July 23. Accessed June 21, 2022. https://thehill.com/homenews/administration /508745-trump-administration-ends-obama-fair-housing-rule/.

Serwer, Adam. 2019. "Trump Is Making It Easier to Get Away with Discrimination." *The Atlantic*, January 4. Accessed May 20, 2022. https://www.theatlantic.com/ideas /archive/2019/01/disparate-impact/579466/.

Shear, Michael. D. 2019. "Trump Expresses Shock at Homelessness, 'a Phenomenon That Started Two Years Ago.'" *New York Times*, July 2. Accessed June 13, 2022. https://www .nytimes.com/2019/07/02/us/politics/trump-homeless.html?searchResultPosition=1.

Steil, Justin P., Nicholas F. Kelly, Lawrence J. Vale, and Maia S. Woluchem. 2021. *Furthering Fair Housing Prospects for Racial Justice in America's Neighborhoods.* Philadelphia: Temple University Press.

Stein, Jeff, Tracy Jan, Josh Dawsey, and Ashley Parker. 2019. "Trump Pushing for Major Crackdown on Homeless Camps in California, With Aides Discussing Moving Residents to Government-Backed Facilities." *Washington Post*, September 12. Accessed May 10, 2022. https://www.washingtonpost.com/business/2019/09/10/trump-pushing -major-crackdown-homeless-camps-california-with-aides-discussing-moving-residents -government-backed-facilities/.

United States Department of Housing and Urban Development. 2020. "Press Release: Secretary Carson Terminates 2015 AFFH Rule." July 23. Accessed May 10, 2022. https:// www.hud.gov/press/press_releases_media_advisories/HUD_No_20_109.

Wilkie, Christina. 2020. "Trump Tells Suburban Voters They Will 'No Longer Be Bothered' by Low-Income Housing." *CNBC*, July 29. Accessed June 10, 2022. https://www .cnbc.com/2020/07/29/trump-suburban-voters-will-no-longer-be-bothered-by-low -income-housing.html.

Wilson, Scott. 2019. "Trump's Proposals to Tackle California Homelessness Face Local, Legal Obstacles." *Washington Post*, September 12. Accessed June 13, 2022. https://www .washingtonpost.com/national/trumps-proposals-to-tackle-california-homelessness -face-local-legal-obstacles/2019/09/12/2ab4a2f0-d58b-11e9-9610-fb56c5522e1c _story.html.

Immigration

At a Glance

U.S. immigration policy is one of the most contentious areas of disagreement between America's two major political parties, raising important civil rights issues in regard to the constitutionality and morality of immigrant detention, pathways to citizenship for illegal immigrants, sanctuary cities for undocumented immigrants, and proposed bans on immigrants from Islamic countries. Both parties have supported detention policies to deter immigration; however, they have taken opposing positions on the other issues. Republicans have opposed providing a pathway to citizenship for aliens arguing that it incentivizes illegal immigration, while Democrats have supported a pathway to citizenship for certain types of aliens. Republicans have opposed sanctuary cities—jurisdictions that do not fully cooperate with federal immigration enforcement—as undermining federal immigration enforcement. Democrats have generally supported sanctuary cities because states are not authorized to enforce federal law. Many Republicans supported a travel ban on Islamic countries arguing that they posed a threat to national security, while Democrats opposed such a policy arguing it was racist and un-American.

According to many Republicans . . .

- Longer detention periods for immigrants deter more immigrants from coming to the United States.
- Providing a pathway to citizenship encourages more illegal immigrants to enter the country.
- Sanctuary cities should lose federal grant money because they are thwarting the enforcement of federal law.
- Bans on individuals from Muslim countries enhance national security.

According to many Democrats . . .

- Longer detention periods for immigrants deter more immigrants from coming to the United States.

- pathway to citizenship should be created for aliens brought to the United States when they were minors.
- Sanctuary cities should continue to receive federal grant money because they cannot be required to enforce federal law.
- Bans on individuals from Muslim countries are un-American and harm the United States by radicalizing Islamists.

Overview

The United States is often referred to as a "nation of immigrants." During the founding era, there were few attempts to limit immigration despite some fears that they would threaten the political culture of the new nation. Indeed, the framers of the U.S. Constitution imposed residency and citizenship requirements for members of Congress and required the president to be a "natural born citizen" to guard against foreign influence. The first law restricting immigration was enacted in 1882 and was nakedly racist in its construction: it prohibited Chinese immigrants from entering the country. Congress continued enacting restrictive immigration laws, many of which limited immigrants from non-white countries, until the United States faced labor shortages during World War II. Congress enacted the Immigration and Nationality Act in 1965, which sought to eliminate racial discrimination in immigration policies and instituted limits on the number of immigrants allowed into the United States. The law gave preference to family members of U.S. citizens.

As immigration increased in the twentieth century, Congress enacted legislation governing two broad areas: admission into the country and restricting and removing immigrants. Admission policies regulating the flow of migration currently allow immigrants to enter the country if they advance the goals of family reunification, contribution to the U.S. labor market, diversity of national origin, and humanitarian assistance. Restricting and removing immigrants involves border enforcement and other enforcement actions, including detention and removal. Federal law also distinguishes between several types of immigrants, but recent political controversy has focused on illegal immigrants and refugees. Illegal immigrants are in the United States without government authorization. Refugees or asylum seekers are unable or unwilling to return to their country of origin because of persecution or fear of persecution. They are eligible to become lawful permanent residents (LPR) after one year of continuous residence in the country. An LPR may reside and work permanently in the United States; however, they may be removed for committing certain crimes. Democrats and Republicans have addressed various immigration issues related to civil rights, including immigrant detention, pathways to citizenship for illegal immigrants, sanctuary cities, and a ban on immigrants from Islamic countries.

Detention

Immigrants were first subject to detention in 1892 at Ellis Island, the primary port of entry for European immigrants from 1892 to 1954, when an estimated twelve million immigrants were processed and approved to live in America. The overwhelming majority were only detained for a few hours to check their health, while a much smaller number were detained for a longer period. After the Immigration Act of 1924 was passed, Ellis Island served as a detention facility for individuals entering the United States without appropriate documentation.

In the 1952 Immigration and Nationality Act (INA), Congress limited an individual's detention to ninety days after the final ruling concerning his or her immigration status. The law also gave the attorney general discretion to extend the detention period and allowed migrants to be detained if they lacked a visa. Facing an influx of immigrants from Cuba and Haiti due to political unrest, Republican president Ronald Reagan initiated a detention program to deter future immigrants from those countries in 1981. Relying on the INA provision that permitted detaining migrants without visas, the Reagan administration took the unprecedented step of detaining all arriving migrants, including asylum seekers, until their status could be verified—a process lasting several years. Democratic and Republican presidents have continued to use detention to deter immigration.

Immigrant detention increased significantly in 1996 after the passage of the Antiterrorism and Effective Death Penalty Act (AEDPA) and the Illegal Immigration Reform and Immigrant Responsibility Act (IIRIRA). AEDPA required mandatory detention for immigrants, legal or illegal, convicted of several different types of crime, including minor drug offenses. IIRIRA stipulated additional crimes for which an immigrant could be detained. These laws subjected a person to mandatory detention even if no prison time was required for the crime they committed. IIRIRA also mandated detention for refugees. A refugee who has a valid claim for asylum and is not considered a flight risk may be released by paying a bail bond, which is often difficult. If immigration officials determine than a refugee lacks a credible claim for asylum, then the individual may be deported through a fast-track or "expedited removal" process. Both the AEDPA and IIRIRA had strong bipartisan support in Congress with AEDPA passing by a vote of 91-8 in the Senate and 293-133 in the House of Representatives. IIRIRA passed the House by a vote of 370-37 and the Senate through a voice vote. They were signed by Democratic president Bill Clinton.

The 1997 *Flores* settlement established federal guidelines for the treatment of unaccompanied migrant children. It requires children to be released from detention without any unnecessary delay to a parent, adult relative, or a licensed juvenile facility willing to accept custody. For minors who are detained for their well-being, the government is required to provide an age-appropriate setting and appropriate standards of care, including food, water, and medical care. Children must also be able to contact family members.

In 2014, Democratic president Barack Obama instituted a detention policy to deter a surge in the number of Central American families arriving at the U.S. border requesting asylum. The policy required all female-headed families to remain in private detention facilities until a determination could be made about whether they could enter the country. Obama also expanded a George W. Bush pilot program known as Secure Communities, which required local law enforcement to share fingerprints of individuals they arrested with federal immigration authorities so that they could deport eligible immigrants. This policy increased the number of immigrants who were arrested in the United States and detained pending deportation proceedings. Republican president Donald Trump, who had taken a hard line against immigration during the 2016 presidential campaign, implemented a "zero tolerance policy," which referred any migrant attempting to enter the country, including those seeking asylum, to the U.S. Department of Justice for prosecution. Trump increased the number of Immigration and Customs Enforcement (ICE) agents to detain and deport individuals who had otherwise been living in the United States lawfully. He also ordered that migrant children be separated from their parents at the border, which led to an unprecedented number of children in detention. This situation strained the capacity of detention centers and aroused great media attention when pictures of small children in dirty cages were published. Civil rights and human rights groups opposed Obama's and Trump's actions for violating the Fifth Amendment's guarantee that any person in the United States is entitled to due process of law.

Citizenship

In 1986, Ronald Reagan signed the Immigration Reform and Control Act, which provided amnesty and a path to citizenship for close to three million undocumented individuals who entered the United States prior to January 1, 1982, and met other requirements such as admitting guilt and paying a fine. The law also provided additional funding for increased border security and civil and criminal penalties for employers who hired individuals who were not authorized to work in the United States. It was billed as a "once and for all" solution to immigration because it combined amnesty with stricter border enforcement. Amnesty was also extended in 1987 to include the children of those eligible for citizenship under the law and other family members in 1990.

When the law failed to be a "once and for all" solution to immigration, both parties argued that immigration reform was necessary but could not agree on a solution. In 2001, the Development, Relief, and Education for Alien Minors Act (DREAM Act) was proposed by Republican senator Orrin Hatch and Democratic senator Richard Durbin. This proposal would allow undocumented immigrants a path to citizenship if they were minors when they entered the country illegally and met other requirements, including having a "good moral character" and educational attainment or military service. Although the act did not pass, the term

"Dreamer" is used to refer to undocumented individuals who entered the country when they were minors. When subsequent attempts to enact DREAM legislation failed, President Barack Obama issued an executive order in 2012 creating the Deferred Action for Childhood Arrivals (DACA) program, which delayed deportation for a two-year period for children brought to the United States by illegal immigrants who met certain requirements. Two years later, Obama issued another executive order, Deferred Action for Parents of Americans and Lawful Permanent Residents (DAPA), deferring deportation for parents of children under DACA and illegal immigrants whose children were American citizens to keep those families together. While neither program provided a path to citizenship, Republicans characterized the programs as providing "amnesty." President Donald Trump attempted to rescind both programs, but the U.S. Supreme Court held that the Department of Homeland Security did not provide a sufficient rationale for ending the programs as required by federal law.

In 2013, the Gang of Eight, a group of four Republican and four Democratic senators, introduced the Border Security, Economic Opportunity, and Immigration Modernization Act, which like the 1986 law, and a series of failed bipartisan bills in the 2000s, would have provided an opportunity for citizenship for undocumented immigrants and stronger border security. The bill stipulated, however, that the requirements for border security, including increased surveillance and border enforcement measures, be enacted prior to extending citizenship to an estimated eleven million illegal immigrants. The bill passed the Senate 68-32 with all the chamber's Democrats voting in favor along with fourteen Republicans; however, the Republican-led House of Representatives did not act on the bill. Democrats argue that immigrants who were brought to the United States as minors and immigrants who have contributed to the U.S. economy or who have served in the U.S. military and who do not have a criminal record should be afforded an opportunity to apply for citizenship. Republicans argue that a path to citizenship attracts more illegal immigrants to the country.

Sanctuary Cities

The concept of sanctuary has ancient origins. In biblical times, for example, "cities of refuge" allowed individuals who accidentally killed someone to seek refuge from their victim's family. While there is no authoritative definition of a sanctuary city in the United States, the term generally applies to a state or municipality that refuses to fully cooperate with federal law enforcement authorities in deporting illegal immigrants. The level of cooperation varies, as some jurisdictions will comply with a request from ICE to detain an immigrant eligible for deportation, while others will even refuse an ICE request for information about an immigrant.

Sanctuary cities in the United States originated with the sanctuary movement of the early 1980s. Churches created havens for Central Americans fleeing violence from civil wars in their respective countries because the Reagan administration denied most asylum requests from these individuals. Oregon created the first sanctuary law in 1987. It prohibited the use of state or local law enforcement resources to find or detain individuals whose only crime was being in the United States illegally. In 1996, IIRIRA prohibited cities from withholding information about an individual's immigration status from federal officials; however, many cities circumvented this provision by not collecting immigration status information.

President Obama's Secure Communities program resulted in an increase in sanctuary cities as local law enforcement refused to cooperate with federal authorities in giving them access to fingerprints of individuals they had arrested. Obama rescinded the policy in 2014 and replaced it with the Priority Enhancement Program, which focused on violent offenders. In 2017, Republican president Donald Trump fulfilled a campaign pledge by issuing an executive order rescinding federal funds to sanctuary cities during the first days of his administration. During the campaign and throughout his presidency, Trump highlighted crimes committed by illegal immigrants and sought tougher enforcement of federal immigration law to deter future crimes. He believed that sanctuary cities should be punished for harboring undocumented individuals. Democratic president Joe Biden overturned Trump's executive order that rescinded federal funds in 2021. Democrats argue that states and localities cannot be forced to implement federal law and that sanctuary cities encourage undocumented immigrants to cooperate with local law enforcement, while Republicans argue that sanctuary cities violate federal law, increase illegal immigration, and put U.S. citizens' lives at risk by allowing criminals to remain in the country.

Muslim Ban

During the 2016 presidential campaign when he was a candidate for the Republican nomination, Donald Trump "call[ed] for a total and complete shutdown of Muslims entering the United States until our country's representatives can figure out what is going on" (Taylor 2015). After two shootings involving immigrants from Islamic countries, Trump argued that a ban would protect Americans from crimes committed by Islamic immigrants. This proposal was criticized by Republicans and Democrats alike. After he was elected, Trump issued a series of executive orders known collectively as the "Muslim ban." The first order barred entry into the United States of individuals traveling from seven Muslim-majority countries. The administration asserted that these countries did not confirm the identities of individuals traveling to the United States, which posed a security risk. In the final order, two non-Muslim countries were added to the list, including North Korea.

In *Trump v. Hawaii* (2018), the U.S. Supreme Court upheld this policy by a 5-4 vote. The Court's ruling emphasized that the president had adequate authority to issue the executive order to protect national security and that the administration conducted a review of relevant facts as a basis for the order. In dissent,

Justices Sonia Sotomayor and Ruth Bader Ginsburg argued that the ruling "leaves undisturbed a policy first advertised openly and unequivocally as a 'total and complete shutdown of Muslims entering the United States' because the policy now masquerades behind a façade of national-security concerns." President Joe Biden reversed this policy on Inauguration Day having referred to it as "morally wrong" during the campaign. While many Republicans opposed the ban, some were also supportive. Democrats opposed the ban labeling it discriminatory and un-American.

Republicans

Detention

Donald Trump began his 2016 presidential campaign by criticizing U.S. immigration policy. He characterized Mexican immigrants as "people that have lots of problems, and they're bringing those problems with us. They're bringing drugs. They're bringing crime. They're rapists. And some, I assume, are good people" (*Time* 2015). As president, Trump pursued a zero tolerance immigration policy bringing criminal charges against those caught crossing the border illegally. The most controversial aspect of the policy called for the detention of families, with children being placed in separate detention facilities. While Trump justified the policy as a deterrent to prevent future immigrants, he faced criticism from members of his own party. Republican senator Ben Sasse urged the president to "immediately end" the policy (Wagner 2018). Even former first lady Laura Bush wrote an op-ed in the *Washington Post* stating that "[o]ur government should not be in the business of warehousing children in converted box stores or making plans to place them in tent cities in the desert outside of El Paso. These images are eerily reminiscent of the internment camps for U.S. citizens and noncitizens of Japanese descent during World War II, now considered to have been one of the most shameful episodes in U.S. history" (Bush 2018).

After a "fierce political backlash," Trump abandoned the policy, which had been in effect for six weeks (Shear and Kanno-Youngs 2019). During that time, 2,816 children were separated from their parents. In an executive order entitled "Affording Congress an Opportunity to Address Family Separation," Trump ordered the indefinite detention of immigrant families who crossed the border illegally (The White House 2018). This violated a 2015 amendment to the *Flores* settlement that children could only be held in custody for twenty days even if they were with their families. If the families remained in custody, the children were treated as unaccompanied alien minors. A request by the Department of Justice to extend the twenty-day time period was denied by a federal judge. A Congressional Research Service report has estimated that between 5,300 and 5,500 children were separated from their families during the Trump administration (Congressional Research Service 2021).

Citizenship

During the 1980s, many Republicans supported amnesty for illegal immigrants. In a 1984 presidential debate, Ronald Reagan stated, "I believe in the idea of amnesty for those who have put down roots and lived here, even though sometime back they may have entered illegally." He also criticized employers who had encouraged illegal immigration by hiring workers at "starvation wages and with none of the benefits that we think are normal and natural for workers in our country. And the individuals can't complain because of their illegal status" (*New York Times* 1984). Reagan supported the bipartisan Immigration and Reform Act (IRA) of 1986. At the bill signing ceremony, he stated, "The legalization provisions in this act will go far to improve the lives of a class of individuals who now must hide in the shadows, without access to many of the benefits of a free and open society. Very soon many of these men and women will be able to step into the sunlight and, ultimately, if they choose, they may become Americans" (Reagan 1986). In 1987, Reagan expanded this policy to include undocumented children of those who had applied for amnesty. George H. W. Bush took similar action when he signed the Immigration Act of 1990. This wide-ranging law increased the number of educated and skilled immigrants allowed into the United States and extended a pathway to citizenship for family members of illegal immigrants covered by the 1986 law. However, because the IRA was not successful in limiting illegal immigration, primarily due to inadequate resources for enforcement, the term "amnesty" has been associated with support for illegal immigration. Republicans are divided over whether to create a pathway to citizenship for illegal immigrants.

President George W. Bush supported a pathway to citizenship and strong border enforcement. Bush was in favor of the Comprehensive Immigration Reform Act of 2007, which was a new version of a 2006 bill cosponsored by Republican senator John McCain and Democratic senator Ted Kennedy. This Senate bill included the DREAM Act, a temporary guest worker program and increased enforcement of the U.S.-Mexico border and outlined a process for citizenship. Many conservative Republicans opposed the bill because of the citizenship provision and concerns that the guest worker program would result in more illegal immigration.

Since 2008, Republicans have emphasized border security over a path to citizenship. During the 2008 election campaign, the Republican nominee, Senator John McCain, stated that he would no longer vote for his own bill. Instead, he proposed a path to citizenship only after governors of border states certified that their borders were secure. Regarding illegal immigrants residing in the United States, he stated, "[m]ake them earn citizenship because they have broken our laws. My friends, that's not amnesty. Amnesty is forgiveness. We're not forgiving anything" (Carter et al. 2008). The 2012 platform characterized securing "the rule of law both at our borders and at ports of entry" as the party's "highest priority" and that "[g]ranting amnesty only rewards and encourages more law breaking."

The political controversy over DACA also involved debate over granting a path to citizenship to Dreamers. During the 2016 presidential campaign, Donald Trump indicated that he was opposed to DACA even when a 2016 Gallup poll indicated that 76 percent of Republicans, and 84 percent of Americans overall, supported a path to citizenship for illegal immigrants (Jones 2016). Indeed, there was more support for a path to citizenship than for Trump's controversial proposed border wall between the U.S. and Mexico, which 62% of Republicans supported (Jones 2016). When President Trump ended DACA in 2017 after eleven states sued claiming the program was unconstitutional, he suggested that Congress find a way to address the issue. Many Republicans supported renewing the program but only with increased border security. In 2017, Republican senator John Cornyn stated that Dreamers "should not be penalized for being brought here illegally through no fault of their own." However, he also stated that "[b]efore we provide legal status to these young people, we must reassure and actually regain the public confidence that we're serious when it comes to enforcing the law and securing our borders" (Meckler 2017).

While the White House and Democrats suggested that a pathway to citizenship should be offered if Congress renewed DACA, some Republicans opposed that idea. In 2020, President Trump reiterated his support for finding a path to citizenship for Dreamers claiming that even conservative Republicans supported the proposal. According to John Binder, writing in *Breitbart*, most conservative Republicans opposed DACA and indicated that "Trump's comments left them 'stunned,' 'appalled,' and 'worried'" (Binder 2020). Indeed, William Gheen, who heads the Americans for Legal Immigration PAC, stated that "[t]here is substantial, strong opposition to this that damages Trump's credibility even further because he campaigned on ending DACA and told us they had to go home in 2016. I believe if Trump signs anything like this for Obama's DACA illegal aliens, it will kill his campaign" (Binder 2020).

In addition to believing that amnesty or a path to citizenship would increase illegal immigration, some Republicans favor eliminating birthright citizenship to prevent the children of illegal immigrants from attaining U.S. citizenship. The Fourteenth Amendment provides that "[a]ll persons born or naturalized in the United States and subject to the jurisdiction thereof, are citizens of the United States and of the State where they reside." During the 2016 campaign, Donald Trump advocated eliminating birthright citizenship, and in 2019, he referred to the constitutional guarantee as "frankly ridiculous" (Lyons 2019). Trump and other conservatives argue that the provision encourages undocumented mothers to give birth to "anchor babies," which would allow the family to gain legal residence. He announced that he was considering ending birthright citizenship. According to many legal experts, the president lacked the authority to do so because a constitutional amendment would be required. Critics of ending birthright citizenship note that the majority of immigrants who have given birth in the United States were in

President Trump Touts the Importance of a Border Wall

A key part of President Trump's immigration policy was a proposed wall between the United States and Mexico. In the excerpt below, Trump explains why a wall is necessary.

My administration has presented Congress with a detailed proposal to secure the border and stop the criminal gangs, drug smugglers and human traffickers. It's a tremendous problem. Our proposal was developed by law enforcement professionals and border agents at the Department of Homeland Security . . . We have requested more agents, immigration judges, and bed space to process the sharp rise in unlawful migration fueled by our very strong economy. Our plan also contains an urgent request for humanitarian assistance and medical support. Furthermore, we have asked Congress to close border security loopholes so that illegal immigrant children can be safely and humanely returned back home. Finally, as part of an overall approach to border security, law enforcement professionals have requested $5.7 billion for a physical barrier. At the request of Democrats, it will be a steel barrier rather than a concrete wall.

This barrier is absolutely critical to border security. It's also what our professionals at the border want and need. This is just common sense. The border wall would very quickly pay for itself. The cost of illegal drugs exceeds $500 billion a year. Vastly more than the $5.7 billion we have requested from Congress. The wall will always be paid for indirectly by the great new trade deal we have made with Mexico. . . . The federal government remains shut down for one reason and one reason only because Democrats will not fund border security. . . . Some have suggested a barrier is immoral. Then why do wealthy politicians build walls, fences and gates around their homes? They don't build walls because they hate the people on the outside, but because they love the people on the inside. The only thing that is immoral is for the politicians to do nothing and continue to allow more innocent people to be so horribly victimized.

Source

Trump, Donald J. 2019. "Address to the Nation on Border Security." American Presidency Project, January 8. Accessed November 22, 2022. https://www.presidency.ucsb.edu /documents/address-the-nation-border-security.

the country at least two years prior to giving birth. Also, even though the children are citizens, if the parents are in the United States illegally, they can be deported.

Sanctuary Cities

Republicans oppose sanctuary cities and have taken executive and legislative action to end them. The party first addressed the issue in its 2008 platform, which asserted that sanctuary cities "endanger the lives of U.S. citizens" and that federal funding should be withheld from those jurisdictions. Every subsequent platform has contained a similar statement.

President Trump attempted to unilaterally end federal law enforcement grants to sanctuary cities in 2017 through an executive order. Specifically, the order cited the "immeasurable harm to the American people and to the very fabric of our republic" sanctuary cities caused by refusing to comply with federal law. After federal courts ruled that the president cannot unilaterally withhold federal funding that had been approved by Congress, Trump suggested moving all illegal immigrants to sanctuary cities or states in 2019.

In a meeting with California officials who opposed the state's sanctuary cities law, President Trump stated, "We have people coming into the country, or trying to come in, we're stopping a lot of them, but we're taking people out of the country, you wouldn't believe how bad these people are. These aren't people. These are animals, and we're taking them out of the country at a rate that's never happened before" (Samuels 2018). Jennifer Rubin, writing in the *Washington Post*, criticized Trump's comments. "Even if he was referring to the tiny percentage of immigrants who commit crimes, his efforts to conflate criminals with all illegal immigrants is repulsive, as is calling any human being an 'animal.' Moreover, it is false that we have never deported so many people; President Barack Obama deported far more. Trump's continued misrepresentation of the numbers seeks to instill fear and prompt egregious action" (Rubin 2018).

Congressional Republicans have proposed legislation such as the Stop Sanctuaries Act of 2015 and the Immigration Detainer Enforcement Act of 2019 to end sanctuary cities. The 2015 bill provided that states or localities refusing to comply with ICE requests would lose federal grant money. Republicans, however, were split on one of the provisions of the bill requiring a mandatory minimum sentence of five years for illegal immigrants who attempted to reenter the United States after deportation. Senator Ted Cruz, who had previously supported mandatory minimums in these situations, stated that "[i]t is legislation that ought to pass 100 to nothing. Every senator, Republican and Democrat, should support keeping this nation safe from criminal illegal aliens" (Kim 2015). Other Republicans were opposed to mandatory minimums for any crimes, including immigration. The 2019 bill also required sanctuary cities to comply with ICE requests but provided incentives to those jurisdictions through federal reimbursement of detention and other costs; however, neither bill was approved.

Muslim Ban

During the 2016 race for the Republican nomination, Donald Trump's proposal for a "total and complete ban" on all Muslims entering the United States was criticized by other Republican contenders. For example, New Jersey governor Chris Christie stated that "[t]his is the kind of thing people say when they have no experience and no idea what they're talking about," while Senator Lindsey Graham tweeted that "every candidate for president needs to do the right thing and condemn" the statement. *Time Magazine* characterized Trump's proposed ban as "an unprecedented proposal by a leading American presidential candidate, and an idea more typically associated with hate groups" (*Time* 2015).

After he issued the executive order, Trump insisted that the order was not a Muslim ban. House Speaker Paul Ryan echoed this characterization saying that the ban was "not a religious test and it is not a ban on people of any religion" (Snell, Demirjian, and DeBonis 2017). Other Congressional Republicans such as Senator Jeff Flake and Congressman Charlie Dent opposed the Muslim ban because of the impact it had on lawful immigrants and family members of U.S. citizens who had been properly vetted. Flake argued that the administration was correct to focus on national security but should not have ascribed "radical Islamic terrorist views to all Muslims" (Snell, Demirjian, and DeBonis 2017). A February 2017 Quinnipiac public opinion poll showed that while 51 percent of Americans viewed the policy as a Muslim ban, most Republicans surveyed (81 percent) did not (Quinnipiac University Poll 2017).

Democrats

Detention

After President Clinton signed the AEDPA and the IIRIRA in 1996, the number of immigrants held in detention centers increased from approximately 8,500 in 1996 to almost 16,000 in 1998. The Obama administration policies also contributed to an increase in immigrant detention. The Secure Communities program, which began as a pilot program under President George W. Bush, required local law enforcement to submit fingerprints of individuals they arrested to federal database to identify illegal immigrants eligible for deportation. Immigrants who had committed minor offenses were arrested by ICE and detained pending deportation proceedings. This program was criticized by law enforcement groups, immigrant rights groups, and civil rights groups. The American Immigration Council, for example, noted that while the program was supposed to target illegal immigrants who had committed serious crimes, 26 percent of those deported did not have a criminal record. The organization was also concerned that the program would lead to racial profiling because local law enforcement would arrest someone to determine whether they were in the United States illegally (American Immigration Council 2011). The program was replaced in 2014 by the Priority Enforcement Program, which focused on detaining and deporting violent criminals, gang members, and immigrants who posed a threat to national security. In a special address on immigration, Obama stated that he would emphasize "[f]elons, not families. Criminals, not children. Gang members, not a mom who's working hard to provide for her kids. We'll prioritize, just like law enforcement does every day" (The White House 2014).

In the summer of 2014, Obama instituted "an aggressive deterrence strategy" following an influx of migrants fleeing violence and persecution in Central America requiring families to be detained to deter others from attempting to seek asylum. Individuals and families were detained even after an immigration judge found that they had a "credible fear of persecution" in their country and that their asylum claims were likely to be granted. Previously, refugees who had received similar rulings were allowed into the country pending an asylum hearing. After a lawsuit by the American Civil Liberties Union (ACLU) arguing that the policy violated the Fifth Amendment's Due Process Clause, a federal judge ordered that the families be released because the policy violated the *Flores* settlement by housing them in deplorable conditions for an indeterminate amount of time.

In 2015, Democratic nominee Hillary Clinton criticized the Obama detention policies for putting the physical and mental health of children and other vulnerable people at risk. She argued that the emphasis should be on detaining individuals who have "a record of violent, illegal behavior" and not on people who are fleeing violence in their home country (Sneed 2015). Immigration activists agreed with her assessment noting that detention exacerbates the trauma that refugees, especially children, have endured.

Democrats also opposed President Trump's policies of separating children from their parents at the border. Democrats were particularly vocal when Trump falsely blamed them for creating the policy (Wagner 2018). Senate minority leader, Democrat Charles Schumer, stated that "everyone who has looked at this agrees, this was done by the president, not Democrats. He can fix it tomorrow if he wants to, and if he doesn't want to, he should own up to the fact that he's doing it" (Wagner 2018).

In 2020, the Democratic platform stated that detention should be "a last resort." It provided that the party would implement "effective and cost-efficient community-based alternatives to detention" particularly for "individuals with special vulnerabilities." That group included those suffering from serious physical or mental illness, the disabled, elderly, pregnant or nursing women, LGBTQ individuals, and those "whose detention is otherwise not in the public interest." It also pledged to improve the conditions of detention facilities and limit the amount of time children were detained.

Citizenship

Democrats support a path to citizenship for some illegal immigrants. During Congressional negotiations of immigration reform legislation through the 2000s and 2010s, Democrats insisted that an opportunity for illegal immigrants to earn citizenship be part of any legislation. Recent party platforms have also articulated this support. The 2016 platform supported DACA and DAPA, and in the 2020 platform, Democrats pledged to "provide a roadmap to citizenship for the millions of undocumented workers, caregivers, students, and children who are an essential part of our economy and of the fabric of our nation."

The Biden administration proposed the U.S. Citizenship Act of 2021, which outlined an "earned roadmap to citizenship for undocumented individuals." The roadmap allowed undocumented immigrants the opportunity to apply for

The Biden White House Touts the U.S. Citizenship Act of 2021

President Biden and Congressional Democrats supported legislation to provide a path to citizenship for illegal immigrants, including Dreamers. This statement summarizes the rationale behind the legislation.

The U.S. Citizenship Act of 2021 establishes a new system to responsibly manage and secure our border, keep our families and communities safe, and better manage migration across the Hemisphere.

President Biden is sending a bill to Congress on day one to restore humanity and American values to our immigration system. The bill provides hardworking people who enrich our communities every day and who have lived here for years, in some cases for decades, an opportunity to earn citizenship. The legislation modernizes our immigration system, and prioritizes keeping families together, growing our economy, responsibly managing the border with smart investments, addressing the root causes of migration from Central America, and ensuring that the United States remains a refuge for those fleeing persecution. The bill will stimulate our economy while ensuring that every worker is protected. The bill creates an earned path to citizenship for our immigrant neighbors, colleagues, parishioners, community leaders, friends, and loved ones—including Dreamers and the essential workers who have risked their lives to serve and protect American communities.

Source
"Fact Sheet: President Biden Sends Immigration Bill to Congress as Part of His Commitment to Modernize Our Immigration System." 2021. The White House, January 20. Accessed November 22, 2022. https://www.whitehouse.gov/briefing-room/statements-releases/2021/01/20/fact-sheet-president-biden-sends-immigration-bill-to-congress-as-part-of-his-commitment-to-modernize-our-immigration-system/.

temporary legal status and the ability to apply for green cards, indicating that they are lawful permanent residents, after five years if they pay taxes and pass criminal and national security background checks. The bill made green cards available immediately for certain groups, including Dreamers, and after three years, all green card holders who passed background checks and demonstrated knowledge of English and U.S. civics can apply for citizenship. Also in 2021, the House of Representatives passed the American Dream and Promise Act specifically geared toward citizenship for Dreamers. It passed by a vote of 228-197 with all Democrats and nine Republicans voting for it. Republicans opposed the plan arguing that it would exacerbate the border crisis by incentivizing immigration. Republican Congressman Chris Jacobs opposed the bill "because we cannot continue to put off strong border security measures and encourage unlawful entry" (Walker 2021).

Sanctuary Cities
Democrats have supported sanctuary cities because they encourage illegal immigrants who are victims of crimes or who have information about criminal activity

to report those to the police. They also prevent otherwise law-abiding individuals from being deported for minor crimes. Additionally, Democrats argue that states cannot enforce federal law. The Obama administration's expansion of the Secure Communities program contributed to the growth of sanctuary cities. He rescinded the policy in 2014 after opposition from state officials and immigrant rights groups.

The Secure Communities program required state and local governments to cooperate with ICE and the Department of Homeland Security in detaining illegal immigrants who had been arrested. As the program continued, more jurisdictions refused to cooperate with federal authorities. Several states, including California, New York, and Connecticut, enacted legislation in 2013 limiting state law enforcement from cooperating with federal immigration authorities in the Secure Communities program. States opposed the policy in part because it cost them millions of dollars to enforce federal law. In 2012, California spent an estimated $65 million holding immigrants pursuant to an ICE request (Brady 2017).Criticism of the program was not limited to public officials. Religious organizations also opposed the policy. The Conference of Catholic Bishops criticized the policy because of the effect it had on separating families. The Seventy-Seventh General Convention of the Episcopal Church passed a resolution in 2012 calling for an end to the program because it "targets communities of color and terrorizes them" (Brady 2017). In 2015, Obama opposed attempts by Congressional Republicans to end federal funding for sanctuary cities.

Muslim Ban
The 2016 platform stated that Democrats opposed the Muslim ban in favor of looking "for ways to help innocent people who are fleeing persecution while ensuring rigorous screening and vetting." Democratic nominee Hillary Clinton characterized the ban as "un-American" and stated that the proposal was "dangerous" because it would strain U.S. relations with partners in Muslim countries to fight terrorists and make it more difficult to build trust with Muslim communities to counter the radicalization of Muslims in the United States. She also argued that Trump's rhetoric was a recruiting tool for ISIS and that it was turning "Americans against Americans," which also benefits ISIS (Beckwith 2016).

The 2020 platform pledged to eliminate the Muslim ban and enact legislation to prevent another president from undertaking such action. During the campaign, Joe Biden stated that the policy was "morally wrong" and racially motivated (Biden 2020). He rescinded it on Inauguration Day 2021. In the presidential proclamation accompanying the order, Biden stated that the orders implementing the ban "are a stain on our national conscience and are inconsistent with our long history of welcoming people of all faiths and no faith at all" (The White House 2021). He also stated that the orders undermined national security because they have "jeopardized our global network of alliances and partnerships and are a moral blight that has dulled the power of our example the world over. And they have separated loved ones, inflicting pain that will ripple for years to come." Biden pledged to "apply a rigorous, individualized vetting system. But we will not turn our backs on our values with discriminatory bans on entry into the United States."

To prevent a future president from implementing travel restrictions based on religion, House Democrats passed the National Origin-Based Antidiscrimination for Nonimmigrants Act (NO BAN Act) in 2021. This bill, which also passed the House in 2019, amended the INA of 1952 and prohibited a president from banning entry of an individual to the United States based on religion. It also restricted temporary bans to those that address specific acts that implicate a compelling governmental interest in protecting national security, human rights, democratic processes, or international stability. The bill also required the president to consult with Congress and provide a follow-up report to it within forty-eight hours or the ban would expire (Visser 2021). The Biden administration issued a statement supporting the legislation arguing that "the prior Administration's haphazard misuse of this authority highlights the need for reasonable constraints" (Executive Office of the President 2021). The statement further asserted that the administration was willing to work with Congress to create a solution that does not allow religious discrimination but that also gives the executive the necessary flexibility to deal with security, public health, and international crises.

Further Reading

Allen, Elizabeth. 2015. "Op-Ed: Why Sanctuary Cities Must Exist." *Los Angeles Times*, September 17. Accessed November 12, 2021. https://www.latimes.com/opinion/op-ed/la-oe-allen-sanctuary-cities-20150917-story.html.

American Immigration Council. 2011. "Secure Communities: A Fact Sheet." November 29. Accessed November 3, 2021. https://www.americanimmigrationcouncil.org/research/secure-communities-fact-sheet.

Beckwith, Ryan Teague. 2016. "Read Hillary Clinton's Speech Criticizing Trump's Muslim Ban." *Time*, June 16. Accessed November 7, 2021. https://time.com/4368907/hillary-clinton-muslim-ban-donald-trump-orlando-shooting/.

Beitsch, Rebecca. 2021. "DOJ Rescinds Trump-Era 'Sanctuary Cities' Policy." *The Hill*, April 28. Accessed November 14, 2021. https://thehill.com/homenews/administration/550675-doj-rescinds-trump-era-sanctuary-cities-policy.

Benton, Grace. 2018. "The Legality of Sanctuary Cities." *Georgetown Immigration Law Journal* 33(1) (Fall): 139–144.

Biden, Joe. 2020. "Joe Biden's Agenda for Muslim-American Communities." Joe Biden for President: Official Campaign Website. Accessed November 16, 2021. https://joebiden.com/muslimamerica/.

Binder, John. 2020. "Grassroots Conservatives View DACA Amnesty as End of the Road for GOP." *Breitbart*, July 15. Accessed December 18, 2022. https://www.breitbart.com/politics/2020/07/15/grassroots-conservatives-view-daca-amnesty-as-end-of-the-road-for-gop/.

Brady, Katlyn. 2017. "Sanctuary Cities and the Demise of the Secure Communities Program." *Texas Hispanic Journal of Law and Policy* 23: 21–50.

Bush, Laura. 2018. "Opinion: Laura Bush: Separating Children from Their Parents at the Border 'Breaks My Heart.'" *Washington Post*, June 17. Accessed November 18, 2021. https://www.washingtonpost.com/opinions/laura-bush-separating-children-from -their-parents-at-the-border-breaks-my-heart/2018/06/17/f2df517a-7287-11e8-9780 -b1dd6a09b549_story.html.

Carter, Shan, Jonathan Ellis, Farhan Hossein, and Alan McLean. 2008. "On the Issues: Immigration." *New York Times*. Accessed November 19, 2021. https://www.nytimes .com/elections/2008/president/issues/immigration.html.

Congressional Research Service. 2021. "The Trump Administration's 'Zero Tolerance' Immigration Enforcement Policy." February 2. Accessed December 18, 2022. https://sgp.fas .org/crs/homesec/R45266.pdf.

Editorial Board of *New York Times*. 2016. "Mr. Obama's Dubious Detention Centers." *New York Times*, July 18. Accessed November 20, 2021. https://www.nytimes.com/2016 /07/18/opinion/mr-obamas-dubious-detention-centers.html.

Executive Office of the President. 2021. "Statement of Administration Policy: H.R. 1333— National Origin-Based Antidiscrimination for Nonimmigrants (NO BAN) Act." April 20. Accessed November 23, 2021. https://www.whitehouse.gov/wp-content /uploads/2021/04/SAP-H.R.-1333.pdf.

Fabian, Jordan. 2017. "Trump Defends Order: It's Not a Muslim Ban." *The Hill*, January 28. Accessed November 24, 2021. https://thehill.com/business-a-lobbying/316703 -trump-defends-order-its-not-a-muslim-ban?rl=1.

Ghosh, Smita. 2019. "How Migrant Detention Became American Policy." *Washington Post*, July 19. Accessed November 26, 2021. https://www.washingtonpost.com/outlook /2019/07/19/how-migrant-detention-became-american-policy/.

Jones, Jeffrey M. 2016. "More Republicans Favor Path to Citizenship Than Wall." Gallup, July 20. Accessed December 18, 2022. https://news.gallup.com/poll/193817/republicans -favor-path-citizenship-wall.aspx.

Kim, Seung Min. 2015. "Immigration Crackdown Splits GOP." *Politico*, August 11. Accessed November 27, 2021. https://www.politico.com/story/2015/08/immigration -gop-rift-mandatory-minimum-senate-cruz-121231.

Lyons, Patrick J. 2019. "Trump Wants to Abolish Birthright Citizenship. Can He Do That?" *New York Times*, August 22. Accessed December 18, 2022. https://www.nytimes .com/2019/08/22/us/birthright-citizenship-14th-amendment-trump.html.

Meckler, Laura. 2017. "Senate Republicans Signal Support for 'Dreamers,' With Conditions." *Wall Street Journal*, October 3. Accessed December 18, 2022. https://www.wsj.com /articles/senate-republicans-signal-support-for-dreamers-with-conditions-15070 71347.

New York Times. 1984. "The Candidates' Debate: Transcript of the Reagan-Mondale Debate on Foreign Policy." October 22. Accessed December 8, 2021. https://www.nytimes .com/1984/10/22/us/the-candidates-debate-transcript-of-the-reagan-mondale-debate -on-foreign-policy.html.

Preston, Julia. 2015. "Judge Orders Release of Immigrant Children Detained by U.S." *New York Times*, July 25. Accessed November 29, 2021. https://www.nytimes.com /2015/07/26/us/detained-immigrant-children-judge-dolly-gee-ruling.html.

Quinnipiac University Poll. 2017. "American Voters Oppose Trump Immigration Ban, Quinnipiac University National Poll Finds; Big Gender Gap as Voters Disapprove of Trump." February 7. Accessed November 30, 2021. https://poll.qu.edu/Poll-Release -Legacy?releaseid=2427.

Reagan, Ronald. 1986. "Statement on Signing the Immigration Reform and Control Act of 1986." Reagan Presidential Library. Accessed November 30, 2021. https://www.reaganlibrary .gov/archives/speech/statement-signing-immigration-reform-and-control-act-1986.

Rubin, Jennifer. 2018. "Opinion: Republicans Are Blowing Their Cover on DACA." *Washington Post*, May 17. Accessed November 30, 2021. https://www.washingtonpost.com /blogs/right-turn/wp/2018/05/17/republicans-are-blowing-their-cover-on-daca/.

Samuels, Brett. 2018. "Trump on Immigrant Gang Members: 'These Aren't People,' They're 'Animals.'" *The Hill*, May 16. Accessed December 2, 2021. https://thehill.com/homenews /administration/388026-trump-on-immigrant-gang-members-these-arent-people-theyre -animals.

Shear, Michael D., and Zolan Kanno-Youngs. 2019. "Migrant Families Would Face Indefinite Detention Under New Trump Rule." *New York Times*, August 22. Accessed December 3, 2021. https://www.nytimes.com/2019/08/21/us//politics/flores-migrant-family -detention.html.

Sneed, Tierney. 2015. "Clinton Criticizes Immigrant Detentions Under Obama." *U.S. News and World Report*, May 6. Accessed December 5, 2021. https://www.usnews .com/news/articles/2015/05/06/hillary-clinton-criticizes-immigrant-detention-practices -under-obama.

Snell, Kelsey, Karoun Demirjian, and Mike DeBonis. 2017. "Facing Intense Criticism, Some Republicans Are Speaking Out against Trump's Refugee Ban: Paul Ryan and Mitch McConnell Aren't among Them." *Washington Post*, January 28. Accessed December 6, 2021. https://www.washingtonpost.com/powerpost/paul-ryan-trumps-refugee-ban -does-not-target-muslims/2017/01/28/e0cf1fe4-e56e-11e6-a547-5fb9411d332c _story.html?utm_term=.90a06c7b2cef.

Taylor, Jessica. 2015. "Trump Calls for 'Total and Complete Shutdown of Muslims Entering' U.S." National Public Radio, December 7. Accessed December 12, 2021. https://www.npr.org/2015/12/07/458836388/trump-calls-for-total-and-complete -shutdown-of-muslims-entering-u-s.

Time. 2015. "Here's Donald Trump's Presidential Announcement Speech." June 16. Accessed December 17, 2021. https://time.com/3923128/donald-trump-announcement-speech/.

University of Texas at Austin. 2019. "The Flores Settlement." *Immigration History*. Accessed December 20, 2021. https://immigrationhistory.org/item/the-flores-settlement/.

Visser, Nick. 2021. "House Votes to Restrict President from Imposing Travel Bans." *HuffPost*, April 21. Accessed December 3, 2021. https://www.huffpost.com/entry/house -democrats-travel-no-ban-act_n_6080da8ce4b05c4290711fc6.

Wagner, John. 2018. "White House Falsely Insists Democrats to Blame for Family Separations, Even as Some in GOP Urge Trump to Reverse Course." *Washington Post*, June 18. Accessed December 3, 2021. https://www.washingtonpost.com/politics/white-house -insists-democrats-to-blame-for-family-separations-even-as-some-in-gop-urge-trump -to-reverse-course/2018/06/18/6626589c-72db-11e8-b4b7-308400242c2e_story .html.

Walker, James 2021. "GOP Says Dream Act Incentivizes Border Surge after Joe Biden Accused of Inviting Crisis." *Newsweek*, March 19. Accessed December 29, 2021. https:// www.newsweek.com/gop-dream-act-incentivizes-border-crossing-crisis-1577275.

The White House. 2014. "Remarks by the President in Address to the Nation on Immigration." November 14. Accessed December 10, 2021. https://obamawhitehouse.archives.gov/the-press-office/2014/11/20/remarks-President-address-nation-immigration.

The White House. 2018. "Affording Congress an Opportunity to Address Family Separation—the White House." June 20. Accessed December 18, 2022. https://trumpwhitehouse.archives.gov/presidential-actions/affording-congress-opportunity-address-family-separation/.

The White House. 2021. "Proclamation on Ending Discriminatory Bans on Entry to the United States." January 20. Accessed December 15, 2021. https://www.whitehouse.gov/briefing-room/presidential-actions/2021/01/20/proclamation-ending-discriminatory-bans-on-entry-to-the-united-states/.

Information Privacy and Internet Freedom

At a Glance

Information privacy has become increasingly important in the United States, given massive data breaches affecting the personal information of millions of Americans. Both parties support stronger information privacy legislation but have disagreed over whether individuals should be able to sue companies that compromise their personal data and whether a federal privacy law should supersede state privacy laws.

The extent to which net neutrality, the equal treatment of information on the internet, should be protected is part of the privacy debate as well. The Federal Communications Commission (FCC) implemented rules to guarantee net neutrality in 2015 and to increase consumer privacy protection in 2016. In 2017, the FCC rescinded the net neutrality regulations while Congressional Republicans rescinded the privacy regulations. Republicans argued that the regulations gave the FCC too much regulatory authority, but the party is divided over the extent to which the internet should be regulated. Democrats argue that net neutrality is necessary for consumers to have fair access to information online and that the FCC has the authority to protect privacy.

Universal broadband internet access has become a more significant issue since the COVID-19 pandemic. Republicans argue that the federal government should play a limited role in providing universal broadband access because private businesses should take the lead. Democrats argue that the government should provide access to affordable universal broadband service because the internet is essential to the U.S. economy and an integral part of modern educational instruction.

According to many Republicans . . .

- Federal information privacy legislation should not include a private right of action because of the detrimental effect lawsuits can have on small companies.

- Federal information privacy legislation should supersede state legislation because Americans' privacy protection should not vary by state.
- The FCC should not implement policies regarding net neutrality because they give the federal government too much control over the internet.
- Universal broadband access should be expanded through the efforts of private companies.

According to many Democrats . . .

- Federal information privacy legislation should include a private right of action to hold companies accountable for data privacy breaches.
- Federal information privacy legislation should respect state privacy legislation because it might provide more protection than federal legislation.
- Net neutrality should be regulated to guarantee a free and open internet.
- Universal broadband access should be expanded through increased government investment.

Overview

In 1890, law firm partners Samuel Warren and future Supreme Court Justice Louis Brandeis wrote an influential *Harvard Law Review* article addressing privacy rights. While their concern was that the press was exposing the personal lives of citizens, the notion that there was a fundamental "right to be let alone" had a significant impact on the development of American privacy law. During industrialization, growing population density in many cities made people more aware of physical privacy. The increase in literacy rates and in the number of mass-circulated newspapers may have resulted in an interest in information privacy and publicity. Finally, technological developments, such as the camera and telephone, allowed people to document and record information about others (Allen and Rotenberg 2016). In the 1920s, states began to classify invasions of privacy as torts, or civil wrongs. In *Griswold v. Connecticut* (1965), the U.S. Supreme Court held that the Bill of Rights protected an implied constitutional right to privacy; however, courts have not extended constitutional protection to information privacy.

A Wave of Information Privacy Legislation

Information privacy, also known as data privacy, involves protecting personal information collected by the government, companies, financial institutions, educational institutions, and other entities. Federal legislation in this area of privacy has been piecemeal and bipartisan. While protecting personal information from becoming public has long been a concern, federal legislation regarding information privacy was not enacted until 1968. Title III of the Omnibus Crime Control and

Safe Streets Act (1968) is a comprehensive law regulating wiretaps and telephone surveillance by the government. In a series of laws passed in the 1970s, Congress addressed specific aspects of information privacy. The Fair Credit Report Act (1970) limits the circumstances under which credit reporting agencies can release information contained in credit reports.

The 1974 Privacy Act, the most significant federal privacy law, sets guidelines concerning the collection and dissemination of information about individuals held by federal agencies. The Family Educational Rights and Privacy Act (1974) protects students' personal and educational information, including restrictions on disclosure of student records to third parties. Congress has continued to enact laws dealing with specific areas of information privacy, such as the Employee Polygraph Protection Act (1988), which prohibits most private employers from requiring their prospective or current employees to take lie-detector tests, and the Driver's Privacy Protection Act (1994), which governs access to car records. More recent legislation has addressed medical privacy, including the Health Insurance Portability and Accountability Act (HIPAA) in 1996, which protects medical records, and the Genetic Non-Discrimination Act (2008), which prevents employers and insurers from discriminating against individuals based on their genetic information.

The contemporary debate over information privacy legislation has been influenced by several highly publicized data breaches of personal information of Americans in the 2010s. In 2013, Edward Snowden, a National Security Agency contractor, leaked information exposing an illegal surveillance program run by the federal government that gathered telephone records, texts, emails, and other information about internet use of U.S. citizens and world leaders. Four years later, Equifax, an American credit bureau, was hacked jeopardizing the personal information of 147 million Americans. And, in 2018, a whistleblower revealed that Facebook allowed Cambridge Analytica, a political consulting firm, to gather personal data from eighty-seven million Facebook users for political advertising.

Democratic president Barack Obama outlined a Consumer Privacy Bill of Rights in 2012 but did not release a bill encompassing the provisions until 2015. Congressional Republicans and Democrats have introduced several bills since 2019 to provide greater protection to Americans' personal information. Industry experts and privacy advocates have been arguing that a federal privacy law is urgently needed particularly since the European Union and some states, including California, have either instituted or enhanced their privacy laws.

Republicans and Democrats agree in principle that information privacy deserves greater protection; however, the parties disagree over the extent to which individuals should be allowed to sue a company that violates a privacy law and whether a federal privacy law should replace, or preempt, state privacy laws. Republicans oppose a private right of action arguing that it results in frivolous lawsuits, while Democrats support it because it enhances corporate accountability. Republicans argue that a federal privacy law should preempt state laws because data privacy should not depend on one's place of residence and businesses should not be forced to comply with a variety of state and federal regulations. Democrats argue that a federal law should not preempt state laws because the states may provide broader privacy protection than the federal government.

Due to the lack of a federal privacy law, government agencies have been given the authority to issue internet privacy rules. The Federal Trade Commission (FTC) has been the primary federal agency dealing with information privacy since Congress charged it with enforcing the Fair Credit Reporting Act. However, the parties disagree as to which federal agency has the authority to regulate internet service providers (ISPs), such as Comcast and AT&T. This has implications for regulating information privacy and net neutrality.

Internet Freedom
Net Neutrality

Columbia University law professor Tim Wu used the term "network neutrality" in a 2003 academic article to both describe and advocate for the free flow of information online without interference from ISPs. Net neutrality requires ISPs to treat all internet traffic equally. At that time, Comcast prohibited its customers from using virtual private networks (VPNs), unless they purchased an upgraded internet package for a significantly higher price. Wu argued that this and other actions violated principles of net neutrality. Specifically, without net neutrality ISPs can slow the transfer of information to websites, known as throttling. They can also speed up transfers to websites through "fast lanes," for which they may charge additional fees. There are concerns that ISPs could use these tactics to limit the availability of some websites to promote their own and that this would allow the censoring of certain viewpoints.

In 2004, due to an increase in restrictions being implemented by ISPs that threatened net neutrality, the Chair of the FCC, Republican appointee Michael Powell outlined Four Internet Freedoms. These included the freedom to access content, freedom to use applications, freedom to attach personal devices, and freedom to obtain service plan information. While the FCC did not adopt formal rules protecting net neutrality, it used the four freedoms as guidelines for evaluating the actions of ISPs. Indeed, in 2008, the FCC issued a cease-and-desist order to stop Comcast from throttling internet traffic to Bit Torrent, a file-sharing website. This was the first time the Commission ruled that an ISP violated net neutrality principles. Comcast challenged the FCC's action and a federal court held that the FCC lacked the authority to regulate ISPs in this manner. The FCC formally adopted net neutrality rules in 2010 by a 3–2 vote, with the Democratic members voting for them and Republicans voting against them. These rules required ISPs to provide transparency regarding their services and prevented ISPs from blocking access to lawful content online and from discriminating in the transmission of lawful network traffic. These rules were challenged by Verizon and invalidated by a federal court in 2014 because the FCC did not have the authority to enact them.

The FCC's power to regulate ISPs stems from the Telecommunications Act of 1934, amended in 1996. The extent of the Commission's regulatory authority depends on how it classifies companies and services under the act. Title I of the law allows the FCC to control "information services," while Title II allows it to regulate "common carriers." After lawsuits, including the Verizon ruling, in which courts held that the FCC lacked Title I regulatory authority over actions taken by ISPs that threatened net neutrality, the Commission reclassified ISPs as common carriers under Title II. This provided a basis for more stringent regulations. The FCC enacted net neutrality rules under Title II in 2015 in the Open Internet Order, which prohibited ISPs from blocking, throttling, or prioritizing website speeds. A year later, the FCC issued privacy regulations requiring ISPs to obtain permission from subscribers before sharing information such as internet browsing history, app usage, location information, and the contents of emails and other electronic communications. Prior to the FCC's actions on net neutrality, ISPs, like all companies, were subject to privacy rules issued by the FTC, which require companies to refrain from "unfair or deceptive" activities. While some policy experts argued that the FTC and FCC rules were similar, others noted that the FCC rules protected more aspects of information privacy; specifically, the FCC's provisions included protection for web browsing history and app usage history.

The 2015 Open Internet Order, like the 2010 order, passed by a 3–2 vote of the Commission. Three Democrats voted for them, while two Republicans voted against them. The Republicans asserted that the FCC had impermissibly expanded its authority, while the Democrats argued that the internet should not be limited by ISPs. When the partisan composition of the FCC changed in 2017, Republican FCC chairman, Ajit Pai, proposed the Restoring Internet Freedom Order to return the regulation of ISPs to Title I and return authority to regulate privacy rules to the FTC. Also in 2017, Congress rescinded the FCC's privacy rules by invoking the Congressional Review Act, which allows Congress and the president to overturn agency rules within sixty days after the rules are enacted. The Senate voted to repeal the rules by a 50–48 vote, while the House vote was 215–205; both votes were along party lines. President Trump signed the bill in April 2017. Several bills were introduced in Congress to protect information privacy and net neutrality, but none have been enacted. In 2021, President Joe Biden issued an executive order encouraging the FCC to restore net neutrality. Republicans argue that net neutrality rules give the FCC too much authority to regulate businesses; however, some Republicans support net neutrality legislation. Democrats support a stronger role for the federal government in protecting net neutrality.

The debate over net neutrality pits the financial interests of ISPs against the public's interest in secure and open communication. Public opinion polls show that most Americans favor net neutrality, including a large percentage of Republicans, putting them at odds with many Republican policymakers who have opposed it. A 2022 poll found that 72.5 percent of Americans supported net neutrality, including 64 percent of Republicans and 82 percent of Democrats (Lima and Schaffer 2022).

Universal Broadband Access

The political debates over information privacy and net neutrality underscore the essential role of the internet in the modern world, deeply intertwined in the worlds of business, education, politics, and culture. The extent to which internet access should be considered a civil right has thus become a subject of increasingly open debate. The digital divide, a term coined in the mid-1990s to describe the gap between those who have internet access and those who do not, now refers to the gap between those who have access to high-speed broadband internet access and those who do not. The COVID-19 pandemic highlighted this problem as Americans were forced to work, attend school, and spend leisure time at home. This created a hardship for the estimated forty-four million Americans who do not have broadband internet access due to either lack of availability or lack of affordability. The digital divide is significant in communities of color. According to a 2021 Pew Research Center poll, Black and Hispanic households were less likely than white households to have broadband access. While 80 percent of whites had broadband access, the percentages for Blacks and Hispanics were lower, with 71 percent of Blacks and 65 percent of Hispanics having broadband access. There were also differences based on income with 92 percent of households earning over $75,000 having broadband access compared to 57 percent of households earning $30,000 or less. Americans living in rural areas were less likely than Americans in urban and suburban areas to have access. Seventy-two percent of those living in rural areas have access, while 77 percent of those living in urban areas and 79 percent of those living in suburban areas do (Pew Research Center 2021).

The federal government has made efforts to make broadband access available and affordable since the mid-1990s. The Clinton administration was the first to propose policies concerning internet access and supported the creation of the e-rate program by the FCC in 1996. The program helps public schools gain access to broadband. The FCC also created the Lifeline program in 1985 to subsidize telephone service to low-income households. While this program was extended to include broadband access in 2016, almost a third of rural households lack access (Pew Research Center 2021).

In January 2018, the bipartisan House Rural Broadband Caucus wrote a letter to President Donald Trump urging him to include broadband in his proposed infrastructure plan after hearing reports that he did not intend to include it. The letter stated that "[r]ural communities must have adequate broadband infrastructure to attract and retain businesses and human resources, close the homework gap for students and teachers, open innovative and convenient pathways to telemedicine for seniors and providers, and help farmers increase efficiencies in their barns and on their land. The future wellbeing of our communities is dependent upon this technology." While Trump did not include broadband access in the infrastructure proposal, he issued an executive order to promote better access in those areas and the Republican majority FCC pledged to make internet access a priority. House Democrats passed the Accessible, Affordable Internet for All Act in 2020, which would have invested federal money in expanding broadband to rural areas and making it more affordable for low-income households. The Republican-controlled Senate did not act on the bill. House and Senate Democrats reintroduced the bill in 2021. In 2021, as part of the bipartisan Infrastructure, Investment, and Jobs Act, $1 billion in grants and loans was made available for the ReConnect Program administered by the U.S. Department of Agriculture. Democrats have supported a stronger role for the federal government in bridging the digital divide, while Republicans have argued that market forces can better address the issue.

Republicans

Information Privacy

Congressional Republicans have initiated and supported legislation to protect data privacy; however, they have opposed allowing states to create their own privacy laws and allowing a private right of action for individuals to sue companies that breach their data. Republicans oppose allowing states to set their own data privacy policies because they say it would be burdensome for businesses in terms of complying with federal regulations and a variety of state regulations.

Throughout Obama's two terms in office, the GOP regularly inveighed against his administration's information privacy record, even making exaggerated claims in its 2016 platform that

> the survival of the internet as we know it is at risk. Its gravest peril originates in the White House, the current occupant of which has launched a campaign, both at home and internationally, to subjugate it to agents of government. The President ordered the chair of the supposedly independent Federal Communications Commission to impose upon the internet rules devised in the 1930s for the telephone monopoly. He has unilaterally announced America's abandonment of the international internet by surrendering U.S. control of the root zone of web names and addresses. He threw the internet to the wolves, and they—Russia, China, Iran, and others—are ready to devour it.

The 2016 platform, which the Republicans also adopted word for word in advance of the 2020 election, also stated:

> We salute the Congressional Republicans who have legislatively impeded his plans to turn over the Information Freedom Highway to regulators and tyrants. That fight must continue, for its outcome is in doubt. We will consistently support internet policies that allow people and private enterprise to thrive, without providing new and expanded government powers to tax and regulate so that the internet does not become the vehicle for a dramatic expansion of government power. The internet's

independence is its power. It has unleashed innovation, enabled growth, and inspired freedom more rapidly and extensively than any other technological advance in human history. We will therefore resist any effort to shift control toward governance by international or other intergovernmental organizations. We will ensure that personal data receives full constitutional protection from government overreach. The only way to safeguard or improve these systems is through the private sector. The internet's free market needs to be free and open to all ideas and competition without the government or service providers picking winners and losers.

The political environment changed dramatically with Donald Trump's narrow presidential victory in the 2016 election. In 2019, the ranking Republican on the House Energy and Commerce Committee, Representative Greg Walden, stated that "[t]here are many policy areas where it makes sense for states to innovate, however the internet does not stop at the state line and neither should innovative privacy and security solutions. Your privacy and security should not change depending on where you live in the United States. One state should not set the standards for the rest of the country" (Neidig 2019). In a 2021 op-ed in the *Washington Times*, Republican senator Roger Wicker (MS) claimed that allowing states to create their own data privacy laws would "raise compliance costs for organizations operating across state lines. This would stifle innovation and threaten small business entrepreneurs. If companies utilizing data struggle to keep up with fragmented state laws, we cannot expect consumers to trust these companies to protect their data" (Wicker 2021).

Republicans Stress Need for a Federal Privacy Standard

In 2021, Republican Senator Jerry Moran reintroduced the Consumer Data Privacy and Security Act. In this news release posted on his website, he argues for a federal privacy standard.

> More and more Americans are recognizing the need for a clear federal standard for data privacy that guarantees them the ability to determine how their personal data is used. Americans need to be able to count on strong baseline responsibilities that businesses must uphold when collecting, processing and protecting their personally identifiable information. Without action from Congress, consumers will continue to be vulnerable to future threats against their personal data, and innovators and job creators will be plagued with regulatory uncertainty resulting from a growing patchwork of state laws. It is clear that Congress needs to act, and I encourage my colleagues to support the Consumer Data Privacy and Security Act as the federal standard for comprehensive privacy legislation.

Source
"Sen. Moran Introduces Bill Creating Clear Federal Standard for Consumer Data Privacy." 2021. U.S. Senator for Kansas, Jerry Moran, April 29. Accessed February 12, 2023. https://www.moran.senate.gov/public/index.cfm/2021/4/sen-moran-introduces-bill-creating-clear-federal-standard-for-consumer-data-privacy.

Republicans also oppose a private right of action. They argue that it will result in numerous frivolous lawsuits that will disproportionately hurt smaller tech companies. Ari Ezra Waldman, director of the New York Law School's Innovation Center for Law and Technology, suggests that a private right of action "would enforce the law and steer companies toward better practices" to avoid lawsuits (Kelly 2019). Republicans believe that strengthening the power of the FTC to enforce privacy rules is preferable to allowing a private right of action. Critics contend, however, that because the FTC can only handle a limited number of cases, the ability of individuals to file lawsuits better protects privacy rights (Kelly 2019).

While Congressional Republicans say they support data privacy legislation, the party repealed the FCC's 2016 privacy rules in 2017. Republicans and the telecom industry opposed the rules arguing that they were costly and confusing. They argued that ISPs would have been subject to restrictions on the collection of personal information that websites and search engines, such as Google and Facebook, which also collect personal information, were exempt from. The Republican House member who introduced the congressional review bill, Marsha Blackburn, supported the repeal arguing that the rules constituted an "overreach" on the part of the FCC and that the appropriate regulatory agency was the FTC (Kang 2017). Critics contended that the FCC rules "are the only thing preventing broadband companies from spying on their customers and selling that data to the highest bidder" (Fung 2017b).

Internet Freedom
Net Neutrality

Congressional Republicans have been divided on net neutrality. After the FCC enacted net neutrality rules in 2015, the House Republican members of the Communications Subcommittee issued a statement criticizing the adoption of the rules, especially by a 3–2 partisan vote. The committee members also stated that they were "willing to come to the table with legislation to answer the calls for legally sustainable consumer protections for the free and open Internet." Republican senator John Thune, who has led efforts for a bipartisan net neutrality bill, favored legislation retaining net neutrality, but limiting the FCC to using Title I to enforce it. According to Volz, many Republicans were more interested in criticizing the FCC action as an example of overreach by the Obama White House than in enacting legislation to address the issue (Volz 2015). Indeed, Republican Representative Doug Lamborn stated that "[t]he FCC, led by three Democrat bureaucrats hand-picked by President Obama, approved a secret plan to fundamentally undermine a free and open Internet. This decision ushers in a new era of government micro-management" (Volz 2015).

After House Democrats passed the Save the Internet Act of 2019, which would have overturned the FCC's 2017 Restore Internet Freedom Order, Republican Senate majority leader Mitch McConnell stated that the bill was "dead on arrival" in the Senate. In response to this comment, a coalition of 103 public interest organizations wrote McConnell asking him to allow the Senate to vote on the bill.

The letter pointed out several examples of the dangers of removing net neutrality regulations. For example, Verizon slowed down a California fire department's data during one of the worst wildfires in the state's history (Birnbaum 2019). The Senate did not vote on the bill.

Universal Broadband Access

Republicans have supported the expansion of broadband access. The first Republican presidential candidate to do so was George W. Bush in the 2004 campaign. Bush emphasized a market-based approach that included providing tax breaks and limiting or eliminating government regulations for companies that expanded broadband infrastructure. Republicans have favored this market-based approach ever since.

During the 2017 discussion of President Trump's infrastructure plan, FCC chairman Ajit Pai argued that broadband was a necessary part of those negotiations. He proposed expanding corporate subsidies and eliminating regulations that deterred private investment (Fung 2017a). In January 2018, President Trump issued an executive order to promote better access to broadband in rural areas. The Streamlining and Expediting Requests to Locate Broadband Facilities in Rural America order provided that the administration would "use all viable tools to accelerate the deployment and adoption of affordable, reliable, modern high-speed broadband connectivity in rural America" (The White House 2018). After this order was issued, Trump proposed a $200 billion infrastructure plan, which excluded broadband. Rural communities were to receive $50 billion for infrastructure projects; however, none of the money was specifically directed to broadband access.

Tom Wheeler, the previous Democratic chair of the Commission, criticized the emphasis on expanding broadband to rural America. Wheeler argued that the attention to rural areas ignored the larger part of the digital divide: lack of affordability. Wheeler, citing a Government Accountability Office report, stated that "the most important reason why the available broadband isn't used is 'can't afford'" (Wheeler 2020).

Some Republicans, who had previously supported broadband as part of infrastructure during the Trump administration, became reluctant to do so when Democratic president Joe Biden included it as part of his infrastructure plan. House Republicans proposed the CONNECT Act ("Communities Overregulating Networks Need Economic Competition Today"), which would limit the use of municipal broadband to promote competition and encourage private investment. Due to lack of private investment, some states and municipalities have paid for broadband equipment on their own to provide service for their residents; however, nineteen states have forbidden state or local governments from doing so. Other Republican proposals have imposed limits on regulatory requirements for ISPs and suggested an expedited approval process for those ISPs who expand broadband availability.

Democrats

The Democratic Party has many factions and constituencies, but virtually all of them are supportive of the following statements of principle in the party's official 2020 platform:

> We will recommit the United States to the principles of an open internet, including net neutrality, and vigorously oppose efforts to digitally silo off countries and populations from the rest of the world. Democrats believe that algorithms and platforms should empower people instead of the surveillance state. We expect technology companies and social media platforms to take responsibility and do more to preserve the openness of democratic societies and identify foreign disinformation, especially including paid efforts to influence American elections through advertising or coordinated inauthentic behavior, and we will take steps to prevent the use of new technologies to facilitate repression, spread hate, or incite violence.
>
> As millions of Americans have stayed at home to prevent the spread of the pandemic, it is plain to see that in the 21st century, an accessible internet is not optional: it is a vital tool for receiving an education and for participating in the economy, and all Americans need access to high-speed, affordable broadband service. Democrats will take action to prevent states from blocking municipalities and rural co-ops from building publicly-owned broadband networks, and increase federal support for municipal broadband while requiring that funding recipients adhere to policies that support good jobs and include strong protections for workers' right to organize. We will increase public investment in rural, urban, and Tribal broadband infrastructure, offer low-income Americans subsidies for accessing high-speed internet, and invest in digital literacy training programs, so children and families and people with disabilities can fully participate in school, work, and life from their homes.

Information Privacy

The Democratic Party's efforts to protect online information privacy began in 1998. Vice President Al Gore announced a plan for an Electronic Bill of Rights in a speech at New York University. Gore stated that "privacy is a basic American value—in the Information Age, and in every age. And it must be protected. You should have the right to choose whether your personal information is disclosed; you should have the right to know how, when, and how much of that information is being used; and you should have the right to see it yourself, to know if it's accurate" (Gore 1998). Despite the early effort to protect information privacy, no legislation was enacted.

Barack Obama sought to make information privacy a priority of his presidency. In 2012, he proposed the Consumer Privacy Bill of Rights providing consumers with more control over the type of data companies collect, greater transparency about how that information is used, and a right to secure and responsible handling of data. When the White House endorsed legislation embodying these principles in 2015, it was criticized by technology companies, privacy advocates, and some Democrats (Sasso 2015). Technology companies were concerned that the legislation would impose regulations that would inhibit the development of new online services that would benefit consumers. Privacy advocates argued that the act did not sufficiently protect privacy interests because tech companies were allowed to write their own regulations subject to the approval of the FTC. To attract Republican votes, the bill also proposed overturning state privacy laws that offered greater data privacy protection. In a letter to President Obama, privacy advocacy organizations set forth several objections to the proposed bill, including that it does not protect "large categories of personal information" or adequately protect information about children and teens. They also objected to the limits on fines that the FTC could impose for privacy violations arguing that they were not large enough to deter big tech companies from violating privacy rules (Sasso 2015). The organizations also criticized the president for not soliciting their input on the legislation. Democratic senator Edward Markey, a party leader on information privacy, stated that the president's proposal "falls far short of what is needed to ensure consumers and families are squarely in control of their personal data" (Markey 2015).

Congressional Democrats have introduced bills to protect data privacy. Democratic legislation differs from Republican legislation in that it emphasizes a private right of action against a company for data breaches and the coexistence of state and federal privacy legislation. Democratic senator Maria Cantwell has argued that "[i]n the growing online world, consumers deserve two things: privacy rights and a strong law to enforce them. They should be like your Miranda rights—clear as a bell as to what they are and what constitutes a violation" (Cantwell 2019). Her bill, the Consumer Online Privacy Rights Act (COPRA), would require that tech companies explain what information they are collecting from users and what they are doing with that data. It specifically protects civil rights by ensuring that personal data about race, sexual orientation, or ethnicity is not used for discriminatory purposes. Her bill proposed strengthening the enforcement powers of the FTC to protect privacy and a "strong" private right of action. She argued that "when consumers have the ability to advocate for themselves, they are better protected against abuse" (Cantwell 2019).

Many Democrats oppose federal preemption of state privacy law because of their concern that a federal law may weaken state laws. Representatives from California have been particularly vocal about preemption since that state enacted the Consumer Privacy Act. The law, which went into effect in 2020, gives consumers the right to know what type of personal information businesses collect and what they do with that information. It also gives consumers the right to delete personal information, the right to opt out of the sale of personal information, and the right to nondiscrimination for exercising those rights. Many of California's fifty-three congressional representatives believe that the provisions of the California law should provide the minimum level of privacy protection (Lima and Hindel 2019). A report by the Brookings Institute has suggested that national preemption would be preferable to a weakened or nonexistent privacy law. The report offered a tiered approach to preemption which "preempts state laws that compete with a national standard, preserves other state privacy laws and rights, and prompts Congress to revisit this question a few years after implementation of the new federal law" (Kerry and Morris 2020). The report suggested that "that significant preemption is the price to pay for establishing strong privacy protections for all Americans" (Kerry and Morris 2020).

Internet Freedom
Net Neutrality

Democrats have consistently supported net neutrality. During the 2008 presidential campaign, Barack Obama expressed support for net neutrality. He argued that if companies were not obligated to protect it, that "destroys one of the best things about the internet, which is that there is incredible equality there" (White House 2014). In a 2014 statement, Obama voiced support for strong net neutrality rules to be implemented by the FCC. He characterized an "open Internet" as essential to the economy and "one of the most significant democratizing influences the world has ever known" (White House 2014).

Congressional Democrats have also supported net neutrality. After Republicans on the FCC repealed net neutrality rules in 2017, House Democrats passed the Save the Internet Act of 2019. The bill sought to restore the FCC's 2015 net neutrality rules and to return oversight authority to the FCC. Frank Pallone, the Democratic Chair of the Energy and Commerce Committee, which had jurisdiction over the bill, stated that "[a] free and open internet is critical to strengthening our nation's economy, and ensuring that everyone has access to a better future. . . . This legislation restores the protections that 86 percent of Americans want and that millions of people demanded when the FCC made its ill-advised decision to strip away those protections two years ago." The act passed the House by a vote of 232–190 but was not considered by the Senate. In July 2021, President Joe Biden indicated his support for net neutrality through an executive order, Promoting Competition in the American Economy, in which he encouraged the FCC to reinstate the 2017 net neutrality rules.

Biden Issues Executive Order Promoting Broadband Access, Internet Affordability, and Net Neutrality

The White House issued a Fact Sheet to accompany the Executive Order on Promoting Competition in the American Economy signed by President Biden. The order addressed a broad range of anti-competitive practices that increased prices for American consumers. This excerpt from the Fact Sheet outlines actions targeted at the FCC to promote internet access and net neutrality.

The Order tackles four issues that limit competition, raise prices, and reduce choices for internet service.

Lack of competition among broadband providers: More than 200 million U.S. residents live in an area with only one or two reliable high-speed internet providers, leading to prices as much as five times higher in these markets than in markets with more options. A related problem is landlords and internet service providers entering exclusivity deals or collusive arrangements that leave tenants with only one option. This impacts low-income and marginalized neighborhoods, because landlord-ISP arrangements can effectively block out broadband infrastructure expansion by new providers.

In the Order, the President encourages the FCC to:

Prevent ISPs from making deals with landlords that limit tenants' choices.

Lack of price transparency: Even where consumers have options, comparison shopping is hard. According to the Federal Communications Commission (FCC), actual prices paid for broadband services can be 40% higher than advertised. During the Obama-Biden Administration, the FCC began developing a "Broadband Nutrition Label"—a simple label that provides basic information about the internet service offered so people can compare options. The Trump Administration FCC abandoned those plans.

In the Order, the President encourages the FCC to:

Revive the "Broadband Nutrition Label" and require providers to report prices and subscription rates to the FCC.

High termination fees: If a consumer does find a better internet service deal, they may be unable to actually switch because of high early termination fees—on average nearly $200—charged by internet providers.

In the Order, the President encourages the FCC to:

Limit excessive early termination fees.

Companies discriminatorily slowing down internet access: Big providers can use their power to discriminatorily block or slow down online services. The Obama-Biden Administration's FCC adopted "Net Neutrality" rules that required these companies to treat all internet services equally, but this was undone in 2017.

In the Order, the President encourages the FCC to:

Restore Net Neutrality rules undone by the prior administration.

Source

The White House. 2021. "FACT SHEET: Executive Order on Promoting Competition in the American Economy." July 9. Accessed February 12, 2023. https://www.whitehouse .gov/briefing-room/statements-releases/2021/07/09/fact-sheet-executive-order-on -promoting-competition-in-the-american-economy/.

Universal Broadband Access

Democrats have supported expanding broadband access and making it more affordable. Democratic Representative James Clyburn created the Rural Broadband Task Force in 2019. The group, composed of Democratic Representatives from primarily rural districts, is developing legislation to "promote high-speed internet accessibility, affordability, and adoption" to ensure all Americans have access to high-speed internet (Clyburn n.d.).

In 2021, Joe Biden proposed to increase broadband access by relying on cities to build networks. During the Obama administration, Democrats unsuccessfully attempted to preempt state laws prohibiting or limiting municipal broadband. Biden's "American Jobs Plan" included policies to make internet access more affordable and more available. The plan included a goal of making broadband 100 percent accessible in the United States by prioritizing municipal broadband (White House 2021).

The cable industry and Republicans have criticized Biden's effort. Michael Powell, a former Republican FCC chair, stated that the Biden administration was taking "a serious wrong turn" by "suggesting that the government is better suited than [the] private sector" to build and operate broadband infrastructure. Other critics of the Democratic approach argue that too much of the emphasis is on expanding broadband access to rural areas when the digital divide is more prevalent in urban areas, where three times as many households lack broadband. Writing in *Wired*, Bhaskar Chakravorti characterized the lack of urban broadband as an issue of "racial justice." He stated that the racial inequity in broadband access puts the "digital divide . . . at the center of numerous pressing racial inequities in health care, education, job security, and well-being" (Chakravorti 2021).

Further Reading

Allen, Anita L., and Marc Rotenberg. 2016. *Privacy Law and Society*. 3rd ed. St. Paul, MN: West Academic Publishing.

Birnbaum, Emily. 2019. "Over 100 Activist Groups Urge McConnell to Take Up Net Neutrality Bill in the Senate." *The Hill*, June 10. Accessed June 5, 2021. https://thehill.com /policy/technology/447768-over-100-activist-groups-urge-mcconnell-to-take-up-net -neutrality-bill-in.

Cantwell, Maria. 2019. "Cantwell, Senate Democrats Unveil Strong Online Privacy Rights." November 26. Accessed June 30, 2021. https://www.cantwell.senate.gov/news/press -releases/cantwell-senate-democrats-unveil-strong-online-privacy-rights.

Chakravorti, Bhaskar. 2021. "Political Bickering Prolongs the Digital Divide." *Wired*, June 10. Accessed June 25, 2021. https://www.wired.com/story/opinion-political-bickering -prolongs-the-digital-divide/.

Clyburn, James. n.d. "Rural Broadband." Representative James Clyburn. Accessed June 4, 2021. https://clyburn.house.gov/legislation/rural-broadband.

Fung, Brian. 2017a. "The Crucial Service Trump Left Out of His Massive Infrastructure Goals, and How the FCC Wants to Fix It." *Washington Post*, March 15. Accessed June 3, 2021. https://www.washingtonpost.com/news/the-switch/wp/2017/03/15/the-crucial -service-trump-left-out-of-his-massive-infrastructure-goals-and-how-the-fcc-wants-to -fix-it/.

Fung, Brian. 2017b. "Republicans Voted to Roll Back Landmark FCC Privacy Rules. Here's What You Need to Know." *Washington Post*, March 28. Accessed June 3, 2021. https:// www.washingtonpost.com/news/the-switch/wp/2017/03/28/republicans-are-poised -to-roll-back-landmark-fcc-privacy-rules-heres-what-you-need-to-know/.

Gore, Al. 1998. "Remarks by Vice-President Al Gore. New York University Commencement." Accessed June 1, 2021. https://clintonwhitehouse2.archives.gov/WH/EOP /OVP/speeches/nyu.html.

Kang, Cecilia. 2017. "At F.C.C., Obama-Era Rules on Chopping Block." *New York Times*, April 5. Accessed June 4, 2021. https://www.nytimes.com/2017/04/05/business/dealbook/fcc-broadband-cable-trump.html.

Kelly, Makena. 2019. "Congress Is Split Over Your Right to Sue Facebook." The Verge, December 3. Accessed June 12, 2021. https://www.theverge.com/2019/12/3/20993680/facebook-google-private-right-of-action-sue-data-malpractice-wicker-cantwell.

Kerry, Cameron, and John Morris Jr. 2020. "Preemption: A Balanced National Approach to Protecting All Americans' Privacy." The Brookings Institute, June 29. Accessed April 14, 2021. https://www.brookings.edu/blog/techtank/2020/06/29/preemption-a-balanced-national-approach-to-protecting-all-americans-privacy/.

Lima, Cristiano, and John Hendel. 2019. "California Democrats to Congress: Don't Bulldoze Our Privacy Law." Accessed February 6, 2023. https://www.politico.com/story/2019/02/21/congress-data-privacy-california-1185943.

Lima, Cristiano, and Aaron Schaffer. 2022. "Poll Finds Republican Voters Support Bringing Back Net Neutrality." *Washington Post*, May 26. Accessed February 11, 2023. https://www.washingtonpost.com/politics/2022/05/26/gop-voters-back-reinstating-net-neutrality-when-given-case-against-poll-finds/.

Markey, Edward. 2015. "Markey: White House Data Privacy Bill Needs to Go Further." February 27. Accessed April 19, 2021. https://www.markey.senate.gov/news/press-releases/markey-white-house-privacy-bill-of-rights-needs-to-go-further.

Neidig, Harper. 2019. "Republicans Push to Block State Privacy Laws." *The Hill*, February 26. Accessed April 20, 2021. https://thehill.com/policy/technology/431631-republicans-push-to-block-state-data-privacy-laws?rl=1.

Pew Research Center. 2021. "Internet/Broadband Fact Sheet." April 11. Accessed September 23, 2022. https://www.pewresearch.org/internet/fact-sheet/internet-broadband/.

Reid, Jon. 2021. "Municipal Broadband War Reignited in Biden's Infrastructure Push." Bloomberg Law, April 1. Accessed April 11, 2021. https://news.bloomberglaw.com/tech-and-telecomlaw/municipal-broadband.

Sasso, Brendan. 2015. "Obama's 'Privacy Bill of Rights' Gets Bashed from All Sides." *The Atlantic*, February 27. Accessed April 17, 2021. https://www.theatlantic.com/politics/archive/2015/02/obamas-privacy-bill-of-rights-gets-bashed-from-all-sides/456576/.

Volz, Dustin. 2015. "The Republican Party Is Divided on Net Neutrality." *National Journal*, February 26. Accessed April 25, 2021. https://www.nationaljournal.com/s/31116/republican-party-is-divided-net-neutrality.

Wheeler, Tom. 2020. "5 Steps to Get the Internet to All Americans: COVID-19 and the Importance of Universal Broadband." The Brookings Institute, May 27. Accessed June 3, 2021. https://www.brookings.edu/research/5-steps-to-get-the-internet-to-all-americans/.

The White House. 2014. "Net Neutrality: President Obama's Plan for a Free and Open Internet." Accessed June 5, 2021. https://obamawhitehouse.archives.gov/net-neutrality.

The White House. 2018. "Presidential Executive Order on Streamlining and Expediting Requests to Locate Broadband Facilities in Rural America—The White House." January 8. Accessed February 12, 2023. https://trumpwhitehouse.archives.gov/presidential-actions/presidential-executive-order-streamlining-expediting-requests-locate-broadband-facilities-rural-america/.

The White House. 2021. "Fact Sheet: The American Jobs Plan." March 31. Accessed April 4, 2021. https://www.whitehouse.gov/briefing-room/statements-releases/2021/03/31/fact-sheet-the-american-jobs-plan/.

Wicker, Roger. 2021. "Protecting Consumer Data during the Pandemic and Beyond." *The Washington Times*, January 27. Accessed June 4, 2021. https://www.washingtontimes .com/news/2021/jan/27/protecting-consumer-data-during-the-pandemic-and-b/.

Wu, Tim. 2003. "Network Neutrality, Broadband Discrimination." *Journal of Telecommunications and High Technology Law* 2: 141–179. https://scholarship.law.columbia.edu /faculty_scholarship/1281.

LGBTQ Rights

At a Glance

LGBTQ (lesbian, gay, bisexual, transgender, queer) rights were first endorsed by the Democratic Party in 1980, and it has consistently advocated for anti-discrimination policies. Democrats have supported hate crimes laws, which increase criminal penalties if a victim was targeted due to their LGBTQ status. Democratic president Barack Obama implemented nondiscrimination polices in many areas, including education and health care. The Republican Party did not address LGBTQ rights until 1992. It has emphasized the issue of homosexuals in the military and protecting the freedom of association of private organizations along with the religious rights of business owners. In 2016, both parties addressed issues affecting transgender Americans for the first time. During the 2020 presidential campaign, the Democratic Party pledged broader protection for LGBTQ rights. The Republican Party argued that it had also made strides in protecting LGBTQ rights; however, President Trump rescinded many of the antidiscrimination policies enacted by Obama. Democratic president Joe Biden has sought to restore and expand upon those policies.

According to many Republicans . . .

- Business owners should not be forced to serve or accommodate LGBTQ individuals if it violates their religious beliefs.
- The military is not a place for "social engineering," and policies concerning personnel should be based on a "traditional military culture."
- LGBTQ individuals are not a protected class and should not have special legal protection.

According to many Democrats . . .

- Discrimination against members of the LGBTQ community should be illegal.

- LGBTQ Americans should be allowed to serve openly in the U.S. military.
- Hate crimes against LGBTQ individuals should carry harsher punishment.

Overview

The Gay Rights Movement in the United States began in the 1970s. Gay rights organizations had existed since the 1950s but did not garner any significant public support or political influence until the 1970s due to the social stigma long associated with homosexuality. In 1969, police raided the Stonewall Inn, a popular Greenwich Village gay bar in New York City. While police raids of establishments where gay people congregated were common, this one was different because the patrons fought back. Over a period of several days, the violent protests drew over two thousand people and ultimately galvanized the Gay Rights Movement.

During the 1970s, several openly gay politicians were elected to local office, and several states and localities implemented antidiscrimination policies. Some of these new policies caused an intense conservative backlash. In 1977, in Dade County, Florida, Save Our Children, Inc. led a successful effort to repeal a county ordinance that prohibited discrimination based on sexual orientation in housing, employment, and public accommodation.

Save Our Children was led by Anita Bryant, a former Miss America, conservative Christian, and nationally known television spokesperson for the Florida Citrus Commission, an alliance of orange juice makers. Bryant was a vocal opponent of the ordinance because she believed that it interfered with her rights as a Christian. Her antigay stances and rhetoric, however, ultimately cost Bryant her position with the Florida Citrus Commission.

During the late 1970s, a new force in Republican politics—the Religious Right—emerged, pushing for conservative, traditional positions on a wide range of social and cultural issues. This influential bloc of voters largely subscribed to the belief that homosexuality is an immoral choice forbidden by the Bible. Many Catholics hold the same view. The tension between LGBTQ rights and religious liberty has been constant in the political debate between the two parties over LGBTQ issues. Religious conservatives have opposed same-sex marriage on the grounds that the Bible specifies that marriage is ordained by God to be between one man and one woman. They have also argued that the government should not force them to sell or provide goods and services to LGBTQ persons because doing so violates their faith. For instance, several Christian business owners that provide services related to weddings argue that it violates their Free Exercise rights to be forced to provide goods and services for same-sex marriages of which they personally disapprove.

In addition to same-sex marriage, which is dealt with separately in this volume, the parties have addressed several other areas of LGBTQ rights, including military service eligibility, antidiscrimination laws, and transgender rights. Democrats have supported LGBTQ rights since the early 1970s and have included provisions articulating that position in their platform since 1980. Republicans have been opposed to LGBTQ rights but did not take an official position until the 1992 GOP platform. In addition to advocating for legal protection for gay marriage after the U.S. Supreme Court limited the right to privacy in *Dobbs v. Jackson Women's Health Organization* (2022), Democrats have focused on antidiscrimination laws; while Republicans initially focused on the issue of gays in the military, they have opposed legal protection for LGBTQ persons.

Military Service

The issue of military service for LGBTQ individuals has been a significant one for both parties. Homosexuals had historically been barred from military service. In 1982, the Defense Department set a uniform policy for all branches of military, which stated in part that "[h]omosexuality is incompatible with military service. . . . [Because the presence of homosexuals] seriously impairs the accomplishment of the military mission." In 1992, the Democratic platform promised "civil rights protection for gay men and lesbians and an end to Defense Department discrimination." While campaigning for president, Arkansas governor Bill Clinton promised to eliminate the ban on homosexuals in the military. The Republican Party first addressed the issue of gay rights in its 1992 platform by supporting "the continued exclusion of homosexuals" from military service. After his inauguration, Clinton sought to rescind the ban on homosexual military service but was immediately met with opposition from both Republicans and conservative Southern Democrats in Congress. The resulting compromise, known as Don't Ask Don't Tell (DADT), was enacted in 1994 and stipulated that military officials were prohibited from discriminating against military personnel on the basis of sexual orientation. Gay or lesbian military personnel were forbidden from disclosing their sexual orientation. According to a Pew Trust poll, 52 percent of Americans supported homosexuals openly serving in the military in July 1994 after DADT was enacted; 45 percent were opposed. This support increased over time and from 2005 to 2010 was close to 60 percent (Pew Research Center 2010).

While Republicans opposed homosexual military service, the party's presidential candidates supported DADT beginning in 2000. As public opinion became more supportive of openly gay individuals serving in the military, DADT was viewed as a compromise and helped candidates with social conservatives and religious voters. Democratic nominees, conversely, opposed DADT because they believed that homosexuals should be allowed to serve openly. In 2008, Senator Barack Obama campaigned on repealing DADT; two years later, he signed the DADT Repeal Act.

Antidiscrimination Laws

Democratic platforms have included statements pledging to end discrimination based on several criteria, including sexual orientation since 1980. Since 2008, the platforms have also vowed to end discrimination based on gender identity. Republican platforms have also contained nondiscrimination provisions but have not included sexual orientation or gender identity as groups that should have legal protection. Republican platforms have also emphasized the religious rights and freedom of association rights of organizations and businesses as it pertains to including or providing services to members of the LGBTQ community.

Congressional Democrats introduced legislation protecting LGBTQ rights in the early 1970s. In 1974, the Equality Act was first introduced by House Democrats. The bill, which did not receive a hearing for six years, would have amended the Civil Rights Act of 1964 to prohibit discrimination based on sexual orientation in employment, housing, and places of public accommodation, such as hotels and restaurants. When Democrats were unable to pass the Equality Act, they proposed a narrower law, the Employment Non-discrimination Act (ENDA), in 1994. This bill would prohibit employers from discriminating against job applicants and employees based on sexual orientation or gender identity. It was introduced in every session of Congress except for the 109th and was last introduced in 2013. The later versions of the bill would have made it illegal to discriminate on the basis of actual or perceived sexual orientation or gender identity. It would also protect employees from discrimination for associating with LGBTQ workers and protect individuals from retaliation by their employer if they complain about discrimination based on sexual orientation or gender identity. Democrats supported this proposed law because it is legal to discriminate against LGBTQ individuals in a majority of states. Republicans opposed it because workplace discrimination laws already exist, and the law does not sufficiently protect religious rights of employers. After the bill was changed to allow a broad religious exemption, many LGBTQ groups withdrew their support for it. Since 2015, the Democratic Party's legislative emphasis has shifted from this narrower law back to the broader provisions of the Equality Act.

In 2000 and 2008, the Republican platform supported the Boy Scouts of America (BSA) and its policy of excluding gay Scout leaders from the organization. In *Boy Scouts of America v. Dale* (2000), the U.S. Supreme Court upheld the policy in a 5-4 ruling because the organization's goal of instilling values in young people would be compromised by allowing homosexuals to hold leadership positions. The Court specifically pointed to the BSA's statement that a scout is required to be "morally straight" and "clean in word and deed." The BSA contended that homosexuality was incompatible with those requirements and that homosexuals are not "desirable role model[s] for Scouts." The Court held that requiring the BSA to allow gay scoutmasters in its organization would impermissibly interfere with its right of freedom of association.

The 2012 Democratic platform touted President Obama's role in protecting LGBTQ rights. In 2009, he signed the Matthew Shepard and James Byrd Jr. Hate Crimes Prevention Act, which expanded existing federal hate crime legislation to include crimes motivated by a victim's actual or perceived gender, sexual orientation, gender identity, or disability. In 2011, he announced that the United States would cut foreign aid to countries that violated the rights of LGBTQ individuals. The 2012 Republican platform criticized each of these actions.

In 2016, Republicans emphasized traditional family values and the religious rights of business owners. The Democratic platform highlighted the repeal of DADT, Obama's initiatives to combat LGBTQ discrimination internationally, and efforts to end discrimination against LGBTQ individuals in numerous areas, including school bullying, immigration, health care, and income inequality. A 2016 Public Religion Research Institute (PRRI) poll indicated bipartisan support for LGBTQ nondiscrimination laws. Indeed, 72 percent of Americans, and over 60 percent of Republicans, favored laws protecting LGBTQ individuals from discrimination in jobs, public accommodation, and housing; however, 80 percent of respondents erroneously believed that federal law already prohibited discrimination on the basis of sexual orientation. The same poll showed that 63 percent of Americans oppose religious freedom laws allowing small businesses to deny services to LGBTQ individuals if doing so would violate the business owner's religious beliefs (Greenberg et al. 2019).

Transgender Rights

The Obama administration sought to protect transgender rights by allowing transgender individuals to serve in the military, prohibiting government contractors from discriminating on the basis of sexual orientation or gender identity, and issuing rules under the Title IX Education Amendments of 1972, which required public schools to allow transgender students to choose the restroom of the gender with which they identified. The Affordable Care Act (2010) also prohibited health care providers from discriminating against LGBTQ persons. In the 2016 election campaign, discrimination against transgender individuals was specifically addressed by the parties for the first time. In their platform, Democrats pledged to end the "crisis of violence against transgender Americans." Republicans, conversely, supported the "original meaning" of Title IX and criticized Obama for "imposing a social and cultural agenda." A PRRI public opinion poll showed that 53 percent of Americans oppose bathroom bills requiring transgender individuals to use the public restroom corresponding with their birth gender. Obama also issued an order allowing transgender individuals to serve in the U.S. military. Both parties also addressed conversion therapy, a controversial practice designed to change the sexual orientation or gender identity of LGBTQ individuals. Hillary Clinton was opposed to conversion therapy, while the Republican platform tacitly approved it.

In 2020, the Democratic Party applauded the U.S. Supreme Court's ruling in *Bostock v. Clayton County*. In a 6-3 decision, the Court held that Title VII of the Civil Rights Act of 1964, which prohibits discrimination "because of sex," includes discrimination based on sexual orientation and gender identity. The platform pledged to enact the Equality Act and further protect the LGBTQ community from discrimination in "housing, public accommodations, access to credit, education, jury service, and federal programs." Democratic nominee Joe Biden pledged to reinstate many of the Obama-era protections that had been eliminated by the Trump administration, such as those in education and health care. Republicans chose to keep the 2016 platform for 2020, which included provisions opposed to LGBTQ rights; however, the Republican Party touted several pro-LGBTQ actions taken by the Trump administration.

Republicans

The Republican Party first addressed LGBTQ rights in its 1992 platform. Early platforms addressing LGBTQ rights focused on military service but have since expanded to include the party's opposition to antidiscrimination legislation supported by Democrats. Since 2000, Republicans have invoked the First Amendment rights of Freedom of Association and Religion as a basis for protecting the rights of private organizations and religious business owners. In 2016 and 2020, the party offered its most comprehensive statement opposing LGBTQ rights. President Donald Trump eliminated many of the protections established during the Obama administration.

In 1992, Republicans supported the exclusion of homosexuals from military service to further the goals of "good order and discipline." The platform also opposed Democratic efforts to make "sexual preference" a protected class at all levels of government, which would allow the enactment of nondiscrimination policies. Republicans argued that homosexuals were seeking preferential or special treatment since rights were being extended to protect them. Some conservatives, including evangelical Christians, argue that homosexuality is a choice that should not be rewarded with special legal protection. At the 1992 Republican Convention, Patrick Buchanan criticized Democratic nominee Bill Clinton's stance on several issues, including gay rights, as "not the kind of change we can tolerate in a nation that we still call God's country" (Buchanan 1992).

From 1996 to 2008, the platforms quoted the Defense Department's policy regarding gays in the military verbatim, "homosexuality is incompatible with military service," and affirmed what it called a "traditional military culture." In 1996, the platform specifically criticized President Clinton for attempting to rescind the ban on gays in the military. In 1995, the eventual Republican nominee Bob Dole was forced to take a more conservative stance on several issues, including gay rights, to appeal to conservative Republican voters. In May 1995, he stated that gay Americans have civil rights and that he had not decided whether homosexuals should be allowed to serve openly in the military. Two weeks later, he wrote a letter to the *Washington Times* in which he stated, "I oppose the special interest gay agenda that runs from gays in the military and reaches as far as to suggest special status for sexual orientation under Federal civil rights statutes." Dole also returned a $1,000 campaign contribution from the Log Cabin Republicans, an organization of gay Republicans, to demonstrate his opposition to LGBTQ rights.

In 2000 and 2004, George W. Bush supported DADT. Public opinion on gays serving in the military had changed since the implementation of DADT. Bush was opposed to same-sex couples adopting children and believed that private organizations such as the BSA should be allowed to refuse membership to gay scout leaders. Bush also opposed the expansion of hate crimes legislation to include crimes based on a victim's sexual orientation because he believed existing state and federal laws were adequate to deal with such crimes.

In addition to the military issue, the 2008 platform supported the decision of the BSA to exclude gay scoutmasters from its organization. John McCain, the 2008 Republican nominee, supported DADT and believed it was unwise to consider changing the policy while the United States was involved in armed conflict in Afghanistan and Iraq. He was opposed to allowing homosexuals to adopt children because he believed that heterosexual parents were better for the family. McCain was the first Republican to receive the endorsement of the Log Cabin Republicans.

The 2012 platform criticized President Obama's repeal of DADT and his executive order regarding foreign aid. During the campaign, several Republican candidates campaigned on restoring DADT. Republican nominee Mitt Romney, however, supported the repeal. He also supported antidiscrimination policies for LGBTQ individuals in the areas of employment and housing; however, he did not support same-sex marriage.

In 2016, after a shooting at a gay nightclub in Orlando, Florida, in which forty-nine people were killed and fifty-three injured, Donald Trump issued statements supporting gay rights. Some were hopeful that Trump's expression of sympathy and support would soften platform language on LGBTQ rights. Indeed, Log Cabin Republican president Gregory T. Angelo stated that Trump was "the most gay-friendly Republican nominee to run for president, ever" (Haberman 2016). The 2016 Republican National Convention was historic from the standpoint that several speakers addressed LGBTQ rights. During his acceptance speech, Trump stated that "Only weeks ago . . . 49 wonderful Americans were savagely murdered by an Islamic terrorist. This time the terrorist targeted our LGBTQ community. As your president, I will do everything in my power to protect our LGBTQ citizens from the violence and oppression of a hateful foreign ideology." After pausing for applause, he continued, "And I have to say as a Republican it is so nice to hear you cheering for what I just said. Thank you."

Trump's comments, the first by a GOP nominee to specifically address LGBTQ Americans, were criticized by several different commentators. Writing in the *National Review*, Alexandra DeSanctis (2016) condemned Trump's last statement because it was "demeaning to conservatives and Republicans" and left the erroneous impression that "Republicans couldn't care less" what happens to LGBTQ people. Eugene Scott in the *Washington Post* noted that critics cited the shooter's loyalty to a terrorist organization, not the protection of LGBTQ individuals, as the motivation for his comments.

Social conservatives created what Gregory T. Angelo called "the most anti-LGBTQ platform in the party's history" (Caplan 2016). The platform pledged to protect the religious rights of business owners who wished to refuse service to LGBTQ individuals and same-sex couples on the basis of their beliefs with the First Amendment Defense Act (FADA). The law would also prohibit the government from taking any action to stop the discrimination. FADA was first introduced by Republicans in 2015 and criticized by Jennifer Pizer, law and policy director at Lambda Legal, an LGBTQ rights organization. Pizer argued that FADA violates the Equal Protection Clause of the Fourteenth Amendment and the First Amendment's Establishment Clause by "elevating one set of religious beliefs above all others and by targeting LGBTQ Americans as a group, contrary to settled constitutional law." The platform continued to criticize Democratic support for gays in the military by stating that the military was not a place for "social engineering." The platform also implicitly endorsed conversion therapy by protecting the "right of parents to determine the proper medical treatment and therapy for their minor children."

The party addressed transgender issues without using the term "transgender." Instead, the platform stated that Republicans "emphatically support the original authentic meaning of Title IX" and accused President Obama of imposing a "social and cultural revolution . . . by wrongly redefining sex discrimination to include sexual orientation or other categories." The platform characterized the bathroom policy allowing transgender individuals to use the restroom of their choice as "at once illegal, dangerous, and ignores privacy issues."

After he was elected, Donald Trump rolled back many of the protections for LGBTQ individuals instituted by the Obama administration. In 2017, Trump tweeted that the U.S. military "cannot be burdened with the tremendous medical costs and disruption that transgender in the military would entail" (Tillett 2019). Ultimately, Trump did not institute a blanket ban on transgender service, allowing individuals who identify as transgender to remain in the military if they retained their biological sex. Anyone who had taken hormones or had sexual reassignment surgery was ineligible for service. This policy rescinded the 2016 Obama policy of allowing transgender individuals to serve. Similarly, in 2020, Trump rescinded a nondiscrimination policy for LGBTQ persons in health care and health insurance. The Affordable Care Act (2010) prohibited discrimination on the basis of "race, color, national origin, sex, age or disability in certain health programs and activities." In 2016, the Obama administration announced that "sex" included LGBTQ persons. The Trump administration defended the change arguing that it restored the "plain meaning" of the law. Trump also opposed the Equality Act.

Former President Trump Argues That Transgender Women Threaten Women's Sports

In his first major speech after he left office, former President Donald Trump addressed the issue of transgender women competing in women's sports at the Conservative Political Action Committee meeting in February 2021.

A lot of new records are being broken in women's sports. Hate to say that ladies, but got a lot of new records, they're being shattered. For years, the weightlifting, every ounce is like a big deal for many years. All of a sudden somebody comes along and beats it by a hundred pounds. Boom. Now young girls and women are in sets that they are now being forced to compete against those who are biological males. It's not good for women. It's not good for women's sports, which worked so long and so hard to get to where they are. The records that stood for years, even decades are now being smashed with these. Smashed. If this is not change women's sports, as we know it will die. They'll end, it'll end.

What coach, if I'm a coach, I want to be a great coach. What coach, as an example, wants to recruit a young woman to compete, if her record can easily be broken by somebody who was born a man. Not too many of those coaches around, right? If they are around, they won't be around long because they're going to have a big problem when that record is we're oh and 16, but we're getting better. No I think it's crazy. I think it's just crazy what's happening. We must protect the integrity of women's sports so important after. And I don't even know, is that controversial? Somebody said, well, that's going to be very controversial. I said, that's okay. You haven't heard anything yet.

Source

"Donald Trump CPAC 2021 Speech Transcript." 2021. Rev. Accessed November 22, 2022. https://www.rev.com/blog/transcripts/donald-trump-cpac-2021-speech-transcript.

Despite these actions, Robert Kabel, chair of the Log Cabin Republicans, argued in an op-ed in *USA Today* that the Republican Party was "delivering real results" for the LGBTQ community. He cited Trump's commitment to end the global criminalization of homosexuality and his administration's decision to distribute medication to prevent the transmission of HIV to uninsured, high-risk HIV individuals. He also noted that Trump had appointed the first openly gay Cabinet member by appointing Richard Grenell, former U.S. ambassador to Germany, as acting director of national intelligence. Trump also appointed two openly gay federal judges. While he expressed his dissatisfaction with the transgender military service ban, Kabel (2020) announced that the Log Cabin Republicans were endorsing Trump.

The Republican Party also asserted that Trump had instituted policies beneficial to the LGBTQ community on its website, which it unveiled during Pride Week in

June 2020. The website provided several facts about Trump's record on LGBTQ issues stating, for example, that he was the first Republican presidential nominee to mention LGBTQ rights in his acceptance speech at the Republican National Convention, and during that speech he said that he would "do everything in his power to protect LGBTQ citizens." The party also cited the appointment of Grenell and increasing support for HIV/AIDS programs ("President Trump Has Taken Unprecedented Steps to Protect the LGBTQ Community | GOP" 2020). Critics suggested, however, that the 2020 Republican Convention was inhospitable to LGBTQ rights noting that in Richard Grenell's speech to the delegates, he neglected to even mention LGBTQ rights. The list of speakers also included numerous anti-LGBTQ advocates, which included evangelist Franklin Graham, North Carolina congressional candidate Madison Cawthorn, who suggested that LGBTQ organizations had pushed for too much after they achieved marriage equality, and Representative Dan Crenshaw, who mocked nonbinary Americans.

Religious conservatives are a key voting block for Republicans, and they have consistently opposed the expansion of LGBTQ rights. While support for nondiscrimination laws has risen in public opinion polls as almost two-thirds of Americans support them, white evangelical Protestants (62 percent) are least likely to favor those laws (PRRI 2021). In 2019, Republicans introduced the Fairness for All Act, a response to the Equality Act, which would ban discrimination against LGBTQ persons in housing and employment but create broad exemptions for religious organizations in areas such as health care and education. For example, a medical doctor could refuse to treat a transgender person undergoing medical procedures related to their transition based on his or her religious beliefs.

Democrats

The Democratic Party was the first to address LGBTQ rights. From 1980 to 1996, the party platforms contained general statements addressing discrimination based on sexual orientation. In 2000, the party asserted its support for specific LGBTQ antidiscrimination policies. The 2016 platform devoted a significant amount of attention to support for LGBTQ policies and was the first to address issues specifically affecting transgender Americans. President Barack Obama initiated several policies to prevent discrimination against LGBTQ persons and President Joe Biden reinstated many of those policies that had been eliminated by the Trump administration. Biden also sought to expand legal protection for the LGBTQ community.

LGBTQ activists lobbied to have the Democratic Party include a nondiscrimination provision in its platform as early as 1972 but faced significant opposition. In 1980, the party platform contained a very general statement pledging to "protect all groups from discrimination based on race, color, religion, national origin, sex, or sexual orientation." During the 1984 campaign, Democratic candidates made an historic and concerted effort to appeal to gay and lesbian voters. The 1984 platform stated that the government has a special responsibility to those who society has historically prevented from enjoying the benefits of full citizenship. It also pledged to "address, document, and end" violence against gay men and lesbians. During his speech at the Democratic National Convention, Jesse Jackson, a key figure in the Civil Rights Movement and candidate for the 1984 Democratic presidential nomination, specifically mentioned gays and lesbians as part of a broader "Rainbow Coalition" of groups who belonged in the Democratic Party.

During the 1988 campaign, Democratic nominee Michael Dukakis was heavily criticized by LGBTQ rights groups. Dukakis refused to promise to sign an executive order barring discrimination in federal employment if elected. He stated that he preferred state and federal nondiscrimination legislation as opposed to executive action. Despite Dukakis's views, the platform stated that Democrats "honor our multicultural heritage by assuring equal access to government services, employment, housing, business enterprises and education regardless of . . . sexual orientation." The platform characterized these rights as "too precious" to be left to Republican-appointed judges and Justice Department officials who were chosen for their "unenlightened ideological views than for their respect for the rule of law."

In the 1992 presidential contest, issues concerning LGBTQ rights were seldom discussed because most of the emphasis during the campaign was on the economy. Nevertheless, Democratic nominee Bill Clinton campaigned on a promise to repeal the ban against homosexuals serving in the military. The 1992 platform condemned "homophobia" and pledged that Democrats would "continue to lead the fight" against discrimination on the basis of sexual orientation. The platform further pledged to "provide civil rights protection for gay and lesbian and an end to Defense Department discrimination."

Democrats vowed to "continue to lead the fight" against discrimination on the basis of sexual orientation in the 1996 platform. In 1994, Democrats first introduced the ENDA in Congress. This law was cited in the 1996 platform as an example of the Democratic Party's attempts to end discrimination against gays and lesbians and to "further their full inclusion in the life of the nation."

In 2000, Democratic presidential nominee Al Gore supported the repeal of DADT even though he was Bill Clinton's vice president. Democrats started to back away from DADT because they argued that the policy was unfair to gay and lesbian service members. The platform supported the enactment of hate crimes legislation. Hate crimes laws increase the penalties for crimes committed on the basis of certain criteria, including sexual orientation. The platform asserted that those crimes are "more than assaults on people, they are assaults on the very idea of America." The platform supported the "full inclusion of gay and lesbian families in the life of the nation." This statement differed slightly from the 1996 platform through its emphasis on families and not just individuals. The party also supported ENDA.

The 2004 platform continued its support for ENDA and stated that members of the armed services should be allowed to serve without being discriminated against.

The Democratic nominee, Senator John Kerry, had a long record of supporting LGBTQ rights. Kerry supported ENDA, partnership benefits for same-sex couples, hate crimes legislation, and changes in immigration and adoption law so that LGBTQ individuals were not discriminated against. He stopped short of endorsing same-sex marriage but did support civil unions. He also supported the repeal of DADT.

The 2008 platform was significant for LGBTQ rights because the party called for the outright repeal of DADT. The party contended that the policy was ineffective because over 12,500 service members had been discharged due to their sexual orientation. Additionally, for the first time the platform stated that discrimination based on gender identity, like sexual orientation, should not be tolerated. The Democratic nominee, Barack Obama, supported ENDA and promised the full support of his administration to pass the law.

In 2012, the platform supported ENDA and touted President Obama's record advancing LGBTQ rights. While previous platforms supported hate crimes legislation that included sexual orientation as protected group, this platform highlighted the enactment of the Matthew Shepard and James Byrd Jr. Hate Crimes Prevention Act in 2009. It also highlighted Obama's 2011 executive order cutting U.S. aid to countries that discriminated against LGBTQ individuals. The order to executive agencies directed them to (1) combat the criminalization of LGBTQ status or conduct abroad, (2) protect vulnerable LGBTQ refugees and asylum seekers, (3) leverage foreign assistance to protect human rights and advance nondiscrimination, (4) ensure swift and meaningful U.S. responses to human rights abuses of LGBTQ persons abroad, (5) engage international organizations in the fight against LGBTQ discrimination, and (6) report on progress. The 2010 Affordable Care Act prohibited healthcare providers from discriminating against LGBTQ persons and made it easier for individuals living with HIV and AIDS to obtain Medicaid. The Obama administration also took steps to ensure equality in housing programs. The Department of Housing and Urban Development's Equal Access Rule outlawed discrimination based on actual or perceived sexual orientation, gender identity, or marital status. The rule also forbade discrimination based on sexual orientation or gender identity in FHA-insured mortgages (Office of the Press Secretary 2016). Obama also allowed transgender soldiers to serve in the military and extended antidiscrimination provisions in federal education legislation to include transgender students.

According to her critics, former secretary of state Hillary Clinton, the 2016 Democratic nominee, was slow to embrace LGBTQ rights during her political career. She repudiated the Defense of Marriage Act and DADT, which were signed by her husband. As secretary of state, Clinton changed the State Department's rules to allow the passports of transgender individuals to reflect their gender. Clinton also supported the Equality Act and opposed conversion therapy for LGBTQ minors.

The 2016 platform offered what was then the party's most extensive LGBTQ plank. Democrats noted that while same-sex marriage had been legalized by the

President Obama Highlights Importance of LGBTQ Rights

President Barack Obama's remarks from an LGBTQ Pride Reception in 2016 illustrate his and the Democratic Party's shift on LGBTQ issues related to changes in military policy, hate crimes legislation, and same-sex marriage. He also makes clear that the Democratic Party sees the LGBTQ fight for equality as an important and moral civil rights cause.

So every year, we set aside this month to celebrate the ways that so many lesbian, gay, bisexual, and transgender Americans have helped to make our union just a little more perfect. We honor the countless nameless heroes who paved the way for progress: The activists who marched. The advocates who organized. The lawyers who argued cases. The families who stood by their loved ones, even when it was tough. Every brave American who came out and spoke out, especially when it was tough. Because of them, because of all of you, there's a lot to be proud of today.

Today, we live in an America where "don't ask, don't tell" don't exist no more. (Applause.) Because no one should have to hide who they love in order to serve the country that they love. We live in an America that protects all of us with a hate crimes law that bears the name of Matthew Shepard. (Applause.) We live in an America where all of us are treated more equally, because visiting hours in hospitals no longer depend on who you are—(applause)—and insurance companies can no longer turn somebody away simply because of who you love. . . .

We now live in an America where all of our marriages and our families are recognized as equal under the law. And that's an extraordinary thing. When you talk to the upcoming generation, our kids—Malia's, Sasha's generation—they instinctively know people are people and families are families. . . . So we live in an America where the laws are finally catching up to the hearts of kids and what they instinctively understand.

Source

Obama, Barack. 2016. "Remarks by the President at LGBT Pride Reception." The White House, June 9. Accessed November 22, 2022. https://obamawhitehouse.archives.gov/the-press-office/2016/06/09/remarks-president-lgbt-pride-reception.

U.S. Supreme Court, LGBTQ individuals were subject to discrimination in many other areas of American life. The platform expressed support for "comprehensive federal non-discrimination protections for all LGBTQ Americans, to guarantee equal rights in areas such as housing, employment, public accommodations, credit, jury service, education, and federal funding." In addition to these areas, the platform addressed specific concerns in education, violence, and income inequality. Democrats promised to end bullying of LGBTQ students and to oppose school disciplinary policies that disproportionately affect LGBTQ youth. They also pledged to protect LGBTQ individuals from violence—"including ending the crisis of violence against transgender Americans." In a similar vein, the platform argued that it was "unacceptable to target, defame, or exclude anyone because of . . . sexual orientation [or] gender identity."

The platform praised Obama's efforts in repealing DADT and in addressing LGBTQ rights globally. It pledged that Democrats would "continue to stand with LGBTQ people around the world" and promised to review discharge records of veterans who had been dismissed under the policy. According to the platform, "[o]ur military is strongest when people of all races, religions, sexual orientations, and gender identities are honored for their service to our country." To counter the Republican argument that religious freedom justified discrimination against LGBTQ individuals, the platform stated that Democrats "support a progressive vision of religious freedom that respects pluralism and rejects the misuse of religion to discriminate."

The 2020 Democratic platform went further than the 2016 platform in advocating for LGBTQ rights. In addition to legal protection in employment and other government services, the party pledged to end discrimination in health care, both mental and physical, for the LGBTQ community. It also promised that all "transgender and non-binary people can procure official government identification documents that accurately reflect their gender identity." Democratic president Joe Biden proposed numerous policies to protect LGBTQ rights, including lifting Trump's ban on transgender military service, appointing LGBTQ people to high-ranking government positions, and reversing Trump's policies that permitted religious exemptions from antidiscrimination policies by social service agencies, health-care providers, adoption and foster care agencies, among others. He accomplished this through an executive order on his first day in office by applying the *Bostock* ruling to executive agencies. He argued that because that ruling interpreted sex discrimination to include LGBTQ discrimination, any federal antidiscrimination policy should also prohibit discrimination against LGBTQ persons. Biden supported the Equality Act and wanted to sign it within his first one hundred days in office. In his first State of the Union Address in March 2022, Biden called for Congress to pass the act; however, Republican Senate opposition has stalled the bill, which passed the House in 2021 by a vote of 224-206. Biden's agenda was criticized by many religious conservatives who had supported Trump. Albert Mohler, the president of the Southern Baptist Theological Seminary, stated that the Equality Act was a "dangerous game changer" that threated religious liberty (Crary and Schor 2020).

Further Reading

Berke, Richard L. 1995. "Dole, in a New Bow to Right, Returns Gay Group's Money." *New York Times*, August 27. Accessed August 19, 2019. https://www.nytimes.com/1995/08/27/us/dole-in-a-new-bow-to-right-returns-gay-group-s-money.html.

Broder, David. 1988. "Gay Activists Confront Dukakis." *Washington Post*, May 15. Accessed August 24, 2019. https://www.washingtonpost.com/archive/politics/1988/05/15/gay-activists-confront-dukakis/02c6d6a4-84ef-43aa-ac31-a2df0a2fcdf6/.

Buchanan, Patrick. 1992. "1992 Republican National Convention Speech." Patrick J. Buchanan Official Website, August 17. Accessed December 19, 2022. https://buchanan.org/blog/1992-republican-national-convention-speech-148.

Burns, Katelyn. 2019. "Republicans Are Introducing a New Compromise LGBTQ Rights Bill: But Everyone Already Hates It." *Vox*, December 9. Accessed October 1, 2022. https://www.vox.com/policy-and-politics/2019/12/6/20997469/lgbtq-discrimination-ban-compromise-religious-exception.

Caplan, David. 2016. "Log Cabin Republicans: GOP Platform the 'Most Anti-LGBT' in Party's History." *ABC News*, July 14. Accessed August 23, 2019. https://abcnews.go.com/Politics/log-cabin-republicans-gop-party-platform-anti-lgbt/story?id=40564850.

Crary, David, and Elana Schor. 2020. "Biden Plans Swift Moves to Protect and Advance LGBTQ Rights." *AP News*, November 28. Accessed December 1, 2020. https://apnews.com/article/joe-biden-donald-trump-barack-obama-discrimination-marriage-fbdd826a46b3c77c265967c73b7ff6e0.

Democratic Party Platforms. 1972–2020. American Presidency Project. Accessed November 22, 2022. https://www.presidency.ucsb.edu/people/other/democratic-party-platforms.

DeSanctis, Alexandra. 2016. "Trump Throws Conservatives Under the Bus on LGBT Issues." *National Review*, July 22. Accessed August 22, 2019. https://www.nationalreview.com/corner/donald-trump-lgbt-convention-speech-conservatives/.

Gailey, Phil. 1983. "Democrats Seek Homosexuals' Votes." *New York Times*, July 25. Accessed August 16, 2019. https://www.nytimes.com/1983/07/25/us/democrats-seek-homosexuals-votes.html.

Greenberg, Daniel, Maxine Najle, Natalie Jackson, Oyindamola Bola, and Robert P. Jones. 2019. "America's Growing Support for Transgender Rights." Public Religion Research Institute, June 11. Accessed August 13, 2019. https://www.prri.org/research/americas-growing-support-for-transgender-rights/.

Haberman, Maggie. 2016. "Donald Trump's More Accepting Views on Gay Issues Set Him Apart in G.O.P." *New York Times*, April 22. Accessed December 19, 2022. https://www.nytimes.com/2016/04/23/us/politics/donald-trump-gay-rights.html.

Johnson, Chris. 2018. "John McCain Leaves Complicated Legacy on LGBT Rights." Pride Source, August 27. Accessed August 16, 2019. https://pridesource.com/article/john-mccain-leaves-complicated-legacy-on-lgbt-rights/.

Johnson, Emily S. 2019. "The Myth That Has Shaped the Christian Right and the LGBTQ Rights Movement for Four Decades." *Washington Post*, June 21. Accessed August 19, 2019. https://www.washingtonpost.com/outlook/2019/06/21/myth-that-has-shaped-christian-right-lgbtq-rights-movement-four-decades/.

Kabel, Robert. 2020. "Log Cabin Republicans Chair: LGBT Americans Belong in Donald Trump's Republican Party." *USA Today*, August 20. Accessed September 15, 2020. https://www.usatoday.com/story/opinion/voices/2020/08/20/donald-trump-lgbtq-lgbt-gay-rights-republican-equality-column/5605491002/.

Loughlin, Sean. 2004. "Gay Support for Kerry on Display at Convention." *CNN*, July 29. Accessed August 24, 2019. https://www.cnn.com/2004/ALLPOLITICS/07/29/dems.dayscene/index.html.

Maxwell, Lesli A. 2016. "Obama Admin. to Schools: No Restrictions on Transgender Restroom Access." *Education Week*, May 12. Accessed August 13, 2019. http://blogs.edweek.org/edweek/rulesforengagement/2016/05/obama_administration_to_schools_no_restrictions_on_transgender_restroom_access.html.

Milligan, Susan. 2016. "Bathroom Bills and Religious Freedom Laws: Losing Battles for the GOP." *US News and World Report*, August 25. Accessed August 24, 2019. https://www.usnews.com/news/articles/2016-08-25/bathroom-bills-and-religious-freedom-laws-losing-battles-for-the-gop.

Murphy, Caryle. 2015. "Most U.S. Christian Groups Grow More Accepting of Homo-sexuality." Pew Research Center, December 18. Accessed August 24, 2019. https://www.pewresearch.org/fact-tank/2015/12/18/most-u-s-christian-groups-grow-more-accepting-of-homosexuality/.

Office of the Press Secretary. 2016. "FACT SHEET: Obama Administration's Record and the LGBT Community." The White House, June 9. Accessed December 19, 2022. https://obamawhitehouse.archives.gov/the-press-office/2016/06/09/fact-sheet-obama-administrations-record-and-lgbt-community.

O'Hara, Mary Emily. 2016. "First Amendment Defense Act Would Be 'Devastating' for LGBTQ Americans." *NBC News*, December 20. Accessed August 25, 2019. https://www.nbcnews.com/feature/nbc-out/first-amendment-defense-act-would-be-devastating-lgbtq-americans-n698416.

Pathe, Simone. 2016. "How Democrats Came Around on Gay Rights." *Roll Call*, July 28. Accessed August 16, 2019. https://www.rollcall.com/news/politics/high-democratic-enthusiasm-gay-rights-wasnt-always.

Pew Research Center. 2010. "Most Continue to Favor Gays Serving Openly in Mili-tary." November 29. Accessed December 19, 2022. https://www.pewresearch.org/politics/2010/11/29/most-continue-to-favor-gays-serving-openly-in-military/.

"President Trump Has Taken Unprecedented Steps to Protect the LGBTQ Community | GOP." 2020. Web, December 26. Accessed December 19, 2022. https://web.archive.org/web/20201226073033/https://gop.com/president-trump-has-taken-unprecedented-steps-to-protect-the-lgbtq-community-rsr/.

PRRI. 2021. "Despite Partisan Rancor, Americans Broadly Support LGBTQ Rights." PRRI, March 23. Accessed October 1, 2022. https://www.prri.org/wp-content/uploads/2021/03/PRRI-Mar-2021-LGBTQ.pdf.

Republican Party Platforms. 1992–2020. American Presidency Project. Accessed November 22, 2022. https://www.presidency.ucsb.edu/people/other/republican-party-platforms.

Reston, Laura, and Alex Shephard. 2016. "The Republican Party Blew It." *New Republic*, July 18. Accessed August 24, 2019. https://newrepublic.com/article/135151/republican-party-blew.

Reynolds, Andrew. 2015. "Why Does the Republican Party Still Oppose LGBT Rights?" *Washington Post*, June 18. Accessed July 23, 2019. https://www.washingtonpost.com/news/monkey-cage/wp/2015/06/18/why-does-the-republican-party-still-oppose-lgbt-rights/.

Scott, Eugene. 2019. "Trump's Response to the Pulse Shooting in 2016 Gave False Hope about His LGBT Agenda." *Washington Post*, June 19. Accessed July 30, 2019. https://www.washingtonpost.com/politics/2019/06/12/trumps-response-pulse-shooting-gave-false-hope-about-his-lgbt-agenda/.

Simmons-Duffin, Selena. 2020. "Transgender Health Protections Reversed by Trump Admin-istration." National Public Radio, June 12. Accessed September 15, 2020. https://www.npr.org/sections/health-shots/2020/06/12/868073068/transgender-health-protections-reversed-by-trump-administration.

Solomon, Marc. 2014. "How Obama Became the Gay-Rights President." *New Republic*, October 12. Accessed August 28, 2019. https://newrepublic.com/article/119801/obamas-gay-rights-record-how- he-became-lgbt-president.

Sosin, Kate. 2020. "Republicans Are Waffling on LGBTQ+ Issues. Will It Matter?" *USA Today*, September 6. Accessed September 15, 2020. https://www.usatoday.com/story/news/politics/2020/09/06/republicans-waffling-lgbtq-issues-matter/5685869002/.

Tillett, Emily. 2019. "Controversial Trump Administration Ban on Transgender Troops Goes into Effect." *CBS News*, April 12. Accessed August 23, 2019. https://www.cbsnews.com/news/transgender-military-ban-trump-administration-ban-on-transgender-troops-goes-into-effect/.

Yurkaba, Jo. 2021. "Biden Issues Executive Order Expanding LGBTQ Nondiscrimination Protections." *NBC News*, January 21. Accessed October 1, 2022. https://www.nbcnews.com/feature/nbc-out/biden-issues-executive-order-expanding-lgbtq-nondiscrimination-protections-n1255165.

Marriage Equality

At a Glance

Marriage equality has been a prominent political issue since the 1990s, when public support for equal rights for LGBTQ Americans steadily climbed in response to wider cultural and societal integration. Initially, both Democrats and Republicans opposed same-sex marriage. The Defense of Marriage Act (DOMA) was a bipartisan law enacted in 1996 to restrict the definition of marriage to one man and one woman, and to allow states to deny recognition of same-sex marriages conducted in states where the practice was legal. The measure passed in the House by 342-67 votes and by a similarly lop-sided margin in the Senate, where it passed by a 85-14 vote. Most states had already enacted bans on same-sex marriage until public opinion on this issue began to shift.

Since 1996, the Democratic Party's stance on the issue has evolved and the party supports marriage equality, while the Republican Party's opposition to it has changed very little despite the U.S. Supreme Court's ruling in *Obergefell v. Hodges* in 2015 invalidating state bans on same-sex marriage. Democrats have supported federal legislation to protect same-sex marriage, while many Congressional Republicans have opposed it.

According to many Democrats . . .

- Marriage equality is a basic human right.
- Marriages between same-sex partners are entitled to the same legal protections as heterosexual marriages.
- Congressional legislation is necessary to protect marriage equality..

According to many Republicans . . .

- Marriage is a union between one man and one woman.
- Same-sex marriage denigrates the institution of marriage because homosexual activity is immoral. Since marriage is a sacrament of the church, same-sex marriage should be banned.

- A traditional family unit is the healthiest way to rear children who deserve both a mother and a father.

———————

Overview

The Gay Rights Movement began in the United States in the 1970s. The early goals of gay rights organizations focused on the repeal of anti-sodomy laws and the enactment of policies to protect homosexuals from employment discrimination. The issue of marriage equality became controversial in the 1990s when three same-sex couples in Hawaii filed a lawsuit challenging the state's ban on gay marriage. In *Baehr v. Lewin* (1993), the Hawaii Supreme Court held that the state must show a compelling interest in banning same-sex marriage. Although Hawaii eventually passed a state constitutional amendment prohibiting same-sex marriage, this ruling sparked a nationwide debate on marriage equality. The U.S. Constitution's Full Faith and Credit Clause requires that states give full faith and credit "to the public Acts, Records, and judicial Proceedings of every other State." In the context of marriage, the clause requires states to recognize marriages performed in other states. The concern in the 1990s was that if some states legalized same-sex marriages, others would be required to afford those marriages legal recognition. In response to these concerns, Congress passed the DOMA in 1996.

DOMA provided that states that prohibited same-sex marriage were not required to legally honor same-sex marriages conducted in states that did. The law also defined "marriage" as "a legal union between one man and one woman as husband and wife" for the purpose of federal benefits. There are over one thousand federal laws that convey benefits based on marital status, including survivorship benefits for Social Security and filing federal tax returns jointly. The law passed both chambers of Congress by overwhelming majorities. It passed the House of Representatives by a vote of 342-67 and the Senate by a vote 85-14. All 14 "no" votes were cast by Democrats. President Bill Clinton signed the bill into law in September 1996 during his bid for reelection.

The DOMA was enacted at a time when most Americans were opposed to same-sex marriage. Gallup began polling on public opinion on the issue in 1996. In its first poll, 68 percent of Americans were opposed to same-sex marriages having the same rights as traditional marriages; only 27 percent supported same-sex marriage. In the 1996 presidential campaign, the Democratic Party platform was silent on both DOMA and same-sex marriage. The Republican Party platform, however, offered unequivocal support for DOMA that same year.

The Democratic Party platform supported gay rights in terms of its opposition to discrimination against homosexuals, but there was no specific mention of same-sex marriage in the platform until 2004. At that point, the party advocated leaving the definition of marriage to the states. The platform also repudiated the federal constitutional marriage amendment supported by Republican president George W. Bush. Bush supported the Federal Marriage Amendment in response to the Massachusetts Supreme Judicial Court's ruling that marriage licenses could not be denied to same-sex couples.

In the 2004 presidential election, Republicans tried to frame the battle to legalize gay marriage as an attack on the traditional institution of marriage. According to some political analysts, the GOP emphasis on the "marriage amendment mobilized enough conservatives to turn out or induced enough swing voters to support Bush, [and] it may have determined the outcome of the presidential election" that year (Klarman 2013a). While Americans had generally supported a variety of equal rights initiatives for same-sex couples, including adoption rights, inheritance rights, and health-care benefits since the late 1980s, the majority continued to oppose marriage equality during this period.

In 2008, a Pew Research Center poll indicated that same-sex marriage was last in a list of issues that were important to voters in the presidential election. Voters were more concerned with the economy, which was cited by 87 percent of respondents as being "very important" to their vote, and energy policy, which was cited by 77 percent of respondents. Only 28 percent of respondents cited same-sex marriage as very important to their vote. This was down from 32 percent toward the end of the 2004 campaign.

During this election, a bare majority (51 percent) of Democratic voters favored same-sex marriage—a 12 percent increase from 2004. On the other hand, 72 percent of Republicans opposed it, including 78 percent of evangelical voters. The views outlined in the party platforms mirrored the views of their respective supporters. The Democratic platform called for full inclusion and equal benefits for gays and lesbians in the life of the nation. While not supporting same-sex marriage, the platform stated that Democrats opposed DOMA. Democratic candidate Barack Obama stated that he favored civil unions and opposed same-sex marriage. Civil unions were considered by some to be an alternative to marriage because they provide the legal benefits of marriage; however, they are not recognized by other states or the federal government, and they do not have to be authorized by a religious institution. By 2008, Vermont, New Jersey, Connecticut, and New Hampshire allowed civil unions.

The Republican platform indicated the party's continued support for DOMA and stern criticism toward Democrats for abandoning a law they had supported. The platform asserted the party's continued support for a constitutional amendment to protect the "traditional definition of marriage." By 2012, Republicans had dropped the language regarding a Federal Marriage Amendment but continued to indicate support for DOMA and opposition to judicial definitions of marriage in court decisions legalizing same-sex marriage. The Republican nominee, Massachusetts governor Mitt Romney, indicated that he was opposed to it. On the Democratic side, however, a clear shift on the issue took place during Obama's first term in office (January 2009–January 2013). By 2011, the Justice Department no longer defended the constitutionality of DOMA against lawsuits by same-sex couples. One year later, the president announced his support for marriage equality. These views were reflected in the Democratic platform, and some argue that his announcement had a significant impact on public opinion. According to a *Washington Post*-ABC News poll, prior to Obama's announcement, 41 percent of Black Americans supported same-sex marriage. That percentage increased to 59 percent after he publicized his support, and overall support for same-sex marriage increased to 53 percent, an all-time high, and 39 percent of those polled were opposed, an all-time low (Clement and Somashekhar 2012). Critics questioned the poll's accuracy. Frank Schubert, the political director for the National Organization for Marriage, which opposes same-sex marriage, stated that "[t]here is not a chance in God's green earth that African Americans support same-sex marriage" and that the president's announcement "created a lot of angst and conflict in that community, but his opinion of same-sex marriage is not going to be changing the opinion of African Americans in a significant way" (Clement and Somashekhar 2012).

In 2013, the U.S. Supreme Court ruled in *United States. v. Windsor* that section 3 of DOMA was unconstitutional. This section denied federal benefits to same-sex couples. The U.S. Supreme Court decided a more significant case pertaining to same-sex marriage in *Obergefell v. Hodges* (2015). In this landmark ruling the Court invalidated bans on same-sex marriage by a 5-4 vote. The 2016 and 2020 Republican Party platforms continued to oppose same-sex marriage and urged for the reversal of these decisions. Republicans opted not to create a new 2020 platform and instead reissued their 2016 platform. The Democratic platform applauded these rulings and stated that they intended to continue working for antidiscrimination legislation to further protect the rights of LGBTQ Americans. A 2020 Gallup poll showed record support for same-sex marriage with 67 percent of Americans supporting it. However, there was a wide gulf in support based on party identification: 83 percent of Democrats versus 49 percent of Republicans (McCarthy 2020).

After the U.S. Supreme Court overturned *Roe v. Wade* in *Dobbs v. Jackson Women's Health Organization* in 2022, there was renewed attention to marriage equality. In *Dobbs*, the Court held that the Constitution did not protect a right to privacy. In a concurring opinion, Justice Clarence Thomas opined that other rights, such as same-sex marriage, which had been recognized by the Court on the basis of the right to privacy, could be reconsidered. House Democrats passed the Respect for Marriage Act in 2022 to protect marriage equality for same-sex couples and interracial couples. All of the chamber's 267 Democrats voted in favor of the bill, while 47 of 211 Republican House members supported it. The Senate delayed a vote on the bill until after the 2022 midterm elections when the bill passed by a vote of 61-36. Forty-nine Democrats and twelve Republicans voted for the bill, while thirty-six Republicans voted against it. One Democrat and two Republicans did not vote. Democratic President Joe Biden signed the bill in December 2022.

Democrats

The Democratic Party's stance on marriage equality has shifted considerably since the issue arose in the 1990s. Initially, Democrats, like Republicans and a majority of Americans, were opposed to same-sex marriage; however, the party was supportive of gay rights generally. By 2012, the Democratic Party fully supported marriage equality and in 2022 Congressional Democrats voted for legislation to ensure its continued legality.

During the 1992 presidential election campaign, the Democratic nominee, and later president, William J. Clinton pledged to eliminate the military's ban on openly gay service members. His decision to support gays in the military was one factor leading to the Republicans gaining a majority of seats in the House of Representatives for the first time in forty years in the 1994 congressional midterm elections. In 1996, when DOMA passed by large majorities in both chambers of Congress, Clinton signed the legislation and indicated that he was opposed to same-sex marriage. The 1996 Democratic Party platform was silent on the issue but included a statement that "[w]e support continued efforts to end discrimination against gay men and lesbians and further their full inclusion in the life of the nation." Very similar language was included in the 2000 party platform with an additional promise to seek an "equitable alignment of benefits" for gays and lesbians. According to one commentator, the party was slow to adopt a definitive position because of conflict among its core constituents. While a majority of gay and lesbian voters were Democrats, a majority of African Americans and working-class Catholics also supported the Democratic Party but opposed same-sex marriage.

Same-sex marriage was first mentioned in the 2004 Democratic Party platform. Here, the party advocated leaving the regulation of marriage to the states—a task they had historically been responsible for. The platform also "repudiated" President George W. Bush's support for a Federal Marriage Amendment and accused him of "politicizing the Constitution." Bans on same-sex marriage were on the ballots in eleven states, and it was a significant issue in the 2004 presidential campaign. With strong Republican opposition, Democrats were compelled to finally take a stand on the issue. Commentators point to the outcome in Ohio, a battleground state, as evidence of the potential impact of the issue. Bush won Ohio by fewer than 2 percentage points, but the same-sex marriage ban passed by 24 percent. "Among frequent churchgoers—the group most likely to oppose same-sex marriage—the increase in Bush's share of the popular vote in Ohio from 2000 was 17 percentage points, compared to just 1 percentage point nationally" (Klarman 2013a).

The first signs of a shift in the Democratic Party's stance came in the 2008 platform. While the party still did not support same-sex marriage, it advocated the repeal of DOMA—a significant change from prior years. While running as the Democratic nominee for president, Senator Barack Obama stated that he favored civil unions and opposed same-sex marriage. While in the White House, President Obama stated that his views were "evolving." In February 2011, Obama ordered the Department of Justice to stop defending DOMA against lawsuits brought by same-sex couples. Attorney General Eric Holder notified Congress that the administration believed laws that treated same-sex couples differently than heterosexual couples should be subjected to strict scrutiny, the highest legal standard used for discriminatory policies. Under that standard, according to the administration, DOMA was unconstitutional. In 2011, polls showed for the first time that a majority of Americans supported same-sex marriage, including 69 percent of Democrats (McCarthy 2018).

In May 2012, President Obama announced his support for marriage equality during a television interview. Two months later, the Democratic Party's platform committee drafted a document supporting it. The final version of the platform stated that Democrats supported marriage equality and equal treatment for same-sex couples. The platform also supported the full repeal of DOMA and the passage of the Respect for Marriage Act. This proposed bill would repeal DOMA and require the federal government to recognize same-sex marriages. Additionally, the party platform supported the freedom of churches to decide how to administer marriage without interference from the government.

In 2013, when the U.S. Supreme Court invalidated section 3 of DOMA, which denied federal benefits to married same-sex couples, Obama stated, "The laws of our land are catching up to the fundamental truth that millions of Americans hold in our hearts: when all Americans are treated as equal, no matter who they are or whom they love, we are all more free" (Raghavan 2013). Two years later, in *Obergefell v. Hodges*, the Court ruled that bans on same-sex marriage violated several constitutional provisions, including the right to privacy. Obama responded that the ruling made "our union a little more perfect" (Neuman 2015).

Democratic support for marriage equality continued in the 2016 election. The platform applauded the decision in *Obergefell v. Hodges* but stated that more work needed to be done in terms of antidiscrimination legislation. The Democratic nominee and former secretary of state Hillary Clinton, like prior nominees, was heavily criticized for her changing views on same-sex marriage. Due to Clinton's long history of public service, she had taken various stances on this issue. This was a disappointment to activist groups who expected her to support same-sex marriage sooner than she did. In 2000, she stated that she supported civil unions and believed that the historic and religious nature of marriage precluded same-sex marriages. During her tenure as secretary of state, she allowed same-sex partners of Foreign Service officers the same travel benefits as married couples; however, her views regarding marriage equality did not change until 2013 (Samuels 2016). In 2020, Democrats did not address marriage equality in their platform, but focused on LGBTQ rights more broadly.

House Democrats introduced the Respect for Marriage Act in 2022 after the *Dobbs* ruling negated a constitutional right to privacy. The bill repealed DOMA and applied to interracial marriages as well as same-sex marriages. Specifically, the bill defined marriage for purposes of federal law as any marriage that is valid under state law. It replaced the provision of DOMA that did not require states to

Democrats Support Legal Protection for Marriage Equality in Wake of Supreme Court Ruling

In this excerpt from the debate in the House of Representatives on the Respect for Marriage Act, Democratic Representative Sheila Jackson Lee argues that the High Court's ruling overturning Roe v. Wade threatened marriage equality.

Mr. Speaker, I am proud to rise in strong support for H.R. 8404, the "Respect for Marriage Act" and the collaboration in the Senate last week that enabled it to pass the Senate and return to the House for today's vote.

I am very concerned that the archaic dictum that the Supreme Court used in *Dobbs v. Jackson Women's Health Organization* to justify overturning the well-established and reaffirmed right to abortion could be further weaponized in the future to strip away other fundamental rights, including the right to marriage equality.

Specifically, in his concurring opinion to the Dobbs decision, Clarence Thomas appallingly stated that other cherished, fundamental rights should be subject to abrogation, writing, ". . . in future cases, we should reconsider all of this Court's substantive due process precedents, including Griswold, Lawrence, and Obergefell." Thomas left no doubt about his regressive, byzantine intentions, adding, ". . . we have a duty to 'correct the error' established in those precedents, . . . After overruling these demonstrably erroneous decisions, the question would remain whether other constitutional provisions guarantee the myriad rights that our substantive due process cases have generated."

To prevent Thomas's dream scenario from inflicting a nightmare on the rest of the country, the Respect for Marriage Act would codify in federal law our essential rights conferring marriage equality for same sex and interracial couples, protecting the rights of Americans to marry who they choose . . .

The Senate's embrace of this legislation, with strong bipartisan support, demonstrates the bill's alignment with bedrock American values and its strong support among the American people, across political ideologies. After witnessing the Senate's passage of the Respect for Marriage Act, I am proud to say that we are on a path to guaranteeing marriage equality for every American. . . .

Marriage Equality is not a right that can be stripped away by a conservative faction of the United States Supreme Court, nor by extremist Republican legislators. It is a fundamental aspect of our democracy . . .

Source

"Congressional Record, Volume 168 Issue 191 (Thursday, December 8, 2022)." Accessed January 3, 2023. https://www.govinfo.gov/content/pkg/CREC-2022-12-08/html/CREC-2022-12-08-pt1-PgH8827-3.htm.

recognize same-sex marriage with a provision that prohibits states from denying the full faith and credit to out-of-state marriages on the basis of sex, race, ethnicity, or national origin. Every House Democrat voted in favor of the legislation. Speaking in support of the bill, Democratic House Speaker Nancy Pelosi (2022) stated, "As radical Justices and right-wing politicians continue their assault on our basic rights, Democrats believe that the government has no place between you and the person you love . . . With the landmark Respect for Marriage Act, we ensure marriage equality remains the law of the land—now and for generations to come." Senate Democrats decided to hold off on a vote on the bill until after the 2022 midterm elections as they hoped to pick up enough Republican votes to pass it. Ultimately, 12 Senate Republicans voted with 49 Senate Democrats. In December 2022, President Joe Biden signed the bill into law.

Republicans

The Republican Party has consistently and steadfastly opposed marriage equality as part of its broader opposition to gay rights in general. Over time, many Republican voters have become more supportive of same-sex marriage, but there is still strong opposition in the party platform and among the most conservative Republicans.

In its 1996 platform, the party specifically endorsed DOMA so that states would not be "forced to recognize same-sex unions." The platform also stated that "sexual preference" should not be among the protected groups in antidiscrimination legislation. In the 2000 platform, the party went even further by articulating "a traditional definition of 'marriage' as the legal union between one man and one woman" and stating that DOMA was based on the belief that the home was the appropriate place "to instill the virtues that sustain democracy itself."

In 2004, President George W. Bush's chief political strategist, Karl Rove, made a concerted effort to appeal to evangelical Christian voters. Rove believed that Bush lost the popular vote in the 2000 presidential election to Democratic candidate Al Gore because millions of evangelical voters did not vote (Abramson, Aldrich, and Rohde 2007, 41). Part of Rove's strategy to increase voter turnout involved emphasizing Bush's stance on moral issues, including his support for a federal constitutional amendment banning same-sex marriage. Bush announced his support for the Federal Marriage Amendment (also referred to as the Marriage Protection Amendment) in February 2004, a few months after the Massachusetts Supreme Judicial Court ruled that denying marriage licenses to same-sex couples violated the Massachusetts Constitution. In the 2004 election, Republicans also strategically placed referenda on the ballots of eleven states, which would ban same-sex marriage in the hopes that more Republican voters would go to the polls to vote for the bans and the president. Bush won nine of the eleven states where same-sex marriage was on the ballot, including the battleground state of Ohio.

The Republican Party's opposition to same-sex marriage was evident in the 2004 platform. There was more discussion of the issue than in previous platforms, and more specific actions against same-sex marriage were delineated. The party platform expressed support for a federal constitutional amendment to protect marriage and asserted that Bush would vigorously defend DOMA because it was a "common sense law."

Despite the lack of congressional and public support for a federal constitutional amendment, the 2008 Republican platform indicated that the party supported such an action to protect the traditional definition of marriage and to prevent judges from imposing their own definition. The platform also criticized Democrats for their stance on repealing DOMA. During the 2008 campaign, the Republican nominee for president, Senator John McCain, was criticized by James Dobson, a conservative evangelical and founder of Focus on the Family, for being slow to announce his opposition to same-sex marriage (Ewers 2008). After this rebuke in June 2008, McCain, who had voted against Bush's constitutional amendment to ban same-sex marriage, announced that he continued to believe the issue should be left to the states and more specifically to the voters rather than judges. In voting against the constitutional amendment in 2004, McCain characterized it as "antithetical in every way to the core philosophy of Republicans [because it] usurps from the states a fundamental authority they have always possessed and imposes a federal remedy for a problem that most states do not believe confronts them" (*CNN* 2004). This issue was not as important to voters as issues such as the economy and energy, but it was characterized as "very important" by 49 percent of white evangelical voters (Pew Research Center 2008).

In 2012, there was no mention of a federal constitutional amendment in the Republican Party platform. Instead, there were familiar references to support for DOMA and opposition to an activist judiciary redefining marriage. Republican nominee Mitt Romney was forced to explain his changing views on same-sex marriage. While running for the Senate in 1994, Romney "promised to be a champion for 'full equality' for gays and lesbians—which many understood to include even gay marriage" (Smith 2012). After Romney was elected governor of Massachusetts, and "had his eye on the White House, he totally flipped" in order for his views to be in line with more conservative Republicans (Smith 2012). An April 2012 Pew poll found that the percentage of Republicans indicating that same-sex marriage was "very important" to their vote in 2012 had fallen 13 points from 49 percent to 36 percent since 2004 (Pew Research Center 2012).

The 2016 Republican platform condemned the U.S. Supreme Court rulings in *United States v. Windsor*, which invalidated the section of DOMA denying married couples of the same-sex federal benefits, and *Obergefell v. Hodges*, which legalized same-sex marriage by invalidating state bans on them. Regarding *Windsor*, the platform stated that the Court's ruling took away congressional authority to define marriage and determine marital benefits. The platform criticized the *Obergefell* ruling as 5 unelected lawyers taking away the rights of 320 million Americans to define marriage as the union between one man and one woman. Further, the platform characterized "natural marriage" as the cornerstone of the family. The platform took the additional step of arguing that the religious rights of business owners who did not want to serve same-sex couples should be protected. By the 2016 election, while more Republicans favored same-sex marriage than in previous polls, "71% of conservative Republicans oppose allowing gays and lesbians to marry legally, more than twice the share of GOP moderates and liberals (34%)" (Pew Research Center 2017).

The Republican Party's opposition to same-sex marriage was reflected in its official party platform for both 2016 and 2020:

> Traditional marriage and family, based on marriage between one man and one woman, is the foundation for a free society and has for millennia been entrusted with rearing children and instilling cultural values. We condemn the Supreme Court's ruling in *United States v. Windsor*, which wrongly removed the ability of Congress to define marriage policy in federal law. We also condemn the Supreme Court's lawless ruling in *Obergefell v. Hodges*, which in the words of the late Justice Antonin Scalia, was a "judicial Putsch"—full of "silly extravagances"—that reduced "the disciplined legal reasoning of John Marshall and Joseph Storey to the mystical aphorisms of a fortune cookie." In *Obergefell*, five unelected lawyers robbed 320 million Americans of their legitimate constitutional authority to define marriage as the union of one man and one woman. The Court twisted the meaning of the Fourteenth Amendment beyond recognition.

In 2022, a majority of House Republicans opposed the Respect for Marriage Act. Of the chamber's 211 Representatives, 157 voted "no" on the bill; 7 members did not vote. Many of the 47 Republicans who supported the bill argued that marriage was a settled right guaranteed by the Equal Protection Clause of the Fourteenth Amendment. Republican representative Nancy Mace, who supported the bill, tweeted that "I'm a big fan of marriage, having done it a few times. And if gay couples want to be as happily or miserably married as straight couples, more power to them" (Sotomayor and Dormido 2022). Republicans who opposed the bill claimed that they objected to how quickly Democrats brought the bill to the floor and the lack of Republican input (Sotomayor and Dormido 2022). 12 Senate Republicans voted with 49 Senate Democrats to pass the bill by a vote of 61-36. Former Florida Representative Ileana Ros-Lehtinen (R), who lobbied for the legislation as part of the organization Conservatives Against Discrimination, suggested that Congressional Republicans "unwisely and incorrectly gauged the nonsupport of their constituents back home" ("How Republicans Got on Board with the Respect for Marriage Act" 2022). She also noted that there were some conservative Republicans who would never accept marriage equality.

Despite such strong official statements from Republican organizations and lawmakers, a 2020 Gallup poll showed record high support for same-sex marriage

Republicans Emphasize Religious Freedom over Legal Protection for Marriage Equality

In this excerpt from the House debate over the Respect for Marriage Act in 2022, Republican Representative Vicky Hartzler tearfully outlined her opposition to the bill.

Mr. Speaker, I rise today to adamantly oppose H.R. 8404, the disrespect for marriage act. This unnecessary and misguided legislation not only disrespects the importance of traditional marriage for the health of a family, but also disrespects people and organizations of faith who have the constitutional right to carry out their mission in accordance with their most deeply held beliefs.

With a crisis at the border, inflation skyrocketing, and a Federal budget that is nowhere to be seen just a week before Christmas, Democrats have made it abundantly clear that this disrespectful policy is their priority.

Let's be clear: *Obergefell* is not in danger, but people and institutions of faith are. This bill only serves to further demonize biblical values by establishing a private right of action against organizations who believe in natural marriage, opening the floodgates for predatory lawsuits against people of faith. The bill's only purpose is to hand the Federal Government a legal bludgeoning tool to drive people of faith out of the public square and to silence anyone who dissents.

Sadly, the Senate rejected three amendments that would have eliminated the private right of action and prevented the government from infringing on the freedom of religion . . .

The bill's implications: submit to our ideology or be silenced. This is yet another step toward the Democrats' goal of dismantling the traditional family, silencing voices of faith, and permanently undoing our country's God-woven foundation. This is the Democrats' priority.

Source

"Congressional Record, Volume 168 Issue 191 (Thursday, December 8, 2022)." Accessed January 3, 2023. https://www.govinfo.gov/content/pkg/CREC-2022-12-08/html/CREC-2022 -12-08-pt1-PgH8827-3.htm.

with a record 49 percent of self-identified Republicans supporting it (McCarthy 2020). A year later, Gallup found that Republican support had increased to 55 percent (McCarthy 2021). According to the poll, Republican support has consistently risen since 2016.

Further Reading

Abramson, Paul R., John H. Aldrich, and David W. Rohde. 2007. *Change and Continuity in the 2004 and 2008 Elections.* Washington, DC: CQ Press.

Clement, Scott, and Sandhya Somashekhar. 2012. "After President Obama's Announcement, Opposition to Gay Marriage Hits Record Low." *Washington Post*, May 23. Accessed

August 19, 2022. https://www.washingtonpost.com/politics/after-president-obamas
-announcement-opposition-to-gay-marriage-hits-record-low/2012/05/22/gIQAlAYRjU
_story.html.

CNN. 2004. "McCain: Same-Sex Marriage Ban Is Un-Republican." July 14. Accessed August
22, 2018. http://www.cnn.com/2004/ALLPOLITICS/07/14/mccain.marriage/.

Democratic Party Platforms. 1972–2020. American Presidency Project. Accessed November
24, 2022. https://www.presidency.ucsb.edu/people/other/democratic-party-platforms.

Ewers, Justin. 2008. "McCain Supports Efforts to Ban Gay Marriage." *U.S. News and
World Report*, June 7. Accessed August 22, 2018. https://www.usnews.com/news
/campaign-2008/articles/2008/06/27/mccain-supports-efforts-to-ban-gay-marriage.

Gerstmann, Evan. 2017. *Same Sex Marriage and the Constitution.* 3rd ed. New York: Oxford
University Press.

Hillygus, D. Sunshine, and Todd G. Shields. 2005. "Moral Issues and Voter Decision Making in the 2004 Presidential Election." *PS: Political Science and Politics* 38, no. 2: 201–
209. Accessed November 24, 2022. http://www.jstor.org/stable/30044276.

"How Republicans Got on Board with the Respect for Marriage Act." 2022. National Public
Radio, December 9. Accessed December 14, 2022. https://www.npr.org/2022/12/09
/1141825989/how-republicans-got-on-board-with-the-respect-for-marriage-act.

Klarman, Michael. 2013a. "How Same-Sex Marriage Came to Be: On Activism, Litigation,
and Social Change in America." *Harvard Magazine*, March/April. Accessed August 31,
2018. https://harvardmagazine.com/2013/03/how-same-sex-marriage-came-to-be.

Klarman, Michael. 2013b. *From the Closet to the Altar: Courts, Backlash, and the Struggle for
Same-Sex Marriage.* New York: Oxford University Press.

Kornacki, Steve. 2015. "Why Bill Clinton Really Signed DOMA." *MSNBC*, October 27. Accessed
July 31, 2018. http://www.msnbc.com/msnbc/why-bill-clinton-really-signed-doma.

McCarthy, Justin. 2018. "Two in Three Americans Support Same-Sex Marriage." Gallup,
May 23. Accessed July 31, 2018. https://news.gallup.com/poll/234866/two-three
-americans-support-sex-marriage.aspx.

McCarthy, Justin. 2020. "U.S. Support for Same-Sex Marriage Matches Record High." Gallup, June 1. Accessed December 1, 2020. https://news.gallup.com/poll/311672/support
-sex-marriage-matches-record-high.aspx.

McCarthy, Justin. 2021. "Record High 70% in U.S. Support Same-Sex Marriage." Gallup,
June 8. Accessed August 23, 2022. https://news.gallup.com/poll/350486/record-high
-support-same-sex-marriage.aspx.

McThomas, Mary, and Robert J. Buchanan. 2012. "President Obama and Gay Rights: The
2008 and 2012 Presidential Elections." *PS: Political Science and Politics* 45, no. 3: 442–
448. Accessed November 24, 2022. http://www.jstor.org/stable/41691359.

Neuman, Scott. 2015. "Obama: Supreme Court Same-Sex Marriage Ruling 'a Victory for
America.'" National Public Radio, June 26. Accessed July 15, 2018. https://www.npr
.org/sections/thetwo-way/2015/06/26/417731614/obama-supreme-court-ruling-on
-gay-marriage-a-victory-for-america.

Pelosi, Nancy. 2022. "Pelosi Floor Speech on the Respect for Marriage Act." Congresswoman Nancy Pelosi, July 19. Accessed September 15, 2022. https://pelosi.house.gov
/news/press-releases/pelosi-floor-speech-on-the-respect-for-marriage-act.

Pew Research Center. 2008. "Section 3: Issues and the 2008 Election." August 21. Accessed
July 31, 2018. http://www.people-press.org/2008/08/21/section-3-issues-and-the
-2008-election/.

Pew Research Center. 2012. "More Support for Gun Rights, Gay Marriage Than in 2008 or 2004." April 25. Accessed July 15, 2018. http://www.people-press.org/2012/04/25/more-support-for-gun-rights-gay-marriage-than-in-2008-or-2004/.

Pew Research Center. 2017. "Changing Attitudes on Gay Marriage." June 26. Accessed July 31, 2018. http://www.pewforum.org/fact-sheet/changing-attitudes-on-gay-marriage/.

Pierceson, Jason. 2013. *Same Sex Marriage in the United States: The Road to the Supreme Court.* Lanham, MD: Rowman & Littlefield.

Raghavan, Gautam. 2013. "Obama Administration Statements on the Supreme Court's DOMA Ruling." June 27. Accessed August 31, 2018. https://obamawhitehouse.archives.gov/blog/2013/06/27/obama-administration-statements-supreme-court-s-doma-ruling.

Republican Party Platform. 1996–2020. American Presidency Project. Accessed November 24, 2022. https://www.presidency.ucsb.edu/people/other/republican-party-platforms.

Roche, Darragh. 2020. "Pete Buttigieg Warns Amy Coney Barrett Could Put 'Marriage Equality Back on the Table.'" *Newsweek*, October 14. Accessed December 1, 2020. https://www.newsweek.com/pete-buttigieg-amy-coney-barrett-marriage-equality-1538928.

Samuels, Robert. 2016. "Hillary Clinton Had the Chance to Make Gay Rights History: She Refused." *Washington Post*, August 29. Accessed August 31, 2018. https://www.washingtonpost.com/local/social-issues/hillary-clinton-had-the-chance-to-make-gay-rights-history-she-refused/2016/08/28/843a5cfc-58cf-11e6-9767-f6c947fd0cb8_story.html?utm_term=.dfb3d3068813.

Savage, Charlie, and Sheryl Gay Stolberg. 2011. "In Shift, U.S. Says Marriage Act Blocks Gay Rights." *New York Times*, February 23. Accessed July 15, 2018. https://www.nytimes.com/2011/02/24/us/24marriage.html.

Smith, Tovia. 2012. "Romney's Views on Gay Marriage: Also Evolving?" National Public Radio, May 10. Accessed August 20, 2018. https://www.npr.org/2012/05/10/152431577/romneys-views-on-gay-marriage-also-evolving.

Sotomayor, Marianna, and Hannah Dormido. 2022. "A Closer Look at the House Republicans Who Broke Ranks for the Marriage Bill." *Washington Post*, August 8. Accessed August 23, 2022. https://www.washingtonpost.com/politics/interactive/2022/republican-marriage-equality-vote-count/.

Police and Criminal Justice Reform

At a Glance

The issues of racial justice and criminal justice have been intertwined throughout American history. Criminal justice polices are primarily implemented by the states; however, the federal role has increased since the 1960s with the federal government providing grant money to states for law enforcement objectives. The death of a handcuffed and prone George Floyd in Minneapolis at the hands of a white police officer on May 25, 2020, triggered protests and isolated rioting over police brutality toward Black Americans—in part because Floyd's death marked only the latest in a series of incidents through the 2010s in which unarmed African Americans, in particular young Black men, had been slain by the police.

The contemporary debate over criminal justice reform has centered on various aspects of police reform, including limitations on chokeholds, no-knock warrants, qualified immunity, and mass incarceration.

According to many Democrats . . .

- The use of chokeholds by law enforcement should be banned with few exceptions.
- No-knock warrants should be banned in drug cases.
- Mass incarceration has been created by systemic racism and should be ended because it unfairly penalizes people of color.

According to many Republicans . . .

- The use of chokeholds by law enforcement should be limited.
- No-knock warrants should be discouraged.
- Mass incarceration should be ended because it is too costly.

Overview

Criminal justice policies regulate law enforcement and corrections. While these policies are primarily implemented by state governments, the federal role has increased since the late nineteenth century. In the aftermath of the Civil War and the end of slavery in the United States, constitutional amendments and federal laws were enacted to protect the rights of Black Americans. Federal law enforcement power increased in the early twentieth century with the creation of the Bureau of Investigation, later named the Federal Bureau of Investigation (FBI), to investigate threats posed by anarchists and criminal activity associated with Prohibition.

During the 1960s, the federal role in criminal justice policy saw a significant increase. President Lyndon Johnson declared a "war on crime," and his successor, President Richard Nixon, declared a "war on drugs." President Ronald Reagan expanded the "war on drugs" during the 1980s, signing bipartisan legislation that increased penalties for drug-related crimes. In 1994, President Bill Clinton signed the largest crime bill in U.S. history. Among its many "tough on crime" provisions were ones that increased jail time for repeat offenders and gave more money to states for law enforcement. Critics argued that the legislation enacted in the 1980s and 1990s led to especially heavy prosecution and mass incarceration of minorities. From 1980 to 2019, the number of Americans imprisoned for drug crimes increased from 40,900 to 430,926. Black men are 6 times as likely, and Latinos are 2.5 times as likely, to be incarcerated than white men (The Sentencing Project n.d.). This criticism, coupled with a wave of high-profile killings of unarmed Black Americans at the hands of the police, led to demands for criminal justice reform and an end to alleged police brutality, especially in communities of color. Contemporary debates over criminal justice policy have centered on police reform and mass incarceration.

Sanctioned Police Violence after the Civil War

The violence against Blacks that was part of maintaining slavery continued even after slavery was abolished. Murder, lynching, and other forms of physical violence against Blacks were often ignored or in some instances perpetrated by law enforcement, which spurred calls for police reform in the early 1900s.

After the Civil War, Congress enacted a series of constitutional amendments to guarantee the rights of Black Americans. The Thirteenth Amendment (1865) abolished slavery, the Fourteenth Amendment (1868) declared that all persons born or naturalized in the United States were citizens and required states to provide due process and equal protection of the law, and the Fifteenth Amendment (1870) allowed Black men to vote. Congress passed the Civil Rights Act of 1871 as a response to a reign of terror from 1868 to 1871 against Black Americans, primarily by Southern whites. The law, known as the Ku Klux Klan Act due to that organization's role in terrorizing Blacks, allows individuals to sue public officials who deprive them of their constitutional rights. This provision is codified in Section

1983 of Title 42 of the U.S. Code, and lawsuits filed on this basis are referred to as Section 1983 suits.

This law, however, did little to end violence against Black Americans who became increasingly frustrated with the unwillingness of law enforcement to protect them. The Silent March of 1917 was the most significant early mass protest by Black Americans. It was a response to the East St. Louis massacre of 1914 in which it is estimated that between fifty and two hundred Blacks were murdered by whites over a three-day period. The killings were spawned by a labor strike in which Black workers had replaced white workers.

Due to the advent of television, police brutality toward Black Americans gained national attention during the Civil Rights Movement. In 1963, police in Birmingham, Alabama, used dogs and fire hoses to attack Black protestors, including schoolchildren. In 1965, after a Black civil rights protestor had been shot to death by a state trooper, Dr. Martin Luther King, Jr. led a march in Selma, Alabama, in which protestors were violently attacked by a white mob, including law enforcement officers. Also in 1965, the Watts Riots in Los Angeles, California, gained national attention when a white highway patrol officer pulled over a Black man for drunk driving, and a six-day riot ensued after rumors about police treatment of Blacks during the arrest. That same year, Democratic president Lyndon Johnson signed the Law Enforcement Assistance Act, which created a direct federal role in state law enforcement by creating a grant agency within the U.S. Department of Justice. This agency provided federal funds to state law enforcement for military-grade equipment to fight crime.

The Rise of "Law and Order" Politics

The American public began to consider crime a national issue in the 1960s due to several events: the assassinations of President John F. Kennedy, his brother and Democratic presidential candidate, Robert F. Kennedy, and civil rights leader Dr. Martin Luther King, Jr., Vietnam War protests, and race riots in urban areas. In this turbulent political and social climate, Republican presidential nominee Richard Nixon emphasized "law and order" during the 1968 presidential campaign. As president, Nixon declared a war on drugs and supported policies such as no-knock warrants as a law enforcement tool. No-knock warrants allow police officers to enter a residence without announcing their presence. In *Miller v. U.S.* (1958) and *Ker v. California* (1963), the U.S. Supreme Court recognized that there are exceptions to the common-law and Fourth Amendment requirement that officers enter a home only after announcing their presence; specifically, there may be instances in which announcing their presence could jeopardize the safety of officers or innocent people or give lawbreakers additional time to destroy evidence. No-knock warrants coupled with the militarization of police weapons led to an increase in violent drug raids by state and local law enforcement.

The Court also effectively upheld the use of another controversial law enforcement practice in *City of Los Angeles v. Lyons* (1983): chokeholds. The case stemmed from a 1976 incident in which Adolph Lyons, a Black man, was pulled over by white Los Angeles Police Department officers for driving a car with a broken taillight. Although he offered no resistance, he was placed in a chokehold after which he blacked out and sustained damage to his larynx. Lyons sued, asking the Court to bar police officers from using chokeholds. Lyons's lawyers pointed out that sixteen people, including twelve Black men, had died from the use of police chokeholds in Los Angeles. The U.S. Supreme Court, however, held by a 5-4 vote that Lyons lacked standing to sue and could not challenge the policy because he could not show that he was likely to be placed in a chokehold again. In dissent, Justice Thurgood Marshall wrote, "Since no one can show that he will be choked in the future, no one—not even a person who, like Lyons, has almost been choked to death—has standing to challenge the continuation of the policy. The city is free to continue the policy indefinitely, as long as it is willing to pay damages for the injuries and deaths that result."

The contemporary political debate over police reform stemmed from several high-profile killings of unarmed Black Americans by white police officers. Michael Brown, an eighteen-year-old Black man, was killed in Ferguson, Missouri, by a white police officer in 2014. Brown was a suspect in a convenience store theft and was fatally shot by Officer Darren Wilson who responded to the call. The circumstances leading to the shooting are disputed; however, the encounter ended with Brown's body lying on the street for four hours as angry crowds gathered. In the aftermath of his death, there were riots in the city that had been plagued by racial tensions between Black residents and the police department.

Later in 2014, Tamir Rice, a twelve-year-old Black child, was killed by a white police officer. Rice was holding a toy gun in a park in Cleveland, Ohio, when police officers responded to a call about an individual in the area pointing a pistol at people. The officers shouted at Rice to put his hands up; instead, he appeared to be drawing a weapon, and Timothy Loehmann, a white officer, shot Rice. The gun lacked the orange-tipped barrel indicating that it was a toy. The officers were cleared of any wrongdoing because investigators determined that they had acted reasonably under the circumstances; however, Loehmann was later fired for failing to disclose that in his previous job as a police officer he was deemed unfit for duty and emotionally unstable.

Two other high-profile killings sparked debate over race and policing in 2020. In March, police officers in Louisville, Kentucky, obtained no-knock warrants related to criminal activity of Breonna Taylor's ex-boyfriend; however, the warrant was later changed to knock and announce. One of the warrants was for her apartment, which officers entered by using a battering ram. When they crashed into Taylor's apartment, her boyfriend at the time shot at the officers, who he believed to be violent intruders. The officers returned fire and shot Breonna Taylor to death. The officers claimed they announced their presence, but Taylor's boyfriend claims that he did not hear them announce that they were police. They found no evidence of criminal activity at her residence and later learned that the man they were looking for—her ex-boyfriend—was already in police custody at the time of the raid. He told police that she had nothing to do with illegal drugs. Prosecutors alleged that the officers obtained the warrant by including false information about her involvement. There are other questions about the shooting, including why the police officers chose to raid her home in the middle of the night when they had already arrested their primary suspect (Oppel, Taylor, and Bolger-Burroughs 2022).

Breonna Taylor's death received renewed national attention after the May 2020 killing of George Floyd, a Black man, by a white police officer in Minneapolis, Minnesota. Floyd, who was suspected of buying cigarettes with a counterfeit $20 bill, died when Derek Chauvin, a white officer with a history of complaints about excessive force, held his knee against Floyd's neck for over seven minutes after he had handcuffed him and forced him to lie face down on the street. After video footage of Floyd's murder was released (Chauvin was later convicted of murder charges on April 20, 2021), protests by Black Lives Matter and other organizations erupted across the United States and around the globe.

Competing Visions of Police Reform

In the wake of these protests, Congressional Democrats and Republicans introduced comprehensive police reform bills during the summer and fall of 2020. House Democrats introduced the George Floyd Justice in Policing Act, while Senate Republicans introduced the JUSTICE (Just and Unifying Solutions to Invigorate Communities Everywhere) Act. The bills contained some similar provisions, including record-keeping requirements for police misconduct, training programs for officers on racial profiling, racial bias, and use of force, federal data collection on use of force incidents, criminalizing sexual conduct by law enforcement with a person in custody, and promoting hiring practices of officers who live in the communities in which they serve.

The bills also addressed some of the same issues such as chokeholds, no-knock warrants, and body cameras; however, the provisions in each bill treated these issues differently. The George Floyd Act favored by Democrats required states and localities that received certain types of federal grants to enact laws banning chokeholds. It also required federal law enforcement officers to refrain from using chokeholds unless conditions for use of deadly force were met. The law narrowed the circumstances under which deadly force could be used—it could only be used as a last resort to prevent death or serious bodily harm, when there is no substantial risk to a third party, and when reasonable alternatives to the use of deadly force have been exhausted. The JUSTICE Act, crafted and championed by Republicans, differed in that it demanded an exception to local and state bans on police chokeholds except when deadly force is authorized. The same policy also applied to federal authorities.

The George Floyd Act proposed a ban on no-knock warrants in drug cases at the federal level and for state and local authorities that received federal funds. The JUSTICE Act did not ban the warrants but rather required state and local law enforcement to report information concerning no-knock warrants issued in their jurisdictions to the federal government. The bills also addressed body cameras with the George Floyd Act requiring their use by federal law enforcement and providing grants for their purchase to state and local law enforcement, while the JUSTICE Act offered grant money to state and local authorities for body cameras but would not require federal law enforcement officers to wear them.

"Defunding the Police"

Proposals to "defund the police" have also been a prominent part of the national discussion on police reform. The term refers to reallocating funding from law enforcement to de-emphasize militarization and reemphasize the community mission of government agencies, including law enforcement agencies. Advocates point out that "defund" does not mean "abolish" and that research shows increased spending on policing does not reduce crime (Henderson and Yisrael 2021). Public polling shows, however, that many Americans do not make such distinctions when they hear Republican lawmakers and conservative media personalities frame "defund" to mean the elimination of police departments, leaving communities to fend for themselves against marauding criminals.

Regardless of public perceptions of what the slogan means, "defund" advocates argue that since most calls to police departments are for nonviolent matters, police are not as well trained as social workers or mental health professionals to handle these situations. They assert that budgets at every level of government should be shifted to reallocate some of that funding toward social services departments that are better equipped to provide those services. While this movement received a great deal of attention after George Floyd's death, neither political party supported defunding police. Republican and Democratic public officials and candidates opposed defunding the police; however, a few progressive Democrats supported it.

A poll taken a year after Floyd's death found that 61 percent of Black Americans believed that police treat minorities more harshly than they do whites. Only 25 percent of whites agreed with that view. The poll showed that since 2015, the overall number of Americans who believed that minorities were treated more harshly by the police had risen seven points to 32 percent. The poll also showed that 50 percent of whites, 17 percent of Blacks, and 40 percent of Latinos had a great deal of confidence in the police to protect them from violent crime, while 6 percent of whites, 23 percent of Blacks, and 13 percent of Latinos had very little confidence in the police to protect them from such crimes (NPR/PBS NewsHour/Marist National Poll 2021).

Republican and Democratic lawmakers attempted to compromise on their differences and create a bipartisan police reform bill in 2021. The two sides were unable to reach an agreement due to their differing views on qualified immunity.

Qualified Immunity

Section 1983 allows individuals to sue state and local law enforcement officials who violate their civil rights. Federal law enforcement officials are also prohibited from violating the civil rights of individuals. In *Bivens v. Six Unknown Named Agents of Federal Bureau of Narcotics* (1971), the U.S. Supreme Court held that federal law enforcement officials may also be sued for damages based on the Fourth Amendment. The doctrine of qualified immunity, however, has imposed limits on these types of suits. The "qualified immunity" doctrine created by the U.S. Supreme Court in that case makes government officials, including police officers, shielded from any lawsuit for actions performed as part of their job. Qualified immunity was created to balance the interest of holding public officials accountable when they violate constitutional rights with the interest of shielding officials from liability when they have reasonably performed their duties.

According to the Court, public officials (like police) are entitled to legal immunity on the job unless their actions violate a "clearly established statutory or constitutional rights of which a reasonable person would have known." Courts have interpreted this standard very narrowly, which has made it more difficult for victims suing police officers for alleged violent or nonviolent offenses to collect damages. Democrats have supported abolishing qualified immunity, arguing that it keeps police officers from being accountable for their actions. Republicans oppose abolishing qualified immunity, claiming that it would be more difficult to hire officers because of the increased fear of being sued.

A 2020 Pew Research Center poll found that 66 percent of Americans believed that civilians should have the ability to sue police officers for use of excessive force to hold them accountable. However, there was a significant split along party lines with 45 percent of Republicans and 84 percent of Democrats agreeing with that statement. The poll also found that 31 percent of Americans believed that police forces do an excellent or good job of holding officers accountable when misconduct occurs compared with 27 percent who believed they do an "only fair" job, while 42 percent believed they do a poor job (Pew Research Center 2020).

Mass Incarceration and Prison Privatization

The United States houses more of its population in prison than any other country in the world largely due to stringent penalties for drug crimes. The federal role in U.S. drug policy expanded during the 1970s with the enactment of the Federal Comprehensive Drug Abuse Prevention and Control Act, more commonly known as the Controlled Substances Act (CSA), in 1970. Federal drug policies during the 1970s emphasized prevention and treatment for drug users, while criminal penalties were meted out to drug traffickers.

Mass incarceration has been exacerbated by policies implemented in the 1980s when Republican president Ronald Reagan declared a "war on drugs." While Republican President Richard Nixon had also used that terminology, Reagan pursued more stringent criminal penalties for drug crimes. During his administration,

Congress enacted a series of laws that included mandatory minimum sentences for drug crimes. Mandatory minimum sentences remove discretion from judges when sentencing defendants because the sentence has been prescribed by law. The Anti-Drug Abuse Act of 1986 established mandatory minimum sentences for cocaine possession. Individuals who possessed five grams of crack cocaine or five hundred grams of powder cocaine received a minimum sentence of five years. The Anti-Drug Abuse Act of 1988 made crack cocaine the only drug for which a defendant received a mandatory minimum for possession for a first offense.

Democratic president Bill Clinton signed the bipartisan Violent Crime Control and Law Enforcement Act of 1994. This law, one of the most significant crime bills in American history, established a "three strikes" policy, which was not limited to drug crimes. The policy provided that an individual convicted of one serious violent felony was eligible for life imprisonment if they committed two more crimes that were violent felonies or serious drug offenses.

From 1975 to 2019, the U.S. prison population jumped from 240,593 to 1.43 million. One in five of these individuals was incarcerated with a drug offense as their most serious crime (Morrison 2021). The impact of mandatory minimum sentences disproportionately affected minorities. "The Black incarceration rate in America exploded from about 600 per 100,000 people in 1970 to 1,808 in 2000. In the same time span, the rate for the Latino population grew from 208 per 100,000 people to 615, while the white incarceration rate grew from 103 per 100,000 people to 242" (Morrison 2021). Black defendants are also more likely to be sentenced to longer prison terms than whites for the same crimes (Holder 2016). Because most crimes are violation of state law, federal policies apply only to federal crimes for which there are fewer individuals incarcerated. Federal policy, however, can identify reforms that may resonate with the states.

The Democratic and Republican Parties have recognized that mandatory minimum sentencing needs to be reformed. Democrats want to eliminate it, while Republicans want to modify it. The parties differ, however, on the issue of prison privatization.

Prison privatization at the federal level began in the 1980s. Initially, the federal government contracted with prison companies to build facilities after the Reagan administration ordered the detention of Haitian and Cuban migrants. After Congress passed the mandatory minimum sentencing laws for drug crimes and the three strikes policy was enacted in 1994, more facilities were needed to house the growing number of federal prisoners.

These policies led to a dramatic increase in the federal prison population. According to a 2016 Congressional Research Service report, the federal prison population ballooned from approximately 25,000 prisoners in 1980 to 205,000 in 2015 (Congressional Research Service 2016). The prison population began to increase as U.S. prison facilities were deteriorating; private prison companies stepped in to build new ones. In 1983, the first private prison corporation was formed and since then it has become a billion-dollar industry. The increased use of private prisons has created a "prison-industrial complex," wherein government spending helps private prison corporations by allowing them to incarcerate prisoners. These corporations, in turn, lobby members of Congress to increase their spending. This allows them to incarcerate more people, which requires more funding. Since 2000, the federal government's use of private prisons increased by 77 percent.

In 2016, the Obama administration, citing a lack of safety and a decline in the federal prison population, attempted to phase out the use of private prisons; however, the Trump administration reversed those decisions in 2017 and used private prisons to house illegal immigrants leading to a significant increase in the number of individuals incarcerated in private prisons. In 2019, private prisons housed 81 percent of immigrant detainees (The Sentencing Project 2021). In 2021, Democratic president Joe Biden issued an executive order that prohibited the Department of Justice from renewing federal contracts with private prisons, but the order did not limit private contracts with immigrant detention facilities (The Sentencing Project 2021). Democrats argue that private prisons are not safe enough and do not result in cost savings, while Republicans argue that private facilities provide the same function as government prisons for lesser money.

Democrats

Democrats have supported police reform legislation that would impose requirements on state and local law enforcement to ban chokeholds and no-knock warrants and to require use of body cameras. They have argued that qualified immunity for police officers should be abolished to hold them more accountable and that mass incarceration is the result of discriminatory sentencing for drug crimes and have proposed reforms to end it. The party has also opposed prison privatization arguing that it has exacerbated mass incarceration of minorities and not reduced the cost of incarceration.

Police Reform

House Democrats passed the George Floyd Justice in Policing Act in 2020; however, since Republicans controlled the Senate, no action was taken on the bill. In 2021, the bill was reintroduced when Democrats held the majority in both chambers. It passed the House by a vote of 220-212, with only one Republican vote. The Senate has not yet acted on the bill.

The bill, as previously noted, banned chokeholds and no-knock warrants and required the police to wear body cameras. It also imposed criminal liability on officers who violated suspects' civil rights, increased the authority of the Justice Department to investigate civil rights violations, and provided funding for independent use of force investigations. The bill sought to prohibit racial profiling at all levels of government and required federal law enforcement agencies to adopt policies to eliminate racial profiling by training state and local police, collecting data on profiling, and requiring the attorney general to submit annual reports on racial profiling to Congress. Finally, the bill would limit the transfer of military-grade equipment to state and local law enforcement.

Characterizing the provisions as "bold reforms," Democratic House Speaker Nancy Pelosi argued that the bill would "address systemic racism, curb police brutality and save lives." Further, she stated that "[s]adly, despite mass protests across America and a renewed focus on the crisis of racial injustice, the epidemic of police brutality continues—with more police killings occurring last year than in the year before, and with communities of color and vulnerable groups disproportionately bearing the brunt of this cruelty. We must act decisively and urgently to end the injustice" ("Pelosi Statement on Re-Introduction of George Floyd Justice in Policing Act" 2021).

The bill was criticized for several reasons. There is some evidence that chokehold bans are ineffective. An investigation by National Public Radio found that chokehold bans in some of the nation's largest police departments were "largely ineffective and subject to lax enforcement" (Evstatieva and Mac 2020). When bans were implemented, officers resorted to a different type of neck restraint to subdue suspects. The chokehold ban was also criticized by William Johnson, the director of the National Association of Police Organizations (NAPO), an association of over 241,000 law enforcement officers. He "strongly" recommended against criminalizing chokeholds arguing that they "are a vital tool for officers to have when necessary to save their life or the life of another" (Johnson 2021). The organization also opposed making chokeholds a per se civil rights violation. NAPO criticized the bill for lowering the legal standard to hold officers criminally liable for the use of force. It supported data collection, training, and certification but noted that the bill did not provide the necessary funds to comply with those mandates. The primary criticism of NAPO was that law enforcement officers were not consulted in reforms proposed by the bill, making it difficult to gain the support of the broader law enforcement community (Johnson 2021).

Qualified Immunity

House Democrats specifically eliminated the qualified immunity doctrine in the George Floyd Justice in Policing Act. They argued that the doctrine makes it more difficult for victims of police violence to sue, which prevents police officers from being held accountable for their actions.

There are several criticisms of qualified immunity. One is that it is a judicially created doctrine. The Court determined that qualified immunity existed based on its interpretation of common law, but several U.S. Supreme Court justices have argued that the modern doctrine "bears little resemblance to common law" (Anderson, Novak, and Lampe 2020). Other criticisms focus on practical aspects of the doctrine. While proponents of the doctrine argue that police officers will be financially accountable and potentially bankrupted without qualified immunity, most police departments indemnify their officers so that the city or county actually pays any monetary damages incurred by lawsuits. Finally, the level of specificity courts require that officers violated a "clearly established right" is difficult to meet. Courts granted qualified immunity to police officers in 57 percent of excessive force cases decided from 2017 to 2019 (Anderson, Novak, and Lampe 2020). An investigative report by Reuters found that the Supreme Court is more likely to hear appeals from police officers arguing they are entitled to immunity than plaintiffs who argued they are not. The Supreme Court almost always rules in favor of granting immunity to the police (Reuters 2020).

In June 2020, a group of Democratic senators led by Senator Cory Booker introduced a resolution to eliminate qualified immunity. In addition to the criticisms listed above, the resolution stated that "the lack of accountability that results from qualified immunity arouses frustration, disappointment, and anger throughout the United States, which discredits and endangers the vast majority of law enforcement officers, who do not engage in the use excessive force" (Congress.gov 2020). The resolution also noted that civil suits are often the only recourse against police brutality because prosecutors are reluctant to file criminal charges against officers and juries are reluctant to convict them (Congress.gov 2020).

Many law enforcement agencies oppose the repeal of qualified immunity. One of NAPO's "most serious concerns" with the George Floyd bill was the provision eliminating qualified immunity for officers. William Johnson (2021) argued that without qualified immunity an officer "can go to prison for an unintentional act that unknowingly broke an unknown, and unknowable right." He also argued that the threat of eliminating qualified immunity had already led both veteran officers and newly hired officers "to question whether the risks of the profession are worth the noble job of serving and protecting their communities" (Johnson 2021).

Mass Incarceration

During the 1980s and 1990s, Congressional Democrats supported drug laws that increased punishment for illegal drugs and imposed mandatory minimum sentences for drug crimes. In 2007, Democrats proposed several bills to reform mandatory sentences by eliminating the discrepancy in sentencing for crack and powder cocaine; however, none were successful. In 2010, Democratic president Barack Obama signed the Fair Sentencing Act, which passed by unanimous consent in the Senate and a voice vote in the House of Representatives. The law changed the weight ratio for possession of crack and powder cocaine and required increased amounts of each to trigger minimum sentences. Under the Anti-Drug Abuse Act, possession of 5 grams of crack cocaine and 50 grams of powder cocaine resulted in a mandatory sentence. This law increased the amount of crack cocaine to 28 grams for a five-year minimum sentence and 280 grams of powder cocaine for a ten-year minimum sentence. The Fair Sentencing Act also eliminated the mandatory five-year sentence for first-time offenders who possessed crack cocaine.

By 2020, Democrats advocated abolishing mandatory minimums sentences. The 2020 party platform pledged to "fight to repeal federal mandatory minimums, incentivize states to do the same, and make all sentencing reductions retroactive so judges can consider past cases when their hands were tied" (Democratic Party Platforms 2020).

Prison Privatization

Congressional Democrats first introduced legislation to eliminate private prisons in 2001. Democratic representative Ted Strickland and Democratic senator Russ Feingold introduced the Public Safety Act of 2001, which would have prohibited states that contracted with private prisons from receiving federal grant money and prohibited the federal government from contracting with private prisons. Senator Bernie Sanders, who campaigned for the 2016 Democratic presidential nomination, introduced a bill to eliminate private prisons. While some Democrats have proposed eliminating private prisons entirely, others have introduced legislation to increase the transparency of the private prison industry. Representative Shelia Jackson Lee introduced a version of the Private Prison Information Act in several different sessions of Congress, most recently in 2017. The bill called for greater transparency of private prison operations by requiring them to comply with Freedom of Information Act requests.

The Obama administration sought to end private prison contracts with the federal government near the end of Obama's second term. In 2016, Deputy Attorney General Sally Yates issued a memo to the acting director for the Bureau of Prisons to reduce, and ultimately end, the federal government's use of private prisons. She noted that while private prisons served an important role when the prison population was increasing, the numbers of incarcerated individuals was declining. Yates also cited a 2015 report by the Justice Department's Office of Inspector General that private prisons "do not provide the same level of correctional services, programs and resources; they do not save substantially on costs and . . . they do not maintain the same level of safety and security" when compared with government-run prisons (United States Department of Justice 2016).

During the 2020 presidential campaign, every candidate for the Democratic presidential nomination opposed prison privatization. Former vice president Joe Biden, the 2020 Democratic nominee, addressed the issue on his campaign website. He pledged that his administration would "stop corporations from profiteering off of incarceration" in part by ending the federal government's use of private prisons ("Joe Biden's Criminal Justice Policy | Joe Biden" 2019). Within a week of his inauguration, Biden issued an executive order to the Justice Department directing the attorney general to allow federal contracts with private prisons to expire. The order, titled "Reforming Our Incarceration System to Eliminate the Use of Privately Operated Criminal Detention Facilities," criticized the system of mass incarceration, which disproportionately affects people of color. The order stated that removing the profit motive for keeping people imprisoned would decrease incarceration levels. It also cited the 2016 Justice Department report that private prisons were less safe for prisoners and correctional staff than government prisons (The White House 2021).

Biden Prohibits Department of Justice from Contracting with Private Prison Companies

In 2021, Democratic President Joe Biden issued an executive order, "Reforming Our Incarceration System to Eliminate the Use of Privately Operated Criminal Detention Facilities" directing the Attorney General to not renew contracts with private prisons. This excerpt from the order explains the reasoning for that decision.

More than two million people are currently incarcerated in the United States, including a disproportionate number of people of color. There is broad consensus that our current system of mass incarceration imposes significant costs and hardships on our society and communities and does not make us safer. To decrease incarceration levels, we must reduce profit-based incentives to incarcerate by phasing out the Federal Government's reliance on privately operated criminal detention facilities.

We must ensure that our Nation's incarceration and correctional systems are prioritizing rehabilitation and redemption. Incarcerated individuals should be given a fair chance to fully reintegrate into their communities, including by participating in programming tailored to earning a good living, securing affordable housing, and participating in our democracy as our fellow citizens. However, privately operated criminal detention facilities consistently underperform Federal facilities with respect to correctional services, programs, and resources. We should ensure that time in prison prepares individuals for the next chapter of their lives.

The Federal Government also has a responsibility to ensure the safe and humane treatment of those in the Federal criminal justice system. However, as the Department of Justice's Office of Inspector General found in 2016, privately operated criminal detention facilities do not maintain the same levels of safety and security for people in the Federal criminal justice system or for correctional staff. We have a duty to provide these individuals with safe working and living conditions . . .

Source
"Executive Order on Reforming Our Incarceration System to Eliminate the Use of Privately Operated Criminal Detention Facilities | the White House." 2021. The White House, January 26. Accessed January 2, 2023. https://www.whitehouse.gov/briefing-room/presidential-actions/2021/01/26/executive-order-reforming-our-incarceration-system-to-eliminate-the-use-of-privately-operated-criminal-detention-facilities/.

Biden was criticized for this action. Fordham University law professor John Pfaff argued that these actions hurt, rather than helped, criminal justice reform. He noted that because the order did not apply to immigrants housed in private detention centers, it was limited and that it was "not likely to lead to any actual change in the total U.S. prison population" since inmates could simply be transferred to federal prison (Pfaff 2021). He also stated that the order did not immediately terminate the contracts between the federal government and private prison corporations. Pfaff also noted that federal prisons also had a profit motive in keeping high numbers of inmates because those prisons were often located in rural areas where residents were dependent on prison jobs. He criticized Biden's comments that the order would reduce the mass incarceration of minorities by pointing out that "[d]isparities in punishment do not arise from where we send the people we've convicted, but from whom we choose to arrest, whom we choose to charge, what we choose to charge them with and the sentences we impose on them" (Pfaff 2021).

Progressive Democrats also argued that the order did little to address racial inequality because it did not address immigrant detainees held in private detention facilities. In a letter to Alejandro Mayorkas, the Department of Homeland Security secretary, and Susan Rice, Biden's domestic policy adviser, twenty-four Congressional Democrats urged the Biden administration to expand the order to include private immigrant detention facilities. They wrote that "[p]rofit incentives to reduce one form of incarceration at the expense of expanding another come at particular cost to Black and Brown immigrants, who are doubly vulnerable to aggressive surveillance and incarceration in the context of both criminal justice and civil immigration enforcement" ("Rep. Omar Leads Letter Urging Executive Action on ICE Detention" 2021).

Republicans

Republicans have supported police reform legislation that would incentivize state and local governments to adopt reforms regarding the use of deadly force, no-knock warrants, and body cameras. They do not support eliminating qualified immunity because police officers need protection from lawsuits. Beginning in 2016, Republicans supported changes to mandatory minimum sentences to reduce mass incarceration; however, they have supported private prisons arguing that they are more cost effective than government-run facilities.

Police Reform

Senate Republicans, led by Senator Tim Scott, the party's only Black senator, introduced the JUSTICE Act in 2020. This bill pledged to "maintain the Constitutionally-limited role the federal government plays in local law enforcement decisions while still affecting significant change" (Scott 2020). As previously noted, this bill proposed requiring state and local law enforcement to gather and report data about the use of force and no-knock warrants and to incentivize the use of body cameras by state and local law enforcement officers. The bill also contained provisions making lynching a federal crime, creating a new criminal offense for falsifying a police report in furtherance of depriving someone of their civil rights, and establishing two commissions to investigate issues and reforms related to law enforcement oversight. In a press release after the bill was introduced, Senator Scott (2020) referenced George Floyd's murder and stated that "action must be taken to rebuild lost trust between communities of color and law enforcement. The JUSTICE Act takes smart, commonsense steps to address these issues."

Democrats, however, criticized the bill. House Speaker Nancy Pelosi stated that "the proposal of studies and reporting without transparency and accountability is inadequate" (Grisales 2020). Senate Democrats blocked the bill in a 55-45 vote in June 2020 citing the opposition of over one hundred civil rights organizations and their belief that the bill did not adequately address systemic racism in policing (Edmonson 2020). Democratic senate minority leader Charles Schumer argued that the Republican bill would not have prevented the deaths of Breonna Taylor or George Floyd because it did not ban no-knock warrants or chokeholds. He stated that the bill would not hold police officers accountable and criticized Republican senate majority leader Mitch McConnell who "has never talked about these issues at all until now, when people are marching in the street and some of his members said we have to do something" (McCammon 2020).

The bill was also criticized by Kanya Bennett, the Senior Legislative for the American Civil Liberties Union (ACLU). She stated that the bill "throws billions of dollars at studies and commissions when we know the real problem at the core of American policing—Black people continue to die at the hands of police without consequence. More talk, more training, and more police is not the solution" (Bennett 2020).

President Donald Trump, who supported the JUSTICE Act, issued an executive order titled "Safe Policing for Safe Communities" on June 16, 2020. The order noted that "[a]ll Americans are entitled to live with the confidence that the law enforcement officers and agencies in their communities will live up to our Nation's founding ideals and will protect the rights of all persons. Particularly in African American communities, we must redouble our efforts as a Nation to swiftly address instances of misconduct" (United States President 2020a). Specifically, the order encouraged police departments to improve training on use of force and de-escalation techniques using independent credentialing services and to improve training for officers in dealing with those who were homeless or suffering from mental illness or addiction. It also created a national database so that federal, state, and local authorities could share information related to police misconduct and called for a ban on chokeholds unless deadly force was necessary. Critics of the order argued that it did not address policies that treat people of color unfairly (Kelly and Naylor 2020). House Speaker Nancy Pelosi characterized the order as "weak" and falling "sadly and seriously short of what is required to combat the epidemic of racial injustice and police brutality that is murdering hundreds of Black Americans" (Kelly and Naylor 2020).

Also in June 2020, Trump discussed defunding the police at a meeting in Dallas, Texas. He stated that "[w]e're not defunding police. If anything, we're going to go the other route. We're going to make sure our police are well trained, perfectly trained." He characterized calls for defunding the police as "'radical efforts brought about by individuals attempting to 'stoke division' and 'push an extreme agenda'" (Martin 2020). Trump also criticized Joe Biden for supporting the defunding the police effort in the September 29 presidential debate. Biden denied the charge

---

Republican Minority Leader Criticizes Democrats for "Defunding the Police"

Republican Senate Minority Leader Mitch McConnell delivered a speech on the Senate floor in November 2022 arguing that Democratic efforts to address crime and to defund the police were dangerous.

. . . After the nationwide murder rate clocked its largest single-year increase in more than a century in 2020, it climbed even higher last year. A record-high majority of Americans report that crime in their communities is getting worse.

This is an area where our two political parties, the two sides of the aisle, have totally opposite instincts about the right way forward.

Republicans are focused on making American communities safer, and we know accomplishing that takes compassion for innocent people, not weak justice for the violent criminals who hurt them.

Meanwhile, Democrats are focused on making it even harder to secure real justice. They've spent two years doubling down on anti-law enforcement rhetoric and putting radical local prosecutors at the center of their plans to make America softer on crime . . .

Here in Washington, things are no different. Our colleague the junior Senator from Connecticut, made this crystal clear a few days ago when he kicked off a fresh wave of Democratic calls to defund the police.

Senator Murphy says that because, in his estimation, "60% of the counties in this country" are friendlier to citizens' Second Amendment rights than Senator Murphy would like, those communities should be punished by defunding their police forces.

Fewer resources for peace officers. Less safety for local communities. Unless every county in America kowtows to Senate Democrats' particular view of the Second Amendment.

Democrats spent all this past year insisting they don't support de-funding the police —but here they go, yet again, proposing to do just that.

Source

"Democrats' Response to Crime: Defund the Police." 2022. U.S. Senator Mitch McConnell, November 22. Accessed January 21, 2023. https://www.mcconnell.senate.gov/public/index .cfm/2022/11/democrats-response-to-crime-defund-the-police.

claiming that Trump was defunding the police by cutting $400 million from the federal budget directed to assisting local law enforcement (USA Today Staff 2020).

Qualified Immunity

Republicans have supported qualified immunity arguing that it is essential to protect police officers from lawsuits. Without qualified immunity, they argue, it would be difficult to recruit police officers because they would be concerned about liability. While many Congressional Republicans were unwilling to consider changes to qualified immunity to pass comprehensive police reform legislation, others suggested that they would consider reforming the doctrine.

Senator Mitch McConnell argued that it would be difficult to hire police officers without qualified immunity. Donald Trump's attorney general William Barr argued that qualified immunity was necessary because "the overwhelming majority of police are good people. They're civic minded people who believe in serving the public." He acknowledged that there are some "bad cops" but stated that their behavior did not mean that the entire organization was "rotten" and that qualified immunity would cause good officers to "pull back" and not do their jobs (*CBS News* 2020). President Trump considered ending qualified immunity a "non-starter" in criminal justice reform legislation (Hoonhout 2020).

Senator Tim Scott had referred to Democratic calls to ending qualified immunity as a "poison pill" for a bipartisan compromise on police reform in 2020; however, in 2021, he stated that he was "open to having conversations on civil qualified immunity as it relates to police departments, cities, and municipalities being held accountable for the actions of those they employ." Other senators echoed that view. Senator Lindsey Graham suggested reforming qualified immunity but not eliminating it entirely. He stated that "[i]f you want to reform it so that municipalities and agencies and organizations running police departments will have some protection but not absolute immunity, let's talk" (Carney 2020).

Mass Incarceration

From the 1980s through the 2000s, Republicans supported mandatory minimum sentences. In 2016, the Republican platform suggested reforms to mandatory minimums that included "nonviolent offenders and persons with drug, alcohol, and mental health issues" (Republican Party Platform 2016). In 2018, President Trump signed bipartisan legislation, the First Step Act, which shortens mandatory minimum sentences for nonviolent drug offenses, gives judges more discretion in sentencing, and applied the provisions of the Fair Sentencing Act retroactively to those convicted prior to the law's enactment. The law also modified the federal "three strikes" policy by replacing the penalty of life imprisonment without the possibility of parole for the third strike with twenty-five years of imprisonment.

Although the First Step Act had bipartisan support, some Republicans have backed away from the law. "With spikes in crime registering as a top concern for voters, Republicans have increasingly reverted back to that 1980s mindset. Talk of additional legislation has taken a back seat to calls for enhanced policing and accusations that Democratic-led cities are veering toward lawlessness" (McGraw 2022).

Prison Privatization

During the 2016 campaign, Donald Trump called American prisons a "disaster" and offered his support for prison privatization saying that "[i]t seems to work a lot better." After these statements, he received significant contributions from companies that owned private prisons (Editorial Board 2017). In February 2017, Trump's attorney general Jeff Sessions rescinded Deputy Attorney General Sally Yates's memo ordering the reduction of the federal government's use of private prisons. He stated that the memo "changed long-standing policy and practice, and impaired the bureau's ability to meet the future needs of the federal correctional system" (Jarrett 2017).

Democratic senator Cory Booker criticized this reversal as "a major setback to restoring justice to our criminal justice system" because "[t]he Bureau of Prisons' own inspector general has found that privately-managed prisons housing federal inmates are less safe and less secure than federal prisons, and these facilities have seen repeated instances of civil rights violations" (Jarrett 2017). The editorial board of the *New York Times* also criticized the decision referring to the private prison industry as "a parasite" feeding "off harsh and shortsighted sentencing policies, such as mandatory minimums and three-strikes laws, that resulted in the largest prison population in the world. By 2014, the top two companies had revenues of $3.3 billion, nearly double what they made in 2006" (Editorial Board 2017).

Private prisons were part of Trump's immigration crackdown. In a 2017 executive order, he broadened the criteria for criminal offenses allowing more illegal immigrants to be detained in private prisons regardless of whether they had been convicted of a crime. The Trump administration increased spending on private prisons paying the GEO Group, a private prison company, $595 million in 2019. By contrast, the Obama administration paid the company $260 million in 2014 (Da Silva 2019). A *USA Today* investigation found that during the Trump administration private prison companies opened at least twenty-four immigration detention centers run by U.S. Immigration and Customs Enforcement (Alvarado et al. 2020). The investigation found that after Trump pursued aggressive immigration policies, there were "more than 400 allegations of sexual assault or abuse, inadequate medical care, regular hunger strikes, frequent use of solitary confinement, more than 800 instances of physical force against detainees, nearly 20,000 grievances filed by detainees and at least 29 fatalities, including seven suicides" at private detention facilities (Alvarado et al. 2020). This situation contributed to national calls to end private prisons.

Most states also have contracts with private prison companies. Montana imprisons half of its prisoners in private prisons, while New Mexico imprisons 45 percent in those institutions. However, twenty-two states do not use private prisons (The Sentencing Project 2021).

Further Reading

Altman, Alex. 2020. "Why the Killing of George Floyd Sparked an American Uprising." *Time*, June 4. Accessed August 15, 2021. https://time.com/5847967/george-floyd -protests-trump/.

Alvarado, Mondy, Ashley Balcerzak, Stacey Barchenger, Jon Campbell, Rafael Carranza, Maria Clark, Alan Gomez, Daniel Gonzalez, Trevor Hughes, Rick Jervis, et al. 2020. "'These People Are Profitable': Under Trump, Private Prisons Are Cashing In on ICE Detainees." *USA Today*, April 23. Accessed June 8, 2021. https://www.usatoday .com/in-depth/news/nation/2019/12/19/ice-detention-private-prisons-expands -under-trump-administration/4393366002/.

Anderson, April J., Whitney K. Novak, and Joanne R. Lampe. 2020. "Police Reform and the 166th Congress: Selected Legal Issues." Congressional Research Service, September 16. Accessed December 18, 2022. https://crsreports.congress.gov/product/pdf/R /R46530/2.

Bennett, Kanya. 2020. "ACLU Statement of Opposition to Sen. Tim Scott's So-Called JUSTICE Act." American Civil Liberties Union, June 24. Accessed December 18, 2022. https://www .aclu.org/press-releases/aclu-statement-opposition-sen-tim-scotts-so-called-justice-act.

Carney, Jordain. 2020. "Republican Rift Opens Up Over Qualified Immunity for Police." *The Hill*, June 20. Accessed July 26, 2021. https://thehill.com/homenews /senate/503496-republican-rift-opens-up-over-qualified-immunity-for-police.

CBS News. 2020. "Transcript: Attorney General William Barr on 'Face the Nation.'" June 7. Accessed September 17, 2021. https://www.cbsnews.com/news/bill-barr-george-floyd -protests-blm-face-the-nation-transcript/.

Congress.gov. 2020. "S.Res.602—A Resolution Recognizing that the Murder of George Floyd by Officers of the Minneapolis Police Department is the Result of Pervasive and Systemic Racism That Cannot Be Dismantled Without, among Other Things, Proper Redress in the Courts." June 20. Accessed December 20, 2022. https://www.congress .gov/bill/116th-congress/senate-resolution/602.

Congressional Research Service. 2016. "Federal Prison Industries: Background, Debate, Legislative History, and Policy Options." May. Accessed August 11, 2021. https:// crsreports.congress.gov/product/pdf/RL/RL32380.

Da Silva, Chantal. 2019. "Trump Administration Has Doubled Private Prison Spending with Most Money Spent on Detaining Immigrants: 'They Are Not a Threat to Public Safety,' Advocates Say." *Newsweek*, September 25. Accessed June 7, 2020. https://www .newsweek.com/u-s-spending-private-prisons-geo-group-increase-immigration -detention-1461067.

Democratic Party Platforms. 2020. American Presidency Project. Accessed November 22, 2022. https://www.presidency.ucsb.edu/people/other/democratic-party-platforms.

Editorial Board. 2017. "Under Mr. Trump, Private Prisons Thrive Again." *New York Times*, February 24. Accessed May 2, 2019. https://www.nytimes.com/2017/02/24/opinion /under-mr-trump-private-prisons-thrive-again.html.

Edmonson, Catie. 2020. "Senate Democrats Block G.O.P. Police Bill, Calling It Inadequate." *New York Times*, June 24. Accessed May 7, 2021. http://www.nytimes.com/2020/06/24 /us/politics/senate-police-bill.

Evstatieva, Monika, and Tim Mac. 2020. "How Decades of Bans on Police Chokeholds Have Fallen Short." National Public Radio, June 16. Accessed October 5, 2020. https://www.npr.org/2020/06/16/877527974/how-decades-of-bans-on-police-chokeholds-have-fallen-short.

Grisales, Claudia. 2020. "Republicans' Police Reform Bill Focuses on Transparency and Training." National Public Radio, June 17. Accessed October 18, 2020. https://www.npr.org/2020/06/17/879082580/republicans-police-reform-bill-focuses-on-transparency-and-training.

Henderson, Howard, and Ben Yisrael. 2021. "7 Myths about 'Defunding the Police' Debunked." Brookings Institute, May 16. Accessed July 2, 2021. https://www.brookings.edu/blog/how-we-rise/2021/05/19/7-myths-about-defunding-the-police-debunked/.

Holder, Eric H., Jr. 2016. "Eric Holder: We Can Have Shorter Sentences and Less Crime." New York Times, August 11. Accessed December 10, 2020. https://www.nytimes.com/2016/08/14/opinion/sunday/eric-h-holder-mandatory-minimum-sentences-full-of-errors.html?searchResultPosition=19.

Hoonhout, Tobias. 2020. "McEnany Reiterates Qualified-Immunity Reform Is a 'Non-Starter.'" National Review, June 10. Accessed September 24, 2021. https://www.nationalreview.com/news/mcenany-reiterates-qualified-immunity-reform-is-a-non-starter/.

Jarrett, Laura. 2017. "DOJ Walks Back Guidance Discouraging Use of Private Prisons." CNN, February 23. Accessed March 8, 2019. https://www.cnn.com/2017/02/23/politics/doj-walks-back-guidance-discouraging-use-of-private-prisons/index.html.

"Joe Biden's Criminal Justice Policy | Joe Biden." 2019. Joe Biden for President. Accessed January 2, 2023. https://joebiden.com/justice/.

Johnson, William. 2021. "Opposition Letter in JUSTICE in Policing Act." National Association of Police Organizations, February 25. Accessed July 2, 2021. https://www.napo.org/files/2116/1480/9575/NAPO_Opposition_Letter_Justice_in_Policing_Act_.pdf.

Kelly, Amita, and Brian Naylor. 2020. "Trump, Hailing Law Enforcement, Signs Executive Order Calling for Police Reform." National Public Radio, June 20. Accessed July 3, 2021. https://www.npr.org/2020/06/16/877601170/watch-live-trump-to-sign-executive-order-on-police-reform.

Lampe, Joanna R. 2020. "Comparing Police Reform Bills: The Justice in Policing Act and the JUSTICE Act." Congressional Research Service, July 6. Accessed August 23, 2022. https://crsreports.congress.gov/product/pdf/LSB/LSB10498.

Long, Heather. 2017. "Private Prison Stocks Up 100% since Trump's Win." CNN Business, February 24. Accessed April 17, 2019. https://money.cnn.com/2017/02/24/investing/private-prison-stocks-soar-trump/index.html.

Martin, Jeffrey. 2020. "Trump Visits Dallas to Talk Policing and Race Relations, but Excludes Top Black Law Enforcement Officials." Newsweek, June 11. Accessed September 21, 2021. https://www.newsweek.com/trump-visits-dallas-talk-policing-race-relations-excludes-top-black-law-enforcement-officials-1510366.

McCammon, Sarah. 2020. "Senate Minority Leader Comments on the Republicans' Failed Police Reform Bill." National Public Radio, June 24. Accessed February 9, 2023. https://www.npr.org/2020/06/24/883017028/senate-minority-leader-comments-on-the-republicans-failed-police-reform-bill.

McGraw, Meredith. 2022. "Trump's Criminal Justice Reform Bill Becomes Persona Non Grata among GOPers." Politico, May 1. Accessed September 25, 2022. https://www.politico.com/news/2022/05/01/trump-republicans-first-step-act-00029104Twenty.

Morrison, Aaron. 2021. "50-Year War on Drugs Imprisoned Millions of Black Americans." *PBS News Hour*, July 26. Accessed September 23, 2022. https://www.pbs.org /newshour/nation/50-year-war-on-drugs-imprisoned-millions-of-black-americans.

NPR/PBS NewsHour/Marist National Poll. 2021. "Race Relations in the United States." Marist Poll, May 17. Accessed October 1, 2022. https://maristpoll.marist.edu/polls /npr-pbs-newshour-marist-poll-race-relations-in-the-united-states/.

Oppel, Richard A., Jr., Derrick Bryson Taylor, and Nicholas Bolger-Burroughs. 2022. "What to Know about Breonna Taylor's Death." *New York Times*, August 23. Accessed September 15, 2022. https://www.nytimes.com/article/breonna-taylor-police.html.

"Pelosi Statement on Re-Introduction of George Floyd Justice in Policing Act." 2021. Speaker Nancy Pelosi, February 24, 2021. Accessed January 30, 2023. https://www .speaker.gov/newsroom/22421-1.

Pew Research Center. 2020. "Majority of Public Favors Giving Civilians the Power to Sue Police Officers for Misconduct." July 9. Accessed September 23, 2021. https://www .pewresearch.org/politics/2020/07/09/majority-of-public-favors-giving-civilians-the -power-to-sue-police-officers-for-misconduct/.

Pfaff, John. 2021. "Private Prisons Aren't Uniquely Heinous: All Prisons Are Abusive." *Washington Post*, February 3. Accessed June 19, 2021. https://www.washingtonpost .com/outlook/2021/02/03/private-prisons-executive-order/.

"Rep. Omar Leads Letter Urging Executive Action on ICE Detention." 2021. Representative Ilhan Omar, March 15. Accessed December 20, 2022. https://omar.house.gov/media /press-releases/rep-omar-leads-letter-urging-executive-action-ice-detention.

Republican Party Platform. 2016. The American Presidency Project. Accessed January 2,2023. https://www.presidency.ucsb.edu/documents/2016-republican-party-platform.

Reuters. 2020. "For Cops Who Kill, Special Supreme Court Protection." May 8. Accessed December 20, 2022. https://www.reuters.com/investigates/special-report /usa-police-immunity-scotus/.

Scott, Tim. 2020. "JUSTICE Act Introduced in United States Senate." U.S. Senator Tim Scott of South Carolina, June 17. Accessed April 26, 2021. https://www.scott.senate .gov/media-center/press-releases/justice-act-introduced-in-united-states-senate.

The Sentencing Project. 2021. "Private Prisons in the United States." March 3. Accessed July 15, 2021. https://www.sentencingproject.org/publications/private-prisons-united -states/.

The Sentencing Project. n.d. "Criminal Justice Facts." Accessed October 7, 2022. https:// www.sentencingproject.org/criminal-justice-facts/.

Sibilia, Nick. 2021. "House Passes New Bill to Abolish Qualified Immunity for Police." *Forbes*, March 4. Accessed August 25, 2021. https://www.forbes.com/sites/nicksibilla /2021/03/04/house-passes-new-bill-to-abolish-qualified-immunity-for-police/?sh= 48e7a4c22daf.

United States Department of Justice. 2016. "Memorandum for the Acting Director Federal Bureau of Prisons." August 18. Accessed December 27, 2020. https://www.justice.gov /archives/opa/file/886311/download.

United States President. 2020a. "Executive Order on Safe Policing for Safe Communities." June 16. Accessed November 23, 2021. https://trumpwhitehouse.archives.gov /presidential-actions/executive-order-safe-policing-safe-communities/.

United States President. 2020b. "Remarks by President Trump at Signing of an Executive Order on Safe Policing for Safe Communities." June 16. Accessed December 17, 2021.

https://trumpwhitehouse.archives.gov/briefings-statements/remarks-president-trump
-signing-executive-order-safe-policing-safe-communities/.

USA Today Staff. 2020. "Read the Full Transcript from the First Presidential Debate between
Joe Biden and Donald Trump." *USA Today*, October 4.

The White House. 2021. "Executive Order on Reforming Our Incarceration System to Eliminate the Use of Privately Operated Criminal Detention Facilities." January 26. Accessed
August 13, 2021. https://www.whitehouse.gov/briefing-room/presidential-actions
/2021/01/26/executive-order-reforming-our-incarceration-system-to-eliminate-the
-use-of-privately-operated-criminal-detention-facilities/.

Religious Liberty

At a Glance

Since the 1960s, issues concerning religious liberty have become increasingly politicized. The rise in clout of the Religious Right within the Republican Party placed issues such as school prayer prominently on the public agenda. After the U.S. Supreme Court's ruling in *Employment Division v. Smith* (1990) limited the free exercise of religious beliefs, Congress passed the Religious Freedom Restoration Act (RFRA) in 1993 with strong bipartisan support to reinstate legal protection for the free exercise of religion. The U.S. Supreme Court's interpretation of this law in subsequent years has been controversial, however, especially as it concerns women's health care and LGBTQ rights. While Democrats emphasize women's access to health care and nondiscrimination policies for LGBTQ individuals, Republicans argue that religious individuals, organizations, and businesses should not be forced to violate sincerely held beliefs to comply with those laws. The Johnson Amendment to the Internal Revenue Service code prohibits nonprofit organizations from endorsing or financially supporting a political candidate. It was a controversial issue in the 2016 election. While Democrats support the amendment, many Republicans argue for its repeal claiming that it violates the free speech rights of pastors.

According to many Republicans . . .

- School prayer does not violate the Establishment Clause of the First Amendment.
- Congress should enact the First Amendment Defense Act (FADA) to protect the rights of religious business owners.
- The Johnson Amendment interferes with free speech rights of clergy and should be repealed.

According to many Democrats . . .

- State-sponsored prayer in public schools violates the Establishment Clause of the First Amendment.

- Congress should pass legislation to clarify that RFRA does not allow limitations on civil rights.
- The Johnson Amendment protects the mission of nonprofit organizations and prevents them from being abused for the purpose of funneling money to political candidates.

Overview

Many of the first American colonists came to the New World seeking refuge from religious persecution. Ironically, some of these same groups, such as the Puritans, later persecuted or expelled from their communities individuals who did not conform to the dictates of their faith.

After America gained its independence, many states collected taxes to support churches. Some lawmakers approved state constitutions that required public officials to be Christians. After Patrick Henry proposed a tax to support the salary of clergymen in Virginia, Federalist Papers coauthor and future president James Madison anonymously wrote "Memorial and Remonstrance Against Religious Assessments" (1785), in which he argued that every man must be free to serve God without interference from civil society and that government cannot regulate a person's religious beliefs. Madison noted he included only one reference to religion in the U.S. Constitution: Article VI's prohibition of establishing any "religious test" for public office.

When it became clear that the Constitution would not be ratified without a Bill of Rights, Madison played a lead role in drafting one to present to the first Congress. He addressed religious liberty in the First Amendment, which contains two religion clauses: the Establishment Clause and the Free Exercise Clause. The Establishment Clause prevents the government from enacting policies that prefer the religious over the nonreligious or one denomination over another. The Free Exercise Clause protects an individual's right to practice religious beliefs, subject to certain limitations. Initially these provisions applied only to the federal government, but after the U.S. Supreme Court incorporated the clauses to apply to state governments, it heard more cases dealing with religious liberty. These rulings are controversial and have political implications as they force public officials, candidates for public office, and political parties to take a stance on those issues.

Landmark Supreme Court Decisions

In 1962, the U.S. Supreme Court held that state-sponsored school prayer violated the Establishment Clause of the First Amendment in *Engel v. Vitale*. The Court ruled that state board of education members could not write a prayer and encourage students to recite it. The Court's ruling is often misunderstood because it did not prohibit voluntary prayer in schools but rather forbade state-sponsored prayer. Further, the Court has held that prayer at graduation ceremonies and at high school football games violates the Establishment Clause, in part because these events are not truly voluntary for all students. A graduation ceremony is an important rite of passage, and football players, cheerleaders, and marching band members are required to attend football games. The Court's school prayer decisions had been consistent in limiting state-sponsored prayer until 2022 when the Court allowed a football coach, a state employee, to lead a prayer in *Kennedy v. Bremerton School District*. The coach, who went to the fifty-yard line to pray after each game, was joined by other coaches and players on his team and the other team. The school district informed the coach that he could no longer continue the practice for fear of a lawsuit based on the Establishment Clause. By a vote of 6-3, the Court emphasized the coach's free speech and free exercise rights over the school district's "hostility" to religion by invoking the Establishment Clause. The dissenting justices criticized the majority for overlooking the facts of the case, which indicated players felt coerced to join in the prayer.

According to public opinion polls, most Americans favor prayer at these events, but that support has declined. A 1999 Gallup poll found that 70 percent of Americans favor daily prayer in the classroom, but by 2014, that support had fallen to 61 percent (Riffkin 2014). A 2021 Pew Research Center poll found that 46 percent of those surveyed opposed allowing public-school teachers to lead students in any type of prayer, while 30 percent supported public-school teachers leading students in Christian prayers. The other 24 percent surveyed were unsure. Among Republicans, 45 percent indicated that they supported teachers leading students in Christian prayers compared with 18 percent of Democrats (Pew Research Center 2021). Member of Congress have proposed constitutional amendments to overturn the Court's ruling in *Engel*, although none have been successful.

The Free Exercise Clause has also been the subject of political controversy. Beginning in *Sherbert v. Verner* (1963), the Court adopted a compelling governmental interest test in evaluating free exercise claims. The Court held that religious freedom is a fundamental right and that when the government enacts a policy that burdens free exercise, it must demonstrate that it is furthering a compelling governmental interest in the least restrictive manner possible. Almost thirty years later in *Employment Division v. Smith*, the Court lowered the standard in free exercise cases and held that a generally applicable law that limited religious free exercise did not violate the Free Exercise Clause. In a 6-3 ruling, Justice Antonin Scalia stated that free exercise "does not relieve an individual of the obligation to comply with a 'valid and neutral law of general applicability.'" Justice Sandra Day O'Connor, who disagreed with abandoning the compelling governmental interest test, wrote that the ruling "departs from well-settled First Amendment jurisprudence, appears unnecessary to resolve the question presented, and is incompatible with our Nation's fundamental commitment to individual religious liberty." The *Smith* ruling shocked legal experts and religious organizations because they feared that without the compelling governmental interest test, states could more easily limit free exercise of religion.

In response to *Smith*, over sixty religious and civil liberties organizations lobbied Congress to overturn the ruling. Congress responded by passing RFRA in 1993. The measure attracted strong bipartisan support, as both parties were eager to court churchgoing voters. It passed unanimously in the House, by a 97-3 vote in the Senate, and was signed by Democratic president Bill Clinton. This law required courts to apply the compelling government interest test in free exercise cases. Congress enacted the law based on its power to enforce the guarantees of the Fourteenth Amendment.

The Supreme Court invalidated RFRA as it applied to the states in *City of Boerne v. Flores* (1997) because Congress had exceeded its power to enforce the Fourteenth Amendment; however, the Court has upheld it as it applies to actions by the federal government. After the *Flores* ruling, Congress enacted the Religious Land Use and Institutionalized Persons Act in 2000 to address two areas not covered by RFRA. This law, also signed by Clinton, provides religious institutions protection from zoning restrictions and guarantees free exercise rights for individuals who are incarcerated. Congress based the law on its power to regulate interstate commerce and its power to tax and spend for the general welfare.

In the Patient Protection and Affordable Care Act (commonly referred to as the Affordable Care Act [ACA] or Obamacare; 2010), President Obama and his administration prioritized women's health by requiring companies to include coverage in their health-care plans for contraceptives. Prior to the law's enactment, Obama addressed concerns of religious employers by signing an executive order to reaffirm that federal funds would not subsidize abortion under the ACA.

Concerns about religious liberty were also raised when the Health Resources and Services Administration (HRSA), an agency of the Department of Health and Human Services, issued guidelines for employers. When HRSA issued a rule pursuant to the ACA (2010) that health-care plans provide coverage for all contraceptive methods and sterilization procedures approved by the Food and Drug Administration (FDA), religious employers were concerned that they would be forced to provide contraceptives contrary to their religious beliefs. HRSA added a religious exemption to the law allowing churches to provide women's health care to the extent that it did not violate their beliefs. The exemption initially did not apply to church-affiliated institutions such as universities and hospitals, which created a great deal of political controversy.

The extent to which RFRA applied to businesses who objected to the contraceptive mandate has been the subject of frequent and intense litigation. In *Burwell v. Hobby Lobby Stores, Inc.* (2014), the Court held in a narrow 5-4 decision that corporations had free exercise rights under RFRA and that the ACA violated those rights when it required businesses to provide health insurance plans that included birth control for their female employees. Hobby Lobby filed suit because its pro-life Christian owners believed that four of the twenty types of contraceptives available to their employees under the health-care plan caused or induced abortions. According to Justice Samuel Alito, the government has a compelling interest in providing health-care coverage, but the contraceptive mandate was not the least restrictive means of achieving that interest. The government could have paid for the contraceptives rather than requiring businesses to provide them or found another method that did not burden the free exercise rights of the company. In dissent, Justice Ruth Bader Ginsburg countered that "[u]ntil this litigation, no decision of this Court recognized a for-profit corporation's qualification for a religious exemption from a generally applicable law, whether under the Free Exercise Clause or RFRA." She also contested the majority's interpretation of RFRA noting that Congress modified women's health-care regulations to require coverage of all FDA-approved contraceptives in 2012, while simultaneously rejecting an amendment that would have allowed an employer to deny coverage based on their religious or moral beliefs.

In response to this ruling, Congressional Democrats introduced the Do No Harm Act in 2017 and reintroduced it in 2019. The law purported to restore the original meaning of RFRA so that religious freedom could not justify denying women access to health care. Democrats were also concerned that RFRA could be used to justify discrimination against the LGBTQ community and have urged passage of the Equality Act to protect LGBTQ rights. Republicans, however, blocked this legislation, arguing that Supreme Court rulings recognizing LGBTQ rights threaten the religious liberty of those who believe homosexuality is immoral. Republicans have sponsored the FADA to protect the rights of individuals and businesses who are opposed to homosexuality and same-sex marriage. This bill sought to prevent the government from what Republicans claimed was "discriminatory action" against individuals or organizations who acted upon their religious or moral belief that marriage is a union between one man and one woman or that sexual relations should be limited to married couples.

The Johnson Amendment was an important religious liberty issue in the 2016 presidential campaign. The amendment, named for then senator and later president Lyndon B. Johnson, was enacted in 1954 and prohibits nonprofit, tax-exempt organizations from endorsing political candidates or collecting funds for candidates or political parties. The Internal Revenue Service could strip organizations that violate the law of their tax-exempt status; however, the law has rarely been enforced since its enactment. Republicans argue that the law hinders free speech rights of clergypersons by forbidding them from endorsing candidates from the pulpit. Democrats argue that the law prevents nonprofits from becoming political entities and destroying their charitable mission. A 2016 public opinion poll found that 66 percent of Americans opposed church endorsements of candidates and that only 33 percent of Republicans and 26 percent of Democrats supported them (Smith 2017).

Republicans

The Republican Party has addressed several issues regarding religious liberty. Republicans have supported a school prayer amendment and have also argued that the ACA has forced religious organizations to violate their beliefs by requiring them to provide insurance coverage for contraceptives and other aspects of women's health care. Likewise, Republicans support the rights of business owners to not comply with LGBTQ antidiscrimination policies if those violate their religious beliefs. Republicans also support the repeal of the Johnson Amendment.

The Republican Party's stance on public policies involving religious freedom have been heavily influenced by the Religious Right. During the 1970s, conservative Christians became increasingly alarmed at policies that they believed threatened their values. The legalization of abortion along with the Women's Rights Movement and the Gay Rights Movement brought evangelical Christians into the political arena. While several Christian groups formed to address these issues, the Moral Majority is among the most prominent. It was founded in 1979 by televangelist Jerry Falwell, minister of the country's largest independent Baptist church. The New Right, as the broader group of evangelical Christians was labeled, became a significant force in American politics through its support of Ronald Reagan in the 1980 presidential election. Prior to 1980, the Republican platform had supported abortion rights and the Equal Rights Amendment. The 1980 platform addressed school prayer for the first time stating that the party supported "Republican initiatives in the Congress to restore the right of individuals to participate in voluntary, non-denominational prayer in schools and other public facilities."

School Prayer

Republicans have supported a constitutional amendment to allow state-sponsored prayer in school on several occasions since the ruling in *Engel*. The two most recent votes on such an amendment occurred in 1984 and 1998. President Ronald Reagan frequently raised the issue of prayer in public schools, often saying that "God isn't dead. We just can't talk to Him in the classroom anymore." In March 1984, the Republican-controlled Senate failed to pass a school prayer amendment that read, "Nothing in this Constitution shall be construed to prohibit individual or group prayer in public schools or other public institutions. Neither the United States nor any state shall compose the words of prayers to be said in the public schools." The vote was 56-44 in favor, but the Constitution requires a two-thirds majority vote of both chambers of Congress to pass an amendment. A total of nineteen Democrats joined with thirty-seven Republicans to support the amendment, while eighteen Republicans and twenty-six Democrats voted against it. Moderate Republicans and a majority of Democrats opposed it, while Southern Democrats along with a majority of Republicans supported it. Critics suggested that Reagan did not lobby enough to help pass the amendment and that he refused to support a proposal for silent prayer that was more likely to pass the Senate.

After the 1994 "Republican Revolution" in which Republicans gained a majority of seats in the House of Representatives in the midterm elections for the first time in forty years, House Speaker Newt Gingrich sought to pass a school prayer amendment. This initiative ultimately failed when competing versions of an amendment from two Republican congressmen, Jim Istook and Henry Hyde, were introduced. Istook's proposal focused specifically on school prayer, while Hyde's was a broader Religious Freedom Amendment that included school prayer. Republicans tried again in 1996 in what was perceived as an attempt to help the Republican presidential nominee, Senator Bob Dole, with the Christian Coalition—a Religious Right organization that had expressed doubts about his stance on abortion. Ultimately, the amendment was not brought to the floor for a vote (Seelye 1996). In 1998, Representative Istook introduced the Religious Freedom Amendment. It stated: "To secure the people's right to acknowledge God according to the dictates of conscience: Neither the United States nor any State shall establish any official religion, but the people's right to pray and to recognize their religious beliefs, heritage, or traditions on public property, including schools, shall not be infringed. Neither the United States nor any State shall require any person to join in prayer or other religious activity, prescribe school prayers, discriminate against religion, or deny equal access to a benefit on account of religion." During the floor debate, Istook stated that "[p]rayer is not divisive. Prayer is unifying. What is divisive is to teach children not to respect the prayers of someone else." Much like the 1984 Senate vote, a majority of House members voted for the amendment, 224-203, but that was 61 votes shy of the two-thirds needed to pass. A total of 197 Republicans and 27 Democrats voted in favor of the amendment, while 174 Democrats, 28 Republicans, and 1 independent voted against it.

The 2000 platform, along with every platform since, has asserted that the party supports voluntary school prayer. In 2003, President George W. Bush issued guidelines through the Department of Education on the religious rights of students and teachers in public schools. The document revised the guidelines issued by the Clinton administration in 1995 and set forth instances of prohibited conduct, including teachers leading students in prayers or Bible study groups, along with examples of permissible conduct, including allowing students to form religious groups and engage in prayer or Bible reading during noninstructional time. In January 2020, President Trump announced that the Department of Education would mail letters to education officials reminding them that students and teachers who wished to pray were protected by the First Amendment. Trump threatened to withhold federal funding from schools that did not respect this right (Marcus 2020). Benjamin Marcus of the Religious Freedom Center criticized the president for making the prayer issue partisan. He quoted Trump's January 2020 speech at a Florida megachurch in which the president stated that his administration would "not allow faithful Americans to be bullied by the hard left" and that he would "safeguard students' and teachers' First Amendment rights" (Marcus 2020). Marcus noted that there are politicians in both political parties that care about religious freedom and who are religious people. He stated that "[t]he guidance document released by the Trump administration last week does not protect rights for students or teachers that have not already been affirmed with bipartisan consensus for decades." Marcus argued that fixating on prayer "feeds a polarizing narrative that only one party cares about the rights of religious Americans. And such myopia stunts important conversations about the full range of issues regarding religion in schools" (Marcus 2020).

Religious Liberty and Discrimination

During the 2012 presidential election, Republican candidates were very critical of the ACA and its provisions regarding women's health care arguing that the contraceptive mandate violated the rights of religious employers. The 2012 Republican nominee Mitt Romney criticized President Obama for the contraceptive mandate and tweeted, "If you've had enough of the Obama Administration's attacks on religious liberty, stand with me & sign the petition." The petition alleged that Obama sought to "impose a secular vision on Americans who believe that they should not have their religious freedom taken away." Writing in the *Washington Post*, journalist Michael Gerson characterized the contraceptive mandate as a "power grab." He also criticized the president for "ambushing" Catholic leaders by implementing a "transparently anti-Catholic maneuver" and stated that "the war on religion is now formally declared." The phrase "war on religion" was used repeatedly during the 2012 campaign even after Obama's decision to expand the religious exemptions under the ACA (Gerson 2012).

Republicans have emphasized the religious liberty of business owners over the civil rights of LGBTQ individuals. The 2008 platform stated that "[f]orcing religious groups to abandon their beliefs as applied to their hiring practices is religious discrimination." In 2012, the platform provided that "[w]e oppose government discrimination against businesses due to religious views" and that "[w]e condemn the hate campaigns, threats of violence, and vandalism by proponents of same-sex marriage against advocates of traditional marriage and call for a federal investigation into attempts to deny religious believers their civil rights." The 2016 and 2020 platforms endorsed the FADA. The bill was first introduced in 2015 and then reintroduced in 2018. Specifically, the platforms stated that the party endorsed the proposed legislation "which will bar government discrimination against individuals and businesses for acting on the belief that marriage is the union of one man and one woman. This Act would protect the non-profit tax status of faith-based adoption agencies, the accreditation of religious educational institutions,

Republicans Support Business Owners Who Refuse to Provide Services to LGBTQ Persons

A key point of contention between Democrats and Republicans on the issue of religious liberty involves LGBTQ rights. Republicans argue that individuals who act on the basis of their faith in denying services to LGBTQ persons deserve legal protection for those actions. Republicans introduced the First Amendment Defense Act, excerpted here, to provide such protection.

First Amendment Defense Act

Prohibits the federal government from taking discriminatory action against a person on the basis that such person believes or acts in accordance with a religious belief or moral conviction that: (1) marriage is or should be recognized as the union of one man and one woman, or (2) sexual relations are properly reserved to such a marriage.

Defines "discriminatory action" as any federal government action to discriminate against a person with such beliefs or convictions, including a federal government action to:

alter the federal tax treatment of, cause any tax, penalty, or payment to be assessed against, or deny, delay, or revoke certain tax exemptions of any such person;

disallow a deduction of any charitable contribution made to or by such person;

withhold, reduce, exclude, terminate, or otherwise deny any federal grant, contract, subcontract, cooperative agreement, loan, license, certification, accreditation, employment, or similar position or status from or to such person; or

withhold, reduce, exclude, terminate, or otherwise deny any benefit under a federal benefit program.

Source

Lee, Mike. 2018. "S.2525—115th Congress (2017-2018): First Amendment Defense Act." Congress.gov, March 8, 2018. Accessed January 30, 2023. https://www.congress.gov/bill/115th-congress/senate-bill/2525.

the grants and contracts of faith-based charities and small businesses, and the licensing of religious professions—all of which are under assault by elements of the Democratic Party." Additionally, the platform argued that the "government could not use subsequent amendments to limit First Amendment rights."

Johnson Amendment

During the 2016 presidential campaign, the Republican Party platform and Republican nominee Donald Trump promised to repeal the Johnson Amendment. The 2016 platform stated: "We value the right of America's religious leaders to preach, and Americans to speak freely, according to their faith. Republicans believe the federal government, specifically the IRS, is constitutionally prohibited from policing or censoring speech based on religious convictions or beliefs, and therefore we urge the repeal of the Johnson Amendment." At the observance of the 2017 National Day of Prayer, Trump stated that he intended to "get rid of and totally destroy the Johnson Amendment and allow our representatives of faith to speak freely and without fear of retribution." Shortly thereafter, Congressional Republicans held hearings on the Free Speech Fairness Act, which proposed to "allow charitable organizations to make statements relating to political campaigns if such statements are made in the ordinary course of carrying out its tax exempt purpose." Trump issued an executive order in May 2017 "to defend the freedom of religion and speech" by limiting the enforcement of the law. Writing in the *Atlantic*, Emma Green suggested that Trump's pledge to repeal the amendment was more about fundraising than religion. She stated that the repeal proposal "seems to serve more of a dog-whistle purpose . . . a signal to religious conservatives that Trump is their champion, and that he cares about religious freedom issues. It might also be a message to rich conservatives, specifically . . . a way to make tax-favored political donations" (Green 2016). The 2020 platform language was identical to the 2016 platform as Republicans opted out of writing a 2020 platform due to the COVID-19 pandemic.

Democrats

Democrats have emphasized efforts to prevent religious discrimination, particularly for religious minorities, which is why they support voluntary prayer in public school but not a school prayer amendment. Democrats argue that the First Amendment protects the exercise of all religions, not just Christianity, and that business owners should not be legally allowed to use their religious beliefs to justify discrimination. Democrats also believe that the Johnson Amendment should not be repealed.

Democrats have opposed the two most recent attempts to add a school prayer amendment to the Constitution. During the consideration of the amendment in the House in 1984, many Southern Democrats joined Republicans in the failed attempt, but most Democrats opposed it. Democratic senator Bill Bradley opposed the amendment for several reasons. He noted that the Constitution already guarantees an individual's right to pray regardless of their location. He argued that he opposed the amendment in order to preserve a "clear division between church and state." He also argued that it is not the role of public school officials to enforce religious practices and that prayer is a private and individual experience. Finally, he stated that it is unfair to force a child to decide whether to conform to a state-sponsored prayer given the religious pluralism that exists in the United States (Perlez 1984).

The school prayer issue resurfaced in the 1990s, and the 1996 platform stated that "Americans have a right to express their love of God in public, and we applaud the President's work to ensure that children are not denied private religious expression in school. Whenever the religious rights of our children—or any American—are threatened, we will stand against it." In 1998, House Democrats opposed the Religious Freedom Amendment. A total of 27 House Democrats voted for it, while 174 voted against it. Representative Barney Frank stated that the "amendment seeks to solve a problem that does not exist. Let's leave religion to the families and to individual choice" (Walsh 1998). In his May 30, 1998, radio address after the Religious Freedom Amendment failed, Clinton highlighted his 1995 Department of Education guidelines on religious activity in public schools. He stated that "since we've issued these guidelines, appropriate religious activity has flourished in our schools, and there has apparently been a substantial decline in the contentious argument and litigation that has accompanied this issue for too long." He also addressed his opposition to the proposed amendment in the House stating that "[f]or more than 200 years, the First Amendment has protected our religious freedom and allowed many faiths to flourish in our homes, in our workplaces, and in our schools. Clearly understood and sensibly applied, it works. It does not need to be rewritten" (Walsh 1998). Unlike Republicans, Democratic platforms have not addressed school prayer since 1996; however, platforms have repeatedly stated that the party opposes religious discrimination. A 2021 Pew Research Center poll showed that 18 percent of Democrats supported allowing public-school teachers to lead students in Christian prayer, while 60 percent opposed allowing teachers to lead students in any type of prayer. The other 23 percent either had no opinion or refused to answer (Pew Research Center 2021).

Religious Liberty and Discrimination

Democrats have sought to expand women's access to health care and prevent discrimination against LGBTQ individuals. Republicans have charged that these actions threaten religious liberty. In 2012, the Democratic platform stated that "[t]he Affordable Care Act ensures that women have access to contraception in their health insurance plans, and the President has respected the principle of religious liberty." President Barack Obama sought to guarantee health care for women in the ACA. One of the most controversial aspects of the law was that it initially only exempted churches from complying with the contraceptive mandate. After being criticized by Mitt Romney and other Republicans for waging a "war on religion," one of Obama's campaign managers tweeted that the mandate was identical to Romney's policies when he was the governor of Massachusetts. Obama modified the law so that insurance companies, and not religious organizations, would guarantee coverage for contraceptives if the religious organizations opted not to—an action that was also controversial. This decision was criticized by Gerson (2012) who wrote that "[i]nstead of being forced to buy an insurance product that violates their beliefs, religious institutions will be forced to buy an insurance product that contributes to the profits and viability of a company that is federally mandated to violate their beliefs. Creative accounting, it seems, can cover a multitude of sins."

The 2012 platform also stated that Democrats support a government that "gives everyone willing to work hard the chance to make the most of their God-given potential." The term "God-given" was added to the platform at the Democratic National Convention on a voice vote with some delegates booing the decision to add the language. The incident led some commentators to suggest that the Democrats had a "God problem." In the *New Republic*, however, Amy Sullivan (2012) pointed out that like the Republican Convention, the Democratic Convention began and ended its daily sessions with prayer and that the 2012 platform included a section labeled "Faith," which noted that "our lives are made vastly stronger and richer by faith and the countless acts of justice and mercy it inspires."

The 2016 Democratic platform supported "a progressive vision of religious freedom that respects pluralism and rejects the misuse of religion to discriminate." In an op-ed for the *Deseret News*, a Utah newspaper, 2016 Democratic presidential nominee Hillary Clinton asserted that "[a]s Americans, we hold fast to the belief that everyone has the right to worship however he or she sees fit." She emphasized her record as secretary of state in protecting the rights of religious minorities around the world. Her views were criticized by Alexandra DeSanctis (2016) in the *National Review*, who argued that Clinton had "made no effort to defend religious freedom . . . in the U.S." and had "actively worked *against* religious minorities for the sake of her cherished causes, specifically expansive access to abortion and the supremacy of LGBT rights," including her opposition to *Burwell v. Hobby Lobby Stores, Inc.*

Congressional Democrats sought to amend RFRA after *Burwell v. Hobby Lobby Stores, Inc.* The Do No Harm Act was first introduced in 2017 and reintroduced in 2019. The bill would amend RFRA and provides that RFRA "should not be interpreted to authorize an exemption from generally applicable law that imposes the religious views, habits, or practices of one party upon another" (Aviles 2019). One of the cosponsors of the bill, Democratic representative Joseph P. Kennedy III, said that "we cannot be equal or free if our government grants select Americans a license to discriminate against their neighbors under the guise of religious freedom" (Aviles 2019). Another cosponsor, Democratic representative Bobby Scott, stated that "[u]nfortunately in recent years, bad faith interpretations of RFRA have been used to deny health care coverage for employees, claim exemptions to civil rights laws and impede justice in child labor and abuse cases" (Aviles 2019). In an op-ed in *USA Today*, Matt Sharp, the senior counsel for Alliance Defending Freedom, an influential Christian interest group, who testified against the Do No Harm Act, stated that RFRA had not been distorted by the courts. He charged that Democrats were motivated to limit the exercise of religious beliefs that they personally disliked and that their true intention was "to deny those disfavored religious groups from even having access to a fair hearing in court" (Sharp 2019).

In the wake of the U.S Supreme Court's ruling in *Bostock v. Clayton County* (2020), which held that Title VII of the Civil Rights Act of 1964 prohibits employment

Democrats Support Law to Protect LGBTQ Persons from Discrimination

Democrats argue that religion should not be used as a shield for business owners to discriminate against LGBTQ individuals., and have introduced the Equality Act as an amendment to the Civil Rights Act of 1964 to protect LGBTQ individuals. The Equality Act is excerpted here.

Equality Act

(3) Lesbian, gay, bisexual, transgender, and queer (referred to as 'LGBTQ') people commonly experience discrimination in securing access to public accommodations—including restaurants, senior centers, stores, places of or establishments that provide entertainment, health care facilities, shelters, government offices, youth service providers including adoption and foster care providers, and transportation. Forms of discrimination include the exclusion and denial of entry, unequal or unfair treatment, harassment, and violence. This discrimination prevents the full participation of LGBTQ people in society and disrupts the free flow of commerce.

Source

"Text—H.R.5—116th Congress (2019-2020): Equality Act." 2019. Congress.gov, 2019. Accessed January 30, 2023. https://www.congress.gov/bill/116th-congress/house-bill/5/text.

discrimination on the basis of sexual orientation and transgender status, Senate Democrats demanded a vote on the Equality Act. This act would limit RFRA by specifically prohibiting the use of religious liberty as a defense in discrimination claims in employment and other areas, including housing and education. Justice Neil Gorsuch's majority opinion in *Bostock* noted that employers were concerned that they might be forced to violate their religious convictions by complying with Title VII. He stated that "[b]ecause RFRA operates as sort of a super statute, displacing the normal operation of other federal laws, it might supersede Title VII's commands in appropriate cases." The Equality Act could eliminate that possibility.

Johnson Amendment

The repeal of the Johnson Amendment was addressed much more by the Republican Party in the 2016 election than by the Democratic Party. In a letter to Republican congressional leadership in 2017, Democratic senator Ron Wyden outlined several key arguments for keeping the amendment. Wyden was concerned that eliminating the amendment would effectively abolish campaign finance laws. "Using charitable causes as shell companies to evade campaign finance transparency and contribution limits would increase the flow of dark money in politics. At the same time, it would force taxpayers to foot the bill for special interests.

Hardworking Americans simply should not be required to subsidize the political spending for our country's powerful few." He also argued that feeding the hungry and ministering to the homeless are not partisan issues and that individuals who donate to those causes are contributing to those organizations for "social good, not political engineering" (Wyden 2017). If even a few charitable organizations contribute money to a political campaign, it undermines faith in the mission of all charitable organizations. While the public at large opposed allowing nonprofits to contribute or advocate on behalf of candidates, Democrats were the least likely to do so with only 26 percent supporting those actions.

Further Reading

Aviles, Gwen. 2019. "Congressional Democrats Reintroduce the Do No Harm Act." *NBC News*, March 1. Accessed July 16, 2020. https://www.nbcnews.com/feature/nbc-out /congressional-democrats-reintroduce-do-no-harm-act-n978101.

Boston, Rob. 2020. "Our Constitution Lacks a School Prayer Amendment—For That, You Can Thank These Champions." *The Humanist*, February 25. Accessed July 6, 2020. https://thehumanist.com/magazine/march-april-2020/church-state/church-state-our -constitution-lacks-a-school-prayer-amendment-for-that-you-can-thank-these-champions.

Clymer, Adam. 1993. "Congress Ponders Bill to Protect Some Religious Practices." *New York Times*, May 10. Accessed July 6, 2020. https://www.nytimes.com/1993/05/10/us /congress-ponders-bill-to-protect-some-religious-practices.html.

Democratic Party Platforms. 2012–2020. American Presidency Project. Accessed November 22, 2022. https://www.presidency.ucsb.edu/people/other/democratic-party-platforms.

DeSanctis, Alexandra. 2016. "Hillary Clinton Is No Champion of Religious Freedom." *National Review*, August 11. Accessed August 28, 2019. https://www.nationalreview .com/2016/08/hillary-clinton-opposes-religious-liberty.

Gerson, Michael. 2012. "Obama's Radical Power Grab on Health Care." *Washington Post*, January 30. Accessed July 7, 2020. https://www.washingtonpost.com/opinions/obamas -radical-power-grab-on-health-care/2012/01/30/gIQANB7XdQ_story.html.

Green, Emma. 2016. "Trump Wants to Make Churches the New Super PACs." *The Atlantic*, August 2. Accessed July 14, 2020. https://www.theatlantic.com/politics/archive /2016/08/how-trump-is--trying-to-put-more-money-in-politics/493823/.

Marcus, Benjamin. 2020. "Don't Get Stuck on Prayers in Public Schools." Freedom Forum, January 23. Accessed July 15, 2020. https://www.freedomforum.org/2020/01/23/dont -get-stuck-on-prayers-in-public-schools/.

Moore, David W. 2005. "Public Favors Voluntary Prayer for Public Schools." Gallup, August 26. Accessed July 12, 2020. https://news.gallup.com/poll/18136/Public-Favors -Voluntary-Prayer-Public-Schools.aspx.

Perlez, Jane. 1984. "5 Senators Oppose School Prayer Measure." *New York Times*, March 16. Accessed July 10, 2020. https://www.nytimes.com/1984/03/16/nyregion/5-senators -oppose-school-prayer-measure.html.

Pew Research Center. 2021. "In U.S., Far More Support Than Oppose Separation of Church and State." Pew Research Center, October 28. Accessed September 23, 2022. https:// www.pewresearch.org/religion/2021/10/28/in-u-s-far-more-support-than-oppose -separation-of-church-and-state/.

Republican Party Platforms. 1980, 2000–2020. American Presidency Project. Accessed November 22, 2022. https://www.presidency.ucsb.edu/people/other/republican-party -platforms.

Riffkin, Rebecca. 2014. "In U.S., Support for Daily Prayer in Schools Dips Slightly." Gallup, September 25. Accessed July 15, 2020. https://news.gallup.com/poll/177401/support -daily-prayer-schools-dips-slightly.aspx.

Seelye, Katharine. 1996. "Republicans in Congress Renew Push for Vote on School Prayer Amendment." *New York Times*, July 16. Accessed July 14, 2020. https://www.nytimes .com/1996/07/16/us/republicans-in-congress-renew-push-for-vote-on-school-prayer -amendment.html.

Sharp, Matt. 2019. "Disagreement Is Not Discrimination: 'Do No Harm Act' Is a Dishonest Act to Eject Religion." *USA Today*, July 4. Accessed July 13, 2020. https://www .usatoday.com/story/opinion/voices/2019/07/04/religious-liberty-attack-do-no-harm -act-column/1622136001/.

Smith, Gregory A. 2017. "Most Americans Oppose Churches Choosing Sides in Elections." Pew Research Center, February 3. Accessed July 6, 2020. https://www.pewresearch.org /fact-tank/2017/02/03/most-americans-oppose-churches-choosing-sides-in-elections/.

Sullivan, Amy. 2012. "Debunking the 'Democrats Hate God' Lie." *New Republic*, September 6. Accessed July 12, 2020. https://newrepublic.com/article/106966/debunking -democrats-hate-god-lie.

Walsh, Mark. 1998. "Religious Freedom Amendment Fails in House Vote." *Education Week*, June 10. Accessed July 14, 2020. https://www.edweek.org/education /religious-freedom-amendment-fails-in-house-vote/1998/06F.

Wyden, Ron. 2017. "Letter to Republican Leadership." U.S. Senate Committee on Finance, May 3. Accessed July 15, 2020. https://www.finance.senate.gov/imo/media /doc/050317%20RW%20to%20GOP%20Leadership%20re%20Johnson%20Amdt .pdf.

School Choice

At a Glance

School choice is a type of education reform by which parents can select the schools their children will attend. The modern school choice movement began in 1991, and since that time, both the Republican and Democratic parties have expressed support for school choice. However, the two parties differ dramatically in the types of school choice programs they support. Democrats support public charter schools and magnet schools while Republicans favor a broad array of school choice options, including vouchers and tuition tax credits for private schools (many of which are closely affiliated with or owned and operated by religious institutions).

According to many Republicans . . .

- Parents should be allowed to use vouchers in private schools, including private religious schools, if that is the best option for their child.
- Competition among schools improves education quality because under-performing schools will have to improve to attract students.

According to many Democrats . . .

- School choice options should be limited to public schools because they are more accountable.
- Funding private schools in school choice programs takes away valuable resources from public schools and violates the Establishment Clause by funding private religious schools.

Overview

Education policy has been an important political issue in the United States since the colonial era. The Puritans established a system of public schools in 1647, primarily to teach children how to read the Bible. By 1800, seven of the sixteen states forming the Union had some provision for education in their state constitutions. Initially, local school districts had great latitude in creating education policy, with the states exercising varying degrees of control. In the twentieth century, however, the states played a more significant role in crafting education policy, including setting requirements for teachers and curriculum.

In the 1960s, the federal government became increasingly involved in public education policy. The Elementary and Secondary Education Act (ESEA) of 1965 was the first significant federal law concerning public education. This legislation was part of President Lyndon B. Johnson's "Great Society" slate of social welfare programs and policies intended to combat poverty and inequality in the United States. The landmark ESEA was meant to promote educational opportunity by providing additional funding to public schools. State and local governments provide over 90 percent of the funding for public schools while federal funds are awarded to the states through grants. ESEA created grant programs for school districts serving low-income students, for textbooks and library books, and for state educational associations to help improve the quality of elementary and secondary education. Since its enactment, Congress has reauthorized and amended the law several times to include provisions concerning school choice.

The basic premise of school choice is that parents can decide which schools their children attend instead of them being assigned to a school based on their residence. Although school choice became a salient political issue in the 1990s, influential conservative economist Milton Friedman addressed the issue as far back as the 1950s. He argued that allowing parents to choose the best schools for their children would pressure underperforming schools to improve or close; market-based competition between the schools would result in a better-educated populace. Critics of the market-based approach, however, countered that not all parents make decisions based on their child's best interests, school closings have negative effects on children's academic achievement, and the best schools are not often viable options because they have waiting lists.

Proponents of school choice argue that in a democracy parents should have the right to choose the best schools for their children. Choice advocates claim that families with financial means can choose to reside in districts that have good schools, which leaves less affluent children stuck in lower quality schools; allowing every parent to choose the best schools for their children is a way to even the playing field. Critics of school choice, though, argue that tax money should be devoted exclusively to improving the quality of education in underfunded *public* schools— not private school. Further, critics charge that choice programs that subsidize private schools do not necessarily improve education because those institutions are not required to meet the same academic standards as public schools.

Public- and Private-School Options
States have created various types of public- and private-school choice options. Public-school choice options include magnet schools, charter schools, and

open-enrollment policies. Magnet schools are public schools that offer a special-ized curriculum to draw students from across a school district. These schools were created in the late 1960s to promote racial integration. The federal govern-ment offered funding for magnet schools specifically for that purpose in 1972. The federal program has evolved into the Magnet Schools Assistance Program, which still provides funds for purposes of integration but also for school choice. Charter schools are public schools that are exempt from state regulations but are generally subject to stricter accountability standards. Minnesota created the first charter school program in 1991, and in 2019, forty-three states and the District of Columbia had charter schools. Students must apply and be accepted into both magnet schools and charter schools. Another type of public-school choice program is open enrollment, also referred to as inter-/intra-district choice. Inter-district pro-grams allow parents to choose a public school outside the school district to which their child has been assigned, while intra-district choice programs allow families to choose a school within their assigned school district.

Private-school options include vouchers, education savings accounts, and tui-tion tax scholarships. Vouchers give parents a specified sum of money to spend toward their child's education in a private school. Parents can spend the money to pay for school, including religious schools, but it may or may not cover the entire cost of tuition. Vouchers typically involve giving private schools tax money that would have otherwise been earmarked for public schools. Wisconsin was the first state to implement a voucher system in 1991. Education savings accounts (ESAs) were first implemented in Arizona in 2011. In this system, money that the state would have spent educating a child in public school is put into an account controlled by parents. Unlike voucher systems, which require that any money not spent on tuition be returned to the state, in an ESA parents can spend money on education-related expenses such as school supplies. Tuition tax scholarships allow individuals to obtain a tax credit for donating to a nonprofit scholarship organiza-tion that provides scholarships to students attending private schools.

Private-school choice options have proven controversial, both legally and polit-ically. From a legal perspective, various types of state aid to parochial schools were challenged as a violation of the Establishment Clause of the First Amendment. The U.S. Supreme Court generally upheld aid that it considered neutral toward religion. The Court, for example, upheld state programs that provided textbooks, comput-ers, and sign language interpreters to parochial schools because these programs benefited the students, not the religion. Opponents of vouchers argued that pay-ments to parochial schools were unconstitutional because the funds subsidized reli-gion. The Supreme Court addressed that issue in *Zelman v. Simmons-Harris* (2002), where it upheld the constitutionality of the school voucher program in Cleveland, Ohio. The Cleveland school district was one of the worst performing school dis-tricts in the country and was placed under state control in 1995. The state imple-mented its Pilot Project Scholarship Program, which gave parents several options when it came to their children's education. The choices included: (1) remain in Cleveland public schools, (2) receive a scholarship (up to $2,250 per year) to attend a private, accredited nonreligious school, (3) receive a scholarship (up to $2,250 per year) to attend a private, accredited religious school, (4) remain in Cleveland public schools and receive a $500 stipend for tutorial assistance, and (5) attend a public school outside the district. The state distributed financial assistance to parents according to financial need. Parents received a check, which they endorsed to pay private-school tuition. Of the students, 96.7 percent chose to attend private religious schools. By a 5-4 margin, the Court held that the policy was neutral toward religion because parents could choose nonreligious schools, and the state did not award vouchers based on religion. The Court noted that the only preference in the policy was for lower-income families, not religion.

From a political perspective, before the parties addressed the broader issue of school choice, they embraced tuition tax credits. The 1968 and 1972 Democratic platforms supported tuition tax credits that would have allowed parents to deduct a portion of the costs of private-school tuition from their income taxes. In 1978, Democratic senator Patrick Moynihan introduced a tuition tax credit bill with the support of twenty-four Democratic senators. The National Education Association (NEA), the largest labor union and professional interest group in the United States representing public-school teachers, had supported President Jimmy Carter's campaign and opposed Moynihan's bill. According to Moynihan, the NEA's influence was instrumental in Carter's opposition to the bill (Emerson 2012).

In 1980, the Republican platform supported tuition tax credits. President Ronald Reagan backed proposed tuition tax credit legislation in 1981. He suggested that it would help struggling private and public schools because the former would receive additional funding and latter would be more efficient with fewer students. Critics of the proposal argued that it would assist "white academies," private schools attended by white students avoiding integrated public schools. The proposal was amended to prohibit aid to schools that discriminated on the basis of race, but a proposal prohibiting discrimination against students who were disabled or who had learning disabilities failed. Reagan also attempted to persuade Congress to amend ESEA to allow vouchers in 1983 and 1985, but these attempts were unsuccessful because there was significant opposition to funding private schools with federal tax dollars (Cavanaugh 2004).

Party platforms did not address school choice until the 1992 presidential campaign. President George H. W. Bush supported vouchers in part to appeal to Catholic and evangelical Christian voters. Catholic schools directly benefit from vouchers, and evangelical Christians were critical of public schools because they taught evolution and prohibited state-sponsored school prayer. The 1992 Democratic nominee, Bill Clinton, also supported public-school choice through the establishment of charter schools but opposed vouchers for private, religious schools. The parties' stances in 1992 have remained consistent with Republicans continuing to argue that competition between schools results in better schools.

They have also consistently favored vouchers for private religious schools. Democrats also support school choice but oppose vouchers. They argue that public schools should be the focus of education reform. Republicans are critical of Democrats for siding with teachers' unions, while Democrats criticize Republicans for advocating polices that hurt public schools.

Republicans

The 1992 platform was the first to address school choice as a method of education reform. The platform emphasized the role of parents in the education of their children and asserted that they should have the "broadest array of educational choices." During the 1992 campaign, President George H. W. Bush unveiled a $500 million school choice policy that would allow poor and middle-income families to choose which school their children attended, including private, religious schools. According to the president, this program would reduce overcrowding in schools and provide students from lower-income families the same educational opportunities as more affluent families. Bush argued that even though federal tax dollars would go to religious schools, the policy was not supporting religion because parents, not the government, were choosing the schools.

Prior to the 1996 campaign, several candidates for the Republican nomination attended the Christian Coalition's 1995 annual convention where school choice was a key issue. In the Christian Coalition's Contract with the American Family, the organization offered a ten-point agenda, including vouchers and tuition tax credits, for school choice (Christian Coalition 1995). During the 1996 presidential campaign, Republican nominee Bob Dole announced his support for a proposal that would spend $5 billion per year on a voucher program allowing parents to choose public, private, or parochial schools. He stated that school choice was "a civil rights movement of the 1990s" (Waggoner 1996). During the first presidential debate, Dole questioned whether President Bill Clinton was fully committed to vouchers because private, religious schools were not included in his school choice program (*Reuters* 1996). The platform encouraged local and state governments to ensure quality education through a system of parental choice among public, private, and religious schools. It specifically supported and pledged to work vigorously for opportunity scholarships, block grants, school rebates, charter schools, and vouchers.

The emphasis changed in the 2000 platform, which stated that the party endorsed Republican nominee and Texas governor George W. Bush's education reforms. The reforms included expanding parental choice and encouraging competition among schools by providing parents with information about their child's school, increasing the number of charter schools, and expanding ESAs so that they could be used from kindergarten through college. During the campaign, Bush acknowledged that the Republican Party was not known for its concern for public schools. He stated that he was deeply devoted to public schools, but he also supported vouchers for private, religious schools. He reasoned that it was preferable for funds to be spent supporting schools where students were learning, as opposed to those which failed to educate children.

Early in his presidency, Bush proposed No Child Left Behind (NCLB), which was enacted in 2001 with bipartisan support in Congress. This law was an amendment to ESEA and significantly increased the role of the federal government in education policy, including school choice. NCLB required states and school districts to provide report cards containing information about the quality of schools. The law also stipulated that students enrolled in schools that needed improvement were required to be given information about public-school choice options.

The 2004 platform stated that "choice creates competition and competition puts the focus on equality." The platform was similar to the 2000 platform in supporting an increase in the number of charter schools and expanding ESAs for use from kindergarten through college. During his second term, Bush proposed additional funding for the Charter Schools Program (CSP) and for magnet schools. While campaigning in 2004, he touted the successes of NCLB and stated that school choice was helping to improve educational quality.

In 2008, the platform stated that the party supported school choice for all families, particularly those with children "trapped in failing schools." The party stated that charter schools, vouchers or tax credits for religious or nonreligious public schools, or homeschooling would provide those options to families. The Republican nominee, Senator John McCain, proposed doubling federal spending on public charter schools. His views on the breadth of school choice options mirrored those articulated in the platform. In a debate among Republican presidential contenders in 2007, McCain argued that choice and competition were critical to success in American education, which meant charter schools, homeschooling, and vouchers. He also supported using federal money for online programs.

The 2012 Republican platform reiterated much of the language from the 2008 platform but supported an even broader range of options. In addition to charter schools, homeschooling, and vouchers, the platform supported open-enrollment requests, college-lab schools, virtual schools, and career and technical education programs. The party characterized helping students in failing schools as "the greatest civil rights challenge of our time." Republican nominee, former Massachusetts governor Mitt Romney, avoided using the term "voucher" on the campaign trail and in the presidential debates. He did, however, state that he would initiate an overhaul of the federal government's education system and provide $25 billion for school choice. He argued that choice would "introduce marketplace dynamics into education to drive academic gains" (Trip 2012).

In 2016, the platform supported more options for school choice. These included: homeschooling, career, technical education, private or parochial schools, magnet schools, charter schools, online learning, and early-college high schools. The platform emphasized support for education savings accounts, vouchers, and tuition tax credits. Unlike other platforms, the 2016 platform was specific regarding funding these programs: namely, through Title I funds for low-income students and through the Individuals with Disabilities Act for special needs children. The money for those programs would go to the parents instead of the schools.

While campaigning for president in 2016, Republican nominee Donald Trump proposed a $20 billion school choice program. According to a report in the *New York Times* published just after the 2016 election, education policy experts were "struggling to read the tea leaves" in terms of predicting Trump's education policy because few specifics were offered during the campaign (Saul 2016). The report cited conservative education policy expert Frederick Hess, director of education policy studies for the American Enterprise Institute, as stating that "'[t]he fundamental issue is that nobody really knows what the Trump administration is about' on education." Hess stated that Trump "should be taken seriously" because he wanted to reduce college costs and improve education. However, he also noted that the $20 billion proposal for school choice "came out of nowhere." The confusion was exacerbated because Trump himself offered only general statements such as being "the nation's biggest cheerleader for school choice" and suggesting that the Department of Education should be eliminated (Saul 2016).

As president, Trump appointed Betsy DeVos as secretary of education. In a statement announcing her nomination, Trump said, "Under her leadership we will reform the U.S. education system so that we can deliver world-class education and school choice to all families" (*Roll Call* 2016). Her nomination was controversial because neither she nor her children had attended public school and she was the first education secretary with no experience in public education. She was also a billionaire who was a significant donor to the Republican Party. According to the NEA, "In Michigan, DeVos fought for tax cuts for the wealthy at the expense of public schools, for vouchers that divert taxpayer funds from public schools to private schools, and to allow for-profit charter school corporations to operate with no accountability while being funded by taxpayers" (Rosales 2017).

During her term as secretary, DeVos proposed Education Freedom Scholarships to expand school choice. The scholarships would be funded by private donors who would receive a dollar-for-dollar tax credit. She claimed that the scholarships would not take money from public schools, but an analysis in the *Washington Post* found that while her statement was technically correct, it would cost taxpayers $5 billion in lost tax revenue (Rizzo 2019). Her plan was not considered by Congress, but in 2020 she supported a similar plan, the School Choice Now Act, which would provide direct federal aid to private-school scholarships during the COVID-19 pandemic and would create up to $5 billion in permanent tax credits for organizations that sponsored scholarship programs (Ujifusa 2020). This proposal also failed to gain the necessary political support for passage.

Trump Says School Choice Is a Civil Rights Issue

In his remarks at the Rose Garden for an executive order on police reform, President Donald Trump suggested that his administration was open to working with Congress to enhance opportunities for Americans in other areas of public policy, including school choice.

> . . . We're fighting for school choice, which really is the civil rights of all time in this country. Frankly, school choice is the civil rights statement of the year, of the decade, and probably beyond—because all children have to have access to quality education. A child's zip code in America should never determine their future, and that's what was happening. So we're very, very strong on school choice, and I hope everybody remembers that. And it's happening. It's already happened, but it's happening. We have tremendous opposition from people that know they shouldn't be opposing it. School choice.
>
> All children deserve equal opportunity because we are all made equal by God. So true . . .

Source

"Remarks by President Trump at Signing of an Executive Order on Safe Policing for Safe Communities—the White House." 2020. The White House, June 16. Accessed January 2, 2023. https://trumpwhitehouse.archives.gov/briefings-statements/remarks-president-trump -signing-executive-order-safe-policing-safe-communities/.

DeVos was also a spokesperson for conservative education ideas and policies during her years in the Trump administration, such as at an October 2020 speech at Hillsdale College: "America's parents agree [with Republicans]. There's a mighty chorus, rising in volume and urgency, supporting parental 'school choice.' . . . At the end of the day, we want parents to have the freedom, the choices, and the funds to make the best decisions for their children. The 'Washington knows best' crowd really loses their minds over that. They seem to think that the people's money doesn't belong to the people. That it instead belongs to 'the public,' or rather, what they really mean—government" (DeVos 2020).

Democrats

The 1992 platform supported public-school choice with "protection against discrimination." The party opposed what it characterized as "the Bush administration's efforts to bankrupt the public school system—the bedrock of democracy—through private school vouchers." Likewise, the Democratic nominee, Arkansas governor Bill Clinton, opposed vouchers because of their effect on public schools. In 1994, Clinton, with the support of a Democratic Congress, amended the ESEA to create the CSP. This program provides federal money to create new charter schools and to provide information to parents about successful charter schools.

The 1996 platform proposed to expand the CSP and also pledged to promote public charter schools that were held to the highest standards of accountability and access. Clinton continued to oppose vouchers and vetoed a law during his second term that would have provided $3,200 vouchers for children in the District of Columbia to attend private schools, including religious schools.

The 2000 Democratic platform proposed to triple the number of charter schools in the United States and ensure that those schools were held accountable to students and communities. The platform repeated the party's opposition to vouchers. The Democratic nominee Vice President Al Gore's first policy speech of his presidential campaign dealt with education reform. Gore favored increasing the role of the federal government in education policy in several areas such as universal pre-school. He also favored increasing the ability of parents to choose a public school for their children. He proposed what he called "full public school choice," which entailed tripling the number of public charter schools. Gore characterized vouchers as "fool's gold" because they would siphon money from public schools and not fully cover the cost of private-school tuition (Finn 2000).

In 2004, most of the campaign was devoted to terrorism and security issues. Nevertheless, the platforms and the candidates addressed education because it was important to a significant number of voters. As in previous platforms, the party explicitly stated its opposition to vouchers for private school and its support for public-school choice, including charter schools and magnet schools. Senator John Kerry, the Democratic nominee, was also opposed to private-school vouchers.

The 2008 platform contained a brief statement supporting those public charter schools that are accountable. The Democratic nominee, Senator Barack Obama, opposed school vouchers. He supported doubling the funding for CSP for additional charter schools in high-need school districts. The funding would only be available to states that improved the accountability of charter schools. Obama also proposed an Innovative Schools Fund to provide funding to states and school districts to create a "portfolio" of successful types of public schools. The fund would supplement state and local funding to enhance school choice among these schools. During the Obama administration, the ESEA's 2010 reauthorization focused support on three models of public-school choice: (1) supporting effective charter schools, (2) promoting public-school choice, and (3) continuing the Magnet Schools Assistance Program.

The 2012 platform emphasized strengthening all schools and expanding public-school options for low-income students, along with a pledge to "promote public charter schools that are accountable." President Barack Obama emphasized, as he had in 2008, that he was opposed to vouchers for private schools. Jason Bedrick, writing in the *National Review*, was critical of Obama's stance on vouchers. He pointed out that the NEA and the American Federation of Teachers were among the top donors to the Democratic Party and argued that Obama was putting the interests of public-school teachers' unions above the needs of low-income minority students with his opposition to vouchers. Bedrick (2016) stated that "[t] he primary beneficiaries of school choice policies are key Democratic constituents: low income minorities."

Critics leveled similar criticisms at 2016 nominee, former secretary of state Hillary Clinton. Larry Sand, also writing in the *National Review*, credited Obama with occasionally opposing teachers' unions but labeled Clinton an "unabashed unionista." He criticized Clinton's changing views on public education, including school choice. Sand pointed out that First Lady Clinton had argued that teachers should be held accountable for their work and that she supported charter schools because she believed parents deserved the opportunity to choose their children's school (Sand 2016). The 2016 platform supported high-quality public charter schools and emphasized that those schools should not replace or destabilize traditional public schools. The party also supported increased transparency and accountability for all charter schools. This platform differed from previous platforms by stating that Democrats "oppose for-profit charter schools" because those schools allow the companies that run them to profit from public resources.

During the 2020 campaign, Democrats expressed more skepticism about charter schools. As the 2020 Democratic presidential nominee, Joe Biden stated that he was "not a charter school fan" and pledged to eliminate federal funding for the for-profit charter schools, which receive 12 percent of CSP funds (Green 2022). As president, Biden came under fire from charter school proponents after the Department of Education implemented new rules for CSP in 2022. While the rules did not prohibit funding for for-profit charter schools, they imposed regulations making it more difficult for them to receive funds. The new regulations also required greater transparency and accountability for schools receiving funds (Strauss 2022). The most controversial rule requires a needs analysis to be part of a CSP application. This analysis must include evidence that the community wants the school and an estimate of student enrollment, including a rationale for how the applicant reached that number. The needs analysis must also provide information about student demographics, including the effect of the school on racial and socioeconomic diversity within the school district, and an assurance that the school would not negatively affect a district's desegregation efforts. Applicants must show that the school does not increase racial segregation; however, this provision does not require schools in racially isolated communities to be diverse (Strauss 2022).

The Network for Public Education, which opposes charter schools, applauded the rules calling them "thoughtful and well-reasoned regulations" (Green 2022). In 2019, the organization released several reports documenting the waste of hundreds of millions of taxpayer dollars directed to charter schools that either never opened or closed (Strauss 2022). School choice advocates criticized Biden's stance on charter schools and the Education Department's new rules for pandering to teachers' unions, which donated over $40 million to Democratic campaigns in the 2020 election cycle (Jacques 2022). The National Alliance for Public Charter

Joe Biden Insists that Charter Schools Must Be Held Accountable

During an interview with the National Education Association during the 2020 presidential campaign, Democratic nominee Joe Biden was asked how he felt about charter schools. This is an excerpt of his response to that question.

I will not, there will be no federal dollars. I'm not Betsy DeVos, nor will my Secretary of Education be anything like her in terms of her attitudes about public schools. No privately funded charter school will receive or private charter school receive a penny of federal money—none.

And any charter school that, in fact, is worthy of being able to be in education would have to be accountable to the same exact school boards, the same exact mechanisms that the public school is accountable to across the board. There has to be transparency.

Now a lot of these charter schools are significantly underperforming, significantly. I can see where you can have a school, for example, a specialty school in the arts or for music. But if you're going to have a charter school, it cannot come at the expense of the public school.

We have to fully fund them. And any charter school that qualifies as essentially a chartered public school has to be accountable to the same standards, the same requirements, the same transparency as the public schools in that district are accountable to, meaning the Board of Education or whatever the mechanism and the controls of that school board.

Source
"Joe Biden on Charter Schools—the NEA Interview." n.d. YouTube. Accessed January 2, 2023. https://www.youtube.com/watch?v=Pd_JTCVsMtk&t=53s.

Schools, which supports charter schools, criticized the rules claiming that they would "dampen interest in applying for federal funds to launch new schools" and "damage individuals who don't have resources" (Green 2022).

Further Reading

Bedrick, Jason. 2016. "Obama's War on School Choice." *National Review*, January 29. Accessed September 12, 2019. https://www.nationalreview.com/2016/01/barack-obama -school-choice-war/.

Bush, George H. W. 1992. "Remarks at a Roundtable Discussion on Education Reform." Public Papers George Bush Library and Museum, June 25. Accessed September 12, 2019. https://bush41library.tamu.edu/archives/public-papers/4487.

Cavanaugh, Sean. 2004. "Reagan's Legacy: A Nation at Risk, Boost for Choice." *Education Week*, June 16. Accessed September 17, 2019. https://www.edweek.org/policy-politics /reagans-legacy-a-nation-at-risk-boost-for-choice/2004/06.

Christian Coalition. 1995. *Contract with the American Family*. New York: Ballantine Books.

Cunningham, Josh. 2016. "School Choice: Vouchers." National Conference of State Legislatures, December 1. Accessed September 12, 2019. https://www.ncsl.org/research/education/school-choice-vouchers.aspx.

Democratic Party Platform. 1992–2020. American Presidency Project. Accessed November 22, 2022. https://www.presidency.ucsb.edu/documents/presidential-documents-archive-guidebook/party-platforms-and-nominating-conventions-3.

DeVos, Betsy. 2020. "Prepared Remarks, Hillsdale College." EIN News, October 20. Accessed November 22, 2022. https://www.einnews.com/pr_news/528803131/prepared-remarks-by-secretary-devos-at-hillsdale-college.

Emerson, Adam. 2012. "What the Democratic Party Platform Used to Say About School Choice." Fordham Institute, September 7. Accessed September 12, 2019. https://fordhaminstitute.org/ohio/commentary/what-democratic-party-platform-used-say-about-school-choice.

Emma, Caitlin. "Trump Unveils $20B School Choice Proposal." *Politico*, September 8. Accessed September 12, 2019. https://www.politico.com/story/2016/09/donald-trump-school-choice-proposal-227915.

Finn, Chester E., Jr. 2000. "What the Candidates Say—The Politics of School Choice. The Battle Over School Choice. Frontline." PBS. Accessed July 16, 2019. https://www.pbs.org/wgbh/pages/frontline/shows/vouchers/theguys/candidates.html.

Friedman, Milton, and Rose Friedman. 1980. *Free to Choose: A Personal Statement*. New York: Harcourt.

Green, Erica L. 2022. "New Biden Administration Rules for Charter Schools Spur Bipartisan Backlash." *New York Times*, May 13. Accessed August 23, 2022. https://www.nytimes.com/2022/05/13/us/politics/charter-school-rules-biden.html.

Greene, Peter. 2020. "Where Is Joe Biden on Public Education?" *Forbes*, September 12. Accessed December 11, 2020. https://www.forbes.com/sites/petergreene/2020/09/12/where-is-joe-biden-on-public-education/?sh=1c5e95b62f9b.

Jacques, Ingrid. 2022. "Teachers Unions May Love Biden's Attack on Charter Schools, but Parents Won't Be Happy." *USA Today*, August 16. Accessed December 15, 2022. https://www.usatoday.com/story/opinion/columnist/2022/08/16/biden-charter-schools-out-step-parents-want/10330628002/?gnt-cfr=1.

Morgan, Dan. 1980. "Reagan, Opponents Differ Sharply on Educational Policy." *Washington Post*, September 12. Accessed November 22, 2022. https://search.proquest.com/historical-newspapers/reagan-opponents-differ-sharply-on-educational/docview/147138075/se-2?accountid=189667.

Nagourney, Adam. 1996. "Dole Backs School Choice Through Vouchers." *New York Times*, July 19. Accessed September 9, 2019. https://www.nytimes.com/1996/07/19/us/dole-backs-school-choice-through-vouchers.html.

Republican Party Platform. 1992–2016. American Presidency Project. Accessed November 22, 2022. https://www.presidency.ucsb.edu/documents/presidential-documents-archive-guidebook/party-platforms-and-nominating-conventions-3.

Reuters. 1996. "A Transcript of the First Televised Debate Between Clinton and Dole." October 7. Accessed September 9, 2019. https://www.nytimes.com/1996/10/07/us/a-transcript-of-the-first-televised-debate-between-clinton-and-dole.html.

Rizzo, Salvador. 2019. "Analysis. Betsy DeVos' Claim about Public Funding for 'Education Freedom Scholarships.'" *Washington Post*, April 8. Accessed November 23, 2020. https://

www.washingtonpost.com/politics/2019/04/08/betsy-devoss-claim-about-public
-funding-education-freedom-scholarships/.

Roll Call Staff. 2016. "Betsy DeVos Tapped for Education Secretary." *Roll Call*, November 23. Accessed November 30, 2020. https://www.rollcall.com/2016/11/23/betsy -devos-tapped-for-education-secretary/.

Rosales, John. 2017. "Betsy DeVos: Dangerous for Students and the Promise of Public Education." *NEA Today*, January 11. Accessed December 1, 2020. https://www.nea.org /advocating-for-change/new-from-nea/betsy-devos-dangerous-students-and-promise -public-education.

Sand, Larry. 2016. "The Unionista." *National Review*, October 24. Accessed September 18, 2019. https://www.nationalreview.com/magazine/2016/10/24/hillary-clinton -education-school-choice-policy-unions/.

Saul, Stephanie. 2016. "Where Donald Trump Stands on School Choice, Student Debt and Common Core." *New York Times*, November 21. Accessed September 10, 2019. https://www.nytimes.com/2016/11/21/us/where-trump-stands-on-school-choice -student-debt-and-common-core.html.

Strauss, Valerie. 2022. "What the Biden Administration's New Rules for Charter Schools Say." *Washington Post*, July 5. Accessed August 23, 2022. https://www.washingtonpost .com/education/2022/07/05/new-rules-us-charter-school-program/.

Trip, Gabriel. 2012. "Vouchers Unspoken, Romney Hails School Choice." *New York Times*, June 11. Accessed September 9, 2019. https://www.nytimes.com/2012/06/12/us /politics/in-romneys-voucher-education-policy-a-return-to-gop-roots.html.

Ujifusa, Andrew. 2020. "GOP Senators Push Big Private School Choice Bill Amid Pandemic Relief Debate." *Education Week*, July 22. Accessed November 23, 2020. https://www .edweek.org/education/gop-senators-push-big-private-school-choice-bill-amid -pandemic-relief-debate/2020/07.

Waggoner, Kristen. 1996. "The Milwaukee Parental Choice Program: The First Voucher System to Include Religious Schools." *Regent University Law Review*. Accessed October 1, 2019. https://www.regent.edu/acad/schlaw/student_life/studentorgs/lawreview /docs/issues/v7/7RegentULRev165.pdf#:~:text=Legislators%20have%20debated%20 the%20adoption%20of%20a%20voucher,%22civil%20rights%20movement%20 of%20the%201990s.%22%209%20Additionally.

Wexler, Natalie. 2018. "Six Reasons Why School Choice Won't Save Us." *Forbes*, April 29. Accessed October 1, 2019. https://www.forbes.com/sites/nataliewexler/2018/04/29 /six-reasons-why-school-choice-wont-save-us/?sh=5d713e01142e.

Wong, Alia. 2018. "Public Opinion Shifts in Favor of School Choice." *The Atlantic*, August 21. Accessed September 9, 2019. https://www.theatlantic.com/education /archive/2018/08/school-choice-gaining-popularity/568063.

Voting Rights

At a Glance

The right to vote is a fundamental right protected by the U.S. Constitution. Throughout American history various groups have fought to exercise this right. Election administration and voting qualifications are regulated by both the federal government and the state governments. While both political parties support voting rights in principle, they differ on several key issues, including the reinstatement of provisions in the Voting Rights Act of 1965, the implementation of voter identification laws, the restoration of felon voting rights, and expanding voting rights to Washington, DC, residents.

According to many Democrats . . .

- The Voting Rights Act should be restored to protect voting rights as it did prior to the U.S. Supreme Court's ruling in *Shelby County v. Holder* (2013).
- Strict voter ID laws suppress turnout among lower-income and minority voters.
- Felons' voting rights should be restored to help them rejoin society after incarceration.
- DC residents should have Congressional representation.

According to many Republicans . . .

- The Voting Rights Act has been reauthorized and prevents racial discrimination in voting.
- Voter ID laws are necessary to prevent voter fraud.
- Felons' voting rights should be restored only after they have been reintegrated into society.
- DC residents should only have Congressional representation through a constitutional amendment.

———————

Overview

The right to vote is among the most important civil rights in the United States because voting allows citizens to hold government officials accountable for their actions. The U.S. Constitution allows the federal government and the states to regulate voter qualifications and election administration. In early American history, states only allowed white, male property owners to vote. In the early 1800s, states began to eliminate the property-owning requirement. After the Civil War, voting rights were extended to Black men in the Fifteenth Amendment (1870) and to women in the Nineteenth Amendment (1920).

Despite the Fifteenth Amendment's guarantee, many states prevented Blacks from voting by employing tactics such as white primaries, racial gerrymandering, grandfather clauses, literacy tests, and poll taxes. White primaries were primary elections in the South in which only whites could vote. The Democratic Party limited party membership to whites and allowed only party members to vote in the primaries; thus, Blacks were disqualified from voting in primary elections. Given the dominance of the Democratic Party in the South, elections were often decided in the primaries since Republican candidates seldom bothered to run. Racial gerrymandering is a practice in which district lines are drawn to minimize the impact of the Black vote. In Tuskegee, Alabama, for example, Black residents outnumbered white residents by a 4 to 1 margin. When the Alabama legislature redrew the city's district lines into a twenty-eight-sided figure, only a handful of Blacks remained in the district. Grandfather clauses, enacted in six states, allowed individuals to vote if their ancestor had voted. If an individual's ancestors had voted, they were exempt from the literacy test. Literacy tests required individuals to prove that they could read before they could register to vote or to vote. Poll taxes made voting contingent upon the payment of a fee. The U.S. Supreme Court invalidated white primaries in *Smith v. Allwright* (1944), blatant racial gerrymandering in *Gomillion v. Lightfoot* (1960), grandfather clauses in *Guinn v. United States* (1915), but poll taxes and literacy tests were legal until the 1960s. Blacks also faced significant intimidation and violence when attempting to register to vote.

The Franchise and the Civil Rights Movement

Dr. Martin Luther King, Jr. organized the 1965 Selma March to draw national attention to racially discriminatory barriers to minorities in America at the ballot box and numerous other areas of American law and culture. After white Southern law enforcement officials brutalized the peaceful marchers, Democratic president Lyndon B. Johnson urged Congress to pass a federal voting rights bill to guarantee the same voting rights for Americans of color as for white Americans. Section 2 of the Fifteenth Amendment allows Congress to enforce the amendment through "appropriate legislation." The Voting Rights Act (VRA) of 1965 was a landmark law providing federal oversight of state voting systems to prevent state laws and election officials from discriminating against Black voters. To secure the bill's passage, the Johnson administration agreed to make several of the provisions temporary, unless Congress acted to reauthorize them. One of the key provisions of the law, Section 5, was controversial because it required states or jurisdictions within a state that had a history of racial discrimination in voting, as determined by a formula outlined in Section 4 of the law, to obtain preclearance from the Justice Department to make any changes to its electoral system. This provision prevented further discrimination by these jurisdictions, but critics suggested that it constituted an overreach of federal power. The Supreme Court upheld the law against such a challenge in *South Carolina v. Katzenbach* (1966). The law also banned literacy tests in certain jurisdictions.

Congress has reauthorized or amended the VRA on several occasions; Republican presidents have signed all four reauthorizations. The most recent reauthorization occurred in 2006 when Congress voted to extend the VRA for twenty-five years. The Fannie Lou Hamer, Rosa Parks, and Coretta Scott King Voting Rights Act Reauthorization and Amendments Act of 2006 passed by a vote of 98-0 in the Senate, 390-33 in the House of Representatives, and was signed into law by President George W. Bush.

In *Shelby County v. Holder*, the U.S. Supreme Court held in a 5-4 ruling that Section 4 of the VRA was unconstitutional. Section 4 applied to certain parts of the country known as "covered jurisdictions." These jurisdictions had a history of racial discrimination in their electoral systems and met the conditions of a formula designed to determine the extent to which the minority vote was underrepresented. Section 5 of the VRA required those jurisdictions to have changes in their voting system approved by the Justice Department prior to their implementation. The Court invalidated Section 4 because the components of the coverage formula had not been updated since the law's enactment. According to Chief Justice John Roberts, the VRA was "a drastic departure from basic principles of federalism." He argued that significant progress had been made in eliminating voting discrimination in the fifty years since the law's enactment. Because the coverage formula had not been updated to reflect these changes, it was unconstitutional. He stated that "Congress may draft another formula based on current conditions." The dissenting justices argued that because Congress had overwhelmingly voted to reauthorize the law, it also reauthorized Section 4's continuation. They also suggested that the Court's ruling would allow states to implement more restrictions on voting rights. Democrats strongly objected to this ruling, arguing it would increase voting restrictions and voter suppression. A 2019 report from the Democrat-led House Administration Subcommittee on Elections charged that "[t]he fundamental right to vote is under attack. The Court's decision in *Shelby County* has served to accelerate the process, giving a green light to historically discriminatory jurisdictions to implement laws once put on hold because they could not clear federal administrative review. Some may seem innocuous on their face, but these laws have a disparate impact on minority voters" ("House Democrats Restore the Vote with H.R. 4, the Voting Rights Advancement Act" 2019). More specifically, the report documented an increase in voter suppression efforts in conservative-controlled states and localities, including implementing voter ID laws, cutting the period for early voting, eliminating same-day voter registration, and increasing restrictions for college students and previously incarcerated individuals. Democrats have introduced legislation to restore the VRA, while Republicans have opposed these efforts.

The VRA is not the only federal law dealing with voting rights. In 1993, the National Voter Registration Act (commonly known as the Motor-Voter law) was enacted to facilitate voter registration by requiring states to allow individuals to register to vote at driver's license centers, through a mail-in form, and at public assistance offices and offices that provide services to disabled individuals. The law also sets requirements for how states manage voter registration lists for federal elections. Most Congressional Republicans voted against the law. Of the Republican House members, only 21 of 167 supported the measure, while in the Senate, only 3 of 40 Republicans voted for the law. Democrat Bill Clinton signed the bill in 1993, and it went into effect in 1995.

The controversy surrounding the 2000 presidential election highlighted serious problems with election administration and resulted in additional federal legislation related to voting. After a series of recounts and two U.S. Supreme Court decisions, George W. Bush was declared the winner of Florida's electoral votes and the 2000 presidential election. Florida's electoral system was heavily scrutinized because the outcome was decided by 537 votes. Among the key concerns was a purge of eligible minority voters from voter rolls prior to the election and antiquated voting machines that made it difficult to determine the candidate for which an individual voted. To address these and other issues, the National Commission on Federal Election Reform, a bipartisan commission with former U.S. presidents Gerald Ford (R) and Jimmy Carter (D) as honorary cochairs, released a report in January 2002 which advocated several reforms to ensure the integrity of elections. These included allowing voters to cast a provisional ballot until their status as a registered voter could be confirmed, an election day holiday, regulations that simplified absentee voting, restoring voting rights to felons after they completed their parole or probation, statewide voter registration to allow individuals to vote anywhere within the state in which they reside, federal standards for voting equipment, and federal assistance for election administration.

Congress implemented some of these reforms in the Help America Vote Act of 2002, which was enacted with bipartisan support. The law provided federal funding to replace outdated voting equipment, allowed for provisional ballots to be cast by voters whose registration was disputed, and required first-time new registrants to provide the last four digits of their social security number or their driver's license number on their voter registration application to verify their identity. The latter provision was noted by the U.S. Supreme Court in a case involving the constitutionality of an Indiana voter identification law. In *Crawford v. Marion County Election Board* (2009) the Court upheld the voter ID law, which required voters to present a state-issued photo identification prior to voting in an election. In its 6-3 ruling, the Court asserted that in the Help America Vote Act, Congress believed photo identification was an appropriate means of establishing an individual's qualifications to vote. The Court also held that even though there was no evidence of in-person voter fraud, the state had an interest in preserving the integrity of elections.

In 2020, thirty-six states had some type of voter ID law. States with strict voter ID laws require voters to present a government-issued photo ID, while non-strict state laws require documentation of residency, such as a bank statement or utility bill. Republicans have supported strict voter ID laws in recent party platforms and in Congressional bills arguing that they prevent voter fraud. Democrats have opposed strict voter ID laws because they disadvantage minority and lower-income voters who are less likely to have the appropriate ID. A 2018 Pew Research Center poll found that 76 percent of Americans favored government-issued photo IDs for voting. The poll also indicated 65 percent of respondents support making election day national holiday, and 69 percent support allowing convicted felons to vote after they served their sentence. In a 2020 poll, mail-in voting was supported by 69 percent of Americans. During the COVID-19 pandemic, many states expanded mail-in voting for the 2020 presidential election. Republicans, including President Donald Trump, were opposed to such measures, arguing that such changes would make it easier to engage in fraudulent voting. Democrats, however, supported those initiatives arguing that appropriate procedural safeguards could guarantee voting rights and protect public health.

During the September 29, 2020, presidential debate, moderator Chris Wallace asked Trump whether he would accept the results of the presidential election. Trump cited mail-in voting as a reason that there would be "fraud like you've never seen." Fraudulent mail-in voting was part of a lie perpetuated by Trump and his Republican supporters that Democrats had stolen the 2020 election through widespread voter fraud. Trump had sown doubt about accepting the election results throughout the presidential campaign. His supporters attempted to "Stop the Steal" in a January 6, 2021, insurrection in which six people were killed after Trump supporters stormed the U.S. Capitol at the president's urging. The violent mob intended to stop Congress from officially counting electoral votes but failed when Congressional leadership reconvened both chambers after law enforcement dispersed the Trump supporters. Congress certified the results, with Joe Biden winning 306 electoral votes to President Trump's 232. Numerous courts and investigations have been conducted concerning the 2020 election, and none have found any evidence of widespread voter fraud.

Voting Rights for DC Citizens

Enfranchising citizens residing in the District of Columbia has been debated throughout American history. DC residents pay federal taxes and are subject to Congressional control but lack Congressional representation. Many view this as a civil rights issue because the city's population has been comprised of a Black majority since the mid-1950s. Congress has considered extending voting rights to DC residents on several occasions. In 1960, Congress approved the Twenty-Third Amendment, which provides the District with three electoral votes in presidential elections. In 1978, Congress approved another constitutional amendment, the District of Columbia Voting Rights Amendment, which would have allowed the District to be treated as though it were a state; however, only sixteen states ratified the amendment falling well short of the thirty-eight required for ratification. A 2007 bill giving the District a single seat in the House of Representatives, along with a new seat for Utah, which argued that undercounting during the 2000 census cost it a House seat, passed the House with broad bipartisan support. A majority of senators also supported the bill; however, the Republican leadership prevented a floor vote claiming that it was unconstitutional. In 2020, Democratic House Speaker Nancy Pelosi proposed a bill to make the District of Columbia the fifty-first state, which would enfranchise the city's seven hundred thousand residents. President Trump and Senate Republicans opposed the bill.

Democrats

During the Civil Rights Movement in the 1960s, President Lyndon Johnson supported voting rights despite the opposition of Southern Democrats. After *Shelby County v. Holder*, Democrats have proposed legislation that would fully restore the VRA. The Democratic Party has also supported voting reforms, including opposing strict voter identification laws, restoring the rights of felons to vote, expanding mail-in voting, and extending statehood to the District of Columbia.

Voting Rights Act

After the Selma March in 1965, President Lyndon Johnson pursued a vigorous legislative strategy to protect voting rights for Black Americans. Johnson had successfully worked with Congress to pass the Civil Rights Act of 1964 as a tribute to slain president John F. Kennedy, who had supported a civil rights bill. Dr. Martin Luther King, Jr. led the march in Selma, Alabama, to protest the overt discrimination Black Americans faced when attempting to register to vote and to pressure lawmakers into enacting legislation to protect voting rights. The marchers were attacked by state and local law enforcement officials who used tear gas and billy clubs to stop the march. Bloody Sunday, as this event is known, had a significant effect on public opinion, and President Johnson responded with a Special Message to Congress on the urgent need for voting rights legislation. While Southern Democrats opposed the law and those in the Senate initiated a filibuster to defeat it, the bill passed with bipartisan support in the Senate by a vote of 77-19 (Democrats 47-17, Republicans 302). The House of Representatives approved the bill by a 333-85 vote (Democrats 221-61, Republicans 112-24). President Johnson signed it on August 5, 1965.

The law had a dramatic effect on voter registration. From 1964 to 1966, the percentage of eligible Blacks registered to vote in Mississippi increased from less than 7 percent to almost 53 percent. In Alabama, the registration rate of Blacks increased by over 30 percent. The political impact of the Democratic Party's support for civil rights was also evident in Black support for Democratic presidential candidates. After he signed the Civil Rights Act, Johnson received 94 percent of the Black vote in the 1964 presidential election. He reportedly told aide Bill Moyers that by supporting the Civil Rights Act of 1964, "I think we just delivered the South to the Republican Party for a long time to come." Republican support in the South increased tremendously among white voters, and overall an average of 54 percent of white voters have cast ballots for Republican presidential candidates since 1976, while no Republican presidential candidate has received more than 15 percent of the Black vote since 1968.

Democratic Party platforms have consistently called for vigorous enforcement of the VRA and its amendments. After the Court's 2013 ruling in *Shelby County v. Holder* effectively eliminated the preclearance requirement, Congressional Democrats proposed several bills to restore the VRA, but none have had bipartisan support. In a speech commemorating the fiftieth anniversary of the Selma March on March 5, 2015, President Barack Obama encouraged Congress to restore the law. Obama characterized the right to vote as "the foundation stone of our democracy." He stated that the "Voting Rights Act was one of the crowning achievements of our democracy, the result of Republican and Democratic effort" and that the reauthorizations of the law were enacted with bipartisan support. He noted that "[o]ne hundred Members of Congress have come here today to honor people who were willing to die for the right it protects. If we want to honor this day, let these hundred go back to Washington, and gather four hundred more, and together, pledge to make it their mission to restore the law this year." In 2016, the Democratic Party platform pledged to "rectify the Supreme Court decision gutting the Voting Rights Act, which is a profound injustice." In 2019, the new Democratic majority in the House of Representatives passed the For the People Act, which included a provision to restore Section 5 of the VRA along with other election reforms. Democrats argue that a strong federal role is necessary to protect voting rights from Republican governors and state legislatures who are implementing regulations, such as strict voter ID laws, that disproportionately affect low-income, older, and Black voters—regulations that would have been blocked by the VRA's preclearance requirement. Republican senate majority leader Mitch McConnell refused to allow the Senate to consider the bill. In 2021, the Democratic House passed the John Lewis Voting Rights Advancement Act by a vote of 219-212. This law, named for

Speaker Pelosi Addresses Republican Opposition to John R. Lewis Voting Rights Advancement Act

Democratic House Speaker Nancy Pelosi issued a statement condemning Senate Republicans for blocking a vote on the John R. Lewis Voting Rights Amendment Act. Pelosi argued that they were blocking the vote for political gain.

Today, Senate Republicans again undermined the sacred right to vote and harmed their own constituents when they blocked the John R. Lewis Voting Rights Advancement Act. Right now, our nation faces the most sinister and severe campaign of voter suppression since Jim Crow. . . . While Republicans in Congress shamefully abandon their oath to defend our democracy and greenlight this brazen assault for their own political gain, Democrats are fighting back. Our House-passed Voting Rights Advancement Act empowered the Justice Department to block voting restrictions imposed by states with dark histories of discrimination so every voter has fair access to the ballot box – a cause to which our beloved John Lewis courageously devoted his entire life. Proudly, the people are with us: on an overwhelming and bipartisan basis, Americans support the passage of this urgent, essential legislation.

Source

"Pelosi Statement on Republican Obstruction of John R. Lewis Voting Rights Advancement Act." 2021. Congresswoman Nancy Pelosi, November 3. Accessed December 21, 2022. https://pelosi.house.gov/news/press-releases/pelosi-statement-on-republican-obstruction-of-john-r-lewis-voting-rights.

civil rights icon John Lewis, also sought to restore the preclearance requirement by creating a new coverage formula. The bill did not have the support of 60 Senators, which made it vulnerable to a filibuster by Republicans, and was not voted on by the Senate.

In 2015, the editors of the *National Review* argued that Democrats were wrong to restore the preclearance requirement because the law still prohibits states from enacting "racially discriminatory election laws." The editors argue that the VRA was successful in eliminating the types of discrimination it was intended to eliminate and that the preclearance requirement infringes on the ability of the states to administer elections. Indeed, "[t]he end of the preclearance regime is in harmony with the progress we have made. . . . Republicans are empowered to do nothing in this matter, and to see to it that nothing is done. The VRA is fine as it is" (Editorial Board 2015).

Voting Reforms

Democrats have supported legislation dealing with various types of voting reforms. Congressional Democrats have introduced bills to prevent states from implementing voter ID laws. In 2008, the Democratic platform stated, "We will vigorously enforce our voting rights laws instead of making them tools of partisan political agendas; we oppose laws that require identification in order to vote or register to vote, which create discriminatory barriers to the right to vote and disenfranchise many eligible voters." In 2012, the platform touted the role of the Justice Department in preventing "states from implementing voter identifications laws that would be harmful to minority voters." The 2016 Democratic platform pledged that the party would "continue to fight against discriminatory voter identification laws, which disproportionately burden young voters, diverse communities, people of color, low-income families, people with disabilities, the elderly, and women."

The 2020 Democratic platform used even stronger language in defending voting rights and warning that Republican efforts to "eliminate voter fraud" were transparent and deeply undemocratic attempts to hinder Democratic-leaning demographic groups from voting:

> Democrats are committed to the sacred principle of "one person, one vote"—and we will fight to achieve that principle for every citizen, regardless of race, income, disability status, geography, or English language proficiency. We stand united against the determined Republican campaign to disenfranchise voters through onerous voter ID laws, unconstitutional and excessive purges of the voter rolls, and closures of polling places in low-income neighborhoods, on college campuses, and in communities of color. Americans should never have to wait in hours-long lines to exercise their voting rights.
>
> Democrats will strengthen our democracy by guaranteeing that every American's vote is protected. We will make it a priority to pass legislation that restores and strengthens the Voting Rights Act, and ensure the Department of Justice challenges state laws that make it harder for Americans to vote. We will make voting easier and more accessible for all Americans by supporting automatic voter registration, same-day voter registration, early voting, and universal vote-from-home and vote-by-mail options. (Democratic Party Platform 2020)

Felon disenfranchisement statutes were enacted at the same time as poll taxes, literacy tests, and grandfather clauses to limit Black voting rights. An estimated six million Americans are denied the right to vote because of a felony conviction, including 13 percent of Black men. In a 2014 speech at the Georgetown University Law Center, Democratic attorney general Eric Holder noted that "although well over a century has passed since post-Reconstruction states used these measures to strip African Americans of their most fundamental rights, the impact of felon disenfranchisement on modern communities of color remains both disproportionate and unacceptable." Holder argued that permanently excluding convicted felons from civic life does not advance any objective of the criminal justice system. The laws have the opposite effect by severing "a formerly incarcerated person's most direct link to civic participation," which causes "further alienation and disillusionment" (Apuzzo 2014). Democrats have proposed federal legislation to restore voting rights to felons in the Count Every Vote Act in 2005 and in the For the People Act in 2019.

Democrats supported mail-in voting before it became an issue during the COVID-19 pandemic. The party first advocated for mail-in voting in its 1988 platform and reiterated its support in 2016. Democratic senators Ron Wyden and Amy Klobuchar introduced legislation to expand mail-in voting and early voting for the 2020 presidential election. In an op-ed in the *New York Times*, Klobuchar stated, "In a democracy, no one should be forced to choose between health and the right to vote." The bill would require every state to allow its citizens to vote by mail more easily. She noted that five states vote almost entirely by mail, while sixteen require voters to provide an excuse to obtain an absentee ballot and six require more than one witness, or a notary, to validate a mail-in ballot. The bill would also require states to have a minimum of twenty days of early voting. She concluded that "if you want to know what it's like to vote in a healthy, safe and secure way—from the comfort of your own home—just ask President Trump. He's been doing it for years" (Klobuchar 2020).

Democrats have included statements supporting statehood or voting rights for the District of Columbia since the 1940 platform. In the 1960 Democratic Party platform, for example, there was a statement supporting a constitutional amendment giving DC residents voting representation in Congress. More recent platforms have not specified whether the party favors a constitutional amendment or federal legislation. The 2016 platform stated that "[r]estoring our democracy . . . means finally passing statehood for the District of Columbia, so that the American citizens who reside in the nation's capital have full and equal congressional rights." On June 26, 2020, the House passed H.R. 51, a bill to grant DC statehood along party lines, by a vote of 252-180. Democratic representative Maxine Waters noted that the District's population is larger than that of Wyoming and Vermont. She stated, "Make no mistake, race underlies every argument against D.C. statehood" and "denying its citizens equal participation and representation is a racial, democratic, and economic injustice we cannot tolerate." The proposed legislation, however, failed to overcome a threatened filibuster from Senate Republicans. Critics contend that an amendment is needed to provide DC representation in Congress because the framers of the Constitution intended for the District to be a neutral zone outside the influence of state politics (Lillis and Brufke 2020).

Democrats have supported other voting reforms such as expanding the time period for early voting, an election day holiday, and automatic voter registration. Public opinion polls suggest wide support for these initiatives.

Republicans

The Republican Party was instrumental in securing the passage of the Fifteenth Amendment in 1870. While Blacks initially identified with the party, this allegiance began to shift during President Franklin Roosevelt's administration as his New Deal policies appealed to a broad array of Americans, including Black voters.

When Democratic presidents John F. Kennedy and Lyndon Johnson advocated for civil rights in the 1960s, and the 1964 Republican presidential nominee Barry Goldwater employed states' rights rhetoric in his campaign, Blacks left the Republican Party. Republican presidents have signed all four of the VRA's reauthorizations, which were supported by Congressional Republicans; however, after *Shelby County v. Holder*, Congressional Republicans have opposed Democratic efforts to restore the law. They insist that the VRA still prevents racial discrimination in voting and are opposed to increased federal oversight of elections. Republicans have also emphasized measures to prevent voter fraud, including supporting voter ID laws and opposing mail-in voting. The party has also opposed statehood for the District of Columbia.

Voting Rights Act

Republicans were part of the bipartisan effort to pass the VRA in 1965. Republican senate minority leader Everett Dirksen played a key role in ending the filibuster initiated by Southern Democrats to defeat the bill. Key provisions of the law were set to expire in 1970 during the Nixon administration. Republican president Richard Nixon relied on a "Southern Strategy" to increase his support among white Southerners by implementing policies detrimental to civil rights. He proposed weakening the VRA by eliminating Section 5. The House of Representatives passed Nixon's bill, but after a bipartisan consensus emerged against it, the VRA was reauthorized and strengthened by banning literacy tests in fourteen non-Southern states, limiting state residency requirements for voters to thirty days, and extending the franchise to eighteen-to-twenty- year-olds. The latter provision was invalidated by the U.S. Supreme Court as it applied to state and local elections; Congress then passed the Twenty-Sixth Amendment to lower the voting age nationwide. Nixon contemplated vetoing the legislation but given the civil unrest over the Vietnam War, including the killing of four students by the National Guard at a protest at Kent State University, he signed it to prevent additional conflict.

In 1975, Republican president Gerald Ford also attempted to weaken the VRA to placate white Southerners. In a bipartisan effort, Congress defeated his proposal and expanded the law to prohibit discrimination against language minority citizens (defined as persons who are American Indian, Asian American, Alaskan Natives, or of Spanish heritage) and extended it for seven more years. Prior to the 1982 reauthorization, Republican president Ronald Reagan favored easing the preclearance requirement, much to the dismay of civil rights activists. However, Reagan also endorsed extending the 1975 provisions requiring bilingual ballots in areas where large numbers of citizens did not understand English, despite pleas from some of his advisers to oppose them. Ultimately, Congress extended the VRA for twenty-five years. When he signed the bill, Reagan stated, "[T]he right to vote is the crown jewel of American liberties, and we will not see its luster diminished" ("Text" 1981) and downplayed his previous opposition to parts of the VRA.

In his remarks for the ceremony celebrating the signing of the VRA Reauthorization and Amendments Act of 2006, President George W. Bush stated that "by reauthorizing this act, Congress has reaffirmed its belief that all men are created equal; its belief that the new founding started by the signing of this bill by President Johnson is worthy of our great nation to continue." Bush also pledged that his administration would "vigorously enforce the provisions of this law, and . . . defend it in court." Jesse Rhodes in the *Washington Post*, however, noted that there were fewer new voting rights lawsuits and a decline in Section 5 enforcement during Bush's presidency (Rhodes 2018).

After the ruling in *Shelby County v. Holder*, Republicans, including those in Congress who had voted for the VRA's reauthorization, echoed the essence of Chief

---

Republicans Outline Opposition to John R. Lewis Voting Rights Advancement Act

Fifteen House Republicans penned a letter to House Speaker Nancy Pelosi arguing that the Democratically sponsored bill should not be brought to the House floor for a vote. The coalition, led by Congresswoman Claudia Tenney, characterized the bill as "highly partisan."

Dear Madam Speaker:

We write today to express our strong concern with and opposition to H.R. 4, the John Lewis Voting Rights Advancement Act. We urge you not to bring this bill up for consideration in the House next week. This bill is yet another highly partisan bill. It masquerades as a cure to end racial discrimination, but instead centralizes election control in the federal government, essentially enacting the worst aspects of H.R. 1. At the very least, you should hold an open Committee hearing on this legislation prior to scheduling a vote so the American people's representatives can debate it fairly and subject its dangerous provisions to greater scrutiny . . .

This past March, you pushed through H.R. 1, the so-called "For the People Act," without any Republican involvement or support. In fact, this bill to fundamentally reshape elections in America was not even debated and marked up in its committees of jurisdiction. H.R. 1 is a purely partisan, unconstitutional power grab that would codify some of these worst policies from the 2020 election, while opening the floodgates for almost anyone, including ineligible voters, to be counted in future elections. H.R. 1 would ban common-sense voter ID laws from being enacted, permit convicted non-citizens and felons to vote, give away taxpayer dollars to fund campaigns, and dramatically expand automatic voter registration—a giveaway to political operatives seeking to boost their ballot harvesting operations. Put simply, this bill is a disaster for election integrity.

Source

"Congresswoman Tenney Leads Letter Urging Pelosi to Reject Federal Takeover of Elections." 2021. Representative Claudia Tenney, August 23. Accessed December 21, 2022. https://tenney.house.gov/media/press-releases/congresswoman-tenney-leads-letter-urging-pelosi-reject-federal-takeover.

Justice Roberts's opinion. Republican senate majority leader Mitch McConnell stated that the core of the VRA remained intact after the Court's ruling because "[w]hat was struck down were the provisions that absurdly treated the South differently." He also dismissed Democratic concerns that state voting laws enacted after the ruling disadvantaged minority voters stating that "[t]here are no serious barriers to voting anymore in America" (Troyan and Page 2016). The Brennan Center, a nonpartisan law and policy organization, noted that twenty-four hours after the Court's ruling in *Shelby County v. Holder*, Texas imposed a strict voter ID requirement that the Justice Department had blocked. Two other states, Mississippi and Alabama, began to impose voter ID laws that had previously been blocked by the Justice Department under the VRA.

Voter Fraud

Preventing voter fraud has been a consistent theme in Republican Party platforms and in statements from Congressional Republicans since 2008. Republicans have supported voter ID laws to prevent voter fraud. The party first addressed the issue in its 2008 platform stating that "[p]reventing voting fraud is a civil rights issue." In 2012, the platform characterized voter fraud as "political poison" and "applaud[ed] legislation to require photo identification for voting" along with requiring proof of citizenship because when "a fraudulent vote is cast, it effectively cancels out the vote of a legitimate voter." The 2016 platform contained similar language but also opposed litigation against states that enacted such measures. Public opinion polls show widespread support for voter ID laws, including 91 percent of Republicans (Bialik 2018). Critics note that in-person voter fraud is extremely rare. An analysis by Julian Levitt (2014), a Loyola law school professor, examined fraud allegations from 2000 to 2014 and found thirty-one credible cases out of one billion votes.

President Donald Trump issued an executive order creating the Presidential Advisory Commission on Election Integrity to investigate voter fraud in the 2016 presidential election. After he won the Electoral College vote 304-227 but lost the popular vote to Democratic nominee Hillary Clinton by 2.87 million votes, Trump charged that he lost the popular vote due to widespread fraud. Voting rights advocates criticized the commission because there was no evidence of fraud. The *New Republic* characterized Trump's claim of fraud as "unhinged" and noted that he "stacked the panel with some of America's notorious opponents of voting rights." After he disbanded the Commission in 2018, Trump tweeted his support for voter ID laws. In his tweets, he stated that the electoral system was "rigged" and encouraged people to "[p]ush hard for Voter Identification" (Tackett and Wines 2018).

Trump also claimed that mail-in voting would allow unprecedented voter fraud. His claims were consistent with previous statements in Republican platforms. The 2012 platform criticized states that allowed all-mail elections because these systems undermined the "integrity of the ballot" since ballots could be "stolen or fraudulently voted by unauthorized individuals." This issue gained renewed attention due to the COVID-19 pandemic. To protect public health, many states expanded mail-in voting options for their residents. On May 28, 2020, Trump tweeted, "MAIL-IN VOTING WILL LEAD TO MASSIVE FRAUD AND ABUSE. IT WILL ALSO LEAD TO THE END OF OUR GREAT REPUBLICAN PARTY. WE CAN NEVER LET THIS TRAGEDY BEFALL OUR NATION." Trump was criticized by Republican Tom Ridge, former Pennsylvania governor and former Department of Homeland Security Secretary, for making false claims about mail-in voting. Ridge cochaired a bipartisan organization, VoteSafe, created to advocate for expanding mail-in voting and promote safe in-person voting procedures. Ridge was concerned that the president's multiple false claims about mail-in voting were designed to delegitimize the election. Trump stated that mail-in voting would hurt Republican candidates, but Ridge noted that neither party gains an electoral advantage through voting by mail. He further asserted that if Republicans did not use mail-in voting, it could prevent Republican candidates from winning elections. In June 2020, Trump tweeted, "RIGGED 2020 ELECTION: MILLIONS OF MAIL-IN BALLOTS WILL BE PRINTED BY FOREIGN COUNTRIES, AND OTHERS. IT WILL BE THE SCANDAL OF OUR TIMES!" Election security experts labeled such claims, which were also made by Attorney General William Barr, "preposterous."

Republicans have opposed legislation providing for DC statehood arguing that a constitutional amendment is necessary to enfranchise the District's voters. The 2016 Republican platform asserted that a constitutional amendment was the only appropriate method for DC to achieve statehood but that "a statehood amendment was soundly rejected by the states when last proposed in 1976 and should not be revived." As a candidate in 2015, Trump was asked about DC statehood and responded that he "would like to do whatever is better for the District of Columbia." In 2020, however, he said that statehood would "never happen" because Republicans were not "stupid" enough to give Democrats more seats in Congress. After the House passed statehood legislation in June 2020, the Republican-controlled Senate refused to vote on it. The White House announced that even if it passed the Senate, the president would veto the bill.

Congressional Republicans have opposed restoring voting rights to felons. In 2018, Senate majority leader Mitch McConnell stated that "voting is a privilege" and "those who break our laws should not dilute the vote of law-abiding citizens." Republican senator Rand Paul, however, proposed legislation in 2015 to restore the voting rights of nonviolent felons after their release. He stated that "[a] criminal record is currently one of the biggest impediments to voting in federal elections" and that he would fight to give "low-level ex-offenders another opportunity to vote" (Paul 2015). Public opinion polls support reinstating felon voting rights, including 55 percent of Republicans.

Republicans have also opposed other voting reforms largely on the basis that they would extend federal power. After the House passed the For the People Act, McConnell refused to schedule the bill for a vote in the Senate. In an op-ed in the

Washington Post, he criticized the bill as being part of the Democratic Party's "far-left proposals to retighten Washington's grip on the country." He criticized the election day holiday, which would make election day a paid holiday for government workers along with six extra paid vacation days for federal employees to serve as poll workers, as an "extra taxpayer-funded vacation for bureaucrats to hover around while Americans cast their ballots."

Further Reading

Apuzzo, Matt. 2014. "Holder Urges States to Lift Bans on Felons' Voting." *New York Times*, February 11. Accessed December 17, 2019. https://www.nytimes.com/2014/02/12/us/politics/holder-urges-states-to-repeal-bans-on-voting-by-felons.html.

Berman, Ari. 2014. "Republicans Used to Support Voting Rights—What Happened?" *The Nation*, April 14. Accessed January 1, 2020. https://www.thenation.com/article/archive/democrats-support-voting-rights-republicans-should-too/.

Bialik, Kristen. 2018. "How Americans View Some of the Voting Policies Approved at the Ballot Box." Pew Research Center, November 15. Accessed December 16, 2022. https://www.pewresearch.org/fact-tank/2018/11/15/how-americans-view-some-of-the-voting-policies-approved-at-the-ballot-box/.

Brownstein, Ronald. 2020. "The Most Important 2020 States Already Have Vote by Mail." *The Atlantic*, April 11. Accessed June 2, 2020. https://www.theatlantic.com/politics/archive/2020/04/voting-mail-2020-race-between-biden-and-trump/609799/.

Clegg, Roger, and Hans A. von Spakovsky. 2018. "There Are Good Reasons for Felons to Lose the Right to Vote." The Heritage Foundation, April 10. Accessed December 6, 2019. https://www.heritage.org/election-integrity/commentary/there-are-good-reasons-felons-lose-the-right-vote.

Cohen, Andrew. 2012. "Voting Rights: This Is What a Strong Party Platform Would Look Like." *The Atlantic*, September 5. Accessed November 7, 2019. https://www.theatlantic.com/politics/archive/2012/09/voting-rights-this-is-what-a-strong-party-platform-would-look-like/261640/.

Dastagir, Alia E. 2019. "What If Election Day Were a Holiday?" *USA Today*, February 1. Accessed June 5, 2020. https://www.usatoday.com/story/news/investigations/2019/02/01/election-day-federal-holiday-mcconnell-democracy-voter-turnout-democrats-republicans-voting-rights/2736634002/.

Democratic Party Platform. 1988–2020. American Presidency Project. Accessed November 23, 2022. https://www.presidency.ucsb.edu/documents/presidential-documents-archive-guidebook/party-platforms-and-nominating-conventions-3.

Editorial Board. 2015. "Leave the Voting Rights Act Alone." *National Review*, August 12. Accessed January 4, 2020. https://www.nationalreview.com/2015/08/voting-rights-act-republicans-anniversary/.

Fuller, Jaime. 2014. "Republicans Used to Unanimously Back the Voting Rights Act. Not Any More." *Washington Post*, June 26. Accessed February 15, 2020. https://www.washingtonpost.com/news/the-fix/wp/2014/06/26/republicans-used-to-unanimously-back-voting-rights-act-not-any-more/+&cd=1&hl=en&ct=clnk&gl=us.

Gardner, Amy. 2020. "As Trump Attacks Voting by Mail, GOP Builds 2020 Strategy Around Limiting Its Expansion." *Washington Post*, June 1. Accessed June 2, 2020. https://

www.washingtonpost.com/politics/as-trump-attacks-voting-by-mail-gop-builds-2020
-strategy-around-limiting-its-expansion/2020/05/31/a17ccfa0-a00d-11ea-b5c9-570a
91917d8d_story.html.

Gross, Terry. 2018. "Republican Voter Suppression Efforts Are Targeting Minorities, Journalist Says." National Public Radio, October 23. Accessed January 9, 2020. https://
www.npr.org/2018/10/23/659784277/republican-voter-suppression-efforts-are
-targeting-minorities-journalist-says.

Hopkins, Dan. 2018. "What We Know About Voter ID Laws." FiveThirtyEight, August 21.
Accessed January 9, 2020. https://fivethirtyeight.com/features/what-we-know-about
-voter-id-laws/.

"House Democrats Restore the Vote with H.R. 4, the Voting Rights Advancement Act."
2019. Office of Majority Leader Steny Hoyer, December 5. Accessed Decem
ber 16, 2022. https://www.majorityleader.gov/content/house-democrats-restore-vote
-hr-4-voting-rights-advancement-act.

Klobuchar, Amy. 2020. "Amy Klobuchar: The Right Way to Vote This November." *New
York Times*, April 14. Accessed July 15, 2020. https://www.nytimes.com/2020/04/14
/opinion/klobuchar-coronavirus-mail-voting.html.

Laloggia, John. 2018. "Conservative Republicans Are Least Supportive of Making It Easy
for Everyone to Vote." Pew Research Center, October 31. Accessed January 9, 2020.
https://www.pewresearch.org/fact-tank/2018/10/31/conservative-republicans-are
-least-supportive-of-making-it-easy-for-everyone-to-vote/.

Levitt, Justin. 2014. "A Comprehensive Investigation of Voter Impersonation Finds
31 Credible Incidents Out of One Billion Ballots Cast." *Washington Post*, August 6.
Accessed December 16, 2022. https://www.washingtonpost.com/news/wonk/wp/2014
/08/06/a-comprehensive-investigation-of-voter-impersonation-finds-31-credible
-incidents-out-of-one-billion-ballots-cast/.

Lillis, Mike, and Juliegrace Brufke. 2020. "House Approves Statehood for DC in 232-180
Vote." *The Hill*, June 26. Accessed December 15, 2022. https://thehill.com/homenews
/house/504746-house-approves-statehood-for-dc-in-232-180-vote/.

McConnell, Mitch. 2019. "Mitch McConnell: Behold the Democrat Politician Protection Act." *Washington Post*, January 17. Accessed January 16, 2020. https://www
.washingtonpost.com/opinions/call-hr-1-what-it-is-the-democrat-politician-protection
-act/2019/01/17/dcc957be-19cb-11e9-9ebf-c5fed1b7a081_story.html.

National Review. 2019. "No, McConnell Isn't 'Moscow Mitch.'" July 26. Accessed May 30, 2020.
https://www.nationalreview.com/2019/07/mitch-mcconnell-isnt-moscow-mitch/.

Newkirk, Vann R., II. 2018. "How *Shelby County v. Holder* Broke America." *The Atlantic*, July
10. Accessed January 4, 2020. https://www.theatlantic.com/politics/archive/2018/07
/how-shelby-county-broke-america/564707/.

Pareene, Alex. 2019. "The Simple, Odious Reason Mitch McConnell Opposes Election
Integrity." *New Republic*, July 31. Accessed May 30, 2020. https://newrepublic.com
/article/154566/simple-odious-reason-mitch-mcconnell-opposes-election-integrity.

Paul, Rand. 2015. "Sen. Paul Introduces Civil Rights Voting Restoration Act." Senator Rand Paul. Accessed May 30, 2020. https://www.paul.senate.gov/news/sen-paul
-introduces-civil-rights-voting-restoration-act.

Penniman, Nick. 2019. "Three Lessons Learned from the for the People Act." *RealClear-
Politics*, March 12. Accessed January 16, 2020. https://www.realclearpolitics.com
/articles/2019/03/12/three_lessons_learned_from_the_for_the_people_act_139724.html.

Rhodes, Jesse H. 2018. "No, Republicans Haven't 'Always' Supported Voting Rights until Now: This Is the Real Story." *Washington Post*, January 12. Accessed January 9, 2020. https://www.washingtonpost.com/news/monkey-cage/wp/2018/01/11/have-republicans-always-supported-voting-rights-until-now-nope-heres-the-real-story/+&cd=1&hl=en&ct=clnk&gl=us.

Ross, Janell. 2018. "It's Time for a New Voting Rights Act." *New Republic*, November 13. Accessed January 4, 2020. https://newrepublic.com/article/152182/its-time-new-voting-rights-act.

Roth, Zachary. 2017. "The New Assault on Voting Rights." *New Republic*, July 18. Accessed May 30, 2020. https://newrepublic.com/article/143598/real-voter-fraud-trump-investigates-illegal-votes-states-rush-to-limit-access-ballot-box.

Tackett, Michael, and Michael Wines. 2018. "Trump Disbands Commission on Voter Fraud." *New York Times*, January 3. Accessed February 18, 2020. https://www.nytimes.com/2018/01/03/us/politics/trump-voter-fraud-commission.html.

"Text of the President's Statement." 1981. *New York Times*, November 7. Accessed February 23, 2020. https://www.nytimes.com/1981/11/07/us/text-of-president-s-statement.html.

Troyan, Mary, and Susan Page. 2016. "Sen. Mitch McConnell Lauds Voting Rights in Memoir, Opposes Update." *USA Today*, June 1. Accessed June 18, 2020. https://www.usatoday.com/story/news/politics/2016/06/01/sen-mitch-mcconnell-lauds-voting-rights-law-memoir-opposes-update/85238536/.

Wilson, Reid. 2016. "GOP Platform Calls for Tough Voter ID Laws." *The Hill*, July 19. Accessed November 7, 2019. https://thehill.com/blogs/ballot-box/288302-gop-platform-calls-for-tough-voter-id-laws.

Wise, Justin. 2019. "McConnell Maintains That Senate Won't Take Up Election Reform Bill." *The Hill*, March 6. Accessed June 5, 2020. https://thehill.com/homenews/senate/432938-mcconnell-on-why-senate-wont-take-up-election-reform-bill-because-i-get-to.

Women's Rights

At a Glance

Women have been politically active throughout American history; however, until women could vote, politicians had no incentive to listen to their views on political issues. After gaining suffrage, women's groups have focused on attaining legal equality. In the 1970s, both parties supported the ratification of the Equal Rights Amendment (ERA). The Republican Party withdrew its support in 1980 in favor of a more conservative social agenda. The ERA was not ratified by the deadline, but supporters have sought to have the ratification deadline modified. Democrats support the ratification of the ERA to provide legal protections for women, but Republicans argue that women have sufficient legal protection under existing law. Republicans have also opposed abortion rights arguing that the unborn child has a right to life, while Democrats argue that women, and not the government, should control their reproductive freedom. Republicans have opposed women serving in combat roles in the military, while Democratic presidents have expanded combat opportunities for women. Both parties have supported the Violence Against Women Act (VAWA) (1994), but partisan differences in 2019 and 2020 regarding extending the law to limit gun sales of perpetrators of gender-motivated violence prevented its reauthorization until 2022, when Democrats agreed to drop their objection on gun restrictions. Democrats support expanding the restriction of gun sales, but Republicans oppose it.

According to many Republicans . . .

- The ERA is unnecessary because women have adequate legal protection against discrimination under existing law.
- Abortions should be banned to protect the lives of unborn children.
- Women should be excluded from combat roles in the military.
- The VAWA should be limited to protect Second Amendment Rights.

According to many Democrats . . .

- Passing an ERA will provide full legal rights to women.
- Women have a constitutional right to obtain an abortion.

- Women should not be denied the opportunity to hold combat roles in the military.
- The VAWA should be strengthened by limiting gun sales to those who stalk or abuse women.

_____

Overview

Long before women were guaranteed the right to vote by the Nineteenth Amendment (1920), they were politically active. During the Revolutionary War, women were instrumental in carrying out a successful boycott of British goods. After independence, many women became involved in politics through church groups, which became important players in the rise of abolition and temperance societies across the United States in the nineteenth century.

When it became clear that they could only effect social change with the right to vote, women organized for that purpose. At the World Anti-Slavery Conference in London in 1840, Elizabeth Cady Stanton met Lucretia Mott, and the two agreed to hold a meeting for the purpose of advancing women's rights in the United States. In 1848, the Seneca Falls Convention was held in Seneca Falls, New York, Stanton's hometown. The delegates to the convention drafted a Declaration of Sentiments and Resolutions modeled after the Declaration of Independence. The suffrage provision generated controversy as many of the women in attendance believed that women should not vote. Frederick Douglass persuaded the attendees to support the provision.

After the Civil War, Stanton and Susan B. Anthony lobbied to have women's suffrage included in the Fourteenth Amendment, but their attempts were rebuffed. Stanton and Anthony were infuriated that suffrage was extended to Black men in the Fifteenth Amendment (1870), but that all women were still precluded from voting. The suffrage movement split over the issue of race, and by the late 1800s, the movement had stalled. In 1910, the suffrage movement gained momentum with a new generation of female leaders, including Carrie Chapman Catt and Alice Paul, and five states enacted laws allowing women to vote in state elections. Suffragists drew attention to their cause through marches and protests. When jailed for protesting, women went on hunger strikes, and the resulting media attention forced President Woodrow Wilson to suggest to Congressional Democrats that an amendment extending voting rights to women was needed.

The Equal Rights Amendment

After the battle for suffrage culminated with the passage of the Nineteenth Amendment in 1920, an ERA was introduced in the House of Representatives in 1923 by Daniel Anthony, Susan B. Anthony's nephew. The amendment was authored by suffragist Alice Paul and introduced for Congressional consideration on the seventy-fifth anniversary of the Seneca Falls Convention. While it was introduced in every session of Congress after 1923, it was only seriously considered once in 1946.

Supporters of early efforts to pass the ERA argued that women and men should be treated equally under the law. Opponents argued that biological differences between the sexes justified protectionist legislation for women and were concerned that the ERA's ratification would end those laws. While these laws varied by state, some prohibited female workers from working at night or in certain occupations due to the dangerous nature of such occupations. Some states enacted minimum wage laws for women before the federal minimum wage was established. During World War II, when women had entered the workforce to take the place of men who were fighting overseas, ERA proponents argued that if the United States was fighting for freedom abroad, it should also extend freedom to its female citizens. With this patriotic sentiment, both the Republican and Democratic parties supported the amendment in their party platforms in 1944. Numerous women's organizations also supported the amendment. In 1945, the amendment passed the House Judiciary Committee, and in 1946, it passed the Senate Judiciary Committee. The National Committee to Defeat the Un-Equal Rights Amendment (NCDURA) argued that the ERA would eliminate protectionist legislation and enlisted high-profile individuals, including Eleanor Roosevelt, to thwart the amendment's progress. The organization also lobbied for legislation that would offer women benefits, such as maternity leave. The proposed legislation, although it was not enacted, helped quash interest in the ERA (DeWolf 2021).

In 1950 and 1953, the Senate passed the ERA with the Hayden rider. This rider, named for Senator Carl Hayden, inserted a provision that would not prohibit protectionist legislation. ERA proponents believed this negated the intent of the amendment—for male and female citizens to be treated equally.

Interest in the amendment was revived when the National Organization for Women (NOW), formed in 1968 in part to advocate for its passage, emerged as a formidable lobbying force. NOW argued that the amendment was necessary for several reasons, such as guaranteeing equal pay and preventing sex discrimination, including pregnancy discrimination, in education and employment. On October 12, 1971, the House of Representatives passed the ERA by a vote of 354-24; the Senate followed on March 22, 1972, approving the amendment by a vote of 84-8. Congress established a March 22, 1979, deadline for ratification. Three months after the Senate vote, twenty states had ratified the amendment and supporters were optimistic about passage.

This momentum was thwarted by an anti-ERA group, led by conservative attorney and activist Phyllis Schlafly, called STOP ERA. STOP was an acronym for Stop Taking Our Privileges. Schlafly and her supporters—from ordinary voters to members of Congress—argued that the ERA would threaten the privileges women enjoyed under federal and state law, force women into the military draft, and usher in government-funded abortions. Leaning on prevailing attitudes about LGBT Americans during that period, STOP ERA also argued that the amendment would legalize gay marriage and the adoption of children by gays and lesbians and eliminate the segregation of public restrooms by gender. By 1977, thirty-five states, three shy of the required thirty-eight, had ratified the amendment. Congress voted to extend the deadline to June 30, 1982, but no additional states voted for ratification. Indeed, five states rescinded their ratification prior to the deadline. Analyses of the amendment's failure have suggested that both sides exaggerated the ERA's pros and cons.

Spurred in part by the Women's March in January 2017 and the MeToo Movement, which urged women who had been victims of sexual assault and sexual harassment to come forward to empower other women, Nevada voted to ratify the amendment in 2017, followed by Illinois a year later. After Virginia ratified the ERA in 2020, the House of Representatives voted to remove the 1982 ratification deadline by a vote of 232-183 with all House Democrats and five House Republicans voting for it.

The battle over the ERA's ratification in the 1970s had a profound impact on American politics. By the end of that decade the Republican Party had withdrawn its support; meanwhile, Democrats added a pro-ERA plank to their 1972 platform and have advocated for its passage ever since. While they remain united in supporting passage of the ERA, most Republicans now oppose it. They argue that women already have sufficient rights and legal protections under existing law.

Abortion Rights

Reproductive autonomy was a significant issue in the women's movement. The ability of women to control their reproduction improved dramatically with the introduction of the birth control pill in 1960. States also began to legalize abortion to that end. Abortion had been banned in every state since 1880. From 1965 to 1972, thirteen states legalized abortion. NOW supported abortion rights and campaigned against restrictive abortion laws. The organization asserted that neither men nor the government had the authority to force women to bear children and that women's personhood and dignity were violated if she could not control her body. Supporters of the ERA hoped that it would protect abortion rights, while those who opposed the ERA were concerned that it would.

In *Roe v. Wade* (1973), the U.S. Supreme Court ruled by a 7-2 margin that the right to privacy protected a woman's decision to terminate her pregnancy. This ruling created a trimester framework that placed limits on the procedure while also protecting a woman's reproductive autonomy. During the first trimester, the decision was left to the woman and her doctor. In the second trimester, the state could impose regulations that were related to maternal health, including specifying the types of facilities in which the procedure could be performed. After viability, which the Court defined as the point at which the fetus could live outside the womb, the state could prohibit abortion, unless the mother's life was in jeopardy.

During the 1970s, the Republican and Democratic parties articulated their views on abortion rights. The 1976 Republican platform acknowledged that Republicans disagreed on the issue, but also indicated that the party supported a constitutional amendment to protect the lives of unborn children. The 1976 Democratic platform noted that there were moral and religious concerns surrounding abortion and merely stated that overturning *Roe* through a constitutional amendment was "undesirable."

After *Roe*, many states enacted restrictions on abortion. Throughout the late 1970s and 1980s, the Court invalidated most of those laws. This began to change during the 1990s reflecting the views of more conservative justices who had been appointed to the Court by Republican presidents Ronald Reagan and George H. W. Bush. In *Planned Parenthood v. Casey* (1992), the Court "reaffirmed the central holding of *Roe v. Wade*" but determined that the trimester framework was not part of the central holding. The Court replaced the trimester framework with the undue burden standard. Under this standard, abortion restrictions would be upheld unless they prevented a significant number of women from obtaining an abortion. In *Casey*, for example, the Court invalidated part of the Pennsylvania law that required married women to sign a statement that they had notified their husbands of their intent to obtain an abortion because it could cause physical or psychological harm to the woman. A twenty-four-hour waiting period, also part of the law, was not an undue burden. Four justices in *Casey* argued that abortion was not a constitutionally protected right.

Thirty years later, in *Dobbs v. Jackson Women's Health Organization* (2022), the U.S. Supreme Court overturned *Roe* when evaluating the constitutionality of Mississippi's law prohibiting abortion after fifteen weeks of pregnancy. The ruling reflected the retirement of Justice Anthony Kennedy, a Reagan appointee who had voted to uphold *Roe*, and the appointment of three conservative justices by Republican president Donald Trump. In *Dobbs*, four justices joined Justice Samuel Alito's majority opinion in which he wrote that abortion is not a constitutionally protected right because there is no right to privacy guaranteed by the Constitution. Alito argued that abortion should be left to the states. Chief Justice John Roberts wrote separately that the law was constitutional; however, *Roe* should not be overturned. The dissenting justices, all Democratic appointees, argued that abortion rights were intertwined with other rights involving bodily autonomy, familial relationships, and procreation and that the majority opinion called those rights into question.

Democrats decried the ruling as a significant loss for women's rights, while Republicans expressed their support for it arguing that it protected the rights of the unborn. Public opinion polls have consistently indicated that most Americans support abortion rights with some limits. Indeed, a 2022 Gallup poll showed that from 1990 to 2022, support for *Roe* averaged 58 percent with a high of 66 percent in 2006 and a low of 53 percent in 2014 (Brenan 2022).

Women in the Military

The controversy of the role of women in the military came to the fore during the debate over the ERA's ratification. Congress passed the ERA during the Vietnam War when men were drafted for combat. Proponents of the ERA argued that women should be drafted as well, while those opposed to the ERA argued that they should not. Although the draft ended in 1974, Congress reinstated the Selective Service System in 1980 due to the threat posed by the Soviet Union's invasion of Afghanistan. President Jimmy Carter, who supported the ERA, recommended that both men and women be required to register in case a draft was needed. In *Rostker v. Goldberg* (1981), the U.S. Supreme Court held in a 6-3 ruling that Congress could require only men to register for the Selective Service because the purpose of registration was to generate a list of candidates for combat. Justice William Rehnquist reasoned that since women were ineligible for combat roles, the law did not discriminate against them. Democrats have consistently supported an expanded role for women in the military, and combat roles were opened to women under the Obama administration in 2016. Most Republicans have consistently argued that women should not have to register for the Selective Service and should be excluded from combat positions.

The Violence Against Women Act

The VAWA is part of the Violent Crime Control and Law Enforcement Act (1994), the largest crime bill in U.S. history, signed by Democratic president Bill Clinton. The law passed by a vote of 235 (188 Democrats, 46 Republicans, and 1 Independent) to 195 (131 Republicans and 64 Democrats) in the House and by a 61-38 margin in the Senate. It made gender-motivated violence a federal crime and provided federal funds for training programs, shelters, and other resources to combat violence against women. The VAWA authorized the creation of the Office of Violence Against Women in the Justice Department and the National Domestic Violence Hotline. The law also created a federal civil remedy allowing victims to sue their attackers in federal court for monetary damages due to the unwillingness of local authorities in some jurisdictions to take these crimes seriously. In *United States v. Morrison* (2000), the U.S. Supreme Court ruled that Congress had exceeded its authority under the Commerce Clause by providing a civil remedy by a 5-4 vote. The Court found no link between commerce and violence against women, despite congressional fact-finding indicating that such crimes cost the United States billions of dollars each year. The law was renewed in 2000, without the civil remedy, and again in 2005 and 2013. While the law and the first two reauthorizations were enacted with strong bipartisan support, the 2013 reauthorization was enacted after a partisan battle due to three provisions. The revised statute specifically prevented discrimination on the basis of sexual orientation or gender identity—the first federal law to outlaw discrimination on those grounds. The law also allowed American Indian tribes to enforce domestic violence laws against non-Natives. Finally, the law provided protections for female illegal immigrants. The 2013 renewal was signed into law by President Obama. The law expired in 2018 due to the inability of Congress to avoid a government shutdown. While the funding for grants and programs continued, the law has not been reauthorized. In 2019, the Democratic-controlled House passed a reauthorization bill that included new provisions such as increased protection for transgendered individuals and a controversial provision expanding a ban on gun sales to include more perpetrators of gender-motivated violence. To pass the reauthorization, Democrats dropped their opposition to the ban on gun sales, and the law was reauthorized in 2022. The Safer Communities Act, which passed later in 2022, prevented abusers of dating violence from obtaining a firearm for five years.

Republicans

The Republican Party was an early supporter of the ERA and was the first political party to address the amendment in its platform in 1940. The party continued to support the ERA through the 1970s, but as the party attempted to appeal to conservative voters, it reversed course in 1980. Republicans have consistently opposed abortion rights, a view reflected in Republican presidential appointments to the U.S. Supreme Court and proposed federal legislation. The party has also staunchly opposed attempts to allow women to serve in combat roles due to concerns about military readiness and using the armed forces as a "social experiment." Republicans supported the VAWA in 1994 and its subsequent reauthorizations, but a 2019 reauthorization bill, which restricted gun ownership for perpetrators of gender-motivated violence was met with Republican opposition.

The Republican Party voiced its support for the ERA for the first time in its 1940 platform, which stated that "[w]e favor submission by Congress to the States of an amendment to the Constitution providing for equal rights for men and women." Platforms continued to offer support for the amendment. In 1974, Republican president Richard Nixon stated that his administration "is committed to providing an opportunity for women to participate on an equal basis with men in our national life. We support the equal rights amendment" ("Nixon" 1974). In the 1976 presidential contest, Republican president Gerald Ford, a longtime supporter of the ERA, stated, "I support ratification of the Equal Rights Amendment and I have urged the adoption of it by the states. . . . As we enter our third century as a Nation, it is particularly important that we reaffirm our commitment to equal opportunities for all our citizens."

The 1976 Republican platform contained a vigorous endorsement of the amendment:

> The Republican Party reaffirms its support for ratification of the Equal Rights Amendment. Our Party was the first national party to endorse the E.R.A. in 1940.

We continue to believe its ratification is essential to insure equal rights for all Americans. In our 1972 Platform, the Republican Party recognized the great contributions women have made to society as homemakers and mothers, as contributors to the community through volunteer work, and as members of the labor force in careers. The Platform stated then, and repeats now, that the Republican Party "fully endorses the principle of equal rights, equal opportunities and equal responsibilities for women." The Equal Rights Amendment is the embodiment of this principle and therefore we support its swift ratification.

However, by 1980, the party reversed course on its support largely due to the influence of the Religious Right, whose members argued that the amendment would provide a constitutional basis for abortion and take away women's rights, such as alimony in divorce cases and exemption from compulsory military service (Kennedy 2020). The 1980 GOP platform did not mention the amendment, but Republican nominee Ronald Reagan actively campaigned against it, and the party has opposed it ever since.

A 2020 Pew Research Center poll found that majorities of both Republicans (66 percent) and Democrats (88 percent) either favor or somewhat favor the ratification of the ERA. More Republican women (75 percent) than Republican men (58 percent) support it. Despite those numbers, 59 percent of Republicans who support the ERA believe that adding it to the Constitution would not make much difference in advancing women's rights.

After Virginia became the thirty-eighth state to ratify the ERA in 2020, the Justice Department released a memo stating that Congress lacks the authority to change the deadline for ratification. The Justice Department also instructed the National Archives and Records Administration that it should not authorize Virginia's vote (United States Department of Justice 2020). In a debate on the House floor over the ratification deadline in 2020, several House Republicans offered various arguments opposing the amendment itself. Jim Sensenbrenner argued that the advantages women enjoyed in terms of lower car insurance rates and lower health insurance rates would be eliminated. Virginia Foxx stated that the ERA "would have a harmful impact on shelters that protect women from violence, eliminate women-specific workplace protections, and destroy women's sports" (Israel 2020). Kay Granger argued that ratification could also lead to taxpayer-funded abortion. Republicans, such as Vicki Hartzler, claimed that there are sufficient legal protections for women without an amendment. Critics of that position, such as journalist Stephanie Russell-Kraft, responded that existing legal protections are insufficient and that the ERA is needed to make those protections permanent and expand their scope. She noted that although "it is true that lawyers have been able to demand pretty expansive protections for women in the courts, they'd be on much more solid footing with a clear constitutional mandate, rather than decades of muddled case law" (Russell-Kraft 2018).

Abortion Rights

After *Roe v. Wade* was decided, the Republican Party initially indicated that it respected the differing views of party members on this issue in its 1976 and 1980 platforms. Those platforms also supported a constitutional amendment to protect the unborn. Since the 1988 platform, the party has consistently supported that proposed amendment along with restrictions on the use of taxpayer funding for abortion and the appointment of pro-life judges. Republicans enacted federal legislation to restrict abortions, such as the Partial-Birth Abortion Ban Act, which prohibited a certain type of late-term abortion.

The 2020 Republican platform, which was identical to the 2016 platform as Republicans opted not to issue a new one, suggested that the Declaration of Independence protected a right to life and emphasized the sanctity of human life. It also asserted that Republicans were "proud to be the party that protects human life and offers real solutions for women" (Republican Party Platforms 2000). In 2022, many Republicans supported the Court's ruling in *Dobbs v. Jackson Women's Health Organization*. Republican senate minority leader Mitch McConnell praised the ruling as being "courageous and correct" and compared it favorably with *Brown v. Board of Education*, which overturned *Plessy v. Ferguson* (McConnell 2022). A Pew Research Center poll conducted shortly after the release of the Court's opinion

---

Republicans Support Overturning *Roe v. Wade*

After the U.S. Supreme Court overturned Roe v. Wade *in* Dobbs v. Jackson Women's Health Organization, *the Republican House leadership, which included House Minority Leader Kevin McCarthy, House Republican Whip Steve Scalise, and House Conference Chair Elise Stefanik, issued a statement supporting the ruling.*

Every unborn child is precious, extraordinary, and worthy of protection. We applaud this historic ruling, which will save countless innocent lives.

The Supreme Court is right to return the power to protect the unborn to the people's elected representatives in Congress and the states. In the days and weeks following this decision, we must work to continue to reject extreme policies that seek to allow late-term abortions and taxpayer dollars to fund these elective procedures.

The people's representatives must defend the right to life, liberty, and the pursuit of happiness for every American—born and unborn. As we celebrate today's decision, we recognize the decades of advocacy from the pro-life movement and we acknowledge much work remains to protect the most vulnerable among us.

Source

"House Republican Leadership's Statement on Dobbs Decision—Republican Whip." n.d. Accessed November 23, 2022. https://www.republicanwhip.gov/news/house-republican-leaderships-statement-on-dobbs-decision/.

showed that 70 percent of Republicans supported the ruling, with 48 percent indicating that they strongly approved of it (Pew Research Center 2022).

Women in the Military

One of the key reasons Republicans have continued to oppose the ERA is to prevent women from having to register for the Selective Service or from being drafted. For the past twenty years, Republican Party platforms have consistently endorsed the "advancement of women in the military" but supported "military women's exemption from direct ground combat units and infantry battalions." In 2000, the platform supported a "candid analysis of the consequences of unprecedented changes in the military," while the 2004 platform called for an end to co-ed basic training. In 2005, Republican representative Duncan Hunter, a Marine veteran, attempted to add a provision to a military spending bill that would have required Congress to approve opening new positions, including combat positions, for women in the military. After his proposal was met with bipartisan opposition, and was opposed by Republican defense secretary Donald Rumsfeld, the House voted to continue to let the military decide which jobs women can have, subject to notifying Congress of any changes. Critics were concerned that the proposal would hurt the retention and recruitment of women.

In 2013, when Defense Secretary Leon Panetta announced that the military would have three years to integrate women into combat units, Donald Trump tweeted, "The Generals and top military brass never wanted a mixer but were forced to do it by very dumb politicians who wanted to be politically C!" In 2015, when the Defense Department announced it was opening all combat roles to women, some Republicans were concerned that doing so would open the door to women having to register for the Selective Service and, potentially, a military draft. In 2016 and 2020, the platform opposed "unnecessary policy changes including Selective Service registration of women for a possible future draft." Republicans also rejected "the use of the military as a platform for social experimentation" and stated that "military readiness should not be sacrificed on the altar of political correctness." In an op-ed for the *Washington Post*, Professor Kara Dixon Vuic argued that "[d]rafting women cannot turn the military into a social experiment, because the military has always been a social experiment. . . . Each time the military has used a conscripted force, it has engaged in social engineering." She noted that no draft has required universal service. Instead, people have been drafted based on certain characteristics (age, sex, physical and mental abilities, educational background, and work skills), while those more valuable to the home front have not been required to serve. Wealthy men were able to buy their way out of service in the Civil War, while farmers and fishermen were exempted in World War I and World War II because their skills were needed at home. Thus, requiring women to register for the Selective Service will be no different than any other form of social experimentation. Importantly, "[w]e can't exclude an entire class of Americans from the obligations and benefits of citizenship" (Vuic 2019).

Republican senator Joni Ernst has opposed her party's view on women in the military. Ernst, a retired lieutenant colonel in the Iowa Army National Guard, disagreed with her party members by supporting women serving in combat roles in the armed forces. In 2015, she issued a statement supporting the Defense Department's announcement about opening combat roles to women. She stated, "I support providing women the opportunity to serve in any capacity, as long as standards are not lowered and it enhances our combat effectiveness. The decision to open up all military occupational specialties to women is one that must be a military decision, and not a political one" (Ernst 2015).

The Violence Against Women Act

The VAWA and the 2000 and 2005 reauthorizations of the law were enacted with bipartisan support. In 2013, Republicans objected to provisions expanding protection for LGBT individuals and Native American women. The bill passed in the Senate by a vote of 78-22, but House Republicans, while hesitant to support the Senate version, could not agree on an alternate bill. Some House Republicans were upset that they were only voting on the Senate bill without going through their regular committee process. However, since President Barack Obama won the female vote by twelve points in the 2012 presidential elections, contributing to the largest gender gap in U.S. history, House Republicans felt pressured to reauthorize the law. In 2019, the Democratic House passed a reauthorization bill that contained a provision closing the "boyfriend loophole" by extending bans on gun sales to include stalkers and dating partners along with husbands, former husbands, and live-in boyfriends. The Republican-controlled Senate refused to support the House bill. Republican senator Joni Ernst and Democratic senator Dianne Feinstein attempted to compromise on a bill that both parties could support. However, these efforts failed when the two sides could not come to an agreement over the boyfriend loophole. The law was reauthorized with bipartisan support in 2022 after Democrats dropped the loophole from the bill. Republican senator Joni Ernst, herself a survivor of abuse, issued a statement following the President Biden's signing of the bill in which she said, "My hope is that with this bill, some women will never have to suffer this horrific, personal abuse, and those that do will have the necessary support and resources in a moment of crisis to cope with and ultimately overcome their trauma" (Ernst 2022).

Democrats

The Democratic Party has supported the ERA since 1972 and continues to advocate for its ratification. The party supports abortion rights and has sought to pass legislation to restore the legal protection for abortion eliminated by the Court in *Dobbs*. It has supported and implemented policies to open combat positions to women in the military. Democrats have also supported and expanded the VAWA to protect women from gender-motivated violence.

The Democratic Party has supported the ERA since Congress approved the amendment in 1972 but has advocated for legislation promoting equality between the sexes, including equal pay, since the 1960s. The 1964 Democratic platform supported "legislation to carry forward the progress already made toward full equality of opportunity for women as well as men." The party's strongest statement on the ERA was in its 1980 platform. "The concerns of women cannot be limited to a portion of the platform; they must be reflected in every section of our Party's policy." The platform went on to point out that "[w]omen are a majority of the population. Yet their equality is not recognized in the Constitution or enforced as the law of the land." The party pledged that in "the 1980s, the Democratic Party commits itself to a Constitution, economy, and society open to women on an equal basis with men. The primary route to that new horizon is fabrication of the Equal Rights Amendment." It argued that states did not have the authority to rescind ratification of the amendment.

In 1984, Walter Mondale stated in his speech accepting the Democratic Party's presidential nomination that "[b]efore the start of the next decade, I want to go to my second Inaugural, and raise my right hand, and swear to 'preserve, protect, and defend' a Constitution that includes the Equal Rights Amendment." Mondale's running mate, Congresswoman Geraldine Ferraro, the first female vice-presidential candidate nominated by a major party, said that "[o]ur dream cannot be realized until our rights are guaranteed under the Constitution." The 1984 platform was particularly critical of Republicans for abandoning the ERA stating, "Nowhere is this Administration's hostility to equal rights and equal justice more apparent than in its attitude to the Equal Rights Amendment. As soon as the Reagan faction took control of the Republican Party at its convention in 1980, it ended that Party's forty-year commitment to passage of the Equal Rights Amendment." The platform characterized the Reagan administration as "an enemy in the White House" to the ERA's proponents.

By the 1988 presidential contest, Democratic support for the ERA was reduced to one sentence in the platform. Future platforms followed suit, except for the 2004 platform, when the party did not specifically endorse the amendment, but emphasized its commitment to equal pay and its belief in the equality of women instead. In 2011, angered by the U.S. Supreme Court's ruling in *Wal-Mart v. Dukes* (2011), a 5-4 decision that made it more difficult for women to sue their employers for discriminatory pay and promotion practices, House Democrats reintroduced the ERA. The Court's ruling, according to then Democratic minority leader Nancy Pelosi, "sets back the cause of equality for women and for all Americans in the workplace and in our society. And it will make it more difficult for workers to come together to fight claims of gender discrimination." Representative Carolyn Mahoney, one of the Democratic cosponsors of the ERA, stated that "[t]he Equal Rights Amendment is still needed because the only way for women to achieve permanent equality in the U.S. is to write it into the Constitution. Making women's equality a constitutional right—after Congress passes and 38 states ratify the ERA—would place the United States on record, albeit more than 200 years late, that women are fully equal in the eyes of the law." When the effort failed, Democrats pledged in the 2016 platform that "[a]fter 240 years, we will finally enshrine the rights of women in the Constitution by passing the Equal Rights Amendment."

In February 2020, House Speaker Nancy Pelosi delivered remarks supporting a bill to remove the deadline for the ERA's ratification. She noted that 2020 marked the centennial of the Nineteenth Amendment guaranteeing women the right to vote and that it was "a shameful reality" that the ERA still had not been "enshrined

---

Democrats Support the Ratification of the Equal Rights Amendment

The following is an excerpt from Democratic Speaker of the House Nancy Pelosi in support of a resolution to remove the deadline for the ratification of the Equal Rights Amendment. In her remarks, she explains why Democrats believe the amendment is still necessary.

This is an historic day. A happy day as the House takes action to move our nation closer to the founding—our founding ideal that all are created equal.

Nearly two hundred—excuse me—nearly one hundred years ago, Alice Paul, a Republican, introduced the Equal Rights Amendment, the first proposed amendment to the Constitution calling for women's equality in America.

Today, by passing this resolution, the House is paving the way to enshrining Equal Rights Amendment in the Constitution. That will achieve justice for women and progress for families, for our children: lowering wage disparity, increasing paychecks so moms can pay for their family's needs such as rent, groceries, childcare, health care.

To those who say the ERA is not necessary, let me quote from a recent statement from the American Association of University Women. It states, "Many Americans mistakenly believe that the U.S. Constitution explicitly guarantees equality between men and women"—perhaps, you think that—"the Equal Rights Amendment would once and for all guarantee constitutional equality between men and women. Its ratification would provide the constitutional guarantee that all men and women are truly equal under the law."

I urge a strong bipartisan vote for this resolution. It would be bipartisan in the United States Senate, when we send it over there shortly. And so, to ensure that women are truly equal under the law in America because we know in America, when women succeed, America succeeds.

I urge a yes vote and yield back the balance of my time.

Source

Pelosi, Nancy. 2020. "Pelosi Floor Speech in Support of Resolution on Equal Rights Amendment." Congresswoman Nancy Pelosi, February 13. Accessed August 23, 2020. https:// pelosi.house.gov/news/press-releases/pelosi-floor-speech-in-support-of-resolution-on -equal-rights-amendment.

in the Constitution." She stated that the ERA "will achieve justice for women and progress for families, for our children: lowering wage disparity, increasing paychecks so moms can pay for their family's needs. . . . The ERA will strengthen America, unleashing the full power of women in our economy and upholding the value of equality in our democracy" (Pelosi 2020).

Critics are concerned with both the ERA's substance and the ratification process because the time limit has expired. The editors of the *National Review* criticized the amendment as adding "seemingly innocuous language into the Constitution . . . that could then be used to force policy changes that the democratic process will not yield." They specifically cite "paid family leave, discrimination on the basis of sexual orientation, and the end of policies that have a disparate impact on women." They also approvingly cited Justice Ruth Bader Ginsburg's view that the amendment would have to begin the process again by passing both Houses of Congress and then be submitted to the states for ratification (The Editors 2020).

Abortion Rights

The Democratic Party has been supportive of abortion rights arguing that abortion is protected by a constitutional right to privacy and that it is a woman's personal health-care choice. After *Roe* was decided, the party indicated in its 1976 platform that many Americans had moral and religious concerns over the issue. The platform did not specifically endorse abortion rights but opposed efforts to overturn *Roe* with a constitutional amendment. Over time, the party's views on protecting abortion rights have strengthened. The 2020 party platform stated that Democrats "believe that comprehensive health services, including access to reproductive care and abortion services, are vital to the empowerment of women and girls" (Democratic Party Platforms 2020).

The *Dobbs* ruling was leaked before the Court officially released it. Democratic House Speaker Nancy Pelosi issued a letter to House Democrats in response to the draft opinion. In this letter, she stated that "[w]hile this extremist Supreme Court works to punish and control the American people, Democrats must continue our fight to expand freedom in America. Doing so is foundational to our oath of office and our fidelity to the Constitution" (Pelosi 2022). After the *Dobbs* ruling, House Democrats passed the Women's Health Protection Act. This bill would restore *Roe* and place limits on the types of abortion restrictions that could be implemented by the states. Due to Republican opposition, the bill will not be considered by the Senate. According to a Pew Research Center poll, 82 percent of Democrats disapproved of the *Dobbs* ruling, with 66 percent strongly disapproving of the decision (Pew Research Center 2022).

Women in the Military

During the debate over ratification, ERA supporters argued that women should be registered for a potential military draft because they wanted full equality. President

Jimmy Carter supported women registering for the Selective Service, although neither Congress nor the Supreme Court agreed. After women served in the Persian Gulf War in 1991, Congress voted to allow women to fly combat missions, and in 1993, Les Aspin, President Bill Clinton's defense secretary, approved allowing women to fly combat aircraft. Aspin also lifted restrictions so that women could serve on Navy warships, while continuing to exclude them from ground infantry. In 2013, Leon Panetta, President Obama's defense secretary, announced that all combat jobs should be opened to women and gave the military three years to study the issue and make recommendations regarding implementation. A Gallup poll taken after Panetta's announcement found that 74 percent of Americans supported the decision to allow women in combat roles, including 83 percent Democrats and 70 percent Republicans (Davis 2013).

In 2015, Defense Secretary Ash Carter announced that combat roles would be open to women by 2016. Obama compared the change to desegregating the military and allowing gays and lesbians to serve openly. He said, "Over recent decades, we've opened about 90 percent of military positions to women who time and again have proven that they, too, are qualified, ready and up to the task. In the wars in Afghanistan and Iraq, our courageous women in uniform have served with honor, on the front lines—and some have given their very lives." Obama believed that these changes strengthened the military by drawing on a broader pool of talent (Obama 2015).

Phyllis Schlafly compared the parties' stances on women in the military in the 2016 platforms. She argued that "[a]ssigning women to combat positions would be a radical social experiment in the redefinition of gender." She cited "new evidence proving what most of us already know, namely that women just can't perform the tasks that combat jobs require, and don't want to anyway." Specifically, she pointed to a media report that found since the Obama administration opened combat roles to women, only one out of seven passed the physical fitness test. She noted that 167 had applied for other jobs in combat units, including intelligence, logistics, and communications, "but those jobs don't require the same level of physical fitness" (Schlafly 2016).

The Violence Against Women Act

Democratic senator and chair of the Senate Judiciary Committee, Joe Biden, cosponsored the original VAWA bill in 1990. Biden stated that the bill had "three broad, but simple, goals: to make streets safer for women; to make homes safer for women; and to protect women's civil rights" (Rueb and Chokshi 2019). He and other Democrats worked with Republicans to address an issue that had been considered a private, family matter. As judiciary chair, Biden scheduled hearings to document the pervasiveness of violence against women. In 1993, he stated that "[t]hrough this process, I have become convinced that violence against women reflects as much a failure of our nation's collective moral imagination as it does the failure of our nation's laws and regulations" (Rueb and Chokshi 2019). Democrats have expanded the protections of the law with every reauthorization.

In his remarks when signing the VAWA 2013 Reauthorization, President Obama touted the law's success but emphasized that the law had been strengthened with every reauthorization. He specifically mentioned provisions allowing tribal nations to hold non-Native Americans accountable for crimes on their reservations and expanding services for LGBT victims. Betsy Woodruff, writing in the *National Review*, criticized Democrats for unnecessarily politicizing what had traditionally been a bipartisan reauthorization process. She noted that attacks on Native American women by non-Native men is a serious issue but that ceding jurisdiction to tribal courts is problematic because, unlike American courts, they do not guarantee constitutional rights. Senator Orrin Hatch, one of VAWA's original sponsors, argued that this provision not only does not guarantee constitutional rights but also does not allow U.S. courts to review convictions. Woodruff (2013) also noted that the new provision requiring additional protections for LGBT abuse victims, while needed, could make shelters vulnerable to lawsuits.

The 2016 Democratic platform vowed to "continue to support the Violence Against Women Act to provide law enforcement with the tools it needs to combat this problem. We will support comprehensive services for survivors of violence and increase prevention efforts in our communities and on our campuses." In April 2019, House Democrats renewed the VAWA with a new provision eliminating the "boyfriend loophole." Democrats were critical of the Republican-controlled Senate for not acting on the bill. Democratic presidential nominee Joe Biden was particularly critical of Republican senate majority leader Mitch McConnell for refusing to bring the House bill before the Senate for a vote. Biden was one of the original sponsors of VAWA and pledged on his 2020 presidential campaign website to continue his leadership to end violence against women. The 2020 Democratic platform echoed his sentiment stating that Democrats would "overcome Republican obstructionism to reauthorize and expand the Violence Against Women Act." In 2022, in order to pass the reauthorization, Democrats agreed to drop the boyfriend loophole, and the reauthorization became law as part of an appropriations bill. In a statement signing the law, Biden noted that there was more work to do to address violence against women. "As long as there are women in this country and around the world who live in fear of violence, there's more we have to do to fulfill this sacred commitment. No one—no one, regardless of gender or sexual orientation, should experience abuse. Period" (The White House 2022).

Further Reading

Brenan, Megan. 2022. "Steady 58% of Americans Do Not Want *Roe v. Wade* Overturned." Gallup Poll, June 2. Accessed September 1, 2022. https://news.gallup.com/poll/393275/steady-americans-not-roe-wade-overturned.aspx.

Davis, Alyssa. 2013. "Americans Favor Allowing Women in Combat." Gallup Poll, January 25. Accessed February 9, 2023. https://news.gallup.com/poll/160124/americans-favor-allowing-women-combat.aspx.

Democratic Party Platforms. 1944, 1976–2020. American Presidency Project. Accessed November 23, 2022. https://www.presidency.ucsb.edu/people/other/democratic-party-platforms.

DeWolf, Rebecca. 2021. *Gendered Citizenship: The Original Conflict Over the Equal Rights Amendment, 1920–1963.* Lincoln: University of Nebraska Press.

The Editors. 2020. "The Equal Rights Un-Amendment." *National Review*, January 31. Accessed September 1, 2022. https://www.nationalreview.com/2020/01/the-equal-rights-un-amendment/.

Ernst, Joni. 2015. "Senator Ernst Statement on Pentagon Announcement Regarding Women in Combat Roles." US Senator Joni Ernst of Iowa, December 15. Accessed September 2, 2022. https://www.ernst.senate.gov/news/press-releases/senator-ernst-statement-on-pentagon-announcement-regarding-women-in-combat-roles.

Ernst, Joni. 2022. "Ernst's Landmark Violence against Women Act Signed into Law." US Senator Joni Ernst of Iowa, March 16. Accessed September 1, 2022. https://www.ernst.senate.gov/news/press-releases/ernsts-landmark-violence-against-women-act-signed-into-law.

Israel, Josh. 2020. "182 House Republicans Vote Against Equal Rights for Women." American Independent, February 13. Accessed July 22, 2020. https://americanindependent.com/house-republicans-equal-rights-amendment-era-constitution-gop-congress/.

Kennedy, Lesley. 2020. "How Phyllis Schlafly Derailed the Equal Rights Amendment." History, March 19. Accessed July 23, 2020. https://www.history.com/news/equal-rights-amendment-failure-phyllis-schlafly.

Klar, Rebecca. 2020. "Biden Marks Anniversary of the Violence against Women Act, Knocks Trump and McConnell." *The Hill*, September 13. Accessed October 15, 2020. https://thehill.com/homenews/campaign/516210-biden-marks-anniversary-of-the-violence-against-women-act-knocks-trump-and.

"Nixon Reaffirms Support of Equal Rights Amendment." 1974. *New York Times*, February 3. Accessed July 23, 2020. https://www.nytimes.com/1974/02/03/archives/nixon-reaffirms-support-of-equal-rights-amendment.html.

Obama, Barack. 2015. "Statement by the President on Women in the U.S. Military." December 3. Accessed July 20, 2020. https://obamawhitehouse.archives.gov/the-press-office/2015/12/03/statement-president-women-us-military.

Pelosi, Nancy. 2020. "Floor Speech on Support of Resolution on Equal Rights Amendment." Congresswoman Nancy Pelosi. Accessed November 23, 2022. https://pelosi.house.gov/news/press-releases/pelosi-floor-speech-in-support-of-resolution-on-equal-rights-amendment.

Pelosi, Nancy. 2022. "Dear Colleague on Legislative Response to Supreme Court Overturning *Roe*." Speaker Nancy Pelosi, June 27. Accessed September 20, 2022. https://www.speaker.gov/newsroom/62722-0.

Pew Research Center. 2022. "Majority of Public Disapproves of Supreme Court's Decision to Overturn *Roe v. Wade*." July 6. Accessed September 1, 2022. https://www.pewresearch.org/politics/2022/07/06/majority-of-public-disapproves-of-supreme-courts-decision-to-overturn-roe-v-wade/.

Press Release Republican Leader. 2022. "The Supreme Court's Ruling Is Courageous and Correct." June 24. Accessed September 1, 2022. https://www.republicanleader .senate.gov/newsroom/press-releases/the-supreme-courts-landmark-ruling-is -courageous-and-correct.

Republican Party Platforms. 1940, 1944, and 1976–2020. American Presidency Project. Accessed November 23, 2022. https://www.presidency.ucsb.edu/people/other /republican-party-platforms.

Rueb, Emily S., and Niraj Chokshi. 2019. "The Violence against Women Act Is Turning 25: Here's How It Has Ignited Debate." *New York Times*, April 4. Accessed December 12, 2019. https://www.nytimes.com/2019/04/04/us/violence-against-women-act-reauthorization .html.

Russell-Kraft, Stephanie. 2018. "Why the Equal Rights Amendment Still Matters." *New Republic*, June 14. Accessed July 20, 2020. https://newrepublic.com/article/149074 /equal-rights-amendment-still-matters.

Schlafly, Phyllis. 2016. "Opinion: Republicans and Democrats on Women in Combat." *The Telegraph*, August 8. Accessed July 20, 2020. https://www.thetelegraph.com/opinon /article/Opinion-Republican-and-Democrats-on-women-in-12599039.

Shanker, Thom. 2005. "House Drops Effort to Put New Limits on Women in Combat." *New York Times*, May 25. Accessed July 21, 2020. https://www.nytimes.com/2005/05/25 /politics/house-drops-effort-to-put-new-limits-on-women-in-combat.html.

Sullivan, Patricia. 2020. "U.S. House Removes ERA Ratification Deadline, One Obstacle to Enactment." *Washington Post*, February 13. Accessed July 23, 2020. https://www .washingtonpost.com/local/legal-issues/us-house-removes-era-ratification-deadline -one-obstacle-to-enactment/2020/02/13/e82aa802-4de5-11ea-b721-9f4cdc90bc1c _story.html.

United States Department of Justice. 2020. "Ratification of the Equal Rights Amendment." January 6. Accessed July 24, 2020. https://www.justice.gov/olc/file/1232501 /download.

Vuic, Kara Dixon. 2019. "Women May Soon Have to Register for the Draft: It Is Long Overdue." *Washington Post*, March 4. Accessed July 22, 2020. https://www.washingtonpost .com/outlook/2019/03/04/women-may-soon-have-register-draft-its-long-overdue/.

The White House. 2022. "Remarks by President Biden Celebrating the Reauthorization of the Violence against Women Act." March 16, 2022. Accessed September 29, 2022. https:// www.whitehouse.gov/briefing-room/speeches-remarks/2022/03/16/remarks-by -president-biden-celebrating-the-reauthorization-of-the-violence-against-women-act/.

Woodruff, Betsy. 2013. "Violence against VAWA." *National Review*, February 14. Accessed December 12, 2019. https://www.nationalreview.com/2013/02/violence-against-vawa -besty-woodruff.

Bibliography

Alexander, Michelle. 2012. *The New Jim Crow: Mass Incarceration in the Age of Colorblindness*. New York: New Press.

Allen, Anita L., and Marc Rotenberg. 2016. *Privacy Law and Society*. 3rd ed. St. Paul, MN: West Academic.

Balko, Radley. 2013. *The Rise of the Warrior Cop: The Militarization of America's Police Forces*. New York: PublicAffairs.

Berman, Ali. 2015. *Give Us the Ballot: The Modern Struggle for Voting Rights in America*. New York: Farrar, Straus, and Giroux.

Bullard, Robert D. 2000. *Dumping in Dixie: Race, Class, and Environmental Quality*. 3rd ed. New York: Routledge.

Bullock, Charles S., III, Ronald Keith Gaddie, and Justin Wert. 2016. *The Rise and Fall of the Voting Rights Act*. Norman: University of Oklahoma Press.

Chemerinsky, Erwin. 2021. *Presumed Guilty: How the Supreme Court Empowered the Police and Subverted Civil Rights*. New York: Liveright.

Cohn, Jonathan. 2021. *The Ten Year War: Obamacare and the Unfinished Crusade for Universal Coverage*. New York: St. Martin's.

Dawes, Daniel. 2016. *150 Years of Obamacare*. Baltimore: Johns Hopkins University Press.

Diffie, Whitfield, and Susan Landau. 1998. *Privacy on the Line: The Politics of Wiretapping and Encryption*. Boston: MIT Press.

Frankenberg, Erica, and Gary Orfield, eds. 2012. *The Resegregation of Suburban Schools: A Hidden Crisis in American Education*. Cambridge, MA: Harvard Education Press.

Gerrard, Michael B. 1994. *Whose Backyard, Whose Risk: Fear and Fairness in Toxic and Nuclear Waste Siting*. Cambridge, MA: MIT Press.

Glenn, Richard A. 2003. *The Right to Privacy: Rights and Liberties under the Law*. Santa Barbara, CA: ABC-CLIO.

Goodman, Adam. 2020. *The Deportation Machine: America's Long History of Expelling Immigrants*. Princeton, NJ: Princeton University Press.

Gould, Lewis L. 2014. *The Republicans: A History of the Grand Old Party*. rev. ed. Oxford: Oxford University Press.

Grabowski, Mark, and Eric P. Robinson. 2021. *Cyber Law and Ethics: Regulation of the Connected World*. New York: Routledge.

Jennings, Jack. 2015. *Presidents, Congress, and the Public Schools: The Politics of Education Reform*. Cambridge, MA: Harvard Education Press.

Kazin, Michael. 2022. *What It Took to Win: A History of the Democratic Party*. New York: Farrar, Straus and Giroux.

Kluger, Richard. 2004. *Simple Justice: The History of* Brown v. Board of Education *and Black America's Struggle for Equality*. rev. ed. New York: Random House.

O'Brien, Ruth. 2001. *Crippled Justice: The History of the Modern Disability Policy in the Workplace*. Chicago: University of Chicago Press.

Smith, Bradley A. 2001. *Unfree Speech: The Folly of Campaign Finance Reform*. Princeton, NJ: Princeton University Press.

Tribe, Lawrence. 1992. *Abortion: The Clash of Absolutes*. New York: W. W. Norton.

Winkler, Adam. 2013. *Gunfight: The Battle over the Right to Bear Arms in America*. New York: W. W. Norton.

Winkler, Adam. 2019. *We the Corporations: How American Businesses Won Their Civil Rights*. New York: Liveright.

Wolbrecht, Christina. 2000. *The Politics of Women's Rights: Parties, Positions, and Change*. Princeton, NJ: Princeton University Press.

Yang, Jia Lynn. 2020. *One Mighty and Irresistible Tide: The Epic Struggle Over American Immigration, 1924–1965*. New York: W. W. Norton.

Index

About the Author and Contributors

Kara E. Stooksbury, PhD, is professor of political science and chair of the Department of History, Political Science, and Sociology at Carson-Newman University in Jefferson City, Tennessee. She has served as coeditor of the first and second editions of the *Encyclopedia of American Civil Rights and Liberties* for ABC-CLIO. She is the 2021 recipient of the Distinguished Faculty Award, Carson-Newman University's highest honor for a faculty member. She has also received the institution's mentoring and research awards.

Stephen Joiner, PhD, is assistant professor of political science at Carson-Newman University. His teaching and research interests include peace studies and political violence. He teaches courses in American politics, comparative politics, and international relations.

Derick Marlow holds a Master of Public Policy and Administration. He is lead instructor in adult education for the Tennessee College of Applied Technology.

www.ingramcontent.com/pod-product-compliance
Lightning Source LLC
Chambersburg PA
CBHW080410270326
41929CB00018B/2973